International Migration, Refugee Flows and Human Rights in North America: The Impact of Free Trade and Restructuring

International Migration, Refugee Flows and Human Rights in North America: The Impact of Free Trade and Restructuring

Edited by Alan B. Simmons

1996
Center for Migration Studies
New York

The Center for Migration Studies is an educational, non-profit institute founded in New York in 1964 to encourage and facilitate the study of sociological, demographic, historical, legislative and pastoral aspects of human migration movements and ethnic group relations. The opinions expressed in this work are those of the authors.

International Migration, Refugee Flows and Human Rights in North America: The Impact of Free Trade and Restructuring

Center for Migration Studies
209 Flagg Place
Staten Island, New York 10304-1199

Library of Congress Cataloging-in-Publication Data
International migration, refugee flows and human rights in North America:
the impact of free trade and restructuring / edited by Alan B. Simmons.
— 1st ed.
    p.   cm.
Includes bibliographical references and index.
ISBN 0-934733-91-0 (p)
    1. Alien labor—North America.   1. North America—Emigration and
immigration.   3. Refugees—North America.   4. North America—Foreign
economic relations.   I. Simmons, Alan B. (Alan Burtham), 1941–
HD8045.I585   1996
331.6'2'097—dc20   95-45597
                                                      CIP

Printed in the United States of America

Contents

Preface   *vii*

Introduction
Research and Policy Issues in the Field of International
Migration and North American Economic Integration
Alan B. Simmons   1

Part I
Social and Political Aspects of Restructuring

1. NAFTA, Civil Society and Neoconservative Restructuring
   Ricardo Grinspun   28

2. The Political Consequences of Economic Liberalization
   Maxwell A. Cameron   46

3. The Rights of Mexican Workers in the Context of NAFTA
   Edur Velasco Arregui   65

Part II
New Trends in International Migration

4. Policies and Migration Trends in the North American System
   Hania Zlotnik   81

5. Visitors and Visa Workers: Old Wine in New Bottles?
   Margaret Michalowski   104

6. Emerging Trade Blocs and Caribbean Emigration
   Jean-Pierre Guengant   123

7. Migration, Development and Peace in Central America
   Manuel Angel Castillo   137

8. The Mexican Dilemma
   Rodolfo Casillas   156

Part III
The Emerging International Division of Labor

9. Labor, Migrants and International Restructuring in Electronics
   M. Patricia Fernandez Kelly   174

10. Female Migrant Labor in North America: Trends and
    Issues for the 1990s
    Monica Boyd   193

11. Household, Gender and Migration in Mexican
    Maquiladoras: The Case of Nogales
    Kathryn Kopinak   214

Part IV
Refugees and Asylum in the Hemisphere

12. Asylum Policies in Developed Countries: National
    Security Concerns and Regional Issues
    Charles B. Keely and Sharon Stanton Russell   229

13. United States Refugee Law and Policy:
    Past, Present and Future
    T. Alexander Aleinikoff   245

14. Refugee Claimants: Canadian Law and North American
    Regionalism
    H. Patrick Glenn   258

15. Haitian Refugees and U.S. Policy
    Lucas Guttentag   272

16. Displaced Central Americans: Mexican NGOs and the
    International Response
    Sergio Aguayo Quezada   290

17. Refugees and the Guatemalan Peace Process
    Carlos Ochoa Garcia   309

    Index   329

Preface

This volume is the product of a collaborative program of research and policy review carried out jointly by the Mexican Academy of Human Rights, the Hemispheric Migration Project at Georgetown University and two institutes at York University – the Centre for Research on Latin America and the Caribbean (CERLAC) and the Centre for Refugee Studies (CRS). The cooperative effort led to a first meeting in Mexico City in early 1992 and a larger meeting of researchers and representatives of human rights NGOs at York University in the fall of that same year. Most of the papers in this volume were selected from the larger number of papers presented in draft form and discussed at the second conference. These select papers were subsequently revised, edited and supplemented by a few other papers to fill in gaps for this collection.

When possible the authors have sought to update their texts to take into account new developments in 1993 and early 1994. The fast evolution of migration and refugee flows, policies and related human rights issues soon goes beyond the most recent analysis. The objective of the volume, then, is to summarize the broader trends and issues, as an aid to interpreting current and future developments.

Many people have contributed to this volume. All papers were sent out to peer review before final revisions. I cannot thank individually all those who assisted, but they know who they are and can be assured of my deep appreciation. A few individuals who played central roles in the institutional collaboration deserve special thanks: Sergio Aguayo

Quezada, Charles Keely, Howard Adelman and Meyer Brownstone. Penny Houghton of the Inter-American Organization for Higher Education (IOHE), who first supported the ideas leading to the book, also deserves special mention. Finally, I thank Farhana Mather, Patricia Landolt and Michelle van Beusekom for support, advice and assistance in the joint work with the donors and the authors to prepare the final text.

Financial assistance for the work leading up to this volume was received from the following institutions: IOHE (The Inter-American Organization for Higher Education), IDRC (International Development Research Centre), Pew Charitable Trusts, SSHRC (The Social Sciences and Humanities Research Council of Canada) and York University. I am most grateful to them for their support.

— *A. Simmons*
Toronto

Introduction

Research and Policy Issues in the Field of International Migration and North American Economic Integration

Alan B. Simmons

The contemporary world is increasingly drawn together through expanding international commerce, cultural linkages and international migration flows. While these elements of "globalization" are linked together, their relationship does not necessarily lead to social and political harmony. In fact, the process of global integration typically produces tensions between economic, cultural and migratory trends. These tensions are associated with a number of related social and political conflicts. The following features are widely observed:

1) During the so-called "adjustment" to new trade patterns, a country or subregion may experience a great loss of jobs and tax revenues for social programs.

2) Regions hard hit by job losses often experience rising social conflicts and even violence over scarce resources or over the failure of the local government to find solutions.

3) Modern international telecommunications and available airline transportation – key technological elements of the global system – permit dislocated workers and victims of social and political conflict to pursue migration as a solution to their problems.

4) International migrants frequently meet hostility and legal barriers to their entry into receiving countries. This is particularly true if the migrants are poor, less skilled and difficult to control or regulate because their international migration is crisis-driven.

5) In regions of migrant destination, conflict may arise between different recently arrived ethnic groups or between migrants and disadvantaged minorities with whom they compete for scarce jobs.

This book concerns the ways in which North America is responding to globalization and associated patterns of inequality, social conflict and international migration. To narrow the focus to a more manageable scope, the book concentrates on particularly important dimensions of the response, namely regional trade agreements and their implications. The scope is North America – Canada, Mexico and the United States – and two immediately adjacent regions – Central America and the Caribbean. Topics emphasized are those which have been given relatively less attention in previous studies. My purpose in this introduction is to clarify the reasoning that led to the selection of particular themes and to outline some major findings and issues for future research and policy action.

NORTH AMERICAN REGIONAL ECONOMIC INTEGRATION

Trade and investment linkages between the United States, as the dominant country in the system, and all other nations in the Northern Hemisphere were strong and well established prior to the development of recent specific trade accords in the region.[1] This system is now changing, in part purely in response to changes in corporate investment strategies, new technologies and new ways of organizing production. Many features of

---

[1] As Weintraub (1992: 509) notes, "Both Canada and Mexico send between 60 and 70% of their exports to the United States; for manufactured goods, the proportion is higher – upward of 80%. More than half the nonoil trade in North America is intrafirm trade, which reflects the large direct investment US multinational corporations have in the two other countries."

these changes were underway before any of the recent trade accords were signed and would have continued independently of such accords, as part of a global market system. At the same time, the emerging patterns of integration are significantly shaped by new North American international trade accords and trade-oriented national policies.

Recent regional accords and policies have been promoted in large part to reduce risks from trade challenges emerging from other parts of the global system. The challenges of the European Economic Community (EEC) and of Japan and its principal trading partners in Asia are commonly cited by those U.S. interests promoting greater economic integration within the North American hemisphere, and within the Americas more generally.[2]

Nations in the new global system often seek to minimize trade risks by pursuing more than one trade policy at the same time, even when these policies are not fully coherent with each other. Thus, the major North American nations continue to promote global trade accords, such as the General Agreement on Tariffs and Trade (GATT). At the same time, they promote regional accords. The Canada-USA Free Trade Agreement (CUFTA) signed in 1987 and first implemented in 1989 was a first step. The North American Free Trade Agreement (NAFTA), agreed to by Canada, the United States and Mexico in 1992, is a very large second step. The proximate regions, Central America and the Caribbean, have sought to reduce tariff barriers and promote expanded trade within their own regions. In this way, these smaller nations seek to reduce the insecurity arising from a fast-changing global trading system dominated by clusters of former colonial nations and their close trading partners in associations such as the EEC and NAFTA.

From the above, we may conclude that North American economic integration must be viewed in the context of global trends in trade and the formation of regional trade blocs. In addition, it is apparent that integration in North America cannot be reduced simply to the new trade accords in this region.

A further conclusion relates to the general research strategy of this volume. NAFTA, the most significant of the new trade agreements, is in a very early stage. Implementation will take place over a 15-year period, as different tariffs and subsidies are gradually eliminated. As a

---

[2]Canadian and Mexican promoters of NAFTA had other objectives. Fearing U.S. protectionism, they have viewed free trade primarily as a way of ensuring access to their most important trading partner, the United States (Weintraub, 1992: 510–511).

result, any forward-looking analysis of likely impacts must be based on what we know about trends and patterns of regional integration and international migration in the recent past. This is the approach followed in the various chapters and this introduction.

PREVIOUS RESEARCH

Although the literature is recent, a fair amount has been written about the relationship between North American economic integration and migration. The objectives of the present volume stem from an appreciation of what has been learned in previous studies and what remains unexplored and hypothetical. The following critical observations regarding this literature are relevant for the questions pursued in this volume.

1) Research on North American integration and international migration takes place within a politically charged context that has in some respects directed and limited the agenda of studies to date. Proponents of NAFTA, for example, have sought to play up the anticipated positive economic advantages and to play down possible undesirable social, migration and environmental impacts. President Salinas de Gotiari of Mexico argued that NAFTA would have positive benefits for Mexico that would slow the flow of Mexican workers to the United States. He said, "We want to export goods [,] not people" (Martin, 1993: 1). While many studies responded immediately to question any assumption that NAFTA would necessarily stem the emigration of Mexican workers in the short term, the approach taken in these studies tended to be set by the restricted frame of reference of the main issues of the political debate, namely labor markets and jobs.[3] Social and political forces giving rise to migration have been relatively ignored.[4]

[3]*See* the following reports: Acevedo and Espenshade (1992); Hinojosa-Ojeda and Robinson (1992); Levy and van Wijnbergen (1992); Martin (1993, 1994); Massey (1988).

[4]Of the reports cited in the previous footnote, only Massey (1988) and Martin (1993) give attention to institutional factors, such as cultural linkages, and the legacy of labor-migration agreements, such as the bracero programs between Mexico and the United States. None of these reports address the broader political-economic context of integration and migration, such as GATT and the structural adjustment policies promoted by the International Monetary Fund and the World Bank. A number of other texts, such as Grinspun and Cameron (1993) do extensively examine social and political dimensions of NAFTA without commenting on links to migration. Weinfield (1992) is one of the few exceptions in which both are covered, at least from a Canadian perspective.

2) Many if not most previous studies are concerned with only one aspect of the relationship between North American regional integration and migration. This aspect is the link between trade and migration. In fact, much of the research is even narrower, considering the impact of NAFTA on migration. These studies have led to the widely shared conclusion that NAFTA will lead to pressures for a significant increase in international labor migration from Mexico to the United States over the next 10 to 15 years, and (more hypothetically) to falling pressure for such migration subsequently.[5] Underlying such conclusions are various assumptions on the short-term and longer-term impact of NAFTA on relative wages and unemployment in Mexico and the United States. This kind of labor-market analysis provides an important base for assessing what is taking place, but it is incomplete. A large part of contemporary movement is driven by social conflict and political violence that cannot be reduced just to labor market considerations.[6]

3) Social and political factors in the international system have not been given the attention they deserve in examining economic integration in North America. Political considerations, particularly social policies governing the distribution of income, health and schooling in the sending and receiving countries, play an important role. So, too, do patterns of social conflict, violence, and human-rights protection. Matters of human rights, individual security and the freedom of political and labor movements are now so important in the flows from adjacent regions to North America that they must be incorporated fully into our analytic frameworks.

4) Research on market integration and international migration affecting North America has tended to focus on one par-

---

[5]The most thorough analysis may be found in Martin (1993) and in Massey (1988).

[6]This point has been made strongly for contemporary international movements in general by Zolberg, Suhrke and Aguayo (1989), who also apply their global paradigm to Central America and other specific regions.

ticular linkage: that between Mexico and the United States. This focus is quite logical in some respectsIt is understood that international migration between Canada and the United States is low to moderate in level. It is also relatively noncontroversial as it involves the movement of people with very similar levels of schooling, occupation and income. Migration from Mexico to the United States is the largest flow in the hemisphere. It is highly controversial. After all, wages in Mexico are about 10 percent of those in the United States.The health, schooling and occupational characteristics of Mexican immigrants to the United States are also make them distinctive. This said, other important and emerging features of the hemispheric system deserve greater attention. These include:

a)   The significant movement of people from Central America to Mexico, making Mexico a country of significant immigration as well as a country of significant emigration.

b)   Voluminous Caribbean migration to both the United States and Canada. This is a movement marked by particular points of tension, such as the ongoing Haitian crisis and exodus of refugees and refugee-like migrants, and the uncertain future migration of Cubans to North America as the Cuban crisis deepens.

c)   Global international migration patterns. The literature on North American economic integration generally considers movements within the region as if they were determined by a closed regional system of forces. In fact, the regional migration system is undoubtedly influenced by migratory flows from Asia and other parts of the world to the United States and Canada, but just how has not been assessed.

5)   Much of what has been studied with respect to North American market integration and migration is rather general in its treatment of the nature of the migrants and the social and political consequences of their movement.Thus, a good deal has been written about gross flows of migrants, but less has been said about their characteristics. What is known in this

field comes from more general studies of the international division of labor in the Americas.[7] However, these analyses leave unstated how the recent push to "structural adjustment" and free trade in North America and adjacent regions will affect the international division of labor and the employment of migrants. How many migrants will be women, and what implications will this have for their employment and the profits of their employers? Will those moving within the North American system and from proximate regions be limited to semiskilled workers, or will many include advanced-level students and professionals? Will movement be increasingly regulated by short-term visas? In the case of Europe, it has been noted that nothing is more permanent than a temporary migrant. Will the same be true in North America?

MAIN ISSUES AND ARGUMENTS

The papers in this book cannot cover all the less unexplored issues noted above. However, they can serve to broaden analytic perspectives in this field by viewing hemispheric integration in terms of its relation to broader global issues, and by giving more attention to social and political aspects of regional integration and migration patterns.The volume is organized into four sections, each of which draws attention to a particular theme that requires further exploration. These themes and the major findings related to them are set out below.

Part I. Social and Political Aspects of Restructuring

The chapters in this section generally support the view that NAFTA, as a new accord reinforcing certain existing trends in hemispheric integration, will likely accelerate the speed and exaggerate the effects of trends in integration observed over the 1980s and early 1990s. Ricardo Grinspun argues, for example, that NAFTA could make worse an already unequal distribution of economic benefits and social programs between participating countries and between social groups and

---

[7]See, for example, Cohen (1987: Ch. 2) and the useful collection of papers edited by Sanderson (1985).

sectors within these countries. In a similar critical vein, Maxwell Cameron notes that the forces promoting economic liberalization and free trade in the hemisphere may lead to unexpected and problematic political consequences. He observes that weaker countries in the international system, such as Mexico and Peru, have tended toward a hybrid of democracy and authoritarian government in order to sustain export-oriented development policies required by the regional and global political-economic system. Edur Velasco Arregui provides details on how the rights of Mexican workers have been affected over the 1980s as Mexico, well prior to NAFTA, began to orient its economic policies toward export-led growth and increasing integration into the international (principally the U.S.) market.

The preceding arguments suggest continuing, perhaps even increasing, pressures for emigration from poorer sending countries in the hemisphere as various measures of economic liberalization and integration, including NAFTA, are implemented over the next decade or so. Motives for emigration from these countries will include a mix of interdependent causes, including limited democracy, restrictions on the free organization of labor, social and political conflict in a context of unequal resources, high unemployment, and threats to personal security from high crime and social tensions.

Of course, whether those wishing to leave will be permitted entry in receiving countries is a separate matter. One of the seemingly paradoxical features of NAFTA and of the wider trend to export-led development and expanded trade is that the international movement of people remains as restricted as ever, while the international movement of capital, material goods and cultural goods is liberalized.

Yet, economic migrants and refugees do not always obey the official rules. Migrant receptivity in the wealthier, more secure countries depends heavily on such factors as historical and cultural linkages between migrants and communities in the destination countries and employment prospects for immigrants once they arrive. These forces often tend to encourage migration, even when official policies oppose it, as the papers in the remaining sections of the book make clear.

Part II. New Trends in International Migration

The papers in this section draw attention to the ways in which regional and global patterns of international migration influence one another.

They also comment extensively on the rise of short-term labor and student visas, and on the expansion of crisis-driven flows of refugee claimants and refugee-like migrants in the system. These new or rising trends have important implications for our understanding of North American integration.

Hania Zlotnik notes how international migration in North America is a subsystem within a larger global dynamic in which movement from less developed countries in Asia, the Caribbean and Latin America (and more recently Africa) is clearly and increasingly predominant. Another recent trend noted by Zlotnik is the extent to which short-term employment and student visas are increasingly employed by both Canada and the United States.

Margaret Michalowski examines in greater detail the rapid rise in the use of short-term visas, noting various trends in the origin of the visitors, their length of stay, and the reasons why they move. Visas seem to be readily available to visitors from other developed regions, such as Europe and Japan, who come to study, work or train briefly in a head office or branch plant, or to explore business and investment opportunities. Officials in both the United States and Canada have also used short-term visas for asylum seekers whose claim to stay permanently is not yet resolved or who, in any case, are not being immediately deported. Of course, those migrants who are granted short-term visitor or employment status do not exhaust the actual number of short-term migrants in North America. For example, very large numbers of undocumented Mexican migrants in the United States are known to frequently move back and forth between the two countries.

If these are the general trends from the perspective of the major migrant receiving countries, what then are the recent trends in adjacent regions, such as the Caribbean and Central America? Jean-Pierre Guengant observes that economic integration in Europe and in North America has particular implications for the Caribbean. Some Caribbean countries are territories or dependent political units of European countries or the United States. Still others are closely integrated into international banking and services. These countries have privileged access to investments and other resources, leading to expanded employment and in-migration from elsewhere. However, this is the case for only certain countries, most rather small in size. The rest of the region, including most of the larger countries, remains poor. Under this scenario, pressures to emigrate from the region will remain high.

Manuel Angel Castillo paints a picture for Central America that is similar to the Caribbean in many respects. The big difference is the extent to which Central American emigration in recent years has been driven by violent social and political conflict, including civil war, in addition to economic deprivation. (The only equivalent Caribbean case of emigration pushed by widespread violence in recent years would be Haiti.) Although peace is now spreading in Central America, the economic problems of the region are as serious, if not more serious, than they were in earlier periods.

Rodolfo Casillas draws attention to the Mexican dilemma. Mexico would like to foster selective immigration of skilled workers and professions to reinforce modernization and economic growth. Yet in the current context, Mexico seems destined to continue receiving large numbers of mostly unskilled rural emigrants from Central America. The Central Americans in Mexico, moreover, are a very diverse group. Some are refugees, others farm workers "pulled" into Mexico for seasonal employment, and still others are transmigrants, waiting for an opportunity to move further north to the United States or Canada. Mexican policy objectives have been far removed from the current reality and are only slowly beginning to address it.

It would seem fair to conclude that migration trends in the hemisphere are congruent with trends in the hemispheric political-economic system, including the movement toward increasing market integration. Just as economic integration in the region has progressed over a long period of investment by the United States (and more recently by Canada) in export-oriented enterprise in other countries of the region, so too international migration patterns within the system have developed historically. The United States has been and continues to be the wealthiest country and by far the most important destination for regional migrants. Canada occupies second place. Mexico is far less developed economically and is traditionally a migrant sending country, but it is more developed and politically stable than Central America, and hence has also become a major receiving country for Central American migrants.

Current migration patterns are characterized by both continuity and change. The major established streams, such as those from the Caribbean to North America and from Mexico to the United States, continue on their own internal dynamics (for example, family members come to join kin who have migrated earlier). Relative conditions in sending and receiving countries within the interdependent system have not changed or have become more polarized. New trends that are beginning to reshape the traditional pattern include the rising significance of asylum-seeking and of short-term work visas. This is consistent with a system that has become increasingly interdependent and accessible, both globally and regionally, to students, seasonal workers, and asylum seekers who are given short-term employment rights while their eventual fate is being determined.

Part III. The Emerging International Division of Labor

This section examines the organization of employment in the system. Attention is given to the way in which international migration and new productive investment in migrant sending and receiving countries influence one another. The rights of the workers and employer preferences with respect to gender and ethnicity are also discussed.

Maria Patricia Fernández-Kelly points out that social and economic impacts on immigrants, women, minorities and regional economies in the system can vary significantly from place to place. She notes, for example, that trends in the electronics sector – one particularly affected by globalization and North American integration – may not be shared by other industries. Moreover, the employment impacts and consequences for female migrant workers and different ethnic minorities (Hispanics, Blacks and Asians) in the electronics manufacturing sites she examines in New York are different from those in the sites she examines in California. This is so even though the electronics industry in both states has been affected by downsizing, polarization into sophisticated planning and engineer firms versus labor-intensive assembly firms, subcontracting of the latter by the former, and rising use of low-wage female immigrant labor in the low-end production sites. Moreover, Hispanic, Asian and Black minority groups are reacting differently to the emerging employment market, providing a base for ethnic conflict.

Monica Boyd observes that many of the employment trends in electronics industries, particularly those relating to the employment of women, are generally true in the United States. They are also evident in the textiles and clothing sector in Canada. She notes that the employment of immigrant women tends to follow the increasingly polarized structure of "flexible" industrial organization in a competitive, trade-oriented international economy. Some immigrant women are in top-level jobs or employed at good wages in sophisticated firms, while the others find themselves in a polar opposite situation.

Kathryn Kopinak examines the women's employment, wages and household economic strategies in the assembly industries (*maquiladoras*) of Sonora, Mexico. Like other free-trade zones in Mexico, employment in Sonora is characterized by high levels of low-wage female employment necessary to maintain minimum living standards for families, given insecure employment and low incomes of other family workers, including men. Increasing economic integration through NAFTA will presumably lead to further changes in the international division of labor within North America. Exactly what changes will occur has been difficult to determine given the fact that other "external" and global factors, including particularly economic competition from Asian producers, will affect within-region patterns.

These papers on emerging trends in the division of labor lead to tentative conclusions. It appears that economic integration and *maquiladora* style "free trade zones" (a kind of precursor to expanded free trade) have had mixed impacts on migrant women and ethnic minorities. When wages and employment fall for both men and women, as they may in an early stage of adjustment to regional or global trade and competition, it seems that women, particularly migrant women, are increasingly sought as low-wage employees. Their wages, while low, may nevertheless be more important than ever before in households where other earners are unemployed or also working at low wages. The net effect is a rise in female employment, although at low wages, and with greater stability than would otherwise be the case. Firms that might disappear under competition stay in business and continue to employ low-wage female workers. This said, the emerging pattern can hardly be termed progress or development. If the pattern tends to attract new investment in low-wage production, the net effect could be the appearance of economic development (rising production and exports) without social development. This would be more likely if the investments come from outside and lead to the export of profits. If the investments are local, the rising profits for local investors and low wages for local workers would simply reinforce class polarization and a widening distribution of income.

Part IV. Refugees and Asylum in the Hemisphere

Traditionally, issues of political persecution and asylum have been treated as a distinct subject having little to do with economic integration and the economic forces driving migration and the international division of labor. However, an examination of the papers in this section shows that they are in fact closely linked. The nature of democracy and local political control over economic and social matters is transformed through market integration and the international accords that support it. Small peasant farmers may rise up in revolt, as they have done recently in Chiapas, when local prices (particularly for coffee) fall in the context of trade liberalization and what they feel is an insensitive, unresponsive political system. Clearly the forces of economic integration are not the sole cause of the uprising—they may be just the most recent event that led to an explosion of frustration and anger. But, as in the case of Guatemala or Haiti, issues of political rights are difficult to separate from issues of access to land, employment and markets. The big question concerns how those who flee abroad to escape the mix of poverty and violence are treated in the communities where they seek asylum.

The answer to the preceding question can be given only tentatively, based on the papers in this section. Charles Keely and Sharon Stanton Russell argue that receiving countries in the system (Canada, the United States and Mexico) have common concerns and can cooperate to develop a shared regional policy on asylum. Moreover, they can develop such a policy in ways consistent with humanitarian action and human rights concerns. The other papers in the section report more on specific legislation and civic action with respect to refugees. These papers tend to support the conclusion that governments in North America tend toward similar viewpoints in this area, even though their specific policies are often quite different. Alexander Aleinikoff points out that despite significant changes in U.S. legislation on asylum, for the most part the out-of-country review of refugee claimants follows a "business as usual" pattern established years back. The big change is in the increasing volume of within-country claimants. The political reaction to rising numbers of refugee claimants pressing their cases for asylum after arrival is fraught with contradictions. The application of traditional standards by the U.S. government has clearly favored admission of some nationals (currently Cubans, in the past Nicaraguans) but not others (Guatemalans, Salvadorians, Haitians). Curiously, those who are not accepted as legitimate refugees are not necessarily returned home. Many are given temporary visas and work permits, and eventually find ways of staying permanently. Lucas Guttentag documents in particular the ambivalence and fluctuating policies of the U.S. government toward Haitians.

The Canadian refugee policy response, as reviewed by H. Patrick Glenn, is similar to that of the United States in some respects and different in others. It is similar in that it tends not to deport most refugee claimants. However, its specific policies are often quite different with respect to reaction to different national origin groups of claimants. For example, Canada has been much more open than the United States to viewing Salvadoran and Guatemalan refugee claimants as legitimate refugees with a right to permanent residence in Canada. However, the same policy dance is evident. Canada generally struggles to deal with two conflicting policy orientations: one, to limit refugee inflows to those who meet narrow criteria of individual persecution; two, to take a humane response to those fleeing violence, even when this does not involve individual persecution. Increasingly, Canada tends to accept refugee status claims from people fleeing diffuse violence and extreme poverty. Mexico may also be following a similar pattern, although the case is difficult to interpret. Mexico has on the one hand formally refused refugee status to Guatemalan claimants. Nevertheless, Mexico has also given temporary refuge to large numbers of these claimants. In addition, by not more vigorously pursuing deportation of undocumented migrants, Mexico has permitted large numbers of Guatemalans to assimilate into Mexican society.

In all migrant receiving countries there is significant public support for refugee claimants, and this can further limit or shape state actions. Sergio Aguayo Quezada details the ways in which civil society in Mexico has organized to assist and protect refugees. Finally, states do not act entirely independently in this field. Carlos Ochoa Garcia and Manuel Angel Castillo, in separate papers, detail the role of international institutions and governments, including the government of Mexico, in facilitating the peace process and in pushing for a return of Guatemalan refugees as part of this.

QUESTIONS AND CONTINUING DEBATES

Several broad questions cut across the various themes discussed above. The following general questions are relevant to future research and policy debate in this field.

Does economic integration increase or decrease international migration and refugee flows?
Frameworks for understanding the links between international trade and migration have not been very thoroughly developed at this point. Philip Martin, who has contributed extensively to this area, notes that trade and migration may either substitute for one another or they may stimulate each other, depending on particular circumstances and the mediation of policies that are in themselves influenced by earlier migration patterns and the flow of remittances (Martin, 1993: 29). Thus, the links are potentially extremely complex and difficult to disentangle.

The debate surrounding NAFTA's impact on migration has tended to concentrate on a question of numbers: how many more Mexicans are likely to move to the United States following the removal of certain Mexican tariffs and subsidies that currently protect employment in the small farm sector of Mexican agriculture? A few studies have estimated that the resultant increased migratory flow – that is the number above already high current flows arising from NAFTA – might be as many as 600,000 in the first year after the policy change (Hinojosa Ojeda and Robinson, 1992; Levy and van Wijnbergen, 1992). Such estimates assume that the principal force generating added migrant numbers will be rising unemployment in Mexico, given that some 3 million small farmers and another 3 million farm laborers face serious job and income loss when the current tariffs and subsidies sustaining the production of corn and beans on small farms in Mexico are withdrawn. However, others have questioned these estimates, suggesting that actual numbers may be far lower. From the perspective of these latter assessments, it may be more reasonable to assume that many small farmers and farm workers will adapt to loss of income from corn and beans by shifting to rely more on other part-time jobs they already have; or they may choose to migrate internally within Mexico to jobs that will be generated in those states benefiting from free trade and new investment (Cornelius and Martin, 1993).

Existing studies are clear in concluding that Mexican migrants move along well-established paths from central Mexico to farm and informal sector jobs in the US southwest. This being the case, the US government has found it very difficult to limit the flows through legislation and policing. Even the employer sanctions of the Immigration Reform and Control Act (IRCA) seem ineffective (Acevedo and Espenshade, 1992: 731).

Additions to the state of current knowledge arising from the chapters in the present volume largely concern the need to view the forces generating migration in broader terms. The impact of market integration on emigration from other regions, such as the Caribbean, has been strong in the past and will continue to be strong. This is the case simply because Caribbean nations do not have the resources to sustain protective tariffs in their own region, and they must lower if not eliminate taxes on imports in order to insure that their own exports will not be blocked by other nations. In addition, labor-intensive agricultural production is in a long and continuing decline in the region. NAFTA is a challenge because it creates preferential treatment for low-wage Mexican industrial exports to North America. To compete effectively with Mexico, the Caribbean would have to significantly improve its efficiency or come to accept lower wages.

What is the role of state policies and the practices of international agencies in the link between North American economic integration and international migration?
The present book also draws increased attention to the importance of policies in establishing the conditions for rising international migration in the context of expanding economic integration. Specifically, North American economic integration promotes expanded international migration through the following migrant push mechanisms.

1) The impact of structural adjustment policies and programs on short-term job dislocation.

2) A tendency in weaker nations to limit democracy and human rights during "painful" periods of adjustment to international markets.

3) Unequal land-tenure and weak income-distribution and social-justice policies in migrant sending countries that concentrate the negative impacts of adjustments to international markets on the poorest classes and on underprivileged ethnic minorities. In consequence the adjustments are born by people who cannot afford them, leading to crisis migration and increased social conflict and violence.

Economic integration also reinforces certain policies that tend to pull migrants to receiving countries and to expand short-term migrant circulation. For example, the intellectual property provisions of NAFTA and other trade agreements tend to reinforce the position of developed countries in the management and control of new productive technology. This has at least three migration effects.

1) Short-term circulation of managers and technical staff for purposes of setting up branch plants abroad and for training branch-plant staff in the developed country is reinforced. This trend is reflected in state policies that provide visas for an expanding range of visitors: students, intracompany transfers, investors, and so on.

2) Brain drain from less developed countries is reinforced, both through the operation of the market and through specific immigration policies favoring skilled migrants in the wealthier nations.

3) Income distribution in the system favors those who manage and control technology, either directly or through financial and legal institutions. Those who are furthest removed from this power are the unskilled workers in poor countries and regions. They will migrate to cities in their own countries and to informal sector jobs abroad.

Of course, these push and pull factors should not be considered to be independent, since they are linked and mutually reinforcing the new system. In addition, not all outcomes of integration will reinforce expanded international migration. For example, extreme social conflict, including violent confrontation between police and minority groups, can also erupt in the multiethnic "global cities," such as Los Angeles, during periods of recession or structural adjustment and the downsizing of firms. Thus, insecurity can rise in both sending and receiving areas. For the moment, the problems of insecurity in sending areas seem to dominate, and arguments outlined below suggest that this could continue to be the case over the foreseeable future.

What is the future scenario if current policies and practices do not change?
If current policies and practices do not change, the following hypotheses seem reasonable. There will likely be:

1) High pressure for continuing international migration at elevated levels. This will include particularly the emigration and circulation of less-skilled individuals from poor sectors in the weaker countries and from border regions facing growing poverty and deep political tensions.

2) Continued opening of immigration criteria in wealthier nations of the system to permit more skilled migrants including investors and entrepreneurs, either on a short-term or a long-term basis, combined with a tightening of immigration targets for less-skilled workers.

3) Rising undocumented migration as those who do not meet immigration criteria in the wealthier nations seek to bypass regulations.

4) Complex patterns of investment in which capital seeks profits in low-cost production. In some cases, low-cost production implies low wages, but this is not necessarily the case since low costs can also be achieved through increasing automation, reduced inventories, and other mechanism. The pattern is complex because investments may flow either to low-wage production in North American countries and/or to regions outside North America where workers willing to work for less are available. But investment may also be structured to entice low-wage workers to migrate from one place to another. Thus, investment and immigration patterns influence one another.

5) High levels of independent migration of women, given the preference of certain kinds of employers for immigrant women in low-wage assembly.

6) Potential for rising conflict between ethnic minorities in receiving countries, including conflict between minorities

who have recently arrived as immigrants (*e.g.*, Salvadorans, Koreans, etc.) and long established minorities, such as, in the case of the United States, blacks.

7) Confusion over criteria for refugee determination, leading to the risk of unjust actions or removal decisions not in accord with principles of human rights.

8) Rising potential for social conflict and violence in poor, migrant-origin regions and countries. This potential is particularly great in very poor communities. When changes in the market lead to losses of jobs and income in such communities, frustration is likely to be very high. There is no social security net or other resource to fall back on.

What are the constraints on and options for policy change?

1) Poor countries and regions in them find themselves facing particularly limited policy options. They must for the most part abide by current rules of the international system: loans must be repaid with interest through exports even if this means cutting social welfare and local wages to the bone. If there is rising production and income in the system, it may not benefit their regions or their workers. Some workers will benefit by moving and may send remittances for the survival of their families, but this is unlikely to generate autonomous development in the home community. The big problem is how to transfer rising wealth in some parts of the system across national boundaries. This task is the mandate of the World Bank and of the International Monetary Fund (IMF). These and other institutions are now examining the possibility of changing their policies, but whether they will be able to do so is not clear.

2) Wealthy countries or countries in which certain regions are generating wealth from economic integration have a greater range of options. They can more effectively transfer resources to poor regions. They can also use social policy in fields such as education to upgrade work skills, address the pressing needs of minorities for jobs and housing, and engage in other steps that will reduce social

conflict and enhance regional, national and minority-group economic prospects. Yet, in a context of adjustment of world-wide competition, taxes necessary to support such transfer payments are more difficult to generate.

3) Opportunities available to international organizations for reducing social conflict in poor countries certainly exist and can be pursued with greater effort. One of the striking features of the global-market system, as well as of the North American regional system, is the extent to which it is increasingly concerned with peacemaking and peacekeeping. If recent efforts by the international community to bring peace to the former Yugoslavia have been a failure, then at least efforts in El Salvador and Nicaragua have been relative successes. Guatemala is also a promising case at the present time. Haiti, at the moment, is still a question mark. The United States, backed by Canada and other nations in the hemisphere, contemplates military intervention, by invasion or invitation, to reestablish democracy and peace, in the hope that this will also bring to an end the exodus of Haitian boat people. In sum, efforts to bring peace and democracy are badly needed and should be expanded, but the terrain is extremely challenging.

4) Why has it been so difficult to include social policy, labor rights and environmental policies into NAFTA? Why has the EEC given greater attention to these matters and achieved more with respect to them? Clearly, inclusion of provisions on these matters would have an enormous impact on Mexican migration to the United States, for example. Weintraub (1992: 521) notes that there was simply no enthusiasm among U.S. and Mexican leaders for inclusion of these items in the accord, but that these concerns "will inevitably grow if the economic objectives of NAFTA are reached." From this perspective, the big question for reopening these policy questions, then, is the speed of progress on economic objectives.

What theoretical approach best suits the understanding of the how policies and social processes affecting migration develop and change? The many ways in which particular strategies of market integration and international migration are linked make it very difficult, if not impossible, to reduce the entire process to neoclassical models of regional economic development or to structural models of class conflict and imperialism. The linkages are more complex than such models imply. At the same time, it appears that certain hypotheses and theoretical perspectives may be particularly useful in understanding the relationship between economic integration and migration.

International economic and migration systems are what might be called "heavy" structures with considerable "momentum" based on particular patterns of information flow, contact, trust, legislation, and practices, at various institutional levels (government, enterprises, families) that have developed gradually over time. Even heavy structures can change quickly, but usually as gradual shifts from a previous path.

Current patterns of economic integration in North America are indeed elaborations of certain deeply rooted patterns. NAFTA, as a particular policy instrument, intensifies and spreads more widely aspects of trade and market penetration that were already in existence. Moreover, many of the trends in specific policies concerning North American economic integration actually predate NAFTA. Here I am not referring so much to other agreements (such as CUFTA, the bracero programs, or the U.S.-Mexican agreement behind the maquiladora free trade zones in North Mexico), but to independent decisions by the various countries in the region over the 1980s to shift to export-led development and to further open internal markets to foreign investment and competition. Even without NAFTA, regional and global processes of economic integration were moving forward, with social outcomes of the kind we have noted. NAFTA has the effect of exaggerating and speeding the process already underway. Similarly, NAFTA cannot be viewed independently of other international agreements, such as GATT, which reinforce economic globalization and affect regional trade as well.

The North American regional market is part of a global transformation of production and intensified struggle for profits. Trade agreements are consistent, necessary elements in efforts to shift production to cost-effective sites, to make labor more flexible though subcontracting, variable job assignment, part-time work, etc., and to make the manufacturing process more responsive to market demand through short production runs, low inventory, rapid change in product design or in actual product.

Applying these various arguments to North America, however, requires that one keep in mind the unique context. While the profit and investment strategies of nations and enterprises show increasing similarity around the world, specific applications and outcomes are often very different between regions. The North American case certainly contrasts in many respects with the European case. In Europe, many nations with greater balances of power between leading actors have sought economic integration in ways that increasingly shut out Third World migrants, while relying when necessary on migrants from former Eastern-bloc countries and on investments into these countries to take advantage of low-cost labor. In North America, one nation – the United States – dominates the others to the point that more serious questions arise on the distribution of gains from free trade. At the same time, the leading countries – the United States and Canada – have long histories of reliance on colonization and immigration to develop lands, to exploit resources and to meet farm and industrial labor demands. This historical tradition and the multiethnic communities to which it has given rise have a certain self-sustaining character that tends to slow efforts to change current international migration policies and patterns. In fact, even when legislation changes, practices may lag behind. For example, as shown in the papers by Aleinikoff and Glenn in this volume, various political, social and even economic reasons make it difficult for the United States and Canada to deport certain classes of undocumented migrants.

It therefore seems useful to examine the North American system, including the links between market integration, migration and related social outcomes, from the perspective of institutional linkages and historical developments, in which current patterns of economic integration through free trade are merely the most recent development. It also makes sense to give particular attention to the current historical moment and the transformation of free enterprise to understand current investment patterns and their implications for migration, minorities, social conflict and stratification. These observations accord generally, although not in detail, with migration models that stress historical interpretation, the centrality of capitalism in social and economic transformation, and an emerging international division of labor with regional and national implications in a global context.[8]

---

[8] Approaches which give priority to the weight of historical-institutional arrangements in explaining international migration include those proposed by Portes and Rumbaut (1990: Ch. 7), Cohen (1987), and Zolberg, Suhrke and Aguayo (1989).

With a few exceptions, the papers in the present volume are not explicitly theoretical, even though particular perspectives are evident in the background of most contributions. In the end, it is this insistence on providing observations based on recent economic or migration statistics, surveys and field observations, that may be most important at this moment. Theory can develop beyond general assumptions and approaches when more is known about the process. It is hoped that the papers published here will serve as important stepping stones for future work on the topic.

TOWARD SOME GENERAL POLICY CONCLUSIONS

Perhaps the clearest overall conclusion concerns the need to put aside simple generalizations, ideologically-based forecasts and conclusions based on preconceptions rather than assessments of trends. This clearly includes the need to put aside extreme preconceived scenarios such as the view that economic integration will quickly lead to rising incomes in all countries, all classes, all gender and ethnic groups, and to a decline in international migration and related problems of regional inequality and conflict. If such a positive outcome does emerge, surely it will be after much time has passed and will depend on other factors, such as social policies in the countries concerned.

Overly simplistic negative scenarios must also be rejected. Evidence presented in this volume suggests that economic integration over the short term will tend toward greater polarization of job opportunities and incomes between regions within countries, between countries, between educational strata, between women and men, and between ethnic groups. It also seems to be the case that the immediate impact of economic integration will be rising pressures for international move-ment of workers and refugees along with expanding ethnic and social conflict associated with economic dislocation. Yet, again, real outcomes are likely to turn out to be more complex, varied and interesting than such simplistic scenarios would imply. Actual outcomes will likely depend heavily on policies in other areas, such as those affecting efforts to bring peace and security to troubled countries, improved human rights to regions where they are weak, and greater education and employment opportunities to vulnerable groups, such as women and less privileged ethnic minorities.

What perspectives, then, emerge from the preceding findings and what considerations for the policy approach that should be taken with respect to hemispheric integration and international migration? These are now major questions confronting nations-states and international organizations.[9]

My own reading of the existing research and the contributions in this volume point to the following new policy directions:

1) Policy should begin from the assumption that the current international system, including efforts to expand regional trade, tends to generate migration. Transition periods are likely to lead to increased overall flows of a crisis-driven nature.

2) Policy should continue to address the specific issues that drive migration. This thrust should draw attention to the human face of migration by pointing to individual cases. Such an approach is required to counter the use of mechanical terms, such as "flood" or "invasion", that are often used to negatively characterize and dehumanize aggregate movements of international migrants.

3) Policy should give increasing priority to human rights considerations. The simplest and most radical way of doing this would be to proclaim that everyone has a fundamental right to stay in the place where he/she currently resides (Meissner et al., 1993: 89). This presumes international safeguards to promote peace, security and basic welfare in all communities in the hemisphere. Migration could then become purely voluntary and, eventually, unrestricted.

4) Policy should increasingly clarify the obligations of all countries in the hemisphere with respect to granting asylum in instances where efforts to insure peace, security and basic welfare have failed.

5) Policy should include the development of "early warning" information systems to detect migrant-producing crises before they erupt and to mobilize resources of the international community to avoid crisis. In cases where ethnic, religious and other social tensions have been aroused to the point of

---

[9]*See*, for example, OECD (1993), Meissner *et al.* (1993), and SOPEMI (1993).

violent confrontation, the response should include efforts to mediate tensions through intensive mass-media programs designed to break down stereotypes and social divisions.

6) Pursuing these strategies implies working against current resistance to incorporating social policies into trade pacts. These social policies should include agreements on the treatment of international migrants and the supports for their integration into host societies.

REFERENCES

Acevedo, D., and T. J. Espenshade
1992   "Implications of a North American Free Trade Agreement for Mexican Migration in the United States," *Population and Development Review*, 18(4):729–744. December.

Bach, R. L.
1985   "Political Frameworks for International Migration." In *The Americas in the New International Division of Labor*. Ed. S. Sanderson. New York and London: Holmes and Meier.

Cohen, R.
1987   *The New Helots*. London: Gower.

Cornelius, W., and P. Martin
1993   "The Uncertain Connection: Free Trade and Rural Mexican Migration to the United States," *International Migration Review*, 27(3):484–512. Fall.

Fawcett, J. M.
1989   "Networks, Linkages and Migration Systems," *International Migration Review*, 23(3):671–680.

Grinspun, R., and M. A. Cameron, eds.
1993   *The Political Economy of North American Free Trade*. Montreal and Kingston: McGill-Queen's Press.

Hinojosa-Ojeda, R., and S. Robinson
1992   "Labor Issues in a North American Free Trade Area." In *North American Free Trade: Assessing the Impact*. Ed. N. Lustig, B. Bosworth and R. Lawrence. Washington, DC: The Brookings Institute.

Levy, S., and S. van Wijnbergen
1992   "Mexican Agriculture in the Free Trade Agreement: Transition Problems in Economic Reform." Technical Papers No. 63. Paris: OECD Development Centre.

Martin, P.
1994   "Migration and Trade: Challenges for the 1990s." Mimeograph. Department of Agricultural Economics, University of California–Davis.

1993   *Trade and Migration: NAFTA and Agriculture*. Washington, DC: Institute for International Economics.

Massey, D.
1988   "Economic Development and International Migration in Comparative Perspectives," *Population and Development Review*, 14(3):383–413.

Massey, D., R. Alacron, J. Durand and H. Gonzales
1987   *Return to Aztlan*. Berkeley: University of California Press.

Meissner, D., R. Hormats, A. G. Walker and S. Orgata
1993   "International Migration Challenges in a New Era." The Triangle Papers No. 44. New York, Paris and Tokyo: The Trilateral Commission.

OECD Development Co-operation Directorate
1993   "Migration and International Co-operation: Challenge for OECD Countries." Paper presented at OECD Conference on Migration and International Co-operation: Challenges for OECD Countries. Madrid, March 29–31.

Portes, A., and R. Rumbaut
1990   *Immigrant America: A Portrait*. Berkeley: University of California.

Randall, S. J., H. Konrad and S. Silverman
1992   *North America Without Borders? Integrating Canada, the United States and Mexico*. Second edition. Calgary: University of Calgary Press.

Richards, A.
1993   "Does Trade Liberalism Influence Migration? Some Evidence from Developing Countries." Paper presented at OECD Conference on Migration and International Cooperation: Challenges for OECD Countries. Madrid, March 29–31.

Russell, S. S., and M. J. Teitelbaum
1992   "International Migration and International Trade." World Bank Discussion Paper No. 160. Washington, DC: The World Bank.

Sanderson, S., ed.
1985   *The Americas and the New International Division of Labor*. New York and London: Holmes and Meier.

Simcox, D. E.
1992   "Immigration and Free Trade with Mexico: Protecting American Workers against Double Jeopardy," *Population and Environment*, 14(2):159–175. November.

SOPEMI
1993   "Trends in International Migration." Paper presented at OECD Conference on Migration and International Cooperation: Challenges for OECD Countries. Madrid, March 29–31.

Weinfield, M.
1992   "North American Integration and the Issue of Immigration: Canadian Perspectives." In *North America Without Borders? Integrating Canada, the United States and Mexico*. Second edition. Ed. S. J. Randall, N. Konrad and S. Silverman. Calgary: University of Calgary Press. Chapter 14.

Weintraub, S.
1992   "North American Free Trade and the European Situation Compared," *International Migration Review*, 26(2):506–524. Summer.

Zolberg, A., A. Suhrke and S. Aguayo Quesada
1989   *Escape from Violence: Conflict and the Refugee Crisis in the Developing World*. New York and Oxford: Oxford University Press.

Part I

Social and Political Aspects of Restructuring

1

NAFTA, Civil Society and Neoconservative Restructuring[1]

Ricardo Grinspun

Introduction

The main thesis of this article is that economic integration as promoted by NAFTA encourages and consolidates profound transformations in state-civil society relations, as well as in the economic, social and political structures of each country, and in particular, of the "junior" countries in the arrangement (Canada and Mexico). The costs of adjustment in labor markets fall inordinately on disadvantaged groups in society. Larger economic inequality brings worsened social conditions and a political process that is even more attentive to the power of large national and international capital.

This paper focuses on common characteristics of the restructuring forces shaping the North American societies. The key idea is that close connections exist between economic restructuring and integration on the one hand and social, political and human development on the other.

[1]This paper is a revised version of Grinspun (1993b) and draws on joint work with Maxwell A. Cameron (Grinspun and Cameron, 1993) and with Robert Kreklewich (Grinspun and Krelewich, n.d.). I am grateful to Max Cameron, Kiaran Honderich, Rob Kreklewich and Alan Simmons for useful comments on an earlier draft. The views presented herein, as well as any errors, are solely my responsibility. I acknowledge grants from the Faculty of Arts and York SSHRC at York University.

The next section focuses on the role of NAFTA as a promoter of neoconservative restructuring. Later sections deal with labor market restructuring, social impact and growing inequality. This short presentation will necessarily remain conceptual and synoptic.

NAFTA AS A PROMOTER OF NEOCONSERVATIVE RESTRUCTURING

The August, 1992, NAFTA agreement focuses mainly on technical issues that, at first sight, would have little relevance to the social and political character of a country. These include tariff and nontariff barriers, rules of origin, customs administration, subsidies to foreign trade, rules of investment, technical standards, sanitary and phytosanitary measures, dispute settlement mechanisms, intellectual property rights, and government procurement. The 2,000-page document barely touches on issues of labor adjustment, and its treatment of environmental barriers to trade is based on inadequate GATT precedent. The document does not address social programs, political systems, or even general economic policies in each country. Certainly, the deeper links of trade negotiations to the structure of civil society are not transparent.

The parties to the 1991–1992 NAFTA negotiation recognized, sometimes reluctantly, that an agreement would have influences in diverse areas, for example, the need for labor-market adjustment and environmental regulation. However, these effects were initially seen either as marginal, or as necessary costs to obtain the so-called "economic benefits" of NAFTA. This narrow perspective on NAFTA was shared by the Mulroney, Salinas and Bush administrations.[2] The Clinton administration's recognition that this vision of NAFTA is narrow and incomplete led during 1993 to the initiation of negotiations on labor and environmental side agreements. Completed during August, 1993, the side agreements do not substantially alter NAFTA, but merely propose a face-saving set of unenforceable principles and inadequate institutions. The labor agreement pays lip service to worker rights such as collective bargaining. The environmental agreement does not address issues such as energy, natural resources and agriculture.

To understand the implications of NAFTA for our civil societies, one must first discuss its economic essence. NAFTA is usually presented as

[2]Such a perspective is presented, for example, in *North American Free Trade: Securing Canada's Growth through Trade*(Canada, n.d.)

a trade-liberalizing agreement. However, the liberalizing effect is weaker and less central to the agreement than first appearances would indicate. Most of NAFTA's 22 chapters focus on issues other than commodity trade. Moreover, the level of trade liberalization achieved between the three countries before NAFTA was negotiated was already quite advanced, due to the Canada-United States Free Trade Agreement (CUFTA) implemented in 1989 and the unilateral process of trade liberalization that Mexico undertook during the De la Madrid (1982–1988) and in particular the Salinas (1988) presidencies (Grinspun, 1993a; Lustig *et al.*, 1992: 117–120). Lastly, in the case of nontariff barriers (NTBs) the liberalization obtained was even more limited, since many NTBs were grandfathered in CUFTA and NAFTA. NTBs remain relevant for Canada and Mexico since these agreements legitimize (subject to the application of a new dispute-settlement mechanism) the unilateral use of US trade law to manage trade flows (Cameron, 1988; CCPA, 1992; Sinclair, S., 1993).

The main impacts of NAFTA at the nation-state level will be to carve a stronger role for transnational capital and to consolidate a neoconservative agenda of structural reforms by engraving the changes in an international treaty. Business spokepersons have readily acknowledged that a key role of NAFTA will be to consolidate these reforms.

Claudio González, chairman of Kimberly-Clark of Mexico and a special adviser to the President on foreign investment, describes the intent of a North American free trade area from the standpoint of Mexico's business community as being "to lock in many of the changes that have taken place in our country." It will convince holders of capital that Mexico's new outward orientation, and its commitment to a deregulated market economy, is permanent (Cook, 1991).

The major effect of NAFTA on the trade flows of the "junior" partners is a disciplining one. They will see their ability to manage their trade through activist policies seriously curtailed. Canada and Mexico will further diminish their ability to subsidize their exports, even indirectly, and to engage in various industrial and development policies. One should recall that the "success stories" in terms of export-led growth are based on aggressive promotion of exports and active government intervention (*i.e.*, South Korea), as well as almost nonexistent intellectual property laws that permitted easy and widespread access to technology (Park, 1988; Gereffy, 1992). Mexico is trying to engage in export-led growth under vastly inferior and restrictive conditions (Grinspun and Cameron, 1993b). Literally hundreds of Mexican government programs have been eliminated in the process of opening the economy for NAFTA.

This handcuffing of the Canadian and Mexican governments works in various ways. A major one is by legitimizing in the agreements the unfair trade laws of the United States. This legislation is used by the United States to attack government programs in other countries that directly or indirectly support exports to the United States. For example, Canadian regional development programs – a necessity in a country with such geographic dispersion and unequal regional development – are constantly being challenged by the United States as "unfair trade practices" (Sinclair, S., 1993). Second, stronger intellectual property laws that will benefit U.S.-based Transnational Corporations (TNCs) have a detrimental economic and social impact. These laws restrict the opportunities for industrial and technological development through the exploitation of cheap foreign (mainly U.S.) technology – a key element in the late industrialization of countries such as Japan and South Korea. These laws constitute also a blow to the Canadian medicare system, since they imply raising medical drug prices (Rotstein, 1993).[3] Lastly, the free trade agreements make Canada and Mexico even more susceptible to pressures from the United States on areas that are not directly covered by the agreements. This may be the explanation, for example, for exchange-rate policies of the Canadian government which have been hugely detrimental for Canadian industry but beneficial for the US balance of payments,[4] and perhaps for a similar overvaluation of the Mexican peso during the NAFTA negotiations.

The main economic effects of NAFTA would be on investment flows and capital mobility. In truth, the free trade agreement (whether CUFTA or NAFTA) is a misnomer; a better and more appropriate name would be a free investment agreement. The liberalization of investment

---

[3]Bill C-91 extending patent protection for pharmaceutical drugs was passed in Canada before the NAFTA negotiations ended, in anticipation of such a requirement with the pending passage of Uruguay Round and NAFTA agreements. By embodying the legislation in international treaties, the legislation becomes, in practice, irreversible.

[4]Macroeconomic policies since the middle 1980s, when CUFTA was negotiated, encouraged high interest rates and an appreciated dollar. These trends made the Canadian industry quite uncompetitive, with very detrimental effects in terms of employment and capacity utilization (Grinspun, 1993a).

(in particular of investments by U.S.-based TNCs in Canada and Mexico) is a key element of CUFTA and NAFTA. Canadian critics have argued that CUFTA is a new economic constitution for the junior partner, Canada.[5] NAFTA would have a similar effect for Mexico. This constitution solidifies a bill of economic rights for large national and transnational capital. The business elite and the corporations they control gain a continental citizenship, permitting them to restructure and rationalize their productive processes at a transnational level, cheapening their costs and gaining competitive positions *vis-à-vis* the threatening Japanese and European capital. This is the essence of the "economic blocks."[6] Capitalist competition transcends the nation-state and assumes a continental basis. This continental citizenship is expressed in the "national treatment" clauses for foreign capital, the dismantling of control mechanisms on foreign investment and the legitimizing of increased capital mobility, the intellectual property laws, the drive toward deregulation and privatization and the diminished role for public initiative, the continental restructuring of financial services, and other measures, which are all elements either in CUFTA, NAFTA, or both.[7] Capital, with its increased mobility, now faces porous international and intranational borders, weakening the ability of governments to apply independent policies. Capital is attracted to places with low costs of production, low taxes, and little regulation. This creates convergence toward the lowest common denominator in terms of economic, taxation, social and labor standards. This is true both across state and province borders as well as across national borders.[8]

A major objective of CUFTA and NAFTA is to create internal and external conditioning mechanisms to promote a neoconservative economic program. The absence of an internal base of support for these

---

[5]Many of the criticisms of CUFTA presented in this paper are elaborated in different chapters of Duncan Cameron (1988). *See also* Barlow (1991) and Barlow and Campbell (1992). The institutional and historical background of NAFTA is analyzed in Grinspun and Cameron (1993a).

[6]A discussion of the evolving North American trading bloc from an international political economy perspective can be found in Ranney (1993).

[7]These and other related themes are developed by various authors in Grinspun and Cameron (1993a).

[8]The dialectic of the process is such that popular forces will react and push for *upward* harmonization of economic and social standards. This popular mobilization was the basis for the Clinton administration's decision to negotiate side agreements on labor and environmental standards, completed during August 1993.

unpopular changes is substituted with an external one (Grinspun and Kreklewich, n.d.). The neoconservative agenda includes the elimination of weak, inefficient industrial sectors. It also includes deregulation of the economy, privatization of public enterprises, dismantling of social and labor programs and lowering tax rates on profits. Lower costs of production (*e.g.*, lower private and social real wages) and the shift of initiative from the public sector toward the private sector (a euphemism for large-scale, internationally-linked, capital) are essential neoconservative objectives.[9] At the macro level, it is necessary to implement recessionary policies both to achieve lower inflation (which is good for financial expansion) and to weaken independent labor unions through greater unemployment.

CUFTA and NAFTA are instrumental in pursuing and facilitating various aspects of this neoconservative agenda. An example is the effective constraint that agreements of this kind impose on the establishment of new government programs (as happened in Canada under CUFTA, and is likely Mexico under NAFTA). One reason is that under the typical terms of such an agreement the government has to compensate U.S. firms that may suffer a financial loss as a result of the new program. Campbell (1993: 92) makes clear the implications of creating a new public program in Canada under CUFTA.

> Article 2010 of CUFTA requires prior consultation with the U.S. government and leaves implementation subject to the nullification and impairment clause (Article 2011), which says that, even if an action is compatible with the agreement, if it reduces benefits otherwise expected by U.S. corporations, then the United States is entitled to compensation. Moreover, Article 1605 requires "fair market compensation" to U.S. firms for measures that are considered "tantamount to expropriation".

Later he adds:

> It is important to note . . . that if CUFTA had been in place in the 1960s, these same provisions and the same corporate pressure would probably have prevented Canada from bringing in its publicly funded and administered medical insurance (p. 102).

---

[9]The term "private sector" tends to lump together actors with divergent interests. Neoconservative reforms favor that segment of the private sector capable of internationalizing operations, either through export-orientation, transnational linkages, and the like. Small domestically-oriented businesses suffer the joint impact of recessionary policies and cheaper imports.

These provisions of CUFTA are a key reason why the government of Ontario scrapped plans for establishing a public auto-insurance system, given the likely claim for compensation to U.S.-based insurance companies for foregone future profits. The United States reacted aggressively to this plan, claiming it would constitute a violation of CUFTA (Barlow and Campbell, 1992).

The proponents of free trade in Canada accuse the detractors of giving too much importance to CUFTA and NAFTA. These agreements, they say, cannot cause by themselves a radical transformation of the economy and society. This criticism is correct. Both CUFTA and NAFTA cannot be analyzed in isolation; on the contrary, they must be understood as key components of a wider neoconservative scheme. This is a scheme to restructure the nation-state and to establish a new relationship between the state and civil society. Private capital, and in particular transnational capital, becomes the engine of economic growth. The state must take a subsidiary role of stabilizing and maintaining appropriate conditions for this new stage of capitalist development. Civil society must be restructured to lower costs of production and to transfer economic and political power to the economic groups allied to North American capital.[10]

LABOR MARKET RESTRUCTURING

One of the outcomes of trade liberalization is the loss of jobs in protected and subsidized sectors. Trade liberalization feeds into both the drive toward regional integration and into GATT-driven global trends. Thus, labor adjustment dictated by North American integration reinforces adjustment deriving from wider forces. One global trend openly encouraged by agencies such as the International Money Fund (IMF) and the World Bank is toward conservative monetary and fiscal policies, and the concurrent application of these macroeconomic policies with trade liberalization intensifies the pain of industrial restructuring. Moreover, capital flows as well as the relocation of production lines promoted by economic integration also contribute to labor dislocation. Given the multitude of local and global forces, the character of restructuring is nationally, regionally and sectorially differentiated.

---

[10]An articulate proposal for this "market-friendly" transformation of the economy and society can be found in World Bank (1991).

Some countries will benefit more than others, and some zones and sectors enjoy the export "boom" while other sectors "bust."

The most visible sign of economic restructuring is large changes in the structure of labor demand. Workers, their families and other weak groups in society will pay the costs of economic restructuring and loose economic opportunities. The burden on workers and the disadvantaged grows in the absence of adequate social and labor adjustment programs. The Mulroney administration did not implement new labor adjustment programs following the implementation of CUFTA, and weakened existing ones, such as unemployment insurance (Brazao, 1992). The Chretien administration, elected during October, 1993, on promises to reverse this trend and engage in job adjustment and creation, will be constrained by a growing fiscal deficit. In Mexico, with an almost nonexistent social safety net, workers and their families coping with the distress of economic restructuring are on their own. In contrast, the Clinton administration is likely to heed the calls for labor adjustment legislation if NAFTA is ratified and implemented, but the real commitment of resources to such programs is uncertain.[11] The labor side agreement completed by the three countries during August, 1993, was strongly criticized by opponents of NAFTA as being ineffectual.

Labor market restructuring in Canada since the implementation of CUFTA has been distressing. This restructuring has promoted massive job dislocation but little – if any – job creation. The situation in the manufacturing sector is particularly worrying, where about a half-million jobs were lost between June, 1989, and March, 1992 – a whopping 26 percent of the total. This figure does not include the shift from full-time to part-time employment during this period. In contrast, the United States had only about 6 percent loss of manufacturing jobs during a similar period.[12] The Canadian restructuring is the combined result of free trade and the accompanying macroeconomic policies (Grinspun, 1993a). The industrial corridor between Windsor and Quebec City has seen the worst depression since the 1930s, with a large increase in structural unemployment caused by plant relocation and permanent job loss.

[11]Hufbauer and Schott (1992: 340) estimate that at least $900 million are required in the United States during the first five years of NAFTA implementation to adequately deal with worker dislocation and retraining. Given Clinton's budgetary problems, actual allocations are likely to be insufficient.

[12]Data from Campbell (1993: Table 6.1).

One essential mechanism of adjustment to economic restructuring is labor migration to places where economic opportunities are favorable. Migratory flows are likely to accelerate both domestically and internationally in response to the restructuring of the labor market. An unfortunate outcome for Canada is the likely loss of qualified labor, in particular to the United States. Although CUFTA does not incorporate significant labor mobility, it includes easier passage for business representatives. Highly trained technicians and professionals are more mobile and more prone to take advantage of new opportunities – with or without CUFTA. This greater mobility of middle and middle-upper classes, and the relative immobility of working-class families is another mechanism by which the burden of the economic restructuring is unequally distributed. NAFTA does not prohibit labor relocation within each country, but it does not include specific measures to alleviate the costs of such adjustment. Also, a major drawback of NAFTA is that it does not deal with labor mobility between countries (in particular between Mexico and the United States).

The burden of job loss falls inordinately on weaker groups in society. In Canada, the economic crisis increases social and economic pressures at the bottom of the income scale. Certain groups of immigrants from less developed countries, lacking education and having poor language skills, are likely to be among the first to lose their jobs. Many immigrants – particularly women – tend to work in low-skill industries such as textiles and apparel, which are heavily affected by restructuring. The Canadian textile manufacturing sector lost 32 percent of the jobs between June, 1989, and March, 1992, and the apparel sector lost 33 percent during the same period (Campbell, 1993). The impact on the disadvantaged has many angles. An important one is that deindustrialization and job loss diminish the tax base upon which social services depend. This is happening in a city like Toronto, which has lost more than 10 percent of its businesses during the current recession. The City of Toronto's tax base shrank during 1992 for the first time in its history, due to the closure or moving out of about 4,200 of the city's 40,000 businesses (Armstrong, 1993). A natural response to "bad economic times" is the tendency to impose new restrictions on inflows of immigrants into the country. Recent policy changes in Canada are consistent with this view. There is an effort to limit the number of asylum seekers and of immigrants that do not have special skills or financial resources, while favoring the wealthy immigrants from places such as Hong Kong. Bills C-55 and C-84, implemented in Canada in 1989 represented an effort in this direction, although the impact on the flow of those arriving as refugee claimants seems to have been shortlived (Simmons and Keohane, 1992). Bill C-86, passed in 1992, encouraged certain economic migrants such as workers in scarce supply, investors and entrepreneurs. At the same time it made family sponsorship of new immigrants more restrictive. The same bill also gives Canadian immigration authorities the power to enter into agreements with other countries, such as the United States, so that refugee claimants who fail to meet admission standards in one country will not have the right to pursue a claim in another (for further details *see* chapters by Glenn and Aleinikoff in this volume).

Mexico during the 1980s provides another example of a boom-and-bust economy where restructuring has thrown labor markets into disarray. Restructuring was initiated as a result of the 1982 crisis and the need to redirect resources to external debt payments. IMF-supported policy packages emphasized fiscal and monetary restraint, with further recessionary impact on the economy. The accession to GATT in 1986 and the hurried drop in duties, import-licenses and other market protections left a vast domestically-oriented industry exposed to the ravages of international competition. Deregulation, privatization and further trade and financial liberalization accelerated during the Salinas administration. As a result of these policies, real salaries dropped more than 40 percent between 1982 and 1988, and the share of salaries in national income dropped from 35 to 26 percent in the same period.[13] Drastic economic restructuring created large disguised unemployment in the form of an exploding informal economy, now representing about one-third of total employment. The rural economy, like that in southern regions with a large indigenous population, has undergone impoverishment and depression. The traditional import-substituting industry has been battered by the joint forces of liberalized imports, lack of governmental support, and depressed macroeconomic conditions. An important element has been a shrinking domestic market as the result of income depressing policies.

Other regions, in particular in the northern border areas, are facing a scarcity of qualified workers. One effect of industrial restructuring in

---

[13]Data in this paragraph is from OECD (1992).

Mexico has been a shift of manufacturing jobs from the central areas to the northern border (Velasco, 1993). The most dynamic industrial sector in the new regime is the *maquiladora* industry, which is an enclave economy situated largely in that border. It is based on a mobile working force, mainly young women, and is still dominated by the typical sweatshop using inexpensive labor to assemble and engage in various low-skill, labor-intensive operations. This industry, organically linked to transnational corporations' global production arrangements, demonstrate dynamism, in contrast to the depressed nature of much of the economy. However, the *maquiladora* industry does not have the capacity to absorb the labor surplus resulting from job loss in traditional import-substituting manufacture and the rural economy. The maquiladora sector employed at its peak less than half a million workers, whereas the need for job creation is much larger: every year there are more than 1 million new entrants into the Mexican labor force (OECD, 1992).

The rural economy presents even larger contrasts. Mexico has a two-tier agricultural economy, one based on traditional technology, the other on highly productive and export-oriented agribusiness. Under NAFTA the likelihood of a growing agricultural export sector concentrates on the northwestern states of Sinaloa, Sonora and Baja California, where the transnational corporations have been the major channel for inflows of agricultural know-how, and where foreign direct investment has concentrated. In contrast, a likely outcome of trade liberalization and the related changes to the constitutional status of *ejido*[14] land are the creation of a landless peasant class and increased migratory flows toward the cities.

Several observers have predicted a likely increase in flows of *indocumentados* to the United States, particularly since the NAFTA agreement did not exempt the crucial maize sector from liberalization (although it stipulated a gradual liberalization, over 15 years). There are still 23 million Mexicans who live in rural areas (INEGI, 1992: 12). Total rural employment is 6 million, of which 1.7 million is in the maize sector (Hinojosa-Ojeda and Robinson, 1992: 89). These farmworkers may see their way of life threatened. A study by Levy and van Wijnbergen estimates that NAFTA may increase projected migration during the next decade from the rural to the urban areas by 700,000 (from 1.2 million to 1.9 million) – a significant amount of which may flow to the

---

[14]The *ejido* is the traditional land-tenure system (OTA, 1992: 67).

United States.[15] This huge migration is fed by policies guided to promote agribusiness and discourage small scale, self-reliant agriculture. As noted earlier, these policies are not formally part of NAFTA but are fully consistent with the larger package of neoconservative reform.

The large majority of small farmers have seen their situation deteriorate during the 1980s as a result of withdrawal of government support, depressed economy, and import liberalization (OTA, 1992). Since 1988, real salaries in agriculture have fallen precipitously, and this follows the drop after the debt crisis in 1982. In 1989, over 46 percent of rural families were officially poor: they earned two minimum wages or less – under U.S.$200 a month (OECD, 1992). The prospects for the future are not better: most *ejido* holdings are in the center of the country, not appropriate for export-oriented growth, and this traditional sector will undergo restructuring as a result of NAFTA and the recent constitutional changes that allow for commercialization of the *ejido* holdings. Poor and dispossessed landless farmers and migrant workers will bear the brunt of the cost of NAFTA in Mexico.

SOCIAL DETERIORATION AND INEQUALITY

Overall, NAFTA promotes a situation where disadvantaged groups in each society are likely to worsen their situation. The growth of structural unemployment, in particular among low-skill workers, hits social groups that have the least protection. NAFTA's costs – unemployment, loss of wages and benefits, need to relocate and impoverishment – are likely to be born by vulnerable groups: by "undocumented" workers, Hispanics and blacks in the United States; by marginalized groups and workers, particularly in rural areas, in Mexico; and by low-skill workers and certain ethnic and native groups in Canada. In addition, the downsizing of government-supported unemployment and social programs – driven both by ideological and fiscal considerations – and the overall shift of power from labor to capital affect mainly the weaker groups.

The fiscal contraction fits nicely within the neoconservative objective of widening the space for unregulated, unfettered market forces. The fiscal crisis also strengthens the call to cut social expenditures – the daily experience in Canada during the early 1990s. This crisis is worsened by a shrinking tax base due to the loss of traditional industrial sectors, as well as by the lowering of effective tax rates on capital. All

[15]Study cited in Hinojosa-Ojeda and Robinson (1992).

these contribute to a more acute economic and social situation for less favored social groups.

In Canada the combination of recession, restructuring, and downsizing of social expenditures has created a very difficult social situation. The recession was officially declared dead late in 1992, but the ensuing recovery has been a jobless one. Unemployment was very high by Canadian standards, reaching 11.6 percent in late 1992, and coming back to that level in the middle of 1993; if one adds those discouraged Canadians who have dropped out of the work force since 1989, one attains 13.3 percent unemployment, and this does not include about two percent of the labor force that has been forced to shift from disappearing full-time jobs to part-time ones in the same period.[16] One distressing impact of restructuring is on hunger. According to information provided by the Daily Bread food bank in Toronto, in early 1993 there were 163,000 people in the city dependent on food banks. More than 90 percent of those said they go without food at least once per month. Children were overrepresented in the group. A key factor in this hunger crisis is economic restructuring: 66 percent of the adults using the food banks had lost their work during the current recession (which started in 1990).[17]

Economic restructuring is inherently unequal, between countries, regions, sectors and social groups. Some will gain and some will loose. Moreover, the economic and social "adjustment costs" in the short and medium terms will affect the majority of the population. In Mexico, these "short-term adjustment costs" have persisted during most of the 1980s and have been devastating for a large part of the population. David Barkin (1990) describes the fall in real wages and in living conditions in Mexico during the 1980s. He emphasizes the loss of food self-sufficiency and the agrarian crisis.

Increasing inequality is not just an undesirable side effect of economic restructuring in Mexico. The essence of the new economic model is to lower production costs through reduction of private and social wages, thus affecting consumption and the purchasing power of the large mass of people. The impact of debt and restructuring on poverty and worsening social conditions during the 1980s has been

[16]Data from Statistics Canada, *Labour Force Survey*, August 1992; quoted in Campbell (1992).

[17]Data based on information sheet entitled "Hunger Profile – Toronto and Area", provided by Daily Bread food bank. Sheet summarized preliminary results of a survey conducted during early 1993, reaching over 1,000 households receiving emergency food assistance.

unmistakable. Mexican income distribution data for the censuses 1984 and 1989 shows growing inequality. The economic and social transformation has served as a mechanism to transfer income to the top 10 percent of rich families, which increased their share of national income by 5 percent (from 32.8 to 37.9%). The concentration of wealth in the same period is likely to have been even stronger.

In contrast, the proportion of families living under the official poverty line increased from 18.7 in 1984 to 28.4 percent in 1989.[18] Since the poverty line in 1989 was the equivalent of a daily family income of U.S.$6.62 (two minimum wages), these numbers underestimate the real incidence of poverty. A realistic estimate is that half the Mexican population, about 44 million, were living in poverty in 1987, of which more than 20 million lived in extreme poverty. Recent developments are unlikely to reverse these worrisome trends. The chances that the current export-oriented model will stop serving mainly the wealthy and significantly improve the standard of living of impoverished Mexicans are slim (Grinspun and Cameron, 1993b).

Increasing inequality and impoverishment is closely linked to a dissolving social contract between workers and capital. In the United States and Canada this social contract, called the "fordist" structure of production, promoted the economic boom during the postwar era. The fordist scheme was based on the simple formula of low-skill, high-wage labor, which permitted the expansion of mass purchasing power and the growth of a mass market. This scheme does not respond to the current needs of restructuring; it is now obsolete, and NAFTA plays an important role in its demise. The increased mobility of North American capital, and the integration with a low wage economy like the Mexican, is eroding this social contract (Kreklewich, 1993).

The ensuing social transformation is deeply antilabor. The pressure is to lower real wages and benefits and create a more flexible labor force. Trade unions stand in the way, though, so that a first objective is clearly to weaken their power in the country. The increasing mobility of capital by itself represents a loss of negotiating power by the unions, and to this must be added the explicit use of government policies (*à la* Reagan-Bush-Mulroney-Salinas) to achieve this goal.

The unequal character of the economic transformation determines its political and social implications. A process that provides benefits to a

---

[18]Data in this paragraph is taken from OECD (1992: 119–121).

minority and charges the costs to a majority cannot be democratic. As the citizens of Ontario have recently experienced, it does not matter that they have democratically elected a government; this government is constrained in its ability to deliver the promised policies because the powerful (undemocratic and unelected) lobby of capital – openly threatening capital flight – opposes it. The transfer of effective economic and political power to a powerful and unelected elite is closely related to the shrinking democratic space for the large majority of the population.

What should be done? The answer is not simple. Coming back to old protectionist and bureaucratic formulas is not a good response. Neither is the recognition of defeat to the neoconservative agenda in North America, which will not bring benefits except for an already enriched minority. The answer is to organize mechanisms of democratic control over markets and capital. The Clinton administration may open some space for reforms in the United States, but reforms will become a reality only through widespread and organized opposition to the power of corporate capital. The overriding objective is to emphasize the development of human beings as the key to economic development. This means that domestic and international competitiveness must be based on a more qualified, educated, informed, powerful, autonomous, working force. And it means that we have to fight to enforce the democratic rights of all sectors of our societies, and in particular the workers and the disadvantaged.

We will move in this direction only if social, labor, intellectual, and popular movements join more hands across borders and continue developing real continental alternatives to NAFTA and the neoconservative agenda.

REFERENCES

Armstrong, J.
1993   "Toronto Tax Base Shrinks, Weak Economy is Blamed," *Toronto Star*. January 7.

Barkin, D.
1990   *Distorted Development: Mexico in the World Economy*. Boulder, CO: Westview.

Barlow, M.
1991   *Parcel of Rogues: How Free Trade is Failing Canada*. Toronto: Key Porter.

———
1990   "The Road Back." In *Crossing the Line: Canada and Free Trade with Mexico*. Ed. J. Sinclair. Vancouver: New Star. Pp. 177–188.

Barlow, M., and B. Campbell
1992   *Take Back the Nation.* Toronto: Key Porter.

Brazao, D.
1992   "Jobless Condemn 'Vicious' U.I. Cuts," *Toronto Star.* December 4.

Cameron, D.
1988   *The Free Trade Deal.* Toronto: Lorimer.

Campbell, B.
1993   "Restructuring the Economy: Canada Into the Free Trade Era." In *The Political Economy of North American Free Trade.* Ed. R. Grinspun and M. A. Cameron. New York: St. Martin's Press.

———
1992   "A Critique of 'The Global Trade Challenge': A Tory Trade Tabloid." Ottawa: Canadian Centre for Political Alternatives.

Canada, Govt. of –External Affairs and International Trade
n.d.   *North American Free Trade: Securing Canada's Growth Through Trade.* Ottawa.

Canadian Centre for Political Alternatives (CCPA)
1992   *Which Way for the Americas: Analysis of NAFTA Proposals and the Impact on Canada.* Ottawa: Canadian Centre for Political Alternatives. November.

Cavanaugh, J. *et al.*
1992   *Trading Freedom: How Free Trade Affects Our Lives, Work and Environment.* San Francisco: Institute for Food and Development Policy.

Cook, P.
1991   "Letting the U.S. Call the Shots," *Globe and Mail,* Toronto, February 20.

Drake, D., and M. Gertler, eds.
1991   *The New Era of Global Competition: State Policy and Market Power.* Montreal: McGill-Queen's.

Ferguson, J.
1993   "Families Forced into Poverty by Deficit-Cutting, Panel Says," *Toronto Star.* May 4.

Gereffy, G.
1992   *Mexico's Maquiladora Industries and North American Integration. North America Without Borders? Integrating Canada, the United States and Mexico.* Ed. S. Randall, H. Konrad and S. Silverman. Calgary: University of Calgary.

Grinspun, R.
1993a   "The Economics of Free Trade in Canada." In *The Political Economy of North American Free Trade.* Ed. R. Grinspun and M. A. Cameron. New York: St. Martin's Press.

———
1993b   "NAFTA and Neoconservative Transformation: The Impact on Canada and Mexico," *Review of Radical Political Economics,* 25(4): 14–29.

Grinspun, R. and M. A. Cameron, eds.
1993a   *The Political Economy of North American Free Trade.* New York: St. Martin's Press.

1993b   "Mexico: The Wages of Trade," *NACLA Report on the Americas*, 26(4): 32–37.

Grinspun, R. and R. Kreklewich
n.d.   "Consolidating the Neoliberal Agenda: Free Trade as a Conditioning Framework," *Studies in Political Economy*. Forthcoming.

Hinojosa-Ojeda, R., and S. Robinson
1992   "Labor Issues in a North American Free Trade Area." In *North American Free Trade: Assessing the Impact*. Ed. N. Lustig, B. P. Bosworth and R. Z. Lawrence. Washington, DC: The Brookings Institute.

Hufbauer, G. C., and J. Schott
1992   *North American Free Trade: Issues and Recommendations*. Washington, DC: Institute of International Economics.

Instituto Nacional de Estadística, Geografía e Informática (INEGI)
1992   *Estados Unidos Mexicanos: Perfil Sociodemografico, XI Censo General de Poblacion y Vivienda, 1990*.

Kreklewich, R.
1993   "North American Integration and Industrial Relations: Neo-Conservatism and Neofordism?" In *The Political Economy of North American Free Trade*. New York: St. Martin's Press.

Lustig, N., B. P. Bosworth and R. Z. Lawrence, eds.
1992   *North American Free Trade: Assessing the Impact*. Washington, DC: The Brookings Institute.

Organización de Cooperación y Desarollo Económicos (OECD)
1992   *Estudios Economicos de la OCDE: Mexico 1991/1992*. Paris: OECD. Available in English as *OECD Economic Surveys: Mexico 1991/1992*.

OTA (*See* U.S. Congress, Office of Technology Assessment)

Park, Y.-C.
1988   "Korea." In *The Open Economy: Tools for Policymakers in Developing Countries*. Ed. R. Dornbusch and F. L. C. H. Helmers. New York: Oxford University Press.

Ranney, D.
1993   "NAFTA and the New Transnational Corporate Agenda." Paper presented at CEESP-URPE International Conference on NAFTA. Mexico City, March.

Rotstein, A.
1993   "Intellectual Property and the Canada-U.S. Free Trade Agreements: The Case of Pharmaceuticals." Paper presented at CEESP-URPE International Conference on NAFTA. Mexico City, March.

Rugman, A.
1989   "U.S. Administered Protection and Canadian Trade Policy." In *International Business in Canada*. Ed. A. Rugman. Scarborough, Ontario: Prentice-Hall. Pp. 106–122.

Simmons, A., and K. Keohane
1992   "Shifts in Canadian Immigration Policy: State Strategies and the Quest for Legitimacy," *Canadian Review of Anthropology and Sociology*, 29(4): 421–452.

Sinclair, J.
1992   *Crossing the Line: Canada and Free Trade with Mexico*. Vancouver: New Star.

Sinclair, S.
1993   "NAFTA and U.S. Trade Policy: Implications for Canada and Mexico." In *The Political Economy of North American Free Trade*. Ed. R. Grinspun and M. A. Cameron. New York: St. Martin's Press. Pp. 219–234.

U.S. Congress, Office of Technology Assessment (OTA)
1992   *U.S.-Mexico Trade: Pulling Together or Pulling Apart?* No. ITE-545. Washington, DC: Government Printing Office.

Velasco, A. E.
1993   "Industrial Restructuring in Mexico during the 1980s." In *The Political Economy of North American Free Trade*. Ed. R. Grinspun and M. A. Cameron. New York: St. Martin's Press.

World Bank
1991   *World Development Report 1991: The Challenge of Development*. New York: Oxford University Press.

The Political Consequences of Economic Liberalization[1]

Maxwell A. Cameron

Introduction

The tension between markets and democracy is an enduring theme in studies of Latin American political economy.[2] Early theorizing suggested a positive correlation between economic growth and the spread of democracy (Lipset, 1960: 24–63).[3] Subsequent work on Latin America challenged this by interpreting the rise of bureaucratic-authoritarian regimes to be part of the distinctive developmental trajectory of Latin America (O'Donnell, 1973, 1988). However, this perspective failed to anticipate the breakdown of authoritarian rule and transitions toward more democratic regimes in the 1980s, a period marked by severe economic stagnation and declining income per capita in the region. It would appear that oscillations between democracy and authoritarianism are endemic to Latin America.

[1]This paper was written in 1992 and revised in early 1993; it does not address subsequent events in Mexico or Peru. However, the victory of PRI candidate Ernesto Zedillo in Mexico, and the prospect of the reelection of Alberto Fujimori in Peru, provides evidence of the consolidation of *dictablandas* in both countries. This research was funded by the Social Sciences and Humanities Research Council of Canada (SSHRCC). The SSHRCC is not responsible for views expressed in this paper. The author is grateful to Alan Simmons and an anonymous reader for comments on an earlier draft of this paper.

[2]*See* Rueschemeyer, Stephens and Stephens (1992); Diamond and Linz (1989); Bollen and Jackman (1983); Smithy (1991); Remmer (1990); North (1989).

[3]*See also* Todaro (1989) for a good review of linear theories of growth.

Various hypotheses have been proposed regarding contemporary trends and future prospects for democracy in the region. These hypotheses have implications for understanding emigration pressures in Latin America. Harkening back to earlier modernization theories, Mitchell A. Seligson (1987: 3–12) argues that there may be a "sociocultural threshold" for democracy beyond which a return to military rule is less likely. However, Seligson's work is out of step with the growing appreciation among social scientists of the need for microfoundations in any theory of political change.[4]

A more promising direction is suggested by Adam Przeworski (1991). He argues that democracy is consolidated when it becomes "self-enforcing, that is when all relevant political forces find it best to continue to submit their interests and values to the uncertain interplay of the institutions. . . . To put it somewhat more technically, democracy is consolidated when compliance-acting within the institutional framework – constitutes the equilibrium of the decentralized strategies of all the relevant political forces (p. 26)."

Democratic political systems are rarely in equilibrium in Latin America, largely because the inequitable distribution of wealth leads to intense distributional conflicts. The perception of threat to core interests and values that arise from these conflicts often encourages authoritarian responses. Military regimes in Latin America have historically been inaugurated after threats to basic property rights, economic privilege, or the military's monopoly of coercion. Indeed, a quid pro quo of the recent democratic transitions was that basic property relations and the military hierarchy were left untouched. The power and privilege of military and economic elites has remained entrenched. Democratic transitions tend to be inherently conservative.

Entrenched political and economic power of elites undermines the ability of Latin American democracies to implement adjustment and stabilization policies within a democratic framework. The model of economic reform pursued in Chile, Peru, Mexico and other Latin American countries entails social costs which are carried by the majority of the population because the influence and privilege of economic elites enables them to shift the burden of adjustment onto others (for example, through capital flight). This obvious fact is frequently ignored in the current debate on democracy and markets in Latin America.

[4]*See* for example, Przeworski (1991) and Elster (1989).

Indeed, an often uncritically accepted view is that democracy and markets are mutually reinforcing institutions.

The idea that markets and democracy are mutually reinforcing and contribute to harmonious hemispheric relations is premised on two interrelated propositions. First, market reforms encourage competition and private enterprise that lead to prosperity – and democratic institutions are more viable under conditions of prosperity. Second, democracy makes rent-seeking and lobbying for special privileges more difficult, thus weakening mercantilism and fostering markets. This optimistic view may be juxtaposed against the harsh reality of Latin America today. Politicians elected to implement neoliberal policies have been just as corrupt as those who pursued populist policies. Corruptions scandals brought down Brazilian President Collor de Mello in October, 1992, and Venezuelan President Carlos Andres Pérez in 1993.

Migration, corruption, rent-seeking, speculation, drug-trafficking, informal economic activities, electoral instability, and even the growth of Protestant sects, reflect the disintegration of domestic political institutions in Latin America that has resulted from a decade of economic crisis. The kinds of policies that have been implemented – economic restructuring designed to reduce regulations, restrain public spending, privatize state-owned firms, decentralize the economy and open the domestic market to foreign competition – in the last decade in Latin America have undermined the traditional bases of collective action and forced Latin Americans to pursue individual survival strategies. Crossing the Rio Grande, taking bribes, evading taxes, buying dollars, joining evangelical sects and voting for renegade politicians without organized parties are all activities with one thing in common: they are individualistic strategies that reflect the failure of political and economic institutions in the region.[5]

This paper compares tensions and contradictions in two Spanish-speaking countries, Peru and Mexico, that are currently pursuing orthodox economic policies within hybrid authoritarian-democratic regimes.

POLITICAL CHANGE AND MARKET REFORMS IN PERU AND MEXICO

Both countries have been criticized by the Organization of American States (OAS) for undemocratic practices; both have centralized discre-

[5]For a further discussion, see Cameron (1991c).

tionary spending power in the hands of the president; both have been criticized by opposition politicians for irregularities in recent electoral processes; and in both instances U.S. criticism has been muted by the need to support the orthodox economic programs being implemented which have made regularly servicing the international debt the principle goal of economic policy. Neither Peru nor Mexico can be described as "democracies." Nor, however, can they be considered "authoritarian regimes." They may represent a new hybrid, often described by Latin Americans as *dictablandas* (soft-dictatorships), which have many of the appurtenances of democracy tacked onto, but without checking, the centralized power of an authoritarian-style president.

The 1988 Political Earthquake in Mexico

The Mexican political system defies straightforward classification as either democratic or authoritarian. Most observers agree that the system is moderately authoritarian. It is not as repressive as the bureaucratic-authoritarian regimes in Brazil or Argentina in the 1970s and tends to be more inclusionary; opposition is often coopted and incorporated rather than repressed.[6] It is an institutional rather than personalistic system, one dominated by civilian rather than military leaders, and organized by the powerful ruling political party, the Revolutionary Institutional Party (PRI). A unique blend of cooptation, selective repression, elite discipline and consensus, interlocking pacts and alliances, a low level of mobilization, and state control over much of the economy, has enabled the Mexican regime to survive over 70 years, prompting Mario Vargas Llosa to label Mexico "the perfect dictatorship."

Historically, one of the features unique to the Mexican state has been its ability to maintain an equilibrium among competing classes, factions, and sectors of the economy. Many disparate groups had access to the rewards distributed by the system, but excessive concentration of

---

[6]For example, when Jesus Silva Herzog criticized the government, he was promptly appointed ambassador to Spain. On November 28, 1990, Herzog had written a letter critical of NAFTA to the President in the House of Deputies, in the Mexican legislature with Adolfo Aguilar Zinser, Jorge G. Castaneda, Carlos Fuentes, Carlos Monsivais, and Lorenzo Meyer. In March 1991 Silva Herzog was appointed ambassador to Spain. According to the *Wall Street Journal*, "Many analysts think the government nudged Mr. Silva Herzog out of the domestic political picture to smooth the way for free trade." (*See* Moffett, 1991.) Jorge Cataneda Jr., another outspoken critic, was physically intimidated by the Mexican police. Castaneda, unlike Silva Herzog, was linked to the opposition PRD.

power in the hands of any clique or faction of the ruling elite was avoided. Thus, for example, the principle of "no reelection" has been faithfully respected since the revolution in 1910. "Access to all, supremacy for none" was the slogan for Mexican corporatism. Presidents could grow rich during their six-year terms, but then they had to go quietly into retirement. The rewards of economic growth were also distributed among members of the popular coalition supporting the PRI. But for many years the demands on the state were kept within limits compatible with growth of the economy. The Mexican state was a rent-seeking apparatus, but it was also developmental (Evans, 1989).

After a decade of playing orthodox debtor and implementing tough austerity measures, the Mexican system entered a dramatic period of political crisis. In 1988 President Carlos Salinas de Gortari was brought to power in elections marred by fraud. "A good showing," Salinas had said before the election, "would be for us to take 60% of the vote."[7] After a week of counting the votes, the PRI claimed Salinas won 50.71 percent of the vote. In many precincts Salinas won by a suspicious 100 percent margin. Opposition candidate Cardenas claimed he won a plurality with 41–42 percent. In Congress, Salinas won 260 out of 500 seats, with the rest going to the opposition. In the fight over the ratification of the presidential elections, much of the opposition walked out of Congress, denying that Salinas was anything more than a de facto ruler without legitimacy. Yet, opposition efforts to prevent the certification of the president failed to ignite popular mobilization against the government.

After taking power Salinas sought to weaken the corporatist pillars of the PRI, to improve relations with business, and to reshape the relation between the president and the masses. According to an analysis by Cornelius, Gentleman, and Smith, "Salinas and his reform-minded advisors are calling for an end to the system of corporatist interest representation, centered on the oficialista labor and peasant organizations created in the 1930s, and its replacement with a territorially based system that would foster a more direct relationship between the PRI and individual citizens" (Cornelius *et al.*, 1989: 29). The choice of Salinas-the second consecutive president to be chosen from the ranks of the *técnicos* rather than the *políticos* in the PRI – and Salinas's

---

[7] "A Talk with Salinas: The U.S. Should Allow More Mexican Exports In," *Business Week*, July 4, 1988, 47.

coolness toward the PRI's party apparatus and the corporatist system, encouraged some to speculate that Salinas would move Mexico toward more liberal, representative democratic institutions during his mandate.[8] These speculations failed.

Market reform does not necessarily undermine the economic and political power of rent-seeking elites (Grinspun and Cameron, 1993b). The privatization of state-owned enterprises in Mexico has reinforced both the concentration of wealth and the authoritarian features of the political system. On February 23, 1993, Salinas met with 30 top business executives and asked each for $25 million in contributions to the PRI. Many of the guests had directly benefitted from government policies: Roberto Hernández, for example, had just bought Banamex; Gilberto Borja Navarrete had contracts to build government tollroads; Jorge Larrea Ortega had bought government mines. There were also representatives of Mexico's largest conglomerates, such as Bernardo Garza Sada, chairman of the Grupo Alfa, and Lorenzo Zambrano, chairman of Mexico's multinational cement company, Cemex.[9] It is important to remember that a few players manage Mexico's economy; 25 companies produce nearly half of the recorded gross domestic product (Schomberg and Bardacke, 1992). The contributions were solicited as a way to guarantee that the benefits from neoliberal economic policies would not be lost by ensuring the survival of the PRI in power. The kickback scheme backfired after a public outcry.

The Salinas government did not embarked on any major initiative to open the political system. In his State of the Nation address in November, 1992, Salinas made no specific proposals for political reform. "If the political parties consider it necessary to change electoral legislation, then go ahead," he said (El Financiero International, November 16, 1992, p. 13). Opposition leaders from the right-wing National Action Party (PAN) to the left-wing Party of the Democratic Revolution (PRD) were disappointed with the unwillingness of the government to discuss concrete steps toward democratic transition. Instead, Salinas insisted "political competition without real points of agreement does not guarantee advancement" (ibid). What was particu-

---

[8]For example, a high-ranking Canadian government official predicted that there would be a move toward political opening in 1992–1993 after the signing of a NAFTA. (Personal communication, Ottawa, September 28, 1990).

[9]For further information about the guest list, see Bardacke (1993: 13).

larly disappointing in these remarks for the democratic opposition was the fact that Salinas was quickly running out of time.[10] Mexican presidents tend to be weakest in the final year of their mandate as attention shifts to the unveiling of the PRI candidate and election of the incoming president.[11] Salinas had promised political reform, but insisted that economic change must come first. Pointing to the dangerous path of the Soviet Union – which simultaneously pursued political and economic openings – Salinas said: "[we will] respond to the call of Mexicans for improved well-being. It's a matter of the two reforms going at different rhythms, but the priority is economics."[12]

In fact, the political system that Salinas designed was entirely compatible with the neoliberal economic agenda implicit in the North American Free Trade Agreement (NAFTA) (Grinspun and Cameron, 1993a: 13–15). Salinas sought a "modernization of the authoritarian system," a leaner, more efficient form of authoritarian rule. As Andrew Reding (1993) argued: "The president who promised to 'modernize Mexican politics' has, in a peculiar twist, instead modernized Mexican fraud." (p. 264) "Without legal and electoral accountability, the corrosive effects of unchecked official greed and ambition pervade society, as elections are rigged and as contracts and justice are bought with political favors and bribes." (p. 270).

NAFTA placed the issue of political reform at the center of a debate in Mexico. For example, the PAN argued that NAFTA should be accompanied by political reform because the centralization of power in the hands of the president was a source of economic distortions that NAFTA sought to address (Moreno, 1991). Likewise, Demetrio Sodi de la Tijera called attention to the likely debate on NAFTA in the U.S. Congress and the lack of debate in Mexico. The potential impact on Mexico was greater, yet the Mexican Congress had no voice. This situation forced some Mexican lawmakers to rethink the role of the

[10]Comments by Representative Jorge A. Calderon, Partido de la Revolucion Democratica Legislative Group, at Centre for Refugee Studies, York University, Toronto, November 21, 1992.

[11]On the authoritarian process of presidential selection, *see* Aguilar-Zinser (1988).

[12]Salinas, interviewed by Tim Padgett ("Reform at Two Different Rhythms," *Newsweek*, December 3, 1990, p. 39). An advisor to U.S. President-elect Clinton put it slightly ethnocentrically: "Mexico is perceived by foreigners as a country that is doing spectacular things economically, but it is still a 'banana republic,' to be very blunt, when it comes to politics." (*El Financiero International*, November 16, 1992).

Mexican Congress.[13] Going a step farther, Porfirio Muñoz Ledo called for a referendum on NAFTA (Zamarripa, 1991).

Salinas sought to reduce the size of the government while increasing the discretionary spending power of the president. The National Solidarity Program, or PRONASOL, provided an example of this tendency. Denise Dresser, in a recent analysis, argued that, while ostensibly a program of assistance to the Mexican popular sectors, its real purpose was threefold: "(1) to adapt the state's traditional social role to new economic constraints and redefine the limits of its intervention in the context of a neoliberal reform strategy; (2) to diffuse potential social discontent through selective subsidies, accommodate social mobilization through 'co-participation,' and undermine the strength of left-wing opposition forces by establishing ties with a commitments to popular movements; and (3) to restructure local and regional PRI elites under an increasing degree of centralized contro." (Dresser, 1991: 1–2). Thus, PRONASOL was branded a new form of populist cooptation and clientelism designed to strengthen the president's hand in the implementation of a neoliberal economic agenda.

Salinas sought economic reform without political reform, perestroika without *glasnost*. Yet, Mexico was touted by the Bush administration – specifically by Secretary of State James Baker – as an example for the rest of the Third World and even the ex-Soviet bloc. Orthodox economic policies and prompt repayment of debt obligations goes a long way toward insulating countries from international criticism for undemocratic domestic practices. As Adolfo Aguilar Zinser (1993) put it:

> Mexico today enjoys a unique international status. It is the only remaining single-party authoritarian system that can practice massive electoral fraud and violate human rights without confronting serious recrimination by the international community. Any other Latin America country with such persistent misconduct would cause an international outcry; Mexico not only escapes the censorship of Western democracies, its leaders are often praised and warmly welcomed in virtually all capitals of the world. Such good standing is possible thanks to a combination of two very powerful circumstances: first, the sweeping economic policies implemented by the Mexican government, which follow current world trends – including negotiations toward NAFTA; and second, and most important, President Salinas, the first authentically pro-United States politician ever to rule Mexico, has the unequivocal support

---

[13]See "Los congresos de EU y Mexico," *La Jornada*, April 19, 1991, p. 8. The same point is made regarding the docility of Mexico's Congress in Enrique Quintana, "TLC: La forma sera el fondo," *Cuadernos de Nexos*, No. 33, March 1991, VI–VII.

of Bush and the Washington establishment. . . . The international "immuni-
zation" of the Mexican regime is also helped by the peculiar ability of Mexican
authorities to deny, hide, or disguise serious violations of the human, civil,
and political rights of its citizens.

The election of Democrat Bill Clinton changed the tone of U.S.-Mexi-
can relations. Clinton's Administration linked a traditional U.S. concern
with stability in Latin America with the need to respect human rights and
democratic reforms (Barber, 1993). Moreover, it held up the implementation of NAFTA until after the negotiation of parallel accords on labor
and the environment. The Mexican executive was clearly rooting for the
Bush campaign, and even supported that campaign by participating in the
public signing ceremony of NAFTA during the election. As *The Economist*
(1993) put it: "The Salinas government reduced its bargaining power
by an inexplicable policy of putting all its bets on George Bush. It was
almost totally unprepared for the Clinton administration; the result is
that the new American president owes Mr Salinas nothing."

The 1990 Political Tsunami in Peru

Market reforms have led to political change in Peru, but not toward
democracy.[14] After two years of economic stabilization measures that
failed to produce growth, the popularity of President Alberto Fujimori
began to decline. Fujimori won the 1990 election promising to not
impose economic "shock" measures. Once in power, he implemented
the harshest stabilization program ever adopted in America. These
measures temporarily stabilized the economy without reactivating
economic activity. Inflation was reduced from an annual rate of 6,000
percent to 150 percent. These measures have been sponsored by the
International Monetary Fund and the World Bank and they are crucial
to the reinsertion of Peru in the international financial system. Peru,
unlike Mexico, had challenged the international financial system under
President Alan García Pérez. Under García, Peru became the country
with the largest arrears with the IMF in the world. A major goal of the
Fujimori government was to restore confidence in Peru in the international financial community.

The social and economic cost of these measures was dramatic. As in
Mexico, real wages fell and poverty increased, sending a flood of immi-

[14]The following is based on field research in Peru, July-August, 1992.

grants in search of jobs elsewhere. A United Nations Children's Fund study found that 13 million Peruvians out of a population of 22 million lived in "extreme poverty."[15] Similarly, the World Bank reported that about half of Peru's population in 1991 "fell below the poverty line with personal spending less than the cost of a basic food basket and selected nonfood expenditures."[16] One response to the crisis was migration. Between October, 1992, and April, 1993, 20,000 Peruvians bribed or smuggled their way into Argentina (Honore, 1993). "This is turning into a demographic disaster," said Juan Cantos, a Buenos Aires priest. Peruvian police trace the exodus to phony travel agencies advertising one-way tickets to lucrative employment in Argentina. Many arriving Peruvians found that all that awaited them in Argentina was a life of prostitution or petty crime. Officials feared that as many as 60,000 Peruvians may ultimately make their way to Argentina. A similar number of Peruvians have found their way to Japan (Larmer, 1993). There are roughly 70,000 Peruvians of Japanese descent. Some have grown rich exploiting their connections with Japan. A market has emerged for false adoptions, marriages and Japanese birth certificates to enable Peruvians to become temporary workers in Japan. One plastic surgeon in Lima operated on 80 patient's eyelids to make them appear to be ethnic Japanese. Unfortunately, many of the Peruvians who managed to get by increasingly tough Japanese immigration officials wound up in the same occupations as their counterparts in Argentina. Internal migration was also common. There are no reliable figures, but the number could be as high as 1 million people displaced by violence and poverty. Many of those who arrived in Lima or other cities were without documents, and without even the most basic essentials for urban life.

The social catastrophe caused by the oscillation between populist and neoliberal policies in Peru generated opposition in Congress, especially from the American Popular Revolutionary Alliance (APRA) led by García. Despite García's disastrous tenure in office, he remained one of the few politicians popular enough to threaten Fujimori. Fujimori did not have a majority of seats in the Senate or the House of Deputies. The Peruvian electoral system makes it easy to be elected president

[15]Agence France Presse wire service, "In Peru, a million children suffer chronic malnutrition," February 7, 1993.

[16]United Press International wire service, "About half of Peru's population is poor, World Bank says," April 28, 1993.

without a majority in Congress. In 1990 Fujimori's *Cambio 90* won 14 seats in a 60-seat Senate and 49 seats in a 180-seat Chamber of Deputies. Peru has a presidential system in which the president is elected directly. Fujimori placed second in the national presidential race; then, in a runoff election, he was able to beat the leading candidate, Mario Vargas Llosa, winning 54 percent of the vote. However, he was unable to build a broad alliance in the Congress to back his government (Cameron, 1991a). When the Congress rejected a package of economic measures, Fujimori decided to act.

An *auto-golpe* (or "self-coup") was announced in Peru on the evening of April 5, 1992. The Constitution was suspended, Congress was closed, and Senators and Deputies were placed under house arrest. In an address to the nation, Fujimori denounced Congress for blocking necessary economic measures and accused it of corruption. Congress had rejected a package of measures presented by the government. Fujimori's announcement was followed by a statement of support from the joint command of the Armed Forces.

In defense of the coup, Fujimori argued that Peru did not have a real democracy, and that he would create a more "authentic democracy." Those who opposed his government were free to leave the country. The de facto president's contempt for democracy was not surprising – indeed, he owed little to democratic institutions in Peru. He was elected without an organized social base (his support came largely from independent voters without partisan loyalties), he did not have a disciplined political party, nor a majority in Congress. Indeed, Fujimori could not even control his own fractious movement. There was a mutiny among his supporters even before Fujimori formed his first cabinet. That cabinet did not include a single member from *Cambio 90*. Fujimori's own vice-president turned against him after the dissolution of the Congress.

The Fujimori government initially underestimated the strength of the international reaction to the April 5 coup. Agusto Blacker Miller, a cabinet official and key architect of the coup, advised Fujimori that the international response would be mild. In the weeks following the coup, Fujimori was forced to revise his position. Fujimori's main goal was to reinsert Peru in the international financial community, yet his coup began to isolate Peru. The United States suspended millions of dollars in economic aid and the International Monetary Fund postponed a $222 million loan. Other South American governments – notably Venezuela and Argentina – harshly criticized the coup. The U.S. government called the authoritarian coup a "regrettable step backwards." Assistant Secretary of State for Inter-American Affairs Bernard Aronson, who was in Lima at the time of the coup, canceled a meeting with the Peruvian president to signal his displeasure.

In April the Organization of American States (OAS) met in Washington to coordinate international reaction to the Peruvian *auto-golpe*. The OAS condemned the coup but stopped short of calling for economic sanctions.[17] U.S. foreign policy makers, aware of the extreme crisis in Peru, were unwilling to impose severe economic sanctions – like those placed on Haiti – because they did not want to jeopardize Peru's market reforms, the war on drugs, and the fight against terrorism. The OAS was reluctant to take measures that would interrupt Peru's fragile economic recovery plan just as some of its elements were perceived to be taking hold. Peru's orthodox economic policies helped insulate it from international criticism of undemocratic practices.

In May, Fujimori met with the OAS and made a commitment to restore democratic institutions through a dialogue with the political parties and the convocation of elections for a constituent assembly. However, the Fujimori government quickly discovered that the OAS felt it had to balance its commitment to democracy with its longstanding opposition to interventionism. Such a balance was not achieved in Haiti, and the OAS wanted to be more cautious in Peru. Thus, for example, it was reluctant to intervene directly in the negotiations between parties and the government. It became clear that the international community was more worried about the blood-thirsty terrorist movement Sendero Luminoso (the Shining Path), fighting drug trafficking, and the program to reinsert Peru into the international financial system, than it was about democracy. It was also reluctant to intervene directly in Peruvian internal affairs.

Thus, Peru discovered a fact about the international system which Mexico had been exploiting for years: paying the debt and implementing orthodox economic policy goes a long way toward insulating a government from international criticism for undemocratic domestic practices. Contact with U.S. government officials made it clear that

---

[17]The Canadian Minister of External Affairs, Barbara McDougall, took a stronger position and demanded economic sanctions.

the United States would not take a strictly constitutionalist position and demand the status quo ante, as it did in the Haitian crisis. Rather, the Fujimori government would have to "get that democratic feeling back."[18] As a result, the Fujimori government was emboldened in its attacks on the political parties, deliberately broke the dialogue, and imposed its own norms for the election of the new Congress. The government imposed a Democratic Constituent Congress (CCD), a unicameral legislative body empowered to function until general elections in 1995. The opposition wanted an assembly only to reform the constitution, with a six-month term, and the autonomy to call general elections. Fujimori was inflexible on this issue and on the issue of the timing of the municipal elections. As a result the "dialogue" between the government and the parties collapsed before any agreement was reached. Two of Peru's major parties – APRA and Popular Action – boycotted the election, and thus had no stake in the new political system.

Fujimori sought to consolidate a *dictablanda*, a hybrid system with a strengthened executive able to enact laws and spend discretionary funds for electoral and other purposes through the Ministry of the Presidency, a fragmented and obsequious parliament without strong opposition parties, and greater manipulation of electoral rules and procedures – in short, a system more like Mexico's. The problem with such a scenario was that Peru is not Mexico and Fujimori was not Salinas. No other revolutionary movement in Latin American history was as brutal and blood-thirsty as Sendero Luminoso and in few countries was the crisis and misery created in recent years so savage.

Fujimori, an outsider with little understanding of how political institutions function, with no organized political base, no coherent political party, and no long-term program or notion of reform, was arguably the worst candidate imaginable to undertake the institutional reforms needed in Peru. The debate over the CCD revolved around such sterile issues as whether there should be 80 or 100 or 120 members. Fujimori argued that there should be 80 members because that will make the congress more "efficient." There is no reason to believe that a congress with 80 members will be more efficient than one with 120. The efficiency of the British parliament, one of the

[18]Statement made on condition of anonymity by a senior State Department official in Washington, D.C., May 6, 1992.

largest in the world, is based on disciplined and cohesive parties, a party-oriented electorate, and the centralization of power in the Cabinet (Cox, 1987). Yet Fujimori – a politician who rose from obscurity, without a program or party – routinely contradicted his own cabinet, attacked the system of political parties (what he called the *partidocracia*) and encouraged the growth of independent candidates.

On November 13, 1992, a coup attempt demonstrated that the post-April 5 political equilibrium was still unstable. Prominent members of the political opposition were involved, and some of them were later forced into exile. Elections for the new congress later in the month resulted in a victory for the official slate (*Cambio 90/Nueva Mayoria*), which won a plurality of the vote and a majority of the seats.[19] Municipal election on January 29, 1993, confirmed that the traditional political parties had little support. Independent candidates were victorious throughout the country. Ricardo Belmont, the independent candidate in Lima, was swept back into office, and his movement, *Obras*, won even in districts of Lima where it did not present candidates due to lack of time: voters simply wrote in their preferences for *Obras* on the ballots.[20]

In April and May, 1993, a year after the *auto-golpe*, the fragility of Peru's new political arrangements was revealed by a dangerous stand-off between the new legislature and the armed forces. The stand-off began on April 2, when Deputy Henry Pease revealed a leaked document that tied seventeen officials in the armed forces to the disappearance and execution of nine university students and a professor at Enrique Guzman y Valle University in Chosica, near Lima. A panel was established to investigate the crime. Pease asked the Minister of Defense, General Victor Malca, to testify before the CCD to explain the armed forces' actions. The armed forces responded by sending more than 100 tanks into downtown Lima near the government palace. The generals issued a communiqué accusing the congressional opposition of orchestrating a campaign against the armed forces and serving as allies of terrorism. Then, in a surprise move, General Rodolfo Robles (who had earlier signed the military communiqué attacking opposition legislators) confirmed that an intelligence unit was responsible for the abductions, and that it was coordinated by Fujimori's chief advisor and

[19]*Resumen Semanal*, No. 696, November 18–24, 1992, p. 2.

[20]*Resumen Semanal*, No. 705, January 17–February 2, 1993, p. 5–6.

top intelligence official Vladimiro Montesinos.[21] Robles also implicated General Hermoza, the chief of the army, before fleeing to Argentina.

President Fujimori was caught between the CCD he created and his principal backers, the armed forces. The stand-off quickly escalated into a constitutional crisis when opposition congressmen proposed a motion to force military officers implicated in the abuses to testify before a CCD panel. When members of the ruling coalition rejected the motion, the opposition walked out of Congress. Deputy Pease said, "The majority has abdicated out of fear [of the military]. We are definitely living in a civilian-military regime." (Powers, 1993). Thus, even after congressional and municipal elections, the new political equilibrium remained unstable because of the ambiguous position of the armed forces as Fujimori's de facto coalition base.

CONCLUSION

There is a tension between markets and democracy in Latin America. The idea that markets and democracy are mutually reinforcing has no foundation in analysis of the Mexican and Peruvian cases. A comparison of these two different countries suggests that there are powerful forces toward centralization of power in the hands of the president, weakening of congress, and the manipulation of electoral and other formal procedures in countries seeking to implement economic liberalization measures.[22] Thus, in different circumstances, both Peru and Mexico have moved toward hybrid democratic-authoritarian systems which have some surprising similarities.

The economic crisis and the application of neoliberal policy solutions have resulted in a deterioration of social conditions and institutional arrangements that are crucial for the stability and maintenance of democracy. At the same time, the nature of the crisis undermines the possibility of collective action by the social forces that are marginalized by neoliberal policies. As a result, individual survival strategies –

---

[21]On Montesinos, *see* Gorriti (1993); Speer (1993).

[22]As this conclusion was being written, President Jorge Serrano Elias of Guatemala dissolved Congress, the Supreme Court and the Human Rights Procurator's Office, and closed the country's three major newspapers. The *auto-golpe*, which followed violent student and trade union protests against austerity measures, bore striking resemblance to the Fujimori coup. Serrano said the crackdown was necessary to fight corruption and stem a breakdown of order, however, the armed forces rejected Serrano's actions and forced him from office. (Tim Golden, "Military brass pushes president out of office," *The Ottawa Citizen*, June 2, 1993, A6.)

whether working in the informal sector, drug trafficking, speculation on black markets, or migration – have been the dominant outcome of the crisis.

The evolution of political systems under circumstances of prolonged crisis may be toward a hybrid of democracy and authoritarian rule. Full-fledged authoritarian coalitions have not emerged because it is not clear how repressive authoritarian rule would resolve the current crisis. Threats to order come less from organized opposition than the incremental disintegration of existing institutions. Moreover, the international system is currently hostile to nondemocratic forms of government. However, the repayment of the debt and implementation of orthodox economic policies approved by the IMF and the World Bank have tended to insulate countries such as Mexico and Peru from intense international criticism for their lack of respect for basic democratic rights and freedoms.

REFERENCES

Aguilar-Zinser, A.
1993   "Authoritarianism and North American Free Trade: The Debate on Mexico."
          In *The Political Economy of North American Free Trade*. Ed. R. Grinspun and
          M. A. Cameron. New York: St. Martin's Press.

———
1988   "Mexico" The Presidential Problem," *Foreign Policy*, 69: 40–60.

Bailey, J.
1991   "Populism and Regime Liberalization: Mexico in Comparative Perspective."
          Paper prepared for presentation at Annual Meeting of the Midwest Political
          Science Association. Chicago, Illinois, April 18–20.

Barber, B.
1993   "Clinton's Foreign Policy Brings New Emphasis to Human Rights," *Christian
          Science Monitor*, April 15, p. 2.

Bardacke, T.
1993   "A Dinner with Money on the Menu," *El Financiero International*, March 22,
          p. 13.

Bollen, K. A., and R. Jackman
1983   "World System Position, Dependency, and Democracy: The Cross-national
          Evidence," *American Sociological Review*, 48: 468–479.

Cameron, M. A.
1992   "Micro and Macro Logics of Political Conflict: The Informal Sector and
          Institutional Change in Peru and Mexico." In *Latin America to the Year 2000:
          Reactivating Growth, Improving Equity, Sustaining Democracy*. Ed. A. R. M.
          Ritter, M. A. Cameron and D. H. Pollock. New York: Praeger. Pp. 209–220.

1991a   "The Politics of the Urban Informal Sector on Peru: Populism, Class, and 'Redistributive Combines'," *Canadian Journal of Latin American and Caribbean Studies*, 16(31): 79–104.

1991b   "Political Parties and the Worker – Employer Cleavage: The Impact of the Informal Sector on Voting in Lima, Peru," *Bulletin of Latin American Research*, 10(3): 293–313.

1991c   "Canada and Latin America." In *After the Cold War: Canada among Nations, 1990–91*. Ed. F. Hampson and C. J. Maule. Ottawa: Carleton University Press. Pp. 109–123.

Castaneda, J. G.
1990   "Salinas's International Relations Gamble," *Journal of International Affairs*, 3(2): 407–422.

Collier, D., ed.
1979   *The New Authoritarianism in Latin America*. Princeton, NJ: Princeton University Press.

Cornelius, W. A., J. Gentleman and P. H. Smith, eds.
1989   *Mexico's Alternative Futures*. La Jolla, CA: Center for U.S.-Mexican Studies, University of California at San Diego.

Cox, G. W.
1987   *The Efficient Secret: The Cabinet and the Development of Political Parties in Victorian England*. Cambridge: Cambridge University Press.

Diamond, L., and J. J. Linz
1989   "Introduction: Politics, Society, and Democracy in Latin America." In *Democracy in Developing Countries: Latin America*. Ed. L. Diamond, J. J. Linz and S. M. Lipset. Boulder, CO: Lynne Rienner.

Dresser, D.
1991   *Neopopulist Solutions to Neoliberal Problems*. La Jolla, CA: Center for U.S.-Mexican Studies, University of California at San Diego.

The Economist
1993   "Mexico: Respect Restored," February 13, p. 8.

Elster, J.
1989   *The Cement of Society: A Study of Social Order*. Cambridge: Cambridge University Press.

Evans, P.
1989   "Predatory, Developmental and Other Apparatuses: A Comparative Analysis of the Third World State," *Sociological Forum*, 4(4).

Gilly, A.
1990   "The Mexican Regime in Its Dilemma," *Journal of International Affairs*, 43(2): 273–290.

Gorriti, G.
1993   "The Unshining Path," *The New Republic*, February 8, p. 22.

Grinspun, R., and M. A. Cameron, eds.
1993a   *The Political Economy of North American Free Trade.* New York: St. Martin's
         Press.

_____

1993b   "Mexico: The Wages of Trade," *NACLA Report on the Americas,* 26(4):
         32–37. February.

Hirschman, A. O.
1979   "The Turn to Authoritarianism in Latin America and the Search for Its
         Economic Determinants." In *The New Authoritarianism in Latin America.*
         Ed. D. Collier. Princeton, NJ: Princeton University Press. Pp. 61–98.

Honore, C.
1993   "False Dreams Sends Peruvians Flooding to Argentina," *The Gazette, Mont-
         real,* April 29, p. A1.

Kaufman, R. R.
1979   "Industrial Change and Authoritarian Rule in Latin America." In *The New
         Authoritarianism in Latin America.* Ed. D. Collier. Princeton, NJ: Princeton
         University Press. Pp. 165–254.

Larmer, B. (w/C. Schmidt)
1993   "Peru's Japan Connection," *Newsweek,* February 8, p. 22.

Lehmann, D.
1990   *Democracy and Development in Latin America.* Cambridge: Polity Press.

Lipset, S. M.
1960   *Political Man.* Garden City, NY: Doubleday, Anchor Books.

Moffet, M.
1991   "Mexicans, Weary of 10-Year Debt Crisis Register Little Opposition to Trade
         Pact, *Wall Street Journal,* May 13.

Moreno, M.
1991   "Teme el PAN que el Tratado Solo Sea un Mercado Comun Estadounidense
         con Transpolacion de Leyes," *El Financiero,* April 8, p. 12.

North, D. C.
1989   "Institutions and Economic Growth: An Historical Introduction," *World
         Development,* 17(9): 1319–1332.

O'Donnell, G.
1988   *Argentina 1966–1973: Triumphs, Defeats, and Crises.* Berkeley, Los Angeles:
         University of California Press.

_____

1973   *Modernization and Bureaucratic Authoritarianism.* Berkeley, CA: Berkeley
         Institute for International Studies.

Pastor, R. A.
1990   "Post-Revolutionary Mexico: The Salinas Opening," *The Journal of Inter-
         American Studies and World Affairs,* 32(3): 1–22.

Powers, M.
1993   "Human Rights Case Unleashes Constitutional Crisis in Peru," *The Reuters
         Library Report,* May 25.

Przeworski, A.
1991   *Democracy and the Market: Political and Economic Reforms in Eastern Europe and Latin America.* Cambridge: Cambridge University Press.

Reding, A.
1991   "The Crumbling of the 'Perfect Dictatorship'," *World Policy Journal*, 8(2): 255–288.

Remmer, K.
1990   "Democracy and Economic Crisis: The Latin American Experience," *World Politics*, 42(3): 315–335.

Rueschemeyer, D., E. H. Stephens and J. D. Stephens
1992   *Capitalist Development and Democracy.* Chicago: University of Chicago Press.

Schomberg, W., and T. Bardacke
1992   "Doing Business with the Big Boys," *El Financiero International*, October 19, pp. 14–15.

Seligson, M. A.
1987   "Democratization in Latin America: The Current Cycle." In *Authoritarians and Democrats: Regime Transition in Latin America.* Ed. J. Mallory and M. A. Seligson. Pittsburgh: University of Pittsburgh Press.

Smith, P. H.
1991   "Crisis and Democracy in Latin America," *World Politics*, 43: 608–638. July.

Speer, L. J.
1993   "Fujimori's Right-Hand Man," *San Francisco Chronicle*, May 24, p. A8.

Todaro, M. P.
1989   *Economic Development in the Third World.* New York: Longman.

Zamarripa, R.
1991   "El TLC Debe ser Revisado en el Senado: Legisladores de Oposicion," *La Journada*, April 12, p. 15.

The Rights of Mexican Workers in the Context of NAFTA[1]

Edur Velasco Arregui

Introduction

This paper concerns the rights of the Mexican working class and how these are changing in the context of increasing integration of the Mexican economy into that of the United States and Canada. In addition to human rights that workers share with everyone, workers as paid employees have throughout the world struggled for specific labor rights to ensure their dignity, safety and just role in a democratic society. The current struggle for labor rights in Mexico reflects a long history of worker exploitation and very unequal power between employees and employers. The constitution and law give important rights to workers, but in practice these rights have often been abused because the state has tended to side with the interests of investors and powerful lobbies. One of the major questions for the future is how the increasing integration of Mexico into a North American regional economy is likely to affect labor rights specifically and social and human rights and democratic practices more generally within Mexico. I approach this

[1] I would like to thank Dick Roman from the University of Toronto, Teresa Healy from Carleton University, and Ricardo Grinspun from York University, for their valuable comments and suggestions on earlier drafts of this paper. This work would not have been possible without their help. I, however, take responsibility for any imperfections which may remain in this work.

65

question by examining the impact of integration over the past decade prior to NAFTA and then speculating on future directions.

Mexican workers, along with those in other countries, have struggled for basic labor rights, including the following five: 1) the right to a job in a fair labor market, a market shaped by policies and practices concerned to distribute the benefits of economic gains across social groups; 2) the right to wage increases in proportion to gains in productivity; 3) the right to a safe workplace; 4) the right to a democratic union and a fair labor law; 5) the right to exercise the first four rights when initially hired, without any distinctions concerning the nationality or migration condition of the worker. These rights are widely recognized in Europe and other advanced industrial societies.[2] Many of these rights are also enshrined in the Mexican constitution and law. In practice, however, they have often been violated.

Violations of labor rights in Mexico are frequent and extensive. In consequence, profits flow in disproportionate amounts to the employers and income is very unequally distributed in the country. Poverty among Mexican workers is very high. Low wages and insecurity limit the democratic participation of workers and their influence on social welfare policies. In the context of NAFTA, weak labor rights in Mexico in turn threaten to limit whatever leverage workers in Canada and the United States have gained in their relationship to capital. To overcome these threats to dignity, fairness and democracy, Mexico must participate in world trade and build a stronger economy. At the same time, it must also promote human rights and democratic practices, including those which relate to workers and employment specifically.

THE FIRST RIGHT: A JOB IN A FAIR LABOR MARKET

Article 23 of the Universal Charter of Human Rights establishes the right of every person to remunerative employment in equitable and satisfactory conditions. The Mexican Constitution also recognizes the right of Mexican citizens to employment with a wage that covers the basic needs of the worker and his or her family.[3] Since full employment is a reality in few countries, it is important to promote social welfare

[2]Workers rights are defined in this article according to the main points of the European Social Charter, signed by member countries of the European Economic Community. (See Sanger, 1991: 12–15.)

[3]While the Mexican constitution grants "social rights" to workers, such as the right to piecework, the right to unionization, and the right to strike, the Mexican state has created a parallel structure

schemes that support unemployed people in periods between jobs. It is also important to reinforce democracy in situations where unemployment may be extremely high due to unjust state policies. In instances where state policies generate economic growth and prosperity for the privileged few, workers must have recourse to fair elections in order to change policies.

From the postwar period up until the early 1980s unemployment remained low in Mexico. This came about through earlier efforts at land reform and through a growing economy. In 1980, only 4 percent of Mexican workers were unemployed (INEGI, 1980c). Although population and labor force growth had been high, the construction industry, petroleum production, industrial expansion, and emigration to the United States provided sufficient opportunity to those seeking work.

Matters changed dramatically in 1982. The Mexican economy entered a period of profound crisis. State and private industries were heavily in debt. Interests rates on foreign borrowings skyrocketed. State revenues, which had been heavily dependent on previously high oil prices, dropped through the floor when oil prices plummeted. A year later, the unemployment rate grew to 12.9 percent of the labor force. In the next two years it increased slowly to 14 percent. In 1986, a second oil price drop pushed the unemployment rate to an alarming level: more than a fifth of workers (20.3%) were unemployed.[4]

In the national elections of 1988, the Institutional Revolutionary Party (PRI) – the party which has been continuously in power since the

---

of institutions and regulatory laws directed at limiting the full exercise of the constitutional rights of workers. Among these institutions, the Secretary of Labor stands out because its common practice of imposing conditions on workers' organizations against their will, by methods ranging from the designation of their leaders to the conditions of collective contracts. During recent years, under the two PRI governments of Miguel de la Madrid and Carlos Salinas de Gortari, trade unions have seen the meager negotiation spaces granted by the Mexican labor regimen even more profoundly limited. In the last ten years, liberalization of trade has been accompanied by increased exploitation of Mexican workers.

[4]Our unemployment estimates were obtained by contrasting the data on the economically active population from the Population Census, and the data on the formally employed population from the Mexican Institute of Social Security (IMSS). A third variable which ought to be considered is the employed population not covered by Social Security. This segment we infer from regarding permanent agricultural producers not covered by the IMSS, as well as from data of products and productivity in the informal nonagricultural sector. Here, employment is equal to the growth of the product divided by the productivity rate. In a period of slow growth of the GNP and stagnant productivity, real employment in the informal sector covers only a minimum percentage of the new job seekers. Of course this method of estimating unemployment is provisional; even so, it is more precise than the official definition, which considers as employed all those who have worked one hour in the week previous to the survey, or those have a promise of work for the next month.

Revolution – confronted widespread dissatisfaction with and opposition to its policies. This is not surprising given that almost 6 million
Mexican workers were without jobs at that time. Yet, the widespread
lack of support for PRI did not lead to its defeat. Why? Opposition
parties claimed that there had been massive fraud and a technical *coup
d'état* by PRI.

In the following years PRI, under President Salinas, tried to recover
some legitimacy with an economic policy which, it was stated, would
provide jobs for the unemployed. Yet the actual results of policy in this
period had an opposite effect. In the first three years of the Salinas
government employment grew faster than the gross national product.
Privatization of the biggest state enterprises such as the telephone company and the banks provided financial resources to support some community programs and expand public employment to a certain degree. At the
same time, however, these policies were overwhelmed by others. Distorted income distribution led to rising imports and foreign investments
in services. The most visible investments were in the construction of big
commercial malls. Many of those with little income survived through
increased migration to a small but growing *maquila* (assembly) industry
on the northern border with the United States, and through survival in
petty commerce (small stores and little services shops) that added little
to national production. Hundreds of thousands of other workers left to
the United States. Yet even these adjustments left a massive number of
workers without jobs. In 1990, there were 4.5 million unemployed
workers in Mexico. Worse yet, many of the "new jobs" that had emerged
during the sale of the state companies and the period of import growth
were short-lived and had begun to disappear.

Over the last two or three years, employment in Mexican industry
has slowed in some areas and stagnated in others. The growth of
employment in the *maquila* industry, as we can see in Table 1, decreased
in 1991 and 1992 to only 3.8 percent annually. This decrease is
significant because the *maquila* industry had been an important gener-
ator of new jobs. In the previous eight years (INEGI, 1982b–1990b)
the *maquila* industry had been responsible for half of all new industrial
jobs in Mexico. Moreover, in certain periods the pace of growth of
employment in the *maquila* industry was extraordinary. For example,
starting from a very small base it grew at 22 percent annually between
July of 1986 and July of 1987. In such periods a new *maquila* plant

was established in border cities like Tijuana, Ciudad Juarez and Mata-moros every 24 hours. Yet this growth now tapered off. The number of *maquila* plants was more or less the same in 1993 as it had been two years previously, in 1991, namely a total of some 2,000 plants. In addition, the drop in employment growth has not been restricted to the northern border industrial districts. It is a much more widespread phenomenon. The stagnation in employment is evident in the manu-facturing sector more generally, and arises in large part from the downswing in employment for the whole of Mexico.

As can be seen in Table 1, only 100,000 jobs were created in the manufacturing sector in the 12-month period between July of 1991 and July of 1992. In the third quarter of 1992, growth in industrial output matched the average increase of industrial productivity in the last 10 years (a growth of 2.8% annually) and in consequence employ-ment did not rise. Such stagnation in employment is very serious in an economy that each year faces 1.1 million new job seekers. If the current tendency does not change, the unemployment rate could again rise to 18 percent or more of the labor force (that is, up to 5.6 million Mexicans without a job), as it did in the worst period in the mid 1980s.

A new element in the labor market in Mexico is the deep recession in the economies of the Sunbelt states of the United States. These states absorbed large numbers of Mexican migrant workers over the past decade, but are now expelling the immigrants from their factories. The unemployment rate among the Hispanic population in the United States was 14 percent in July of 1992 (*Monthly Labor Review*, August, 1992). That figure is concentrated among newcomers, who are rela-tively recent entrants in the U.S. labor market. Thus, if we take the whole Mexican labor force in the two labor markets, the Mexican and the United States, one in five "Mexican" workers does not have a job.

Another problem that is reinforced by the downswing in the employ-ment trend is discrimination by gender and race in the labor market. Gender discrimination is demonstrated by the low participation of women in the Mexican labor market. Only 29 percent of Mexican women work outside the home. Racial discrimination is manifested in the low employment levels of graduates from public universities (most of whom are mestizos); their low levels of employment are evident in the private sector, and even in the public sector (STPS, 1991: 30). With the internationalization of the economy, populations of strong indige-

TABLE 1

EMPLOYMENT IN MEXICO
NATIONAL ECONOMY, MANUFACTURES, AND *MAQUILA* INDUSTRY

	National Economy (Thousands)	Manufacture Industry (Thousands)	*Maquila* Industry	Unemployed Workers (Thousands)
1985	19,338	2,384	211,307	3,153
1986	18,610	2,403	255,609	4,730
1987	18,920	2,477	307,866	5,299
1988	19,171	2,617	377,511	5,961
1989	20,738	2,832	440,795	5,342
1990	22,122	2,997	472,271	4,941
1991	23,680	3,078	471,214	4,405
1992	23,967	3,061	509,000	5,198

Source: Instituto Nacional de Geografia Estadistica e Informatica *Caudernos de Informacion Oportuna: 1986–1992*, Mexico; BANAMEX-IMSS, Mexico Social, Mexico 1991.

nous background are increasingly marginalized. In earlier periods, young mestizo working-class people could be upwardly mobile by studying engineering at the National Politechnic Institute, a public institution which favored students from working-class families. But with the decline in the job market, engineers graduating from the National Politechnic Institute find themselves working at jobs below their skills, for example as service attendants in gas stations. In the changed economic context of the last decade, the public educational system has been less able to promote social mobility among mestizos. The 6-week strike in the IPN Mechanical Engineering School during October and November of 1992, demanding a fair deal for the school's graduates, shows how rising ethnic tensions in the labor market can be reflected in open social conflicts.

THE SECOND RIGHT: WAGE INCREASES IN PROPORTION TO PRODUCTIVITY GAINS

A hidden side of the expansion of employment during the first half of the Salinas regime was foreign investors' decisions to profit in the short run from cheap Mexican labor. From 1980 to 1990 Mexican workers experienced a 53 percent drop in their real hourly wage (*Encuesta*

Industrial Mensual, 1980 and 1990). That explains why the wage share in the national income remains around 25 percent despite the increase in employment between 1988 and 1991 (INEGI, 1989a: 35 and Banxico, 1991: 135, 267). The wage share in the Mexican economy is the lowest among the three countries that participate in NAFTA. In the United States the wage share was 59.7 percent of GDP, and in Canada it was 57 percent. If one considers that 75 percent of the Mexican labor force are wage-earners, the low contribution of their total wages to GDP demonstrates the extremely unequal distribution of income in Mexican society. As indicated in Table 2, hourly industrial wages[5] in Mexico fell in 1980 and 1990 in those industrial sectors that are major international exporters. Wages dropped by 50 percent or more in such sectors as autos, cement, beer and glass.

From 1980 to 1991 in Mexico, the annual average increase in labor productivity was 2.6 percent (INEGI, 1980a–1991a). This indicates that during the last eleven years the labor unit cost was reduced by 62 percent as a consequence of the combined effect of rising productivity and falling wages. Yet, clearly, the international competitiveness of Mexican industry was primarily a result of a major reduction in real wages, and only somewhat the result of a small rise in productivity. The failure of state policies and the Mexican industrial bloc to build and operate a modern industrial machine led to a squeeze on labor as the easiest procedure to maintain a share of the international market. Low labor costs were achieved not only through low salaries, but also through low investments in health and safety at the workplace.

THE THIRD RIGHT: A SAFE WORKPLACE

High unemployment rates and low wages create a continuous instability and disorder on the shop floors of Mexican factories. This is evident in the following areas: 1) a high annual labor turnover rate that reaches 200 per cent in the maquila industry, and rates above 40 percent in capital-intensive industries such as steel (Laurell and Noriga, 1989: 197) a practical absence of training programs to raise the skill level of the workforce; 3) a cyclical dissolution of personal working relationships, solidarity and or-

[5]The hourly wage is a statistical figure. One of the few restrictions on companies in Mexican Labor Law is the existence of the daily wage, guaranteeing workers the pay of eight hours of a very low hourly pay. One of the possible modifications of labor law is to introduce the hourly wage, which could be a catastrophe for workers, as they might only receive pay for few hours of work at a very unfair rate.

TABLE 2

HOURLY WAGES IN MEXICAN MANUFACTURE INDUSTRY, 1980–1990

Industrial Sector	1980 Hourly Wages (1990 US$)	1990 Hourly Wages (1990 US$)
Preserved Fruits and Vegetables	1.84	0.83
Beer	2.75	1.63
Broadwoven Cotton Mills	3.12	1.65
Paper Pulp Mills	3.03	1.60
Tires and Related Products	7.33	4.00
Glass Containers	2.70	1.40
Hydraulic Cement	4.05	2.34
Blast Furnace and Steel Mills	4.36	2.07
Electric Household Equipment	2.63	1.15
Motor Vehicles	4.65	2.15
Manufacture Industries	3.14	1.46

Source: Instituto Nacional de Estadistica Geografia e Informatica Encuesta Industrial Mensual, *Resumen Anual*, 1980 and 1990.

ganization of workers;[6] 4) the widespread use of unsafe and poorly designed machinery; and 5) the lack of attention to safety.

As a result of these factors, the Mexican shop floor is a high-risk workplace. During the period between 1980 and 1990, 16,000 workers died from work-related accidents and illness, and 180,000 were disabled by accident or illness. These alarming official figures may in fact underestimate the problem, since it has been noted that the Social Security System is prone to grossly underestimate labor accidents and work-related illness (Laurell and Noriga, 1989: 160). The common practice of companies is to ignore the health and safety aspects of collective bargaining agreements. Cost-cutting and dangerous practices

[6]In the last twenty years, Mexico has had a cyclical recession every six years: The first in 1976–1977, the second in 1982–1983, the third in 1986–1987, and the fourth in 1993–1994. During these recessions the factories fire thousands of workers. The plant closures and the resultant unemployment destroy the solidarity links built before among workers in the shop floor and between the unions of diverse industries. (*See* Ortega and Solis del Alba, 1991.)

include poor lighting on the shop floor; lack of ventilation equipment near noxious fumes and emissions; poor maintenance of moving machinery; worker exposure to hazardous industrial materials. The workers pay with life and limb for these calculated cost-saving practices.

A comparison of the Mexican figures on injuries and illness in the workplace with their equivalents in Canada and the United States (Table 3) shows that the Mexican facilities are at least twice as dangerous as those in the other two countries. Each year during the late 1980s, more than 8 percent of Mexican workers suffered accidents and illness. The rates for workers in the United States and Canada were 3.8 and 5.0 percent, respectively. In 1988 on-the-job death rate was 2.2 per ten thousand in Mexico, but only 0.9 (far less than half the Mexican level) in Canada and the United States. Within NAFTA, there is a clear danger that Mexican workers will compete in part by being obliged to accept extremely unsafe and dangerous working conditions.

THE FOURTH RIGHT: DEMOCRATIC UNIONS AND A FAIR LABOR LAW

The Mexican government maintains tight control over the internal life of trade unions. In 1948, with the military occupation of the Railroad Union headquarters in Mexico City and the imprisonment of their democratically-elected officials, a system of direct and repressive controls over internal union life was established to supplement processes of cooptation and repression.[7] During the next four decades a recurrent cycle of firings, imprisonments and even murders of dissident leaders of the labor movement took place, a brutal harvest to insure that unions would be submissive to the Mexican government.

The union leadership which emerged was in effect imposed by the state and acted on behalf of the state to control worker demands. Labor leaders accorded those who worked for them many important benefits, such as low- or no-interest loans, promotions to higher positions, control over the hiring process and so on. The authoritarian leadership of many unions, known as *charros*, used these "soft" mechanisms to consolidate an iron hand of repression. When the rank and file members

[7]The Social Research Institute of the UNAM years later published a document which stated: "In 1948 occupation of the Railroad Union headquarter the colonel Carlos I. Serrano commanded all the action, with the participation of police special services and selected members of the army. At the same time other four locals of the Railroad Union were occupied by armed squads. Valentin Campa and several democratic leaders were imprisoned." (Serrano, 1980: 323).

TABLE 3

WORK INJURIES AND WORK DEATHS IN THE NAFTA COUNTRIES

	United States	Canada	Mexico
	Work Injuries and Illness per 100 Workers		
1985	3.7	4.9	7.9
1986	3.8	5.1	9.1
1987	3.9	5.1	8.6
1988	4.0	5.0	7.8
	Work Deaths per 10,000 Workers		
1985	1.1	.83	2.0
1986	1.0	.78	2.4
1987	1.0	.92	2.2
1988	0.9	.94	2.2

Sources: U.S. Bureau of Census, *1990 U.S. Statistical Abstract*; Statistics of Canada, *1992 Canada Year Book*; INEGI, Mexico, *Anuario Estadistico 1988–1989*.

of a union have attempted to regain control of their organization, gang members organized by the corrupt leadership in conjunction with police squads, have used violence to dissolve the meetings (Bensusan and Garcia, 1989: 35).

Unions control labor in the big factories and big companies. Half of organized labor is in the public sector, and the biggest union in the country is the Teachers' Union, with 600,000 members. Given the potential power of unions, the government has been particularly concerned with how to maintain control over them and to ensure the tacit support of their members. This has had the paradoxical effect of discouraging further growth of organized labor. Compared with other countries, relatively few Mexican workers outside select public sectors and large factories are unionized. As Table 4 shows, the relative level of union membership of Mexican workers is well below the US level, and represents less than half of the Canadian level.

In the early 1990s the Salinas government has sought to give more guarantees to foreign capital and to encourage foreign investment in the Mexican economy by introducing reforms to law which would further limit the power of organized labor. The Mexican House of Repre-

TABLE 4

UNIONIZATION RATE IN THE NAFTA COUNTRIES

Economic Activity	United States (1988)	Canada (1989)	Mexico (1990)
Agriculture, Forestry, and Fishing	2.0	25.2	2.1
Mining and Oil Industry	18.7	30.8	73.6
Manufactures	22.1	36.3	22.2
Construction	21.1	53.5	0.6
Transports	33.1	53.4	26.7
Finance and Banks	2.6	3.2	29.4
Trade	6.7	11.5	8.4
Services	5.9	34.6	8.4
Public Administration	36.7	79.1	80.1
Total	16.8	34.3	16.1

Sources: U.S. Department of Commerce, Bureau of the Census, *1990 U.S. Statistical Abstract*; Statistics Canada, *Labour Unions 1989* (Ottawa, 1992); STPS, Cuadernos de Informacion Oportuna, *Boletin de Informacion 1992 e INEGI*.

sentatives formed a committee in August, 1989, with the purpose of modifying the labor law and the Constitution in order to remove some of the few rights that the labor movement has on paper. These legal rights create an awkward position for the government, as they run counter to current efforts by the state to limit work rights. As is well know to Mexican historians, the labor rights in the Mexican Constitution were written in 1917 in the context of a revolution which sought many progressive changes. At that time, the Mexican bourgeoisie accepted the right of workers to form trade unions and their right to strike. These were viewed as steps required to bring social harmony and to assure workers that the revolution, which in other areas was less radical than expected, was nevertheless in their interests.

The objectives of the current efforts at changing laws are to facilitate the introduction of all the "flexible procedures" that allow a restructuring of the labor force, restriction of the right to strike, the elimination of trade union control of hiring and firing procedures, the elimination of rigid tasks and positions on the shop floor and the legal settlement of hourly tasks and hourly wages.

One of the arguments of the procapital faction in the Congress is the necessity of "harmonization" of Mexican law with the "right to work" laws in the United States. But the harmonization ends there. The Mexican government is not interested in harmonizing health standards for the workplace. The same could be said about the working week: the Mexican government wishes to preserve the 48-hour work week.

THE FIFTH RIGHT: MIGRANT WORKERS AND HUMAN RIGHTS

The crisis of the 1980s in Mexico produced an intense emigration flow to the southern states of the United States. The dramatic decline in living conditions in many urban areas of Mexico forced many workers to look for opportunities elsewhere. The rural areas, which had for decades a zone of even poorer economic prospects, did not offer a solution. In fact, migration from Mexico to the United States was for many years primarily a movement of rural workers. A big difference with the migration phenomena of the 1970s was that now the main current of migrant workers come from urban areas of Mexico.

By comparing the 1980 and 1990 Census of Population in Mexico and the United States, we can estimate the permanent emigration of Mexicans to the United States over this period at 3 million people. It is estimated that in fact far more people moved and that some people moved back and forth many times, seeking seasonal jobs in the United States. A total of eight million moves may have taken place over the 1980s between Mexico and the United States (*El Financiero*, August 4, 1992). This means that a very large number of unemployed Mexicans and a significant part of the impoverished population attempt to cross the 2,000 mile border at least once a year. Up to one third of the Mexican labor force participates in the U.S. labor market at least for a few months every year.

The immense presence of Mexican workers in the southern states facilitated the development of a dynamic service sector in the southern United States. This cheap immigrant labor has been at times a decisive source of profits and major stimulus for investment. Low-wage employment of Mexican immigrants has also contributed to the relocation of many American industries to the southwest. The absence of organizing rights for Mexican immigrant workers has changed the income distribution in states such as California. In this state, for example, the share of wages of the Gross State Product fell from 64 percent in 1970 to 59 percent in 1990.

According to the U.S. census, in 1991, 3.5 million workers of Mexican and Latin American origin (Hispanic workers, as the Census labels them) participated in U.S. manufacturing, construction and mining. Mexican workers represented 13 percent of those employed in those activities. In terms of the Mexican community itself, 56 percent of the males and 18.2 percent of all adult Mexicans in the United States labored in industrial activities. Overall, while only 29 percent of the white labor force participated in industrial activities, 41 percent of the Mexican labor force in the United States participated as industrial workers.

The drop in the rate of unionization in California from 1983 to 1988 from 21 percent to 14 percent presumably reflects many factors, including the location in this region of many new "flexible" industries which were hostile to unions and which offered to establish plants only on the condition that the workers they employed would not seek to organize. Yet, this trend may also reflect how the immigration of both documented and undocumented migrant labor reduces the power and attractiveness of unions. The drop in union membership can be observed in Texas. In 1983, 12.4 percent of workers in Texas were unionized. By 1988 this had fallen to 4.9 percent (Cumer, 1990: 22, 25).

CONCLUSIONS

The reality of labor's rights in Mexico is a far cry from the words written in the constitution and in labor legislation. Workers face three major challenges. First, they face very high unemployment. At least 6 million workers were unemployed in 1993, a tragic outcome, aggravated by economic crisis and stagnation in the southwest United States, the return of thousands of Mexican migrants from the United States, and the recession of the Mexican economy. Second, they face a situation in which income distribution and sources of income are extremely distorted. Workers receive only a relatively small share of the income which their work generates. In Mexico, the total salaries received by workers are only half as important in relation to the drop in the Gross Domestic Product as they are in Canada and the United States. Finally, Mexican workers face a relatively high risk of work-related injuries and illness, due to cost-cutting industrial practices which place a reduced value on human life. All of the above stems from the historical development of a political system which has limited the democratic rights of labor, controlled major unions in key sectors, and sought to minimize the spread of organized labor to other sectors. In the recent past, the Mexican state has frequently intervened to weaken the power and autonomy of labor. When this is not sufficient, it exercises open and brutal repression against dissident groups of workers.

Efforts by the Mexican state to limit the right of labor have not diminished over the past decade in which the Mexican economy has become increasingly integrated into the North American hemisphere. If anything, the promise of expanding *maquiladora* industry and hopes for new foreign investment for export and domestic production have led to intensified efforts by the current government to further limit the role and influence of labor. Thus, rights which currently exist (even if seldom recognized in past practice) may be removed. For example, when Mexican workers demonstrate that their income has deteriorated in relation to the growing profits of the companies, Mexican legislation recognizes the unrestricted right to strike without waiting for the biennial revision of collective contracts. In this area, U.S. legislation is more restrictive, allowing labor to strike legally only when a contract has expired. If Mexican legislation were to be "harmonized" with the more restrictive U.S. legislation, then organized labor in Mexico, already without much influence, would be further weakened. Of course, this is not a necessary outcome. Much will depend on the joint action of organized labor and progressive political parties across all three countries in NAFTA. The weak position and further erosion of labor rights in Mexico has implications for the dignity, status and well-being of workers, and for related democratic practices in the entire NAFTA region. Recognition of these implications, it is hoped, will serve to change the direction of policies and practices as they have been evolving recently.

REFERENCES

Aguilar Garcia, J.
1982   *La Politica Sindical en Mexico*. Mexico: Editorial ERA.

Alvarez, A.
1987   *La Crisis Global del Capitalismo en Mexico*. Mexico: Editorial ERA.

Banco de Mexico (Banxico)
n.d.   *Informes Anuales 1980–1992*. Mexico.

Bensusan , G., and C. Garcia
1989   *Estado y Sindicatos: Crisis de una Relacion.* Mexico: UAM-Xochimilco.

Bensusan Areous, G.
1992   *Las Relaciones Laborales y el Tratado de Libre Comercio.* Mexico: Miguel
            Angel Porrua Editores.

Bernard, E.
1991   "Labour and Politics in the US and Canada." In *Labor in a Global Economy.*
            Ed. S. Hecker and M. Hallock. Eugene: University of Oregon Books.

Bortz, J.
1986   *El Salario en Mexico.* Mexico: Editorial FCE.

Cumer, M.
1990   "Union Membership and Contract Coverage in the United States,
            1983–1988," *Industrial and Labor Relations Review*, 44(1). October.

Davis, M.
1990   *City of Quartz: Excavating the Future in Los Angeles.* London and New York:
            Verso.

De la Garza, E.
1992   "Reestructuracion y Polarizacion Industrial en Mexico," *Revista El Cotidiano*,
            50(8).

Edwards, R., and M. Rodgursky
1986   "The Unraveling Accord: American Unions in Crisis." In *American Unions in
            Crisis and Beyond.* Ed. R. Edwards *et al.* London: Auburn House Publishing
            Company.

Gastelum Gaxiola, M.
1991   *Migracion de los Trabajadores Mexicanos Indocumentados.* Mexico: Univer-
            sidad Nacional Autonoma de Mexico, Facultad de Derecho.

Gregory, P.
1986   *The Myth of the Market Failure: Employment and the Labor Market on
            Mexico.* Baltimore and London: World Bank and the Johns Hopkins Univer-
            sity Press.

Instituto Nacional de Estadistica Geografia e Informatica, Mexico (INEGI)
1980a–   *Sistema de Cuentas Nacionales de Mexico.* Mexico.
1992a

1982b–   *Cauadernos de Informacion Oportuna.* Mexico.
1992b

1970c–   *Censos de Poblacion.* Mexico.
1990c

Laurell, C., and M. Noriega
1989   *La Salud en la Frabrica.* Mexico: Editorial ERA.

Lopez, C.
1990   *En la Modelo: un Modelo de Huelga.* Mexico: Centro de Asesoria Sindical
            Valentin Campa Salazar.

Montiel, Y.
1992   "Volkswagen: Contradicciones ante la Modernizacion." Paper presented at Tercer Coloquio of Jalapa on "Productive Restructuring and Social Reorganization." October 7–10.

Ortega, M., and A. Solis del Alba
1992   *Mexico: Estados y Sindicatos, 1983–1988*. Mexico: Mesa Obrero-Sindical, MCCLP.

Poole, M.
1986   *Industrial Relations: Origins and Patterns of National Diversity*. London: Routledge and Kegan Paul.

Quiroz, J. O., and L. Mendez
1992   "En Busca de una Nueva Legislacion Laboral," *Revista El Cotidiano*, 50(8).

Sanger, M.
1991   *Free Trade and Worker's Rights: The European Social Charter*. Ottawa: Canadian Centre for Policy Alternatives.

Secretaria del Trabajo y Prevision Social (STPS)
1991   *Encuesta Nacional de Educacion, Capacitatcion y Empleo 1991*. Mexico.

Serrano, C. I.
1980   *Memorias del Encuentro sobre Movimiento Obrero*. Puebla: Universidad Autonom de Puebla. Vol. 2.

Stanford, J.
1991   *Going South: Cheap Labour as an Unfair Subsidy in North American Free Trade*. Ottawa: Canadian Centre for Policy Alternatives.

Velasco-Arregui, E.
1992   "Labour Markets, Productivity and Trade Unions in the North American Free Trade Agreement Countries." Paper presented at Congress on "Economic Interpretation Between Unequal Partners." Athens University of Economics and Business, August.

———
1989   "El Resurgimiento del Cuarto Estado: Los Asalariados y su Ciclo." In *La Clase Obrera y el Sindicalismo Mexicano*. Ed. A. Alvarez. Mexico: Universidad Nacional Autonoma de Mexico, Facultad de Economia.

Part II

New Trends in International Migration

Policies and Migration Trends in the North American System[1]

Hania Zlotnik

Introduction

At the global level, Canada and the United States are major attraction poles for international migrants. Both can be characterized as traditional countries of immigration, since they are among the handful of countries in the world that continue to admit foreigners for permanent settlement. Both countries, like other countries in the Americas, were largely populated by European migrants but, in contrast with other important migrant-receiving countries in the hemisphere, both have maintained strong immigration programs. Their economic prosperity has ensured that during most of this century they have not lacked a ready supply of potential immigrants. Changes in their immigration policies have also contributed to their continued attraction by reducing their reliance on immigration from developed countries. Thus, once they opened their doors to immigrants from developing countries, both Canada and the United States became the core of a truly global migration system having linkages with almost every world region (Zlotnik, 1992).

---

[1]The views and opinions expressed in this paper are those of the author and do not necessarily represent those of the United Nations.

This paper analyses the evolution of migration links between the North American core countries (Canada and the United States) and other world regions in terms of different types of migration and in view of the policies that have given rise to migration trends. Particular attention is given to the North American migration system and the major role played by Mexico as a source of undocumented migrants to the United States. The passage of the North American Free Trade Agreement (NAFTA), which will lead to even greater economic interdependence between Canada, Mexico and the United States, is likely to have a significant effect on migration flows between the three countries.

MIGRATION TO THE CORE COUNTRIES COMPARED

Both Canada and the United States have evolved relatively complex systems for the admission of foreign migrants. The complexity stems from the fact that each country admits both immigrants, that is, foreigners granted permission to stay indefinitely in their territories, and nonimmigrants, that is, foreigners allowed to enter and stay only temporarily. The latter are usually subject to a number of restrictions that vary according to the class of admission. In addition, both countries receive persons who are not legally admitted and those who are seeking asylum. Furthermore, they generate emigrants and returning migrants when their citizens or permanent residents go abroad for a significant period or return after having been abroad for a lengthy period. A complete analysis of migration trends in the system would demand that all these components be considered and compared – a far from straight-forward task, mainly because of data deficiencies.[2]

Immigration statistics concerning the number of persons granted permanent residence rights in a given year are useful for comparative analysis. However, care must be taken in interpreting different trends. Whereas the vast majority of immigrants to Canada obtain residence rights before entering the country, in the United States a very significant proportion of those granted permanent residence in a given year have already resided in the country for some time. Thus, in fiscal year 1986 (the year ending on September 30, 1986), 37 percent of those granted

---

[2]Canada and the United States lack data on the in- and out-migration of their citizens, and have no mechanism in place to gather information on emigration, be it of their own citizens or of immigrants. Consequently, available statistics reveal at best only gross gains through the immigration of foreign born. Losses or net gains can only be conjecture.

permanent residence in the United States were only "adjusting" their status from within the country. In 1990, when the results of the regularization drive instituted by the Immigration Reform and Control Act (IRCA) of 1986 were still being felt, a full 72 percent of all immigrants admitted were adjusting their status. That is, admission is not equivalent to entry. Hence annual immigration statistics, particularly for the United States, are not adequate reflections of actual population gains through immigration on a year-by-year basis.

Immigration for Permanent Settlement

Bearing the preceding caveats in mind, consider the data presented in Table 1 comparing the average annual number of admissions of permanent immigrants by Canada and the United States over the past 30 years. Although during 1960–1990 Canada's total population was roughly about one-tenth of that of the United States, the number of immigrants Canada admitted has been, at its lowest, 20 percent of those admitted by the United States (in 1980–1984) and has reached nearly 51 percent (in 1960–1964) at its highest. That is, although in absolute terms immigration to Canada has always been considerably lower than that to its neighbor to the south, it has been considerably greater in relative terms. Indeed, according to the censuses carried out in the early 1980s, the foreign-born population accounted for over 16 percent of the total enumerated in Canada and for only about 6 percent of that enumerated in the United States.

The data in Table 1 also indicate the diverse sources of immigrants admitted by these two receiving countries. During the early 1960s, immigrants to Canada showed a much greater concentration by region of birth than those to the United States, with 88 percent having been born in developed countries. In the United States, in contrast, only 58 percent of the immigrants admitted during 1960–1964 were born in developed countries; a further 27 percent came from Central America (including Mexico) and the Caribbean. That is, some diversification of migrant sources had already occurred in the United States prior to the enactment of the 1965 Amendments to the 1952 Immigration and Nationality Act. Nevertheless, the measures taken by both core countries towards the mid-1960s to put the selection of immigrants on a more universal footing contributed to an accelerated diversification during the 1970s when, as Table 1 indicates, a steady decline in the

proportion of immigrants originating in the developed world was counterbalanced in great measure by the gains made by Asia, particularly
Eastern and Southeastern Asia and, to a considerably lesser extent, by
Central America and the Caribbean. As a result of such trends, by
1985–1989, 65 percent of all immigrants to the United States originated
in Eastern and Southeastern Asia or in Central America and the Caribbean. The equivalent proportion was 41 percent in the case of Canada.

Another facet of the diversification experienced by the core countries is the increasing number of immigrant source countries. During
the 1940s and 1950s, 75 percent of the migration to Canada originated
in eight countries. Seven of those were European: the United Kingdom
(27%), Italy (11%), Germany (10%), the Netherlands (9%), Poland
(8%), France and Yugoslavia (2% each).[3] The United States itself was
an important source of immigrants to Canada (6%). By 1970–1974, the
list of countries accounting for three-quarters of all immigrants to
Canada had grown to 27. The United Kingdom and the United States
occupied first and second places, but developing countries were also
high in the list, particularly India, the Philippines, Hong Kong and
China, all of which were in the top ten. By 1985–1989 the two
top-ranking ones had become Hong Kong and India. The Philippines,
China and Jamaica occupied prominent places and Viet Nam had
emerged as a major source. The United Kingdom and the United States
had moved to sixth and seventh places, surpassed among the developed
countries only by Poland.

In the United States, diversification was also evident in the increasing
number of countries of origin accounting for three-quarters of all
immigrants admitted in different periods. Thus, whereas in 1946–1955
the list included only 14 countries, by 1985–1989 it had grown to 23.[4]
Although the rank of most countries changed from period to period,
Mexico headed the list between 1956–1960 and 1985–1989. Before
1970, Canada, Germany, Italy and the United Kingdom ranked consistently high, but since then China, Cuba, India, the Philippines and the
Republic of Korea largely displaced them. In addition, since 1975, Viet
Nam became a major source of immigrants to the United States.

---

[3]For this data, see Canada, Employment and Immigration Canada, *Immigration Statistics*, various
years.

[4]For this data, see U.S. Immigration and Naturalization Service, *Statistical Yearbook*, various years.

TABLE 1

AVERAGE ANNUAL NUMBER OF IMMIGRANTS ADMITTED BY CANADA AND THE UNITED STATES BY
REGION OF BIRTH AND PERIOD OF ADMISSION, 1960–1994

	1960–1964	1965–1969	1970–1974	1975–1979	1980–1984	1985–1989	1990–1991
Canada[a]	Numbers						
Sub-Saharan Africa	794	2,217	5,819	5,707	3,585	6,174	—
Northern Africa and Western Asia	3,146	6,534	4,698	6,858	4,878	9,829	—
Southern Asia	1,365	5,815	11,713	10,450	11,361	16,990	—
Eastern and Southeastern Asia	1,816	11,525	20,467	26,120	35,080	41,444	—
Central America and the Caribbean	2,381	8,947	16,490	13,244	9,822	15,176	—
South America	1,031	2,555	7,139	8,773	5,452	7,492	—
Oceania (Developing)	324	434	1,113	1,148	690	578	—
Developed countries	77,151	143,950	91,418	57,828	43,187	40,227	—
Total	88,008	181,976	158,857	130,127	114,056	137,910	—
United States							
Sub-Saharan Africa	1,106	1,888	3,655	7,315	11,175	14,111	16,191
Northern Africa and Western Asia	5,348	9,652	14,438	18,358	20,851	21,162	26,521
Southern Asia	1,387	5,393	16,761	23,156	39,497	51,775	64,553
Eastern and Southeastern Asia	13,272	34,925	81,512	131,690	208,765	193,855	213,775
Central America and the Caribbean	76,977	123,664	132,704	158,239	162,136	198,006	178,201
South America	20,026	23,844	20,935	30,848	36,925	42,215	46,732
Oceania (Developing)	734	1,172	2,020	2,489	1,896	1,924	1,866
Developed countries	164,951	158,409	112,658	87,445	83,761	82,625	132,220
Total	283,803	358,947	384,683	459,541	565,007	605,674	680,058
Canada[a]	Percentage Distribution						
Sub-Saharan Africa	1	1	4	4	3	4	—
Northern Africa and Western Asia	4	4	3	5	4	7	—
Southern Asia	2	3	7	8	10	12	—
Eastern and Southeastern Asia	2	6	13	20	31	30	—
Central America and the Caribbean	3	5	10	10	9	11	—
South America	1	1	4	7	5	5	—
Oceania (Developing)	0	0	1	1	1	0	—
Developed countries	88	79	58	44	38	29	—
United States							
Sub-Saharan Africa	0	1	1	2	2	2	2
Northern Africa and Western Asia	2	3	4	4	4	3	4
Southern Asia	0	2	4	5	7	9	9
Eastern and Southeastern Asia	5	10	21	29	37	32	31
Central America and the Caribbean	27	34	34	34	29	33	26
South America	7	7	5	7	7	7	7
Oceania (Developing)	0	0	1	1	0	0	0
Developed countries	58	44	29	19	15	14	19

Sources: Canada, Employment and Immigration Canada, *Immigration Statistics*, various years; U.S. Immigration and Naturalization Service, *Statistical Yearbook*, various years.

[a]For Canada, the first period is considered 1961–1964.

These observations suggest that even though the core countries have many characteristics in common, there are others setting them apart. In particular, the United States has a longer tradition of admitting immigrants from its immediate region of influence, Central America, Mexico and the Caribbean, and has generally been a more likely destination for emigrants from that region than has Canada (United Nations, 1990: 221). This said, migration from Central America and the Caribbean to Canada has become very important in the 1970s and 1980s, a trend which continues. In addition, especially during the late 1970s and early 1980s, when developed countries experienced a recession, immigration to Canada dropped substantially while that to the United States continued to rise. Significantly, in the late 1980s and early 1990s, immigration to Canada again rose. As will be discussed later, such a difference in trends was due not only to economic factors but also to a host of other developments that effectively led to important differences in the two countries' immigration policies.

Temporary Migration

Both Canada and the United States have provisions allowing the admission of aliens on a temporary basis. In Canada, there are four categories of persons granted permission to stay for substantial, albeit limited, periods: 1) visitors, 2) students, 3) temporary workers, and 4) holders of minister's permits (Michalowski and Fortier, 1990). Minister's permits are usually granted on humanitarian, compassionate, or national-interest grounds. Since temporary migrants can hold more than one type of permit at a time, the four categories are not mutually exclusive. Michalowski and Fortier have estimated the number of temporary migrants present in Canada for every year of the period 1982–1988. Their estimates indicate that the annual number of temporary migrants fluctuated between 134,000 and 144,000 during 1982–1986 and increased thereafter to reach nearly 176,000 in 1988. The number of persons holding work permits rose consistently, passing from 58,000 in 1982 to 112,000 in 1988. The number of students fluctuated between 48,000 and 61,000, whereas that of persons holding minister's permits varied over a narrower range: 32,000 to 37,000. Visitors accounted for the lowest numbers, ranging from 17,000 to 21,000.

Table 2 presents the estimated number of temporary migrants in Canada by region of last permanent residence for 1982, 1985, and

TABLE 2

TEMPORARY MIGRANTS IN CANADA BY REGION OF LAST PERMANENT RESIDENCE FOR SELECTED YEARS

Region	1982		1985		1988	
	N	Percent	N	Percent	N	Percent
Europe	26,581	20	22,708	16	34,804	20
Africa	7,625	6	8,955	6	14,835	8
Asia	51,244	38	55,922	40	70,206	40
Australasia	1,504	1	1,468	1	2,533	1
North and Central America	18,484	14	18,980	14	27,963	16
Caribbean	18,686	14	17,112	12	11,939	7
South America	9,640	7	12,983	9	11,224	6
Oceania	517	0	516	0	1,937	1
Unspecified	7	0	22	0	139	0
Total	134,288	100	138,666	100	175,580	100

Source: Michalowski and Fortier, "Two Neglected Categories of Immigrants to Canada: Temporary Immigrants and Returning Canadians," *Statistical Journal of the United Nations Economic Commission for Europe*, 7(3): 175–240 (1990).

1988. Those data indicate that, just as with regard to immigration flows, persons originating in Asia accounted for most of the temporary migrants in Canada (about 40%). Although the available classification does not distinguish between migrants originating in the United States and those originating in Mexico and Central America, the estimates suggest that, among temporary migrants, those originating in Central America and the Caribbean account for a larger proportion than they do among immigrants, with the converse being likely with respect to migrants originating in developed countries. Unfortunately, data on region of origin are not available for the migrant categories distinguished above.

In the United States, information on temporary migration is obtained from entry records collected mostly at airports. The statistics published refer therefore to the number of entries of aliens by visa category. Several of those categories allow relatively prolonged periods of stay in the country, but there is no guarantee that all the aliens counted actually stay for lengthy periods. In addition, multiple entries during a given year result in multiple counts of the same person. Despite these deficiencies, the data in Table 3 approximate the likely trends and characteristics of temporary migration to the United States.

The nonimmigrant categories under which stays of a few months or more are possible include: 1) students, 2) temporary workers and trainees, 3) exchange visitors (*i.e.*, persons working for a short period in specialized areas), 4) intracompany transferees, 5) treaty traders and investors, and 6) fiancés of U.S. citizens and their children. As Table 3

TABLE 3

AVERAGE ANNUAL NUMBER OF NONIMMIGRANTS ADMITTED BY THE UNITED STATES BY
CATEGORY, REGION OF ORIGIN, AND PERIOD OF ADMISSION

	Average Annual Numbers			Percentage		
	1974–1979	1983–1986	1987–1990	1974–1979	1983–1986	1987–1990
All Nonimmigrants						
Developed countries	3,673,039	5,545,999	9,671,419	47.1	56.3	63.9
Central America and Caribbean	2,774,815	1,849,754	2,507,909	35.6	18.8	16.6
South America	619,831	925,573	1,141,592	7.9	9.4	7.5
Eastern and Southeastern Asia	283,889	654,625	934,653	3.6	6.6	6.2
Northern Africa and Western Asia	174,370	326,054	356,568	2.2	3.3	2.4
Southern Asia	172,237	201,047	236,390	2.2	2.0	1.6
Sub-Saharan Africa	72,714	142,672	146,279	0.9	1.4	1.0
Oceania (Developing)	30,944	210,000	150,998	0.4	2.1	1.0
Total	7,801,839	9,855,723	15,145,808	100.0	100.0	100.0
Students						
Developed countries	36,039	72,907	125,230	26.3	28.2	40.5
Eastern and Southeastern Asia	16,615	55,181	75,203	12.1	21.4	24.3
Central America and Caribbean	26,002	32,976	31,521	19.0	12.8	10.2
South America	14,606	30,576	21,869	10.7	11.8	7.1
Northern Africa and Western Asia	12,416	33,676	23,049	9.1	13.0	7.5
Southern Asia	22,008	16,003	20,735	16.1	6.2	6.7
Sub-Saharan Africa	6,847	11,594	8,687	5.0	4.5	2.8
Total	136,809	258,144	308,860	100.0	100.0	100.0
Spouses and Children of Students						
Developed countries	3,295	3,878	4,903	23.3	13.4	18.3
Eastern and Southeastern Asia	1,673	8,832	11,820	11.8	30.5	44.2
Northern Africa and Western Asia	2,397	8,041	4,580	16.9	27.7	17.1
Southern America	2,050	3,146	1,706	14.5	10.9	6.4
Southern Asia	2,166	1,672	1,659	15.3	5.8	6.2
Central America and Caribbean	1,541	1,559	1,176	10.9	5.4	4.4
Sub-Saharan Africa	940	1,278	719	6.6	4.4	2.7
Total	14,153	28,981	26,757	100.0	100.0	100.0
Temporary Workers and Trainees						
Developed countries	21,105	39,498	64,139	43.8	52.4	51.6
Central America and Caribbean	19,443	21,587	32,435	40.4	28.7	26.1
Eastern and Southeastern Asia	4,606	5,841	12,697	9.6	7.8	10.2
South America	1,487	3,222	6,287	3.1	4.3	5.1
Northern Africa and Western Asia	591	1,881	3,156	1.2	2.5	2.5
Southern Asia	419	1,427	3,245	0.9	1.9	2.6
Sub-Saharan Africa	396	812	1,782	0.8	1.1	1.4
Total	48,182	75,342	124,255	100.0	100.0	100.0

TABLE 3 (CONTINUED)

AVERAGE ANNUAL NUMBER OF NONIMMIGRANTS ADMITTED BY THE UNITED STATES BY
CATEGORY, REGION OF ORIGIN, AND PERIOD OF ADMISSION

	Average Annual Numbers			Percentage		
	1974–1979	1983–1986	1987–1990	1974–1979	1983–1986	1987–1990
Spouses and Children of Temporary Workers and Trainees						
Developed countries	3,906	7,738	14,243	42.4	64.5	63.9
Central America and Caribbean	4,038	718	1,314	43.8	6.0	5.9
Northern Africa and Western Asia	248	1,049	1,694	2.7	8.8	7.6
South America	420	801	1,623	4.6	6.7	7.3
Eastern and Southeastern Asia	338	734	1,768	3.7	6.1	7.9
Southern Asia	138	560	1,043	1.5	4.7	4.7
Sub-Saharan Africa	118	255	491	1.3	2.1	2.2
Total	9,221	11,989	22,278	100.0	100.0	100.0
Exchange Visitors						
Developed countries	25,472	64,090	111,563	53.5	60.3	66.9
Eastern and Southeastern Asia	3,699	11,946	17,468	7.8	11.2	10.5
South America	7,355	6,122	8,309	15.4	5.8	5.0
Northern Africa and Western Asia	3,506	8,975	8,126	7.4	8.4	4.9
Central America and Caribbean	2,736	5,834	10,109	5.7	5.5	6.1
Sub-Saharan Africa	2,489	4,687	5,806	5.2	4.4	3.5
Southern Asia	2,191	3,131	4,455	4.6	2.9	2.7
Total	47,626	106,334	166,828	100.0	100.0	100.0
Spouses and Children of Exchange Visitors						
Developed countries	10,522	15,091	18,939	56.2	51.0	50.3
Northern Africa and Western Asia	2,119	4,629	4,202	11.3	15.6	11.1
Eastern and Southeastern Asia	1,003	4,097	7,636	5.4	13.8	20.3
South America	2,447	1,925	2,455	13.1	6.5	6.5
Southern Asia	1,012	1,295	1,721	5.4	4.4	4.6
Central America and Caribbean	925	1,129	1,418	4.9	3.8	3.8
Sub-Saharan Africa	680	994	1,081	3.6	3.4	2.9
Total	18,738	29,589	37,687	100.0	100.0	100.0
Intracompany Transferees						
Developed countries	12,289	43,572	47,184	75.6	67.9	74.0
South America	1,709	6,188	5,434	10.5	9.6	8.5
Eastern and Southeastern Asia	552	5,192	4,518	3.4	8.1	7.1
Central America and Caribbean	921	5,067	3,325	5.7	7.9	5.2
Total	16,256	64,165	63,773	100.0	100.0	100.0
Spouses and Children of Intracompany Transferees						
Developed countries	9,839	27,570	28,528	77.5	66.2	72.8
South America	1,111	3,959	3,491	8.8	9.5	8.9
Eastern and Southeastern Asia	414	3,936	2,660	3.3	9.5	6.8
Central America and Caribbean	719	3,360	2,155	5.7	8.1	5.5
Total	12,689	41,619	39,161	100.0	100.0	100.0

TABLE 3 (CONTINUED)

AVERAGE ANNUAL NUMBER OF NONIMMIGRANTS ADMITTED BY THE UNITED STATES BY
CATEGORY, REGION OF ORIGIN, AND PERIOD OF ADMISSION

	Average Annual Numbers			Percentage		
	1974–1979	1983–1986	1987–1990	1974–1979	1983–1986	1987–1990
Treaty Traders and Investors						
Developed countries	33,850	78,282	112,247	82.9	81.7	85.2
Eastern and Southeastern Asia	3,437	9,318	11,116	8.4	9.7	8.4
Total	40,819	95,872	131,781	100.0	100.0	100.0
Fiancés of U.S. Citizens and Their Children						
Eastern and Southeastern Asia	2,463	3,293	2,922	34.1	43.6	43.1
Developed countries	3,136	2,411	2,099	43.5	31.9	31.0
Central America and Caribbean	974	872	860	13.5	11.5	12.7
South America	297	376	361	4.1	5.0	5.3
Total	7,215	7,559	6,774	100.0	100.0	100.0

Source: U.S. Immigration and Naturalization Service, *Statistical Yearbooks*, various years.

Note: Data for 1974–1979 are classified by place of birth. Those for the other two periods are classified by citizenship.

indicates, the numbers of entries of temporary migrants in these categories are relatively small in comparison to the entries of all nonimmigrants, which range in the millions. The latter, however, consist mostly of entries of temporary visitors for pleasure or business.

Students account for the largest number of temporary migrants. Furthermore, their numbers have been rising steadily to reach an annual average of over 300,000 in 1987–1990. The distribution of foreign students by region of origin has changed markedly during the period considered. In the 1970s nearly 74 percent of all student entries corresponded to persons from developing countries. By the late 1980s that proportion had declined to about 60 percent and its distribution among the developing regions had become more skewed, with nearly 35 percent of all students originating in Eastern and Southeastern Asia or in Central America and the Caribbean. Southern Asia, in particular, had seen its share of foreign student entries decline substantially. Interestingly, there were important differences between the trends and distribution of the spouses and children of students and those of the students themselves. Whereas the latter increased with time, the former declined between 1983–1986 and 1987–1990. Furthermore, students from Eastern and Southeastern Asia as well as those from Northern Africa and Western Asia were more likely to be accompanied by spouses and children than were their counterparts from other regions. Better economic standing among students from those regions is probably responsible for that pattern.

Among temporary migrants entering the United States, those in the categories of temporary workers and trainees, exchange visitors, intra-company transferees, and treaty traders and investors are granted permission to work. However, whereas the second, third and fourth categories include mostly skilled workers or professionals, the first includes both "aliens of distinguished merit or ability" and unskilled agricultural and nonagricultural workers. During 1988–1990, the latter accounted for about 30 percent of all temporary workers and trainees (U.S. Immigration and Naturalization Service, 1991).

As Table 3 indicates, steady increases have been registered in three categories: temporary workers and trainees, exchange visitors, and treaty traders and investors. The fourth category, intracompany trans-ferees, increased fourfold between 1974–1979 and 1983–1986 but has remained fairly stable since then. The various categories of highly skilled or specialized workers include very high proportions originating in the developed world. Four out of every five treaty traders and investors have come from developed countries. The proportion is closer to three out of every four among intracompany transferees and to three out of every five among exchange visitors. Consequently, the developing regions are the source of relatively few specialized workers. The category of temporary workers and trainees constitutes an exception in that, although the proportion from developed countries is still high (about half), so is that from Central America and the Caribbean. The latter region is the source of an important number of unskilled workers, particularly those working in agriculture.

Unfortunately, the figures presented in Tables 2 and 3 relative to temporary migration to Canada and the United States are not compa-rable since the former indicate stocks of persons staying in the country for at least a year and the latter are overestimates of flows. However, the figures suggest that the ratio of temporary migrants in Canada to that in the United States may be about one to five, indicating again that in relative terms Canada admits more temporary migrants than the United States. Furthermore, in the United States temporary migrants from developed countries rank first in terms of number of entries, whereas in Canada temporary migrants of Asian origin hold that rank. One must point out, however, that the difference may be due mostly to the fact that temporary migrants from developed countries travel more often into and out of the United States than do their counterparts from other regions.

Undocumented Migration

Perhaps one of the most important differences between Canada and the United States is that only the latter has experienced high levels of undocumented migration. Concern about the inflow of undocumented migrants and the need to control it led the United States to adopt in 1986 the Immigration Reform and Control Act (IRCA). Among other things, IRCA laid the grounds for legalization of aliens who had resided in an unlawful status in the country since before January 1, 1982. It also created a new classification for seasonal agricultural workers and provisions for the legalization of some of those workers (U.S. Immigration and Naturalization Service, 1991: A1–A19). As a result of IRCA, nearly 2.5 million persons were granted permanent-resident status during 1989–1991. The overwhelming majority of those legalized through IRCA (75%) have been Mexican. Salvadorans, Guatemalans and Haitians have occupied the second, third and fourth places respectively, accounting for nearly one-tenth of all the legalizations carried out thus far.[5] In contrast with general permanent immigration patterns, migrants from Asian countries have accounted for relatively few of those regularized.

The main goal of IRCA was to reduce and control undocumented migration through legalization measures, by imposing sanctions on employers who knowingly hire undocumented migrants, and by reinforcing the border patrol. However, it is difficult to assess the effectiveness of IRCA. Although the legalization drive did reduce the undocumented population in the United States, it did not eliminate it altogether. It has been estimated that by 1988 between 1.7 and 2.9 million undocumented migrants remained in the country and that the undocumented population increased between 1986 and 1988 (Woodrow and Passel, 1990).

THE IMMIGRATION POLICIES OF THE CORE COUNTRIES

The context in which migration takes place is highly conditioned by the adopted policies of the countries of destination to control the inflows

[5]For this data, *see U.S. Immigration and Naturalization Service, Statistical Yearbook*, 1989–1991.

of foreigners. Although it is generally accepted that Canada and the United States have adopted a number of immigration policies having many elements in common, differences exist. A major one arose when the shortage of labor during the World War II prompted the United States to adopt in April 1943, an act that provided for the importation of temporary agricultural workers from North, South, and Central America. This program was later extended through 1947 and served as the legal basis of the Mexican bracero programs which lasted through 1964 (U.S. Immigration and Naturalization Service, 1991: A1–A9). In fact, the United States had begun resorting to Mexican labor earlier in the century when in 1917 after the United States entered World War I, 72,000 Mexican contract workers had been imported (Fogel, 1982). U.S. statistics indicate that during the 1920s nearly half a million Mexicans were admitted as immigrants. That movement can be seen as both a consequence and a cause of the strong links between Mexico and the Southwestern states of the United States that had been annexed by the latter in the nineteenth century.

Mexican immigration to the United States was already of major importance by the time the Immigration and Nationality Act Amendments of 1965 were passed. The latter abolished the national origins quota system originally established by the Immigration Act of 1924 and modified by the Immigration and Nationality Act of 1952, which had effectively restricted the admission of immigrants from developing countries, particularly those from Asia. Although in Canada the liberalization of immigrant admission policies began in 1962 and culminated in 1967 with the adoption of a new selection system which was meant to avoid all discrimination in terms of national origins (Samuel, 1991), the system did not become a reality in terms of immigrant admissions until the 1970s (*see* Table 1).

Both the Canadian point system and the United States system of immigrant preferences gave high priority to family reunification as a basis for immigrant admission. In the United States, the 1965 Amendments to the Immigration and Nationality Act established seven preference categories, four of them for relatives of U.S. citizens and permanent-resident aliens. A limit of 290,000 was put on all preference categories and about 74 percent of all places were allocated to the family preferences (Reimers, 1982). In addition, immediate relatives of U.S. citizens could be admitted without numerical limitation (U.S.

Immigration and Naturalization Service, 1991: A1–A15). In contrast, the 1976 Immigration Act adopted by Canada that came into effect in 1978 established a point system that, although favoring family reunification, was better suited to fine-tune immigrant admissions to economic need. Canada's act also established that the number of immigrant admissions was to be controlled by "planning levels" established at least one year in advance. Although planning levels were not quotas in the sense that they might not be met strictly, the possibility of changing them and using them as targets gave Canadian policy added flexibility. During 1979–1986, however, actual immigrant admissions matched planning levels in only three years out of seven.

Despite the similarity of their policies, the immigration trends recorded by Canada and the United States differed considerably. Not only did Canada experience a decline in immigrant admissions during 1975–1984 while the United States experienced a steady increase, but there were also substantial differences in the composition of the intake: during 1980–1989, nearly 70 percent of all immigrants to the United States were admitted by virtue of their family ties with either U.S. citizens or permanent residents, whereas the equivalent proportion in Canada during 1981–1987 was 52 percent. In addition, whereas during the 1980s only 9 percent of immigrants to the United States belonged to the occupational preferences, in Canada the "independent class," consisting of immigrants with needed skills or capital and their dependents, accounted for nearly one-third of all those admitted during 1981–1987 (United Nations, 1992: 176).

Partly because of concern that immigrant admissions under family preferences were leaving little room for the admission of immigrants with needed skills, the United States adopted the Immigration Act of 1990 which establishes increased intakes of employment-based immigrants and a "hard cap" of 714,000 annual total immigrant admissions for the period 1992–1994. That figure includes 465,000 places allocated to family immigrants; 55,000 for the immediate relatives of persons legalized under IRCA; 40,000 for nationals of countries underrepresented in previous admissions ("adversely affected countries," such as Ireland); 12,000 for Hong Kong nationals who are high-level employees of large U.S. multinationals having subsidiaries there, and 140,000 for immigrants having needed skills. Since immediate relatives of U.S. citizens are still admitted without limitations, the hard cap is maintained by allocating to family immigrants who are not in that category 465,000 places minus the number of immediate relatives admitted the previous year plus any unused slots for the employment-based immigrants. The resulting number cannot, however, drop below 226,000 or the difference will be made up by borrowing from other categories. Starting in 1995 a soft global cap of 675,000 is established, but that cap may be pierced to assure that at least 226,000 places are available for family immigrants who are relatives of permanent residents and U.S. citizens (Papademetriou, n.d.)

It is noteworthy that Hong Kong nationals are singled out for special treatment by the United States. Provisions of a similar nature have been adopted by Canada which, as a member of the British Commonwealth, has closer ties to the Crown Colony. Not coincidentally, therefore, Hong Kong became the main country of origin for immigrants to Canada in 1985–1989.[6]

The U.S. Immigration Act of 1990 also established a new method to select employment-based migrants. In a move similar to that taken by Canada early on, the U.S. Department of Labor is charged with identifying up to ten occupations where there are shortages or surpluses of workers and issuing blanket certification for immigrants in occupations experiencing shortages. In Canada, the points system takes account of information on needed occupations produced by Employment and Immigration in consultation with the Provinces. Clearly, the intention of the 1990 U.S. Immigration Act is to give greater weight to economic considerations in selecting immigrants.

THE ASYLUM AND REFUGEE POLICIES OF THE CORE COUNTRIES

Both Canada and the United States have a long history of admitting refugees for permanent resettlement, but until the late 1960s both countries had adopted ad hoc programs for the admission of persons in need of protection. The first instances of refugee resettlement occurred in the aftermath of World War II, when Canada admitted 186,000 persons from Western Europe and the United States approximately 640,000. In 1956, when the Soviet army invaded Hungary, Canada and the United States responded by admitting 37,000 and 31,000 refugees from that country, respectively (Adelman, 1990: 172–223; U.S. Immi-

[6]See Canada, Employment and Immigration Canada, *Immigration Statistics*, various years.

gration and Naturalization Service, 1991: 108). The Hungarian crisis occurred at the height of the cold war, when both Canada and the United States considered that the admission of refugees from Eastern bloc countries buttressed their foreign policy aims in combatting communism.

The next crisis also concerned a communist regime, but this time within the immediate sphere of influence of the United States. In 1959, Castro took over the government of Cuba: The United States, considering his regime a threat to its economic, political and security interests, initiated a long-drawn offensive against the Castro regime that would include sabotage, assassination attempts, economic blockades, the creation of an army in exile, and the admission of thousands of Cubans (Zolberg *et al.*, 1989: 185). According to U.S. statistics, 132,000 Cuban asylees and refugees were admitted during the 1960s.

The 1965 Amendments to the Immigration and Nationality Act formalized U.S. refugee policy by "establishing that 6 percent of all ordinary immigrants were permitted to enter as refugees if they could satisfy four requirements: 1) they had departed from a Communist country or a country within the general area of the Middle East; 2) they had departed in flight; 3) the flight was caused by persecution or fear of persecution on account of race, religion, or political opinion; 4) they were unable or unwilling to return." (Zucker and Zucker, 1990) The United States thus incorporated the universally recognized concept of refugee, albeit with geographic and ideological limitations, into its statutory law. Further, in 1968 it became a party to the United Nations Protocol Relating to the Status of Refugees. One year later, Canada signed the United Nations Convention and its Protocol (Adelman, 1990: 193). From then on, the policies of both countries, though converging in certain respects, also evinced important differences.

During 1972–1973, for instance, Canada was called upon to resettle about 7,000 Ugandan Asians who had been expelled by Idi Amin. The United Kingdom was instrumental in obtaining Canada's involvement in the resettlement, but the United States was not involved. Then, in September 1973, the overthrow of the Allende Government in Chile elicited fairly different responses from the two core countries. Although both Canada and the United States were in favor of a change of government in Chile, the latter had been involved in bringing about such a change and had no interest in undermining the military regime that had taken over the country by accepting large numbers of refugees. Consequently, only 420 Chilean refugees were admitted by the United States during the 1970s. In contrast, Canada, albeit at first reluctantly, responded to internal pressure from humanitarian and other groups to establish a special program for Chilean refugees and admitted about 7,000 from Chile and other South American countries during the 1970s (Adelman, 1990: 195). This policy move had important implications: for the first time Canada received appreciable numbers of Latin American immigrants. Subsequently, refugee flows from Central America further increased the number of Latin Americans in Canada.

In 1975, the end of the Viet Nam War and the conflicts that followed led to a massive outflow of people in need of asylum. The United States, having been a party to the conflict, responded by resettling the Vietnamese who had been its allies. As conflict in the region spread, other groups of Indochinese were also resettled. By 1990, the United States had admitted 475,000 Vietnamese, 165,000 Laotians and 122,000 Cambodians as refugees (U.S. Immigration and Naturalization Service, 1991: 109). Canadian policy, though tepid towards the resettlement of Indochinese refugees at the beginning of the outflow, became committed to it towards the end of the 1970s after the 1976 Immigration Act had come into effect. The act, which incorporated for the first time into Canadian statutory law the principles of the Geneva Convention, also established two classes of refugee admissions: Convention refugees and persons in the designated classes, so-called because they included groups of persons who, not qualifying entirely as Convention refugees, were nevertheless in need of protection. The latter were admitted provided private sponsorship for them could be found. In the case of the Indochinese refugees, the government itself helped mobilize such sponsorship, which soon surpassed the government's own efforts (Adelman, 1990: 211–212). By 1989, Canada had admitted 37,000 Vietnamese, 19,000 Cambodians and 16,000 Laotians, mostly on humanitarian grounds.

In 1980, the United States adopted a new Refugee Act incorporating for the first time into statutory law a definition of refugee fully consistent with United Nations instruments, establishing a federal policy for refugee admissions, and institutionalizing resettlement assistance for refugees. No sooner had the act come into effect than it was tested by an unprecedented outflow of asylum seekers from Cuba, the Mariel boatlift. Since the Act was based on the principle of individual adjudication of refugee status and the *Marielitos* numbered in the thousands, the U.S. government decided to bypass the Refugee Act of 1980 and create instead a special status for all Mariel arrivals: special entrant. That status applied to all undocumented Cubans within the United States before October 10, 1980. Although the special entrants could not at first apply for permanent-resident status, most *Marielitos* were eventually allowed to become immigrants (Zucker and Zucker, 1990: 229).

In fact, the Refugee Act of 1980 has failed to change the policy considerations underlying refugee admission and determination procedures in the United States. Among the million or so refugees admitted during 1956–1979, only 0.3 percent originated in noncommunist countries or countries outside of the Middle East; since 1980 that proportion has remained at 0.2 percent (U.S. Committee for Refugees, 1992). The continuing influence of ideological considerations in refugee determination in the United States is reflected most clearly in the differential treatment accorded Central American asylum seekers. Since the overthrow of the Somoza regime in Nicaragua and the takeover by the Sandinista regime in 1979, U.S. policy, especially during the Reagan Administration, was to combat the latter by providing arms and aid to the so-called Nicaraguan "freedom fighters." Under such policy, the granting of refugee status to Nicaraguans indicated that the Sandinista regime persecuted its people. In contrast, actual persecution by the rightist governments of El Salvador and Guatemala was largely ignored in order not to undermine such regimes. Thus, during 1984–1990, among the asylum seeker cases adjudicated by U.S. authorities, 26% of those filed by Nicaraguans were approved compared to only 2.6% among those filed by Salvadorans and 1.8% of those corresponding to Guatemalans. Such differential outcomes were the basis of a lawsuit in U.S. courts that led to a review of asylum claims by Guatemalans and Salvadorans, and that was instrumental in securing until 1992 temporary protected status for Salvadorans present illegally in the country.

Although Canada's policy towards Salvadoran refugees has been "cognizant of U.S. policy towards . . . [Central America]" (Adelman, 1990: 216) and of the United Nations High Commission on Refugees position favoring the temporary protection of Central American refugees within the region, Canada has, in fact, admitted considerably larger numbers of Salvadorans and Guatemalans as refugees than has the United States.

During the 1980s, emigration from Central America has probably been one of the most distinctive components of the North American migration system. If, as Gibney (1990) argues, U.S. foreign policy has been responsible to a significant extent for both the economic problems facing poor Central American countries and the repressive measures taken by some of their governments, its policy has ultimately led to an exodus fueled by both economic deprivation and massive human rights abuses. The exodus, however, has affected not only the United States but has spilled over into several countries in the region. Thus, during the 1980s Mexico became for the first time a less-than-willing first country of asylum, hosting some 300,000 Guatemalans recognized as refugees and an unknown number of other Central Americans, mostly Salvadorans, considered undocumented aliens. Costa Rica, Guatemala, Honduras and Nicaragua have also received considerable numbers of refugees, and a large number of persons remain "displaced" within the region because their status as refugees has not been recognized.

CONCLUSION

The end of the cold war and the move towards economic globalization have unleashed forces that may lead to increased population mobility. In the economic arena, the creation of trading blocs in which barriers to trade are reduced or dismantled is likely to strengthen the various types of linkages between countries, linkages that have given rise to migration in the past. Thus, although NAFTA eschews almost any mention of migration, it fosters various types of exchanges between Canada, Mexico, and the United States, exchanges that are unlikely to occur without increasing the transnational mobility of people. Following recent trends, we arrive at the following tentative conclusions:

1. The United States has for a long period been the major destination for migrants from the Caribbean, Mexico, Central America and South America. These patterns will be sustained by NAFTA and other efforts to increase intraregional trade.

2. Canada has become increasingly integrated into the international migration system in the hemisphere. The proportions of immigrants and temporary visitors from the

Caribbean, Central America and South America rose dramatically in the 1970s and remain significant – even if lower than the inflow from Asia. NAFTA and expanding intraregional political, economic and cultural contacts will tend to sustain this pattern.

3. A rising proportion of mobility within the hemispheric system, as in the world more generally, will be temporary in nature and may fit within channels already in existence (such as the admission of temporary workers and trainees, intracompany transfers, or treaty traders and investors). The flow of students on short-term study visas will be a continuing important part of these flows and will tend to reinforce cultural and economic links between developing and core countries in the hemisphere.

4. The effects of free trade on migration between Mexico and the United States are likely to vary over time, probably leading to increased emigration pressures in Mexico over the short run but reducing those pressures in the long run. To the extent that avenues for legal migration are restricted, undocumented migration will continue to be significant, responding to structural conditions that create a need for cheap labor in the receiving country.

5. While Canada is now an established destination for hemispheric migrants from the Caribbean and a few Central American and South American countries where refugee flight is or has been important, it is not as yet an important destination for Mexicans. Given the strong historically developed migration links between Mexico and the United States, it does not seem likely that NAFTA will have much direct influence on the flow of Mexicans to Canada. Modest numbers of Mexican farm workers, however, have been coming to Canada on work visas for some years. Just as this eventually led to larger flows in the case of the United States, these modest flows and other contacts facilitated by NAFTA, could lead to an expansion of migration between Mexico and Canada.

6. Strong economic linkages have not and will not be maintained exclusively within the North American region. Indeed, the two core countries have stronger trade, financial and political

ties with overseas developed countries than they do with Mexico. Migration ties between the core countries and Asia are also very strong. These ties, which in the past led to long-term migration, are increasingly being translated into short-term exchanges, mostly of skilled workers. This trend will continue and may become strong with respect to developing countries, especially those embarking successfully in development.

The end of the cold war, rising pressure against international immigration in Europe, and the violence associated with political reorganization and ethnic tensions in various parts of the world will continue to create challenges for the immigration policy in both Canada and the United States.

To a greater or lesser extent, the challenges just described are faced by most industrialized countries today. However, the North American core countries are probably in a better position to face them because of their consistent commitment to the admission of immigrants. Despite current misgivings about international migration, North America's doors remain open and it is in the long-term interest of the region for that openness to prevail.

REFERENCES

Adelman, H., ed.
1990   *Refugee Policy: Canada and the United States.* Toronto: Centre for Refugee Studies.

Bean, F. D., B. Edmonston and J. S. Passel, eds.
1990   *Undocumented Migration to the United States: IRCA and the Experience of the 1980s.* Washington, DC: The Urban Institute.

Burstein, M.
1991   "Immigration in Canada: A Statistical Report for the Continuous Reporting System on Migration of the OECD (SOPEMI)." Ottawa: Employment and Immigration Canada. Mimeograph.

Canada
1990   *Annual Report to Parliament: Immigration Plan for 1991–1995.* Ottawa: Immigration Canada.

Chiswick, B. R., ed.
1982   *The Gateway: U.S. Immigration Issues and Policies.* Washington, DC: The American Enterprise Institute.

Fogel, W.
1982   "Mexican Migration to the United States." In *The Gateway: U.S. Immigration Issues and Policies*. Washington, DC: The American Enterprise Institute. Pp. 193–211.

Gibney, M.
1990   "U.S. Foreign Policy and the Creation of Refugee Flows." In *Refugee Policy: Canada and the United States*. Ed. H. Adelman. Toronto: Centre for Refugee Studies. Pp. 81–112.

Hawkins, F.
1989   *Critical Years in Immigration: Canada and Australia Compared*. Montreal: McGill-Queen's University Press.

Michalowski, M., and C. Fortier
1990   "Two Neglected Categories of Immigrants to Canada: Temporary Immigrants and Returning Canadians," *Statistical Journal of the United Nations ECE*, 7(3): 175–204.

Papademetriou, D. G.
1991   "SOPEMI 1991: United States Report." Washington, DC: U.S. Department of Labor. Mimeograph.

_____
1990   "Contemporary Approaches to Reforming the U.S. Legal Immigration System." Papers prepared for NYU/Rockefeller Foundation Conference on Migration, Ethnicity and the City. Arden Homestead, New York, November 2–4.

_____
n.d.   "The Immigration Act of 1990." Washington, DC: U.S. Department of Labor. Mimeograph.

Reimers, D. M.
1982   "Recent Immigration Policy: An Analysis." In *The Gateway: U.S. Immigration Issues and Policies*. Washington, DC: The American Enterprise Institute. Pp. 13–53.

Samuel, T. J.
1991   "Contemporary Immigration Policies: Canada: the United States and Mexico." Paper presented at "Facing North/Facing South: A Multidisciplinary Conference on Contemporary United States – Canadian – Mexican Relations. Calgary, the University of Calgary, May 1–5.

United Nations
1992   *World Population Monitoring 1991*. New York: United Nations.

_____
1990   *World Population Monitoring 1989*. New York: United Nations.

U.S. Committee for Refugees
1992   *World Refugee Survey 1992*. Washington, DC: American Council for Nationalities Service.

U.S. Immigration and Naturalization Service
1991   *Statistical Yearbook of the Immigration and Naturalization Service, 1990*. Washington, DC: Government Printing Office.

Weintraub, S.
1992   "North American Free Trade and the European Situation Compared," *International Migration Review*, 26: 506–524.

Weintraub, S., and S. Diaz-Briquets
1992   "The Use of Foreign Aid to Reduce Incentives to Emigrate from Central America." Geneva: International Labour Office, World Employment Programme Working Paper.

Woodrow, K. A. and J. S. Passel
1990   "Post-IRCA Undocumented Immigration to the United States: An Assessment Based on the June 1988 CPS." In *Undocumented Migration to the United States: IRCA and the Experience of the 1980s*. Washington, DC: The Urban Institute. Pp. 33–76.

Zlotnik, H.
1992   "Empirical Identification of International Migration Systems." In *International Migration Systems: A Global Approach*. New York: Clarendon Press. Pp. 19–40.

Zolberg, A., A. Suhrke and S. Aguayo
1989   *Escape from Violence*. New York: Oxford University Press.

Zucker, N. L., and N. F. Zucker
1990   "The 1980 Refugee Act: A 1990 Perspective." In *Refugee Policy: Canada and the United States*. Ed. H. Adelman. Toronto: Centre for Refugee Studies. Pp. 224–252.

5

Visitors and Visa Workers: Old Wine in New Bottles?[1]

Margaret Michalowski

Introduction

Over recent decades the number of temporary workers in foreign countries has been rising rapidly in the world system. This paper examines these trends in North America, with particular attention to Canada in comparison with the United States. It is noted that the contribution to the Canadian economy through the labor of visa workers in 1990 was greater than that through new immigration, even though 1990 was a year of relatively high immigration to Canada. The United States has a longer tradition of relying on visa workers. The contribution of visa workers to the U.S. economy rose in the 1980s. These trends raise a number of questions. Are visa workers replacing immigration as the key mechanism for solving short-term labor deficits? How does such a trend relate to other forces of globalization and economic integration?

MEASURING A STREAM OF VISITORS AND PERMIT HOLDERS

Data limitations make difficult attempts to assess the importance of nonpermanent residents (foreigners with temporary status) in North

---

[1]Views expressed in this paper are those of the author, and do not necessarily reflect those of Statistics Canada.

America. The term nonpermanent resident refers usually to those who are in the country legally but on a temporary basis. It encompasses such diverse groups as: visitors for pleasure (tourists), visitors for business, foreign students, treaty traders and investors, temporary workers, seasonal workers, domestic workers, highly skilled professional trainees, managerial and technical workers on assignment to a North American branch of their corporation, refugee status claimants, and spouses as well as dependents of all those belonging to these groups. Members of these diverse groups may be staying in the country for varying periods of time and, in many instances, they are part of the host country's labor market.

Most countries, including Canada and the United States, gather only limited data on nonpermanent residents. Moreover, the data collected in Canada is somewhat different than that collected in the United States, making comparisons difficult. With respect to Canada, all foreign citizens seeking temporary residence status in Canada are required to make an application for and obtain a visa or authorization to enter the country before they appear at a port of entry. There are four types of documents in the possession of foreigners legally resident in Canada: visitor's visa, employment authorization (workers), student authorization (students at all levels of study) and minister's permit (granted for humanitarian, compassionate or national interest reasons). Those documents are registered in the Visitors Data System administered by Employment and Immigration Canada. However, this system does not include all foreigners living in Canada. Due to exemptions specified by Canadian law, not all visitors to Canada require a visa. U.S. citizens can enter Canada freely with only personal identification. Many nationals enter Canada as visitors without a visa requirement simply by showing their passport at their port of entry. Also "refugee claimants" – that is individuals who enter Canada without documentation and claim refugee status after arrival – do not immediately have any kind of visa. Their rights with respect to employment prior to assessment of their claim (which may take many months) have shifted over time. In addition, foreigners with temporary status can apply for an extension of their original document or apply for another type of document, which is then registered in the system. Despite these deficiencies, available statistics on nonpermanent residents – both flows (new arrivals) and stocks (the total number at any given moment) – in Canada are mostly based on this system.[2]

In assessing stocks of nonpermanent residents, an effort was made to avoid multiple countings of the same person due to extension of this person'soriginaldocumentauthorizinglegalstayinanadaÿÿÿlsexiÿÿÿystem when their permit expires, hence the figures do not account for possible shortening of a temporary stay. Moreover, in the case of workers, the estimate represents the number of foreigners for temporary stay who are authorized to work and should not be considered as the number of actually employed foreigners.

A prime source of information on foreigners admitted to the United States for a temporary stay is the Nonimmigrant Information System. Unlike Canada's Visitors Data System, the U.S. system maintains records of admission and departure of nonimmigrants. Statistics on annual admissions based on this system reflect multiple entries by nonimmigrants who were issued visas during that year, as well as in previous years.[3] Such U.S. data are not directly comparable to the Canadian data presented in this paper, but they can be used to approximate the inflow dynamics of foreigners for temporary stay in the United States.

Another source of information used in this paper consists of the United States Department of State statistics on visa issuances to nonimmigrant aliens authorized to work in the United States. These data provide an overestimation of the persons in the country through inclusion of multiple visa issuances to the same foreigners. However, in the situation when data on foreigners staying temporarily in the country are not available, and statistics on admissions of nonimmigrants cannot be directly compared with statistics on admissions of immigrant workers, the number of visa issued to nonimmigrants seems to be the best approximation of visa workers in the United States.

To derive the estimate of visa workers presented in this paper three types of visa were combined: visas for temporary workers (H-1 and H-2), visas for industrial trainees (H-3) and visas for intracompany transferees (L-1). Additionally, so-called exchange visitors (with spouses and children excluded) (J-1, J-2) who enter temporarily to

---

[2]A description of this system can be found in Michalowski and Fortier (1990).

[3]Detailed description of this system can be found in U.S. Immigration and Naturalization Service (1991: 118–128); Kraly and Warren (1991).

study, teach or conduct research were taken into consideration. Other foreigners/holders of visas which authorized them to work in the United States but for whom the work is incidental (students for example) were not considered.

In general, no attempt was made to introduce the dimension of undocumented migration into this discussion. Undocumented migrants are deemed to be of no significance in the Canadian case. As for the United States, their estimates are vague and uncertain.

ARRIVALS OF FOREIGNERS FOR TEMPORARY STAY IN CANADA IN THE 1980s

In the 1981–1990 period, over 2.5 million foreigners arrived in Canada for temporary residence (Table 1). In total, arrivals in the first half of the 1980s were quite stable, around the level of 220,000 foreigners annually. The second half of the 1980s witnessed a very significant increase in arrivals. It is interesting to note that this general tendency was triggered by different dynamics in each of the admission categories. A generally declining tendency in arrivals was displayed by two categories – documented visitors (those with visas) and minister's permit holders. For documented visitors, however, the decline was not very pronounced, and Canada experienced almost stable levels of visitor admissions over the period. For the latter, the only exception to the general downward tendency was in 1986, when in comparison to 1985 the number of minister's permit holders doubled. The inflow of visa workers and visa students deserves more detailed analysis.

In general, visa workers showed the biggest upsurge in admissions. A particularly dramatic arrival acceleration took place in the second half of the 1980s, with almost 20 percent of all worker arrivals occurring in 1989. The most important reasons for this acceleration seem to be the recovery of the Canadian economy after the recession of the early 1980s, and the 1985 Supreme Court of Canada interpretation of the Chapter of Rights and Freedoms known as the *Singh* decision. The first reason implies a labor market in which growing demand has been met through the recruitment of visa workers. The latter resulted in issuing general, not employer or job-oriented, employment authorizations to "in Canada exempted" groups such as refugee status claimants, applicants for landing, and convention refugees. Other factors contributing to the increased arrival in the worker category could be initiatives aimed

TABLE 1

VISA AND PERMIT HOLDERS BY CATEGORY OF ADMISSION: CANADA, 1981–1990

Category of Admission	N (Thousands)	%	1981	1982	1983	1984	1985	1986	1987	1988	1989	1990
	1980–1991											
			Percentage of Total for 1981–1991									
Total[a]	2,584.4	100.0	9.0	8.3	8.8	8.2	8.6	9.6	10.2	10.5	15.3	11.5
Documented Visitors	970.3	100.0	11.0	10.0	11.1	9.8	9.7	9.2	9.6	9.5	10.2	9.9
Workers	1,286.3	100.0	7.6	7.0	7.4	7.3	8.1	10.1	10.6	10.7	19.3	11.9
Students	396.7	100.0	9.0	8.2	7.2	6.9	7.5	8.4	10.0	12.6	15.2	15.0
Minister's Permit Holders	149.5	100.0	10.2	8.5	8.4	7.4	8.0	14.7	12.3	10.2	10.7	9.6
			Proportion in Each Category									
Total[a]		100.0	100.0	100.0	100.0	100.0	100.0	100.0	100.0	100.0	100.0	100.0
Documented Visitors		37.5	45.9	45.2	47.4	44.9	42.3	36.0	35.3	34.0	25.0	32.3
Workers		49.7	42.0	42.0	41.9	44.3	46.9	52.4	51.7	50.7	62.8	51.5
Students		15.3	15.3	15.1	12.6	12.9	13.4	13.4	15.1	18.4	15.3	20.0
Minister's Permit Holders		5.8	6.5	5.9	5.5	5.2	5.4	8.9	7.0	5.6	4.0	4.8

Source: Demography Division, Statistics Canada estimates based on the Visitors Data System.

[a]As foreigners, entering the nonpermanent population in possession of more than one document authorizing their temporary stay, the total does not represent the sum of arrivals in four categories.

at establishing rules of reciprocity in the areas of business, the performing arts, research, training and education, and changes in regulations affecting the employment of foreign students and their spouses. Announced at the beginning of 1988, these changes in general resulted in relaxation of previous limitations. They made it possible for students' spouses to hold jobs and students to be employed after graduation, without going through the job validation procedure, which ensures that employment prospects of Canadian citizens and permanent residents are not jeopardized.

The inflow of visa students followed the pattern characteristic of workers only in the second half of the 1980s, as a decline in arrivals in the first half of the 1980s is documented. As in the case of visa workers, it seems that foreign student arrivals may also have been affected by the 1985 Supreme Court ruling which granted the right to free access to education in Canada to the children of refugee status claimants (asylum seekers) awaiting determination of their status. Another explanation for the recent increase in the student category is suggested by the more aggressive recruitment of foreign students by Canadian educational institutions. Changes in recruitment strategies were a response to the persistent decline in the number of foreign students from the beginning of the 1980s.

VISA WORKERS VS. IMMIGRANT WORKERS FROM A CANADIAN PERSPECTIVE

The legislative framework for the migration of visa workers in Canada is provided by the Employment Authorization Programme introduced in 1973. Like the labor recruitment programs of other countries, its purpose was to respond to specific demands of the Canadian labor market. Its creation aimed at forging a closer link between foreign worker migration and the demands of employers for labor through a guestworker model of international migration. Admission to Canada granted on a labor market basis must be authorized by a validated employment offer to ensure that the employment and career opportunities of permanent Canadian residents are not affected. However, employment authorization can also be issued to persons already in Canada whose entry was granted on the basis of social or humanitarian considerations. Such authorization is exempted from the labor market validation procedures. Evidence from other studies indicates a trend for employment authorizations going to persons already in Canada.[4] By 1985, over half of all employment authorizations were in this category. Thus, even before the 1985 Supreme Court decision which clearly resulted in an increased number of visa workers with exempted authorization granted from "within Canada," the program had become increasingly shaped by family reunification, refugee claimant needs for employment and other humanitarian concerns, and could no longer be considered just a labor recruitment program.

Regardless of the category of their employment authorization, visa workers are a part of the labor market in Canada. The question is how to evaluate their importance. The most logical approach would be to compare them with the other stream of international migration – landed (permanent) immigrants destined to enter the labor market upon their arrival in Canada. The difficulty with such an approach is in

---

[4]Studies done so far cover only the first decade of the existence of the Employment Authorization Programme which coincided with the economic crisis of 1973 accompanied by the recession and ends with the skyrocketing unemployment rates of the beginning of the 1980s; see, for example, Wong (1984); Boyd et al. (1986). This unfavorable economic situation was apparently the rationale behind the moderate, controlled levels of both visa worker admissions and landed immigration for the same period.

choosing a measure which would make such a comparison meaningful.[5] An estimate of the average "stock" (population) of visa workers in a particular year would seem to serve this objective well. Unless otherwise stated, this measure will be used in further analyses.[6]

The numbers presented in Figure 1 indicate considerable dynamism in the growth of the visa worker population in the 1980s – especially in the second half of the decade. Over the whole period, the number of visa workers increased fourfold, reaching the level of 250,000 persons in 1990. At the beginning of the 1980s, the number of visa workers and the annual number of new immigrants in the economically active age range (20 to 64 years) were approximately the same. Over the early 1980s, however, the number of visa workers grew very quickly. By 1985, visa workers outnumbered immigrants aged 15–64 by a ratio of 2.5 to 1 (Table 2). With the exception of 1989, the second half of the 1980s witnessed a nearly stable ratio of 2: 1 in favor of visa workers. In 1989, a 60 percent increase in the number of visa workers raised temporarily the ratio between this and the immigrant worker population. This shift was caused by the decision to issue an exempt employment authorization to almost 100,000 persons in Canada who claimed refugee status before that date and who were awaiting review of their claims.

Canada experienced a significant recession in the early 1980s. In consequence, restrictions were introduced in 1982 affecting all foreigners applying for work visas in occupations having experienced massive lay-offs of Canadian workers (Boyd et al., 1986). Yet, this reduction was more than counterbalanced by an increase in the exempt category – that is, foreigners whose employment visa requests were considered on the basis of social or humanitarian considerations. Consequently,

---

[5]Canadian studies have evaluated the visa worker flows using two measures. One is the number of employment authorizations issued to foreigners; see Wong (1984); Satsewich (1990). The other is the number of person-years of employment; see Marr (1985); Boyd et al. (1986). As both measures serve certain objectives, their application does not allow meaningful comparison with immigrant worker flows in the addressing of such essential issues as, for example, the degree of permanentcy of residence of visa workers in Canada.

[6]The following observations justify the choice of the measure: 1) unlike its permanent counterpart, the visa worker population experiences significant turnover due to large number of entries into and departure from the population during a one-year period; 2) monthly trends in the size of the visa worker population indicate that the midyear point estimate represents an average size of the population for a given year, and (given 1 above), this estimate can be conceptualized as an approximation of the net annual gain from visa worker flows; and 3) although data on re-migration of immigrants are not available, the same-year level of re-migration of immigrant workers is expected to be low allowing consideration of the annual flow of immigrant workers as the net gain from immigrant worker flows.

Figure 1.   Visa and Immigrant Workers to Canada: 1981–1990

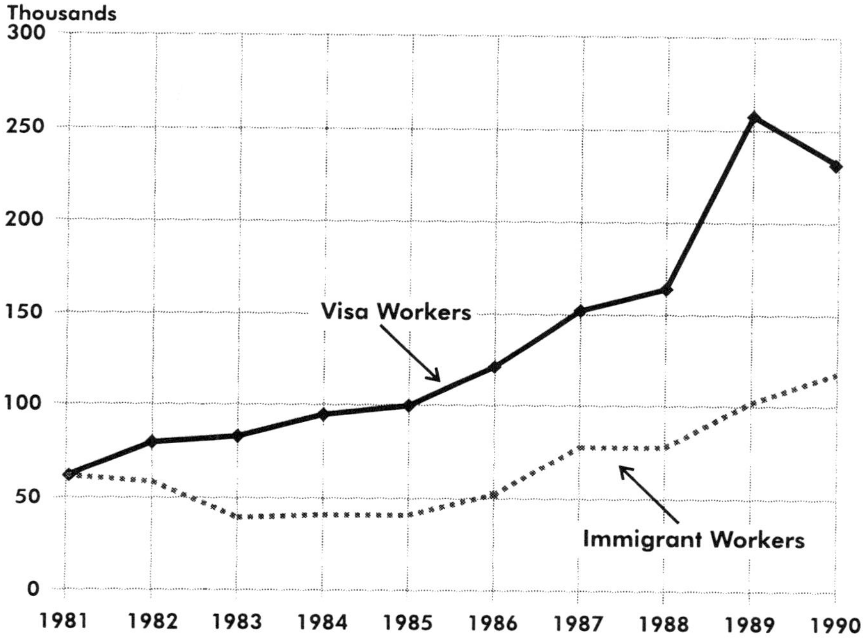

Source: Demography Division, Statistics Canada estimates based on the Visitors Data System;
Employment and Immigration Canada statistics.

TABLE 2

VISA WORKERS AND IMMIGRANT WORKERS IN CANADA: 1981–1990

Category of Admissions (Thousands)	1981– 1990	Year (% of 1981–1990 Total)									
		1981	1982	1983	1984	1985	1986	1987	1988	1989	1990
Visa Workers	1,324.4	58.5	76.5	80.2	90.5	96.6	117.1	150.1	161.6	259.5	233.8
Imigrant Workers	537.0	57.0	55.5	37.1	38.5	38.5	48.2	76.7	76.3	98.2	114.0
Immigrants Age 20–64 years	881.2	82.7	79.8	58.7	58.8	56.2	67.2	102.2	103.9	127.5	145.2
Proportion (%) of Workers:											
Nonpermanent residents	56.0	40.9	42.1	44.0	48.4	51.6	56.4	60.9	60.3	66.0	63.3
Immigrants	48.2	44.3	45.8	41.6	43.7	45.7	48.6	50.4	47.1	51.1	53.7
Ratio (%) between Visa Workers and:											
Immigrant workers	207	103	138	216	235	251	243	196	212	264	205
Immigrants age 20–64 years	150	71	96	137	154	172	175	147	156	204	161

Source: Demography Division, Statistics Canada estimates based on Visitors Data System; Employment and Immigration
Canada statistics.

over the first half of the 1980s, there was an increase in the inflow of temporary workers, despite the recession. This resulted in generally positive growth in the total inflow of workers to Canada in the 1980s (Employment and Immigration Canada, 1992).

NONIMMIGRANTS, VISA WORKERS AND IMMIGRANT WORKERS IN THE UNITED STATES

In the second half of the 1980s, the United States admitted almost 90 million foreigners for temporary stay (Table 3). Admissions increased over the whole period, especially after 1986. The overall volume of admissions almost doubled between 1984 and 1990. Although temporary visitors for pleasure are by far the largest category of admission, other categories such as visitors for business, students, treaty traders and investors, and temporary workers and trainees also contribute significantly to the inflow of foreigners into the United States. The number of foreigners in the last four categories, which are related directly or indirectly to economic activity in the United States, increased 1.5 times between 1984 and 1990. Temporary worker arrivals grew the most rapidly, at the same rate as admissions of all nonimmigrants. Arrivals of these foreigners – who are admitted to the United States to perform services of an exceptional nature requiring specialized skills or to perform temporary services (with inclusion of agricultural workers) where U.S. citizens or resident aliens cannot be found to perform the job – numbered 145,000 arrivals in 1990.

It seems that, as in the Canadian case, recent temporary migration streams to the United States, and especially labor-related migration, are gaining importance. In order to better assess the dynamics of labor-related temporary migration, or visa worker migration in Canadian terms, the number of visas issued to the four groups of foreigners applying for work authorization in the United States was analyzed in relation to the levels of immigration of permanent workers in the United States.

Visa workers encompass the following groups: temporary workers (H-1 and H-2), trainees (H-3) and intracompany transferees (L-1). Due to lack of statistics, the estimate of permanent (immigrant) workers had to be generated. This estimate was produced to correspond as closely as possible to the concept of "immigrant worker destined to the labor force" used in the Canadian statistical system. It

TABLE 3

ADMISSIONS OF NONIMMIGRANTS TO THE UNITED STATES BY CATEGORY: 1984–1990

Category of Admission	1984–1990		Year						
	N		Percentage of Total for 1981–1991						
	(Thousands)	%	1984	1985	1986	1987	1988	1989	1990
Total	89,886.8	100.0	10.3	10.6	11.6	13.7	16.2	18.0	19.6
Selected Categories									
Temporary visitors for business	15,079.7	100.0	10.8	11.9	12.9	14.1	15.8	16.9	17.6
Treaty traders and investors[a]	817.8	100.0	11.1	11.8	12.7	14.0	15.4	17.0	18.0
Students	1,981.1	100.0	11.5	13.0	13.1	13.2	15.8	16.9	16.5
Temporary workers and trainees[a]	726.0	100.0	9.5	10.3	11.8	13.3	15.6	19.5	20.0
All Selected Categories	18,604.6	100.0	10.8	12.0	12.8	14.0	15.7	17.0	17.6

Source: U.S. Immigration and Naturalization Service statistics.

[a]Includes spouses and children.

encompasses the following classes of admission: professional or highly-skilled immigrants (third preference), married sons/daughters of U.S. citizens (fourth preference), brothers or sisters of U.S. citizens (fifth preference), needed skilled or unskilled workers (sixth preference), ministers; employees of U.S. government abroad, Cuban refugees (CU6), Indochinese refugees (IC6), refugee parolees (R86), refugees (RE6), asylums (AS6), Amerasian new arrivals, and other adjustments.[7]

Arrivals of visa workers increased significantly over the second half of the 1980s, reaching a level of 78,000 in 1989 (Figure 2). The figure for admissions in 1990 indicate a continuation of this trend. Occurring simultaneously with the rising visa worker inflow was a growing inflow of exchange visitors. Both streams resulted in the presence of over 200,000 temporary workers in the United States in 1989. While permanent immigration to the United States was bringing larger numbers of workers as well, the rate of increase was lower. Indeed, with the exception of 1988 – which witnessed 40,000 more persons who can be classified as immigrant workers than the previous year – the level of immigrant worker migration increased from 120,000 to 130,000 between 1984 and 1990.[8] Given the threefold increase in the level of immigration to the United States over the same period, the observed

[7]For data *see* U.S. Immigration and Naturalization Service (1991: 54–57).

[8]The exceptional 1988 increase in the number of immigrant workers was brought about mostly by a change in immigration law on eligibility for Section 249. Prior to fiscal year 1987, to be eligible foreigners must have entered before July, 1948. In 1987, the new date was set to be January, 1972, which increased significantly the number of those eligible for admission.

Figure 2.   Visa and Immigrant Workers to the United States: 1984–1989

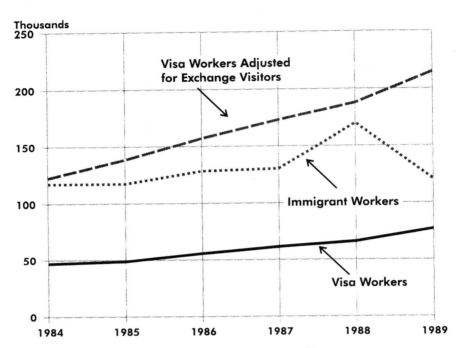

Source: U.S. Immigration and Naturalization Service; U.S. Department of State statistics.

tendency in immigrant worker arrivals implies a diminishing role of this category in permanent immigration, and indicates a shifting of priorities in United States immigration policy in the second half of the 1980s.

When contrasting the Canadian and American situation in the second half of the 1980s, it is evident that the inflow of visa workers in both countries became increasingly significant for their labor market. What distinguishes the countries is the importance of visa workers in relation to their permanent counterparts. Canadian visa workers apparently play a more important role than they do in the United States. Over the whole period in Canada, the visa worker population was twice the size of the immigrant worker population, while in the United States even though the ratio of visa workers to immigrant workers was increasing, it was still significantly below the Canadian level at the end of the period (Table 4).

This finding remains unchanged when comparing visa-workers to the total annual new arrivals of immigrants of working ages (20–64). This

TABLE 4

VISA WORKERS AND IMMIGRANT WORKERS IN THE UNITED STATES: 1984–1989

Category of Admission (Thousands)	1984–1989	1984	1985	1986	1987	1988	1989
Visa Workers[a] and Exchange Visitors	1,008.8	125.6	140.7	159.5	176.2	191.9	214.8
Immigrant Workers	795.5	119.1	119.1	129.9	132.2	172.7	122.5
Immigrants Aged 20-64 Years	2,785.3	357.2	380.3	400.6	406.6	445.8	794.8
Ratio (%) between Visa Workers and Exchange Visitors and:							
Immigrant workers	127	105	118	123	133	111	175
Immigrants aged 20-64 years	36	35	37	40	43	43	27

Source: U.S. Immigration and Naturalization Service (data on immigrants); U.S. Department of State (data on visa workers).
[a]Included are temporary workers (H-1, H-2), trainees (H-3), and intracompany transferees (L-1).

second comparison indicates an even more significant discrepancy: in relative terms, visa workers are four times more important in Canada than in the United States.

THE MIGRATION OF VISA WORKERS: GLOBALIZATION OR REGIONALIZATION?

International migration, and particularly labor migration, is widely recognized to be a response to global inequality in terms of population and economic growth. Despite the tendency towards a declining rate of population growth in most developing countries, their demographic situation over the next 15–20 years is already fairly well defined (United Nations, 1989). This future will bring a continuation of population growth and an unprecedented accelerated increase of persons entering the labor force. As a result, the employment problems experienced in developing countries will prevail and in some cases worsen, and are likely to lead to continued migration pressure in the form of permanent, temporary and illegal flows. Within this scenario, it is anticipated that migration will undergo further streamlining, confined mostly to a south-north direction, with a growing importance of south-south direction within newly developed migration networks (Zolberg, 1989; Salt, 1992). Based on evidence from the past pointing to the importance of geographical proximity in the initial stage of development of migration streams, it might be expected that migration from Latin America and the Caribbean to the United States and to Canada will increase, leading to regionalization of temporary labor migration.

In the Canadian case, the dynamics of visa-worker flows do not clearly support the regionalization hypothesis, indicating the significance of other than geographical proximity factors (Table 5). Although the inflows of temporary workers have increased, their origins have diversified, resulting in a decline in the proportion of visa workers from the American region among the total visa-worker population. This decline occurred mostly during the second half of the 1980s. Losses from the American region were distributed unequally between its four subregions. The biggest loser in terms of their share of visa workers was North America (which includes the United States and Mexico), followed by the Caribbean. South American losses were the smallest, and were defined by the patterns of inflow characteristic of the second half of the decade. Central America – a major origin of refugee claimants to Canada in the 1980s – occupied a special position in as much as it was the only subregion among the four American subregions to have experienced an increase in its share of the total visa worker population. Most of the work visas given to Central Americans living in Canada were given for humanitarian reasons – to permit their employment during a very long review of their claim for refugee status. Only the Asian continent experienced a relative increase greater than that of Central America.

The situation in the United States can only be described in very general terms, as observations must be based on admissions by region of visa-workers origin (Kraly and Warren, 1992; U.S. Immigration and Naturalization Service, 1991). Between 1974 and 1990, admissions of visa workers underwent significant transformation (Figure 3). Interestingly, this transformation has followed the Canadian pattern: the importance of the American region decreased (from one-third to one-fourth of all admissions), and Central America was the only subregion which increased its share in the inflow of visa workers to the United States. North America's stream displayed even more dramatic decreases in its share than was estimated in the case of visa workers in Canada. The only difference in this evolution of the visa-worker populations to both countries is in the proportion of Europeans – they were gaining in relative importance in the stream destined to the United States and declining in migration to Canada. The relative importance of the European stream to both countries may change in the near future. Up to now, Eastern European countries, and particularly the former Soviet Union, have taken little part in international migrations. They have, however, the potential for an enormous impact as it is suggested that possibly 2 to 3 million Soviet workers might seek temporary jobs

TABLE 5

VISA WORKERS IN CANADA BY REGION OF LAST PERMANENT RESIDENCE: 1981–1990

Region	1981	1982	1983	1984	1985	1986	1987	1988	1989	1990
	Percent Distribution									
Europe	23.1	24.8	21.1	18.8	18.8	21.3	19.8	18.9	15.6	15.2
Africa	4.3	4.3	4.6	4.6	4.8	5.7	7.3	7.7	7.9	7.7
Asia	26.0	26.3	27.7	29.6	31.8	33.7	34.5	36.4	36.2	37.5
American Region	44.6	42.9	44.6	43.9	43.7	36.7	35.8	33.6	37.9	30.7
North America	20.5	19.0	17.2	15.2	14.3	13.1	12.1	13.0	9.2	9.7
Central America	1.2	1.6	1.9	2.4	3.0	2.6	6.6	6.5	8.2	7.4
Caribbean	15.6	14.9	16.3	16.0	14.9	12.4	9.2	8.0	12.6	8.5
South America	7.3	7.4	9.2	11.3	10.5	8.6	7.9	6.1	5.9	5.1
Other	2.0	1.7	2.0	1.9	1.9	2.4	2.4	3.0	2.7	2.7
Total[a]	100.0	100.0	100.0	100.0	100.0	100.0	100.0	100.0	100.0	100.0

Source: Demography Division, Statistics Canada estimates based on Visitors Data System.

[a]As information on region of last permanent residence is not available for all workers, for some years percentages do not add up to 100.0.

Figure 3.   Admissions of Visa Workers to the United States by Region of Last Permanent Residence: 1974 and 1990

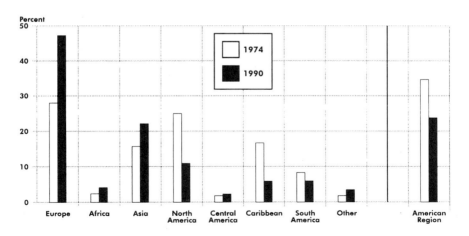

Source: U.S. Immigration and Naturalization Service.

in the Western countries (Shevtsova, 1992). Canada and the United States could be influenced by these pressures.

The above findings lend support to a hypothesis of shifting directions of international labor migration within the American continent. Notwithstanding the significance of the United States market, analysis of the situation in both countries could indicate an increasing intensity of interregional migration related to labor market exchanges between South American and Caribbean countries (Pessar, 1988; Portes and Walton, 1981). In fact, as the most recent studies demonstrate, Latin America in general is a minor receiver of intercontinental labor migration. It is, however, an area of interregional worker migration which occurs between countries at different stages of modernization (for example, streams from Colombia to Venezuela, and from Chile, Bolivia and Paraguay to Argentina). Moreover, the fact that in Canada the Asian stream dominates while in the United States it is the European direction which prevails, suggests different priorities in both countries towards accepting and/or recruiting temporary workers from outside the America region. Granting temporary work permission to Canada's asylum seekers reinforces the undoubted importance of the Asian stream of workers to this country. In Canada, this significant stream prevailed throughout the 1980s.

Based on the example of both countries, it seems that directions in recent documented international labor migration are determined mostly by migratory networks which are dependent more on political and economic linkages between states than on their geographical proximity. The United States' experience with undocumented flows confirms the significance of political and economic factors. In this context, globalization of international processes has resulted so far in a certain redefinition of regional networks of labor migration.

CONCLUSIONS

Nonpermanent migration and factors which give rise to this phenomenon are part of a broader context involving movement and exchange of capital, goods, information and communication. As this broader mobility is not a recent phenomenon, nonpermanent migration is not a new form of geographical mobility. What is new, however, is the dynamic development of this form, particularly its labor-defined part, in response to increased intensity of international trade and movements of capital accompanied by more restrictive immigration policies in the major receiving countries. Canada and the United States, although different in some aspects of the temporary migration phenomenon, are prime examples of these developments. Other new aspects of visa worker migration are: changes in distribution by origin of this movement (directions) and changes in level of qualifications which it represents. For the American region, it has translated into a decreasing intensity of documented temporary migration from within the region to Canada and the United States and an accelerated reinforcement of streams to both countries originating outside the American region. When asylum seekers are excluded from this picture, it has also defined a larger involvement of highly-skilled migrants in labor migration among the rest of the migrant groups.

For the future, it seems that several major factors will influence the development of temporary migration and its part in the changing labor market in the America region. First, ratification of the North American Free Trade Agreement is expected to intensify labor migration between North American countries. Although migration was deliberately excluded from the negotiations of this agreement, it is likely that a provision for facilitating the migration of technical and managerial personnel in connection with cross-border direct investment will be included following the provision which exists in the Free Trade Agreement between Canada and the United States. The observed importance of economic and politically based migratory networks could also be a factor in an increase of labor migration from outside of the American region. And undoubtedly, national immigration policies will continue to exercise very important influence over the international movement of visa workers.

REFERENCES

Appleyard, R.
1991   *International Migration: Challenge for the Nineties*. Geneva: International Organization for Migration.

———
1989   *The Impact of International Migration on Developing Countries*. Paris: OECD.

Boyd, M., and C. Taylor
1986   "The Feminization of Temporary Workers: The Canadian Case," *International Migration*, 24(4).

Boyd, M., C. Taylor and P. Delaney
1986   "Temporary Workers in Canada: A Multifaceted Program," *International Migration Review*, 20(4).

Briggs, V. M.
1986   "The 'Albatross' of Immigration Reform: Temporary Worker Policy in the United States," *International Migration Review*, 20(4).

Employment and Immigration Canada
1992   *Profile of Permit Holders and Visitors in Canada, 1989, 1990, 1991*. Ottawa.

─────
1990   *Annual Report to Parliament, Immigration Plan for 1991–1995*. Ottawa: Supply and Services.

Escobar-Navia, R.
1991   "South-North Migration in the Western Hemisphere," *International Migration*, 29(2): 223–230.

Hawkins, F.
1989   *Critical Years in Immigration: Canada and Australia Compared*. Kingston and Montreal: McGill-Queen's University Press.

Kraly, E. P. and R. Warren
1992   "Demographic dimensions of Southern Migration to and from the United States in the 1970s." In *Proceedings of the Peopling of the Americas Conference*, Vol. 2. Vera Cruz, Mexico: IUSSP. Pp. 219–236.

─────
1991   "Long-term Immigration to the United States: New Approaches to Measurement," *International Migration Review*, 25(1): 60–92.

Kritz, M. M.
1987   "International Migration Policies: Conceptual Problems," *International Migration Review*, 21(4).

Lim, L. L.
1989   "Processes Shaping International Migration Flows." In *Proceedings of the IUSSP International Population Conference*, Vol. 2. New Delhi: IUSSP.

Marr, W.
1985   "The Canadian Temporary Visa Programme as an Alternative to the European Guest Worker Scheme," *International Migration*, 23(3).

Massey, D. S.
1991   "Economic Development and International Migration in Comparative Perspective." In *Determinants of Emigration from Mexico, Central America, and the Caribbean*. Ed. S. Diaz-Briquets and S. Weintraub. Boulder, CO: Westview.

Michalowski, M.
1992   "The Dynamics of Recent South-North Flows of Temporary Workers: A Canadian Case Study." In *Proceedings of the Peopling of the Americas Conference*, Vol. 2. Vera Cruz, Mexico: IUSSP. Pp. 255–276.

1991　　　"Foreign Temporary Residents to Canada: Short-Term Movers on Long-Term Immigrants?" Paper presented at Annual Meeting of the Population Association of America. Washington, DC, March 21–23.

Michalowski, M., and C. Fortier
1990　　　"Two Neglected Categories of Immigrants to Canada: Temporary Immigrants and Returning Canadians," *Statistical Journal of the United Nations ECE*, 7(3): 175–204.

Molle, W. T. M., *et al.*
1992　　　"Can Foreign Aid Reduce East-West Migration in Europe? With Special Reference to Poland." WEP Working Paper. Geneva: ILO.

Pessar, P. R., ed.
1988　　　*When Borders Don't Divide: Labor Migration and Refugee Movements in the Americas.* New York: Center for Migration Studies.

Portes, A., and J. Walton
1981　　　*Labor, Class and the International System.* New York: Academic Press.

Reubens, E. P.
1986　　　"Temporary Foreign Workers in the U.S.: Myths, Facts and Policies," *International Migration Review*, 20(4).

Salt, J.
1992　　　"The Future of International Labor Migration," *International Migration Review*, 26(4).

Samuel, J.
1991　　　"Contemporary Immigration Policies: Canada, the United States, and Mexico." In *Facing North/Facing South: A Multidisciplinary Conference on Contemporary United States-Canadian-Mexico Relations.* Calgary: University of Calgary.

Sassen, S.
1993　　　"Economic Internationalization: The New Migration in Japan and the United States," *International Migration*, 31(1).

Satsewich, V.
1990　　　"Rethinking Post-1945 Migration to Canada: Towards a Political Economy of Labor Migration," *International Migration*, 28(3).

Shenstone, M.
1992　　　"World Population Growth and Population Movements: Policy Implications for Canada," *Policy Planning Staff Paper*, No. 92/7.

Shevtsova, L.
1992　　　"Post Soviet Emigration Today and Tomorrow," *International Migration Review*, 26(4).

Tapinos, G.
1991　　　"Les Migrations Extra-Communautaires et l'avenir des Populations Etrangeres." Paper presented at the conference "Le Capital Europeen a l'aube due XXIe Siecle." Luxembourg, November 27–29.

United Nations
1989   *World Population Trends and Policies: 1988 Monitoring Report*. New York: United Nations.

U.S. Immigration and Naturalization Service
1991   *Statistical Yearbook of the Immigration and Naturalization Service, 1990*. Washington, DC: Government Printing Office.

Weiner, M.
1985   "On International Migration and International Relations," *Population and Development Review*, 11(3).

Weintraub, S.
1992   "North American Free Trade and the European Situation Compared," *International Migration Review*, 26(2): 506–529.

Wong, L. T.
1984   "Canada's Guest Workers: Some Comparisons of Temporary Workers in Europe and North America," *International Migration Review*, 18(1).

Zolberg, A. R.
1989   "The Next Waves: Migration Theory for a Changing World." *International Migration Review*, 23(3).

6

Emerging Trade Blocs and Caribbean Emigration[1]

Jean-Pierre Guengant

Introduction

From an economic point of view, the contemporary Caribbean presents a paradoxical picture. On one hand most Caribbean countries appear fairly well integrated in the world economy. But the Caribbean region itself appears more fragmented than ever. Each country has its own privileged trade ties to former colonial and other developed nations in Europe and North America, but economic links within the region are weak. This is the result of a long historical evolution.

In the sixteenth and seventeenth centuries, Caribbean countries became integrated in the North Atlantic segment of the then-emerging world economy. Structured as plantation economies, they specialized in the export to the metropoles of sugar and other primary commodities and had to import everything else. The very profitable nature of the "colonies" made the Caribbean a battlefield for the European powers up to the beginning of the nineteenth century.

By the late nineteenth century, thanks to massive U.S. investments – noticeably in the sugar industry, the banana plantations, and in related infrastructure (ports, transportation, etc.) – the Caribbean region became somewhat more integrated. As a result of the uneven distribu-

[1]The author would like to thank Professor Alan B. Simmons, York University, for his assistance and encouragement.

tion of those investments large numbers of migrants moved from one country to another. After the Spanish-American War in 1898, American economic and political control over the region was unchallenged; during the first half of the twentieth century the Caribbean is often referred to as the "American sea."

After the end of World War II, the collapse of plantation and peasant agriculture, as well as political changes in the region, led again to fragmentation. The Caribbean began to split apart as each country developed its own commercial and migratory links to different North American and European metropoles. In this period, the quest for regional economic and political integration has been fraught with difficulty.

This paper will address trends and prospects for integration of Caribbean countries in the present world economy. It will give particular attention to shifting economic opportunity, employment prospects and population movements within the integration process. Some attention will be given to the possible impact of two emerging trade blocks – the European Economic Community (EEC) and North American Free Trade Agreement (NAFTA) – on economic development and migration in the Caribbean.

INTEGRATION

The integration of the Caribbean into the present world system, including the integration of Caribbean countries between themselves may be considered in terms of three major dimensions: political, economic (trade and investment), and human resources (migration).

From a political point of view, the countries of the region appear still largely dominated and controlled by the colonizing metropoles, and hence poorly integrated among themselves. Out of the 31 distinct geopolitical entities which constitute the Caribbean – all the Caribbean islands, plus Bermuda, the three Guyanas and Belize – half, fifteen, are still politically dependant in one way or another on a northern country. Puerto Rico, and the U.S. Virgin Islands are U.S. dependencies. Guadeloupe, Martinique and French Guyana are French territories. The Netherlands Antilles – Curaçao, Aruba, Bonaire, and Saint Maarten – are tied to the Netherlands. Anguilla, Bermuda, the British Virgin Islands, the Cayman Islands, Montserrat and the Turks and Caicos Islands are dependent on the United Kingdom. Nevertheless, with the exception of the French territories, which as Overseas Departments of

France have very limited local powers, all these dependent countries enjoy a large control over local affairs.

The economic consequences and the effects on people's mobility of political dependency differ from one country to another. For example, the currencies used in the Netherlands Antilles – the Antillean guilder – and those used in the British colonies are linked with a fixed parity to the US dollar and not to the Netherlands and United Kingdom currencies. In fact most Caribbean currencies are or have been linked to the U.S. dollar, except again for the French territories, where the French franc is the legal currency. In terms of mobility, political dependency guarantees free movements between the colonies and their metropoles, except for the British colonies, whose natives cannot settle freely in the United Kingdom.

For the sixteen independent countries, independence is a new phenomenon. Only three countries achieved independence before World War II: Haiti in 1804, the Dominican Republic in 1844, and Cuba in 1902. But all three have been occupied by American troops in the twentieth century, and their economies have been more dominated by American capital than those of the other countries. The remaining thirteen countries all gained their independence over the past 30 years, twelve from the United Kingdom, and one, Suriname, from the Netherlands.

The twelve former British colonies along with Montserrat constitute the Caribbean Common Market (CARICOM). Among these countries one traditionally distinguishes three groups. First, the four MDCs (More Developed Countries), Jamaica, Trinidad and Tobago, Guyana and Barbados, so called because of their more diversified economies compared with those of the LDCs (Less Developed Countries). Second are the seven members of the OECS (Organization of Eastern Caribbean States) referred to as LDCs, which have in common the EC dollar, with a fixed parity with the US dollar, as is the case for the Barbadian dollar. These countries correspond to two subgroups. The Windward Islands comprise, from south to north, Grenada, Saint Vincent and the Grenadines, Saint Lucia and Dominica. The Leeward Islands comprise Antigua and Bermuda, Montserrat and Saint Kitts-Nevis. Third and last, the Bahamas and Belize, whose currencies are also linked to the U.S. dollar.

However, it should be noted that the categorization between the MDCs and LDCs does not correspond to today's economic realities.

Indeed, during the 1980s the economic growth of the LDCs has been faster than those of the MDCs, and Guyana and Jamaica in particular have now GDP per capita lower than those of the LDCs.

CARICOM, established in the early 1970s, represented a valuable attempt to foster regional economic integration and development. But its membership is limited, and its results have been far behind expectations. Intra-Caribbean trade between members has not grown as expected, and continues to represent a small percentage of each country's exports and imports. Moreover, it has been dominated by the exports of oil from Trinidad and Tobago.

As for political traits, economic characteristics of the integration of the Caribbean countries into the world economy reflect a strong legacy of the colonial past, the double allegiance to the U.S. and the European colonizers, and poor regional integration. Overall, Caribbean economies remain undiversified, dependent, and open. Exports often remain limited to a narrow range of products. Exports as well as imports represent for many countries about 50 percent or more of their Gross Domestic Product (Chernick, 1978). Caribbean trade partners are mainly North American and European countries, but the United States is the main trade partner for most countries. However, the United Kingdom remains a major partner for the CARICOM countries, and of course France is the main trade partner for the French territories.

In the 1980s, many Caribbean countries continued to enjoy preferential trade agreements with both European and North American countries for their products. This is the case for sugar and banana production with the European Community under the Lomé convention and for manufactured products under the U.S. Caribbean Basin Initiative (CBI) and Canada's CARIBCAN (World Bank, 1993). However, several Caribbean countries have been able to find new niches of profitable integration in the world economy, notably tourism and other offshore business services. The Bahamas, the United States and British Virgin Islands, the Cayman Islands, the Turks and Caicos Islands and Anguilla in particular have been very successful in taking advantage of tourism and banking. By contrast, Jamaica and Guyana, still largely integrated according to the old "colonial economic order", i.e., exporting agricultural and mineral products, have had great difficulty maintaining a stable income from these exports.

Political and economic dependency on the metropoles appears to have gone hand in hand with preferential admission of Caribbean migrants to Europe and North America. Interestingly enough, this is not the result of free movement from the dependent countries to their metropoles, but more the result of the economic transformation of the Caribbean economies in a changing international environment. Indeed the massive exodus from the Caribbean to the metropoles registered since the end of World War II has affected all countries. Also, it has been one of the main component in the adaptation of the Caribbean to the new world economy.

POPULATION MOVEMENTS

Mobility integration is defined here as integration of Caribbean labor markets into the labor markets of the metropoles and between themselves. One proxy indicator of this integration is for a given country, the ratio between the number of emigrants and its total population.

The total loss of Caribbean population due to net migration out of the region between 1950 and 1990 can now be estimated at 5.6 million (Guengant, 1993). This represents 32 percent of the population of the region in 1950, and 16 percent of the population of the region in 1990. No other region of the world experienced such heavy losses due to sustained emigration in the same period. The loss during the 1980s is estimated at about 1.4 million, only slightly less than the 1.7 million losses estimated for the 1970s and the 1960s (*see* Table 1).

The top sending countries are logically among the most populated countries of the region. Haiti and Jamaica, with about 1 million lost each over the past 40 years, is followed by Puerto Rico (about 800,000 lost), Cuba and the Dominican Republic (about 700,000 lost each), then Guyana and Trinidad and Tobago (about 300,000 lost).

However, the greatest proportional loss of population due to emigration is found in five small CARICOM states: the four Windward Islands – Grenada, Saint Vincent, Saint Lucia and Dominica – and Saint Kitts-Nevis. For these countries, loss due to net migration between 1950 and 1990 represent more than 80 percent of their 1950 population. In fact the thirteen CARICOM countries, with the exception of the Bahamas – one of the few net migration gain countries over the period – were all severely affected. The CARICOM countries lost 62 percent of the 1950 population as a result of negative net migration.

TABLE 1

INTERNATIONAL MIGRATION BALANCES, CARIBBEAN COUNTRIES

	Migration Balances by Decade (Thousands)				
	1950–59	1960–69	1970–79	1980–89	Total
Cuba	-10.0	-475.0	-222.6	-19.9	-727.5
Dominican Republic	-54.0	-175.0	-220.0	-240.0	-689.0
Haiti	-70.0	-220.0	-350.0	-400.0	-1,040.0
Puerto Rico	-469.8	-211.9	-41.1	-110.1	-832.9
Jamaica	-165.1	-289.5	-270.8	-246.5	-971.9
Trinidad & Tobago	-0.4	-110.1	-94.7	-75.0	-280.2
Barbados	-20.2	-38.2	-14.7	-10.7	-83.8
Guyana	-4.3	-53.1	-129.5	-121.6	-308.5
Grenada	-12.4	-18.5	-21.4	-19.5	-71.8
St. Vincent	-9.3	-20.0	-15.1	-13.1	-57.5
St. Lucia	-13.4	-17.8	-18.5	-13.0	-62.7
Dominica	-5.5	-9.7	-12.5	-15.8	-43.5
Antigua	-2.7	-5.0	-7.1	-7.1	-21.9
St. Kitts/Nevis	-6.1	-16.9	-8.0	-7.4	-38.4
Montserrat	-4.5	-2.6	0.8	-1.6	-9.5
Belize	-0.8	-7.1	-19.5	-14.7	-42.1
Bahamas	13.6	23.9	3.9	7.4	48.8
Bermuda	0.0	0.0	-2.3	-1.1	-3.4
Curaçao	-4.5	-18.3	-16.9	-20.4	-60.1
Aruba	-13.0	-9.9	-5.5	-5.6	-34.0
Suriname	-4.4	-27.8	-97.6	-33.5	-163.3
Guadeloupe	-3.4	-25.3	-50.3	14.0	-65.0
Martinique	-4.5	-30.9	-46.5	-4.3	-77.6
French Guyana	2.5	8.2	7.9	25.7	44.3
REGION	-863.2	-1,724.0	-1,651.8	-1,338.3	-5,577.3

Caribbean migration has been massively directed to the northern metropoles. This reflects the increasing integration of the Caribbean labor markets into those of the metropoles, particularly into the U.S. and Canadian labor markets. Whereas European metropoles, namely the United Kingdom, France and the Netherlands, have received less than 1 million Caribbean migrants over the past 40 years, the United States and Canada have admitted 2.7 million legal immigrants from all Caribbean countries, mainly since the mid-1960s (Guengant, 1990). If we add to this figure Puerto Rican emigration to the United States, we arrive at about 3.5 million "documented" Caribbean migrants who have settled in North America.

By comparison intra-Caribbean migrations appear marginal, reflecting a lessening of the integration of Caribbean labor markets compared to what it was at the beginning of the century. A plausible estimate of intra-Caribbean migration (permanent change in residence) is around half a million over the past 40 years (Simmons and Guengant, 1992a). This is about double the number of Caribbean-born individuals enumerated in 1980 in a country of the region not their country of birth. Such an estimate would mean that intra-Caribbean movements represented about 10 percent Caribbean emigration over the past 40 years. Countries of origin and destinations where intra-Caribbean movements are significant are not many. Haiti is the main provider of intra-Caribbean migrants to a number of countries in the region (Allman and May, 1982). Yet the majority of Haitians emigrants go to North America. Next are the four Windward Islands with a similar pattern: multiple countries of destination but with a majority of emigrants going to the United States and Canada. On the receiving side only a handful of countries have registered net migration gains over the past 40 years as a result of these movements. These are the Bahamas, French Guyana, the U.S. Virgin Islands, Saint Maarten, the Cayman Islands, the British Virgin Islands and the Turks and Caicos Islands. All are countries which have been very successful in taking advantage of new niches in the world economy. For example, French Guyana hosts the European space center at the Kourou base.

The movements described above are the result of a variety of factors, whose importance varies over time. Previous research covering the 1950s, the 1960s and the 1970s, identified the percentage of the labor force in agriculture at the beginning of each decade as the main determinant of Caribbean emigration (Simmons and Guengant, 1990). As a result of declining employment in agriculture (due to declining farm production and increasing farm mechanization), rural workers have been subject to pressure to move to urban areas – where they displace urban workers – and to migrate, at least seasonally, to work outside their country. This is particularly true for the twelve CARICOM countries which experienced net migration losses during the 1970s. In their case, for example, the percentage of the labor force in agriculture in 1970 explains 59 percent of the variation in their net-migration rates over the following decade.

Indeed, the decline of the agriculture sector in the Caribbean over the past 40 years – both in plantation and peasant agriculture sectors – is a key factor in explaining the timing and magnitude of the Caribbean exodus to the metropoles. This decline is linked to the increasing competition from other Third World countries, and to the emergence of a new role for the Caribbean in the world economy, including the role of manpower provider for the labor markets of the metropoles.

Massive emigration started early in countries where the plantation sector was first liquidated, and where there were few possibilities for resistance in the peasant sector by agricultural workers faced with the deterioration of earnings and employment conditions. Puerto Rico and Montserrat are typical examples of this. But in countries such as the Dominican Republic, Haiti, the Windward Islands, Guyana and Belize, with a sizeable peasantry at the end of World War II, emigration developed later when the crisis of the plantation sector deepened, making subsistence agriculture more precarious, and when first groups of emigrants in the metropoles facilitated further emigration.

THE LIKELY IMPACT OF THE EEC AND NAFTA ON CARIBBEAN INTEGRATION AND DEVELOPMENT

The marginalization of Caribbean agricultural workers and peasants needs to be interpreted as a new step in the integration of the Caribbean countries, and the Caribbean as a whole, into the world economy.

The Caribbean occupies an ambiguous place in the new international division of labor (Anderson, 1985; Simmons and Guengant, 1992b). It is definitively no longer an attractive place for expansion of agriculture activities on large estates. But it is not really an attractive place either for investments in offshore industrial activities. Industrial salaries in the

Caribbean are higher than in other Third World countries. The labor force is less docile. And in several countries, especially those with lower wages, political instability is a force which discourages investment. Nevertheless, the region still has some relative advantages for the development of certain service activities in tourism and offshore banking, for example. In contrast, the major relative advantage of the Caribbean is its relatively well trained and healthy manpower, "ready for use" wherever jobs are available.

During early movements within the Caribbean Basin (to Panama, Cuba, etc.) and, in the later part of the nineteenth, century to the United States, the British and French colonies of the Eastern Caribbean, Jamaica and Haiti, served as reservoirs of manpower for the other countries of the region. In the process, Caribbean people developed a "culture" of migration (Marshall, 1982) which facilitated further movements. Over the past 40 years, with the progressive marginalization of the Caribbean in the world economy as a producer of agricultural and primary commodities, the whole Caribbean has served as a reservoir of manpower for both the European and the North American metropoles.

However, integration of the Caribbean countries into the world economy is uneven. This is reflected in both varying migration rates and huge differences in GDP per capita – from a mere US$300 or $400 for Haiti and Guyana, to more than US$10,000 for Bermuda, the Bahamas, the U.S. Virgin Islands, the French Antilles, and some other small islands. Recent levels of performance for Caribbean economies are also diverse, and reflect the success or failure of their efforts to benefit from a mixed international environment and to adjust to the emerging new international division of labor.

Interestingly, the smaller countries have fared much better than the larger ones. The smallest countries of CARICOM – the Windward Islands, Antigua, Saint Kitts-Nevis, Montserrat, Belize and the Bahamas, as well as the British Virgin Islands and Anguilla were foremost among the high growth economies, recording rates of growth in GDP per capita of 5 percent or more per annum between 1981 and 1990 (Samuel, 1992). This was due largely to vibrant and growing tourism industries, coupled with the good results of the banana sector in the case of the Windward Islands. By contrast, the larger countries either revealed contracting economies during the 1980s (Guyana, Haiti, and Trinidad and Tobago) or low economic growth of between 0 and 2 percent per year (Barbados, the Dominican Republic and Suriname), or at best moderate growth of between 2 and 3 percent per year (Jamaica, Cuba and Puerto Rico).[2] The lower economic growth of the larger countries is surprising since they have relatively diversified economies, often with a substantial manufacturing sector.

Taking into consideration population growth and inequality in income distribution, these results suggest that at least in the Dominican Republic, Haiti, and Suriname and in the previously MDCs of CARICOM (Jamaica, Trinidad and Tobago, and Guyana, and perhaps in the past 2 to 3 years Barbados) people have recently become poorer. Among the other countries, thanks to the economic growth during the 1980s, GDP per capita has increased substantially. In a number of small economies devoted to tourism and offshore business services such as Bermuda, the Bahamas, the Cayman Islands, the British Virgin Islands, GDP per capita is now above US$10,000 (Blackman, 1990). In countries with less or no tourism, such as the Windward Islands and Belize, GDP per capita is around US$2,000.

During the 1980s, most of the countries with poor or modest economic performances have gone through severe structural adjustment programs. As a result, governments have been forced to divert resources away from local expenditure, resulting in disproportionate cuts to social services. Guyana and Jamaica in particular suffered particularly severely from externally imposed adjustment programs. For the most part, the faster growing economies have been spared the debilitating effects of externally imposed programs. But many of them have undertaken self-imposed adjustment programs to reduce their fiscal expenditures. During the 1980s, many of these countries achieved surpluses on their current account. This enabled them to undertake social infrastructure and other investments projects. The emphasis was on "productive" capital expenditure, and slightly less on social investment. Thus the programs may have resulted in a slight shift in the balance away from social infrastructure. However for these countries, on average, government expenditures on health and education remained roughly constant.

Despite differing performances among Caribbean countries, virtually all of them experienced dramatic increases in open unemployment rates (Deere, 1990). Paradoxically this has also been the case among

---

[2]*See* Boland (1992). All this section draws largely from Barbara Boland's paper as well as from Wendell A. Samuel's paper (1992).

the countries with massive emigration rates. Indeed, a major consequence of the integration process at work over the past 20 to 30 years has been to make increasing numbers of Caribbean workers available for external labor markets: mainly in the metropoles, sometimes in the "new niche" economies of the region.

What then is likely to be the impact of the emergence of two major trading blocks – the European Community's single market and the North American free trade area – on the Caribbean economies, and on migration from the Caribbean?

The primary objective of establishing trade blocs is to foster trade and economic development between members. Thus, the first consequence of the establishment of the EEC and NAFTA will be to further expose Caribbean economies to global competition and to exacerbate the competitive pressures facing Caribbean economies. In the process, the preferential trade agreements the Caribbean economies enjoy from European and North American countries may be in jeopardy.

However, with regard to migration, the establishment of the EEC and NAFTA is not likely to change present trends. Since the mid-1970s EEC members have largely closed their borders to "foreign" labor immigration (that is, migration from outside Europe). EEC arrangements allow free movements of people within the Community only for nationals of, and foreigners legally admitted to, the member countries. Given the present high rates of unemployment and the mounting xenophobia observed in virtually all European countries, this is not likely to change soon. Thus, Europe will probably continue to be largely closed to Caribbean migration, except for the few West Indians holding French or Dutch passports. By contrast, Caribbean migrants are likely to continue to have access to American and Canadian labor markets under conditions similar to those in recent years. NAFTA is only a trade agreement, and does not contain any provisions on international migration. This means that the United States and Canada will continue to define their own immigration policies according to their national interest. Both countries have recently demonstrated growing interest in receiving skilled migrants, as opposed to the traditional preference given to family relatives. For many Caribbean potential migrants this shift will not be a problem, given their levels of education. They will have to compete with other educated candidates noticeably from Asia, and to a lesser extent from Latin America as in recent years. But NAFTA will not put them in competition with Mexican workers.

CONCLUSIONS

In the 1980s, the Caribbean economies became more vulnerable as a result of their continued integration in the world economy.

Despite varying results from one country to another, the World Bank notes that: "The Caribbean region is still among the more rapidly growing regions of the world. Exports of goods and non-factory services have been expanding rapidly in part because of preferential trade agreements, and in part because the Caribbean countries have been able to find 'niches' in the world market for their good and services, notably tourism."[3] However, this success has not prevented continued outflow of people from the region through the 1980s.

According to the same source, the outlook for the 1990s does not appear promising. Traditional sources of external financing for the Caribbean countries will be scarce. Agricultural prospects depend largely on the fate of the preferential trade agreements. For sugar, it is assumed that the preferences will continue for some time. But the situation with respect to bananas is deemed more vulnerable. Indeed, it is far from certain that Caribbean bananas – those produced in the French Antilles and those produced in CARICOM countries, mainly in the Windward Islands – will continue to enjoy protected access to French and British markets (for the latter fall under the Lomé Agreement). In 1992 and 1993, American companies challenged this protection by introducing in European markets much less expensive bananas produced in Latin America. The ensuing "banana war" eventually ended with a reaffirmation of preferential treatment for Caribbean bananas, but Caribbean producers encountered huge financial losses, and the long-term future for banana agents from the Caribbean remains clouded.

Turning to the manufacturing sector of the Caribbean economies, the prospects for its three components – the agro-processing sector, the import-substitution sector and the enclave sector – are not so great either (Samuel, 1992). The agro-processing sector is characterized by varying degrees of efficiency because of primitive technology and variability of product quality. The import-substitution sector is characterized by a high import content in the production process and is

[3]See World Bank (1993). This section draws largely from this document.

deemed uncompetitive. Lastly, the enclave sector is dominated by foreign garment manufacturers and highly specialized electronics firms. They export mainly to the United States, and are competitive in the global market. But these firms are inclined to move frequently seeking cost advantages, and they cater to very volatile export markets in which recession and technological changes can decimate the sector in a short space of time. They also employ mainly female workers at low wages, workers who may be increasingly tempted to migrate to North America to earn more, possibly in better jobs. Indeed wage pressure from tourism is a permanent threat to this sector, and may force a shift to higher value-added activities, from apparel manufacturing to data processing, for example.

Overall, to take advantage of the available "niches" in the world market, the Caribbean economies will not only have to compete with other Third World countries, but also among themselves. This is likely to increase the fragmentation of the region between the "better off" and the "left behind" countries. The first group will probably continue to attract migrants from their poorer and unsuccessful neighbors. The second group will continue to serve as reservoirs of manpower for both the better-off countries of the region and the metropoles. This will be particularly the case for Haiti and, to a lesser extent, the Dominican Republic and the Windward Islands. Nevertheless, for all countries, emigration is likely to continue to be a mobility strategy for many youths, irrespective of the economic performance of the countries of origin. In fact, if increased integration of the Caribbean in the world economy means increased vulnerability of the Caribbean economies, it means also increased mobility and circulation for Caribbean people.

REFERENCES

Allman, J., and J. May
1982   "Haitian Migration: 30 Years Assessed," *Migration Today*, 10(1).

Anderson, S. E.
1985   *The Americas in the New International Division of Labor*. New York: Holmes and Meier.

Blackman, C. N.
1990   "Tourism and Other Services in the Anglophone Caribbean." Working Paper No. 26. Washington, DC: Commission for the Study of International Migration and Cooperative Economic Development.

Boland, B.
1992   "Population Dynamics and Development in the Caribbean." Paper presented at Meeting of Government Experts on Population and Development in Latin America and the Caribbean, sponsored by the United Nations, ECLAC, UNFPA and CELADE. Saint Lucia, October 6–9.

Chernick, S. E.
1978   "The Commonwealth Caribbean: The Integration Experience." A World Bank Country Economic Report. Washington, DC: World Bank. Baltimore and London: The Johns Hopkins University Press.

Deere, C. D., ed.
1990   *In the Shadow of the Sun.* Boulder, CO: Westview, A PACCA Book.

Guengant, J.-P.
1993   "Whither the Caribbean Exodus?: Prospects for the 1990s," *International Journal, Canadian Institute for International Affairs*, 48(2): 335–354. Spring.

_____
1990   "Les Emigrations Caraïbéennes." In *La Grande Encyclopédie de la Caraïbe.* Vol. 9, *Economie.* Pointe à Pitre: Editions Caraiba.

Marshall, D.
1982   "The History of Caribbean Migrations," *Caribbean Review,* 11(1).

Samuel, W. A.
1992   "A Socio-Economic Scenario for the Eastern Caribbean." Paper presented at Population and Development Symposium organized by the University of the West Indies, USAID and UNFPA. Antigua, July 19–22.

Simmons, A. B., and J.-P. Guengant
1992a   "Recent Migration Within the Caribbean Region: Migrants, Origins, Destinations and Economic Roles." In *The Peopling of the Americas*, Vol. 2. Veracruz, Mexico: International Union for the Scientific Study of Population. Pp. 419–441

_____
1992b   "Globalisation et nouveaux régimes demographiques dans la Caraïbe." Paper presented at Colloque Fécondité et Insularité. Saint-Denis, May 11–15.

_____
1990   "Caribbean Exodus: Explaining Country Variation in Net-Migration Balance." Paper presented to ORSTOM, Pointe a Pitre, and the Centre for Research on Latin America and the Caribbean. York University. May.

World Bank
1993   "The Caribbean Region, Current Economic Situation, Regional Issues, and Capital Flows, 1992." In *A World Bank Country Study.* Washington, DC: World Bank.

Migration, Development and Peace in Central America

Manuel Angel Castillo[1]

Introduction

At the end of the 1970s, the migratory patterns in Central America underwent a radical change. Until that time the great part of population movements – as was the case in other Latin American contexts – took place within the nations of the region or, at most, were movements of workers between neighboring countries. Internal migration was affected by the development of rural businesses and the accompanying disorder of *campesino* economy and readjustment to the new framework of relations. In some cases, the movements of the *campesino* population were temporary, to work at harvest time on plantations with export crops. In others, migration formed part of a program for expansion of the agricultural frontier. In yet others, the loss of land for subsistence farming – partially due to mounting pressure on the land because of increases in population, but above all because of the absence of effective measures to change the pattern of property-holding and access to agricultural land – brought about the exodus of many among the rural population to the cities, mainly to the capitals of their respective countries (CSUCA, 1978).

[1]The author wishes to acknowledge the valuable comments made on his text by Rómulo Caballeros, and the welcome help of Timothy Edwards in translation. The author assumes sole responsibility for its contents.

Population movement outside the area was of little importance as a social phenomenon. There were indeed some important movements in the border areas, occurring for trade reasons or forming part of well-established movements back and forth, such as the annual flow of Guatemalan workers to coffee plantations near the Mexican border in Soconusco, Chiapas.[2]

Social and political conflicts also determined emigration from Central American countries in specific historical circumstances. However, these cases were not only few but also frequently solved by the granting of political asylum. Individuals involved in these processes generally had professional characteristics that not only enabled them to incorporate themselves easily into the host society, but also ensured a positive reception of their contribution to the social, scientific and cultural development of the country of resettlement.

The majority of countries in the area and those that were liable to become the destination of the politically persecuted generally recognized the principal contents of the different regional instruments related to political asylum.[3] Furthermore, a central fact in this period was the controlled and selective nature of persecution and of fear for life and personal security. It was basically focused on individuals who were leaders of some kind or who were politically active, and in certain cases might extend to the members of their respective families.

STRUCTURAL INEQUALITY AND SOCIAL CONFLICT

Contemporary social structure and dynamic of the Central American countries is deeply marked by their history since the colonial period and by the difficulties they experienced in creating independent states. The successive models of domination were based on particularly disadvantageous relations not only for the original inhabitants but also for the social groups that emerged later.[4]

---

[2]See, among others, Spenser(1984); Paniagua (1983); Fabregras et al. (1985); Castillo (1990).

[3]See the 1928 Havana, 1933 Montevideo, and 1954 and 1981 Caracas Conventions, as well as the 1939 Montevideo Treaty on Asylum and Refugees, and the Montivideo Treaties on International Penal Law of 1889 and 1940.

[4]For this reason, the case of Costa Rica differs from that of the other countries. The form of the crisis, its development projects, their consequences (including migration) and the possible solution are all different.

Independence from Spain and subsequent fragmentation into the present-day small countries did not imply any change whatsoever in this situation (Pinto, 1989). Quite the contrary, local groups recreated the relations of domination to their own advantage, and national economies were subordinated to the forces of the world market. In international economy Central America was basically an exporter of primary consumer goods, particularly those of what one author has appropriately called "after dinner economies" (coffee, sugar, bananas,[5] among others) (Garcia Laguardia, 1971).

Liberal reforms initiated at the end of the last century attempted to create juridical and institutional bases and to implement a transformation of these feudal-like relations into capitalist ones. However, limitation of resources and the lack of alternative technological capacity, as well as resistance by some of the traditional power groups, gave rise to a specific economic development and to political regimes that left intact many preexisting relations (Pinto, 1983).

The integration of the Central American economies into external markets manifested a high degree of dependence and vulnerability to uncontrollable fluctuations (Torres-Rivas, 1970; 1981). Within each economy, this structural weakness and a frequently authoritarian model of domination resulted in an incapacity to build internal markets that would offer the possibility of a strategy of "development inwards."

Central America's relation with contemporary dominant consumer markets and the presence of foreign capital were important factors in the evolution of the economy and of the political regimes. This situation is summed up in the continued existence of a pattern of social inequalities, plainly evident in the extremely high concentration of resources and the profits obtained from their exploitation in the hands of a minority group (Table 1).

The years after World War II saw a modification in the role of the economies supplying primary goods, and some countries managed to develop important quantitative and qualitative changes. There were significant rates of growth in their gross domestic product (GDP) (Table 2) as well as a diversification of economic activity, albeit limited (Mayorga Quiros, 1983). However, income distribution and access to the benefits of this economic growth and diversification did not extend to the majority of social sectors. Levels of poverty and social inequality

[5]On banana growing, *see* Ellis (1983).

TABLE 1

CENTRAL AMERICA: LAND DISTRIBUTION PER UNIT SIZE (PERCENTAGES)

	Central America		Guatemala	
	Units	Area	Units	Area
Total	100.0	100.0	100.0	100.0
Less than 0.7 hectares	22.4	0.8	31.4	1.3
0.7–7 hectares	54.2	9.2	56.7	14.9
7–35 hectares[a]	17.1	18.3	9.3	18.7
35–350 hectares[a]	5.8	38.5	2.3	30.7
351 hectares and more[a]	0.5	33.2	0.3	34.4

Sources: Central America data according to most recent (at the time of edition) agricultural censuses in Mayorga Quiros, 1983. For Guatemala, 1979 Agricultural Census in AID/Washington-Development Associates, 1982: Annex I, Table 2B..

[a]For the Guatemalan case, because of available data, these intervals are 7–44.8, 44.8–450, and 450 and more hectares, respectively.

TABLE 2

CENTRAL AMERICAN COUNTRIES: RATE OF GROWTH OF GROSS DOMESTIC PRODUCT, INDICATED PERIODS (CONSTANT 1970 PRICES)

	Mean Annual Rates					
	Central America	Costa Rica	El Salvador	Guatemala	Honduras	Nicaragua
1950–1955	4.4	8.3	4.5	2.3	2.4	8.3
1955–1960	4.8	6.0	4.8	5.3	4.6	2.3
1960–1965	6.5	6.5	6.7	5.3	5.5	10.1
1965–1970	5.3	7.0	4.5	5.8	4.5	3.8
1970–1973	6.0	7.6	5.1	6.6	5.0	4.8
1973–1978	5.2	5.6	5.6	5.7	4.6	3.6
1978–1983	-0.9	-1.1	-5.5	0.5	-0.2	-1.5

Source: ECLA, 1985: Table 1, p. 7.

remained stable and in some cases deepened. This situation is evident in the continued existence of an extreme pattern of social inequalities, plainly evident in the extremely high concentration of land and other resources in the hands of a small but powerful and wealthy elite.

GENERAL CRISIS, POPULAR STRUGGLE AND POPULATION DISPLACEMENTS

Economic growth of the first half of the 1970s (Table 2) was reversed in the second half of the decade. The economies of the Central American countries felt the effects of international crises such as the oil crisis, since they are highly dependent on oil imports, as well as an escalation of foreign debt and the obligations that accompanied it (Table 3).

By this time the project for regional economic integration, the Central American Common Market,[6] had run up against countless difficulties. Efforts at implementation were reduced to the renewal of some agreements, and the best results were achieved in merely bilateral terms. In any case, the obstacles confronting the region's economies did not change the pattern of inequality described above. The concentration of property and of the benefits of the growth that some economies still enjoyed in the 1970s not only remained stable but in the majority of cases became more acute.[7] Poverty and extreme poverty affected broad levels of the population (Table 4). The most important economic activity continued to be agriculture (Table 5) and the majority of the population employed in this sector did not have access to sufficient productive land in order to satisfy their basic needs.

Nicaragua was the first country to undergo a radical change in its political regime. The movement headed by the Sandinista Front of National Liberation (Frente Sandinista de Liberación Nacional or FSLN), which united opposition forces and forged alliances with economically powerful sectors, overthrew the last of a long line of Somoza family governments.

Later, a long-drawn process of armed struggle took place in El Salvador between the Farabundo Martí Front for National Liberation (Frente Farabundo Martí de Liberación Nacional or FMLN) and successive civilian and military governments without reaching any solutions to the social and political-military conflicts. The struggle took on the character of a civil war, to the extent that the international community acknowledged the belligerent status of the opposition forces. The

[6]The Central American Common Market's overall results were really negative at this juncture, due both to factors within and external to the region. (*See* ECLA, 1981.)

[7]There are difficulties in obtaining information and statistical records about the concentration of property (Table 1). Economic censuses are very irregular. However, the study carried out by AID/Washington-Development Associates, based on the 1979 Guatemalan Agricultural Census is a useful and detailed example (AID/Washington-Development Associates, 1982)

TABLE 3

CENTRAL AMERICAN COUNTRIES: RELATION OF TOTAL FOREIGN DEBT TO POPULATION,
PRODUCTION, AND EXPORTS, YEARS INDICATED AND MEAN GROWTH RATES OF
TOTAL FOREIGN DEBT FOR PERIODS INDICATED

	1970	1975	1978	1980	1983
Foreign debt per inhabitant ($)	88	190	307	417	600
In relation to GDP (at current prices, as percentages, in $)	24.9	33.8	35.1	42.0	71.4
In relation to exports of goods and services ($)	104.4	122.7	125.0	154.4	306.9
Years	1970	1973	1978	1981	1978
	-73	-78	-81	-83	-83
Mean growth rates (%)	12.7	25.1	19.8	14.7	17.7

Source: ECLA, *Centroamérica: El finaciamiento externo en la evolución económica, 1950–1983*
(LA/MEX/L.2), Mexico, March 4, 1985, Table 15, p. 54 and Table 17, p. 60.

TABLE 4

CENTRAL AMERICAN COUNTRIES: PROPORTIONS OF POVERTY IN **1980** AND **1990**
(PERCENTAGES OF TOTAL POPULATION)

	Poverty		Extreme Poverty	
	1980	1990	1980	1990
Central America	60	68	38	46
Costa Rica	25	20	14	11
El Salvador	68	71	51	52
Guatemala	63	75	32	52
Honduras	68	76	57	63
Nicaragua	62	75	35	42

Sources: ECLA, *Bases para la transformación productive y generación de ingresos de la población pobre del Istmo Centroamericano* (LC/MEX/G.3), México, December 3, 1991, Table p. 12, based on ECLA, *Satisfacción de las necesidades básicas de la población del Istmo Centroamericano* (E/CEPAL/MEX/1983/L.32), November 1983. For 1990, estimates of ECLA based on official data for Costa Rica and on the results of surveys on homes in Guatemala, Honduras, and urban areas of El Salvador, compiled by PREALC in 1989. The remaining estimates are based on the data at FLACSO, for 1985, projected through 1990 and adjusted for the evolution of the income per inhabitant.

FMLN managed to occupy territory that it maintained under its control until the signing of the peace agreements.

Around 1978 Guatemala underwent an escalation of generalized violence. From that moment on, armed opposition groups have been involved

TABLE 5
CENTRAL AMERICAN COUNTRIES: SOME ECONOMIC INDICATORS IN THE 1970S

	1970	1975	1987	1980
Growth rate of GDP per inhabitant (1970 prices)	—	-0.4	0.5	-1.4
Proportion to GDP of some economic activities (%)				
Agriculture	29.1	—	26.8	26.2
Manufactures	15.9	—	17.1	16.9
Trade and finances	22.4	—	22.9	22.7
Community, social, and personal services	15.2	—	15.2	16.1
Growth rates of products of some economic activities (%)				
Agriculture	—	—	4.9	-2.0
Manufactures	—	—	5.2	1.7
Trade and finances	—	—	2.5	0.9
Community, social, and personal services	—	—	3.3	5.1

Source: ECLA, *La evolución de la economía centroamericana en 1980* (CEPAL/MEX/1053), Mexico, July 24, 1981, Tables 1, 2, and 3, pp. 27–32.

in a long period of confrontation with the army. Even though there have been ups and downs, the insurgent groups have, as a general tendency, increased their capacity and territorial extension in the military struggle. The nature of the confrontations is different from the Salvadorean case, but there are zones in the country with high levels of combat.

Honduras, although it did not participate in this generalization of regional conflicts in the same way, played an important role as an operational and training base for the armed groups opposing the Sandinista regime. A North American military base was also installed in Honduran territory, from which periodic military operations and exercises were carried out with the evident aim of pointing out to the Sandinista regime that the U.S. government considered it an enemy within "its own backyard."

This crisis, if it can be partially explained by reasons of an economic nature that became more acute with the international crisis of the 1970s, also has roots in the structural historical conditions, and the characteristics of the traditional political systems. With the exception of Costa Rica, authoritarianism and the absence of democratic channels of expression and political participation for the majority of the population in the Central American countries also contributed to deepening the crisis.

The inability to satisfy social demands and the impossibility of the affected sectors' direct participation brought about confrontation. Government's reply to the popular mobilization was persecution and repression. Initially, these actions were directed against the "visible heads" of the discontent, but later they were transformed into a process of generalized violence.

Armed insurgent movements constituted a way of protesting against and confronting the absence of legal channels. The Salvadorean and Guatemalan armies launched several counterinsurgency campaigns, in which they benefitted from ample foreign economic, material and technical support. In each case, military operations affected sectors of the civilian population, in part as a logical result of their presence in zones of conflict. But, even worse, the armies decided to treat the civilians as military objectives since they considered that they provided social and logistical support for the guerrilla organizations.

In Nicaragua, the Sandinista regime established a war economy and rapidly increased the size of its army in order to confront essentially foreign-based aggression. These decisions told against the regime in the long run. The relative weight of the defence budget influenced the deterioration of the economy, with the consequent impossibility of meeting the social demands of the population that had put its trust in the regime. Expanding the size of the armed forces by draft was a bone of contention for many Nicaraguan families and many sought to avoid the obligation, probably to a greater degree than in the other two countries where the armies also made use of this measure.

This overall situation fostered a series of population displacements that affected all countries in the region and that spread to others outside the area. Figure 1 provides an overview of migrations within Central America in the 1980s. The migratory pattern was radically modified. Rural-urban migrations intensified as a result of the exodus of internally displaced persons seeking refuge in the capitals. But there were also movements within the rural areas, and others, of greater importance because of their international repercussions, of refugees who fled to neighboring countries.

Segundo Montes *et al.* (1992) say that

> In the past decade, more than 1 million Central Americans emigrated to other countries in the region and to Mexico and Belize. Internal displacements

involve 1 million people. Around 14 percent of the total populations of Guatemala, El Salvador and Nicaragua have left their country for other countries in the region or have been displaced internally.[8] (Free translation)

The nature of the migration was variable. One of the flows that most attracted the attention of the international community was that of collective movements, entire communities that left their countries of origin and settled in camps. They were later recognized by their host governments and by international organizations such as the United Nations High Commissioner for Refugees (UNHCR). Official recognition – not immediate in all cases – did not always mean the acceptance of a juridicial status corresponding to their status as refugees, in accordance with the terms of the United Nations Convention and Protocol or with the broadest terms of the Declaration of Cartagena.[9]

However, these were not the only international migrations.[10] Individuals and families from different countries, but especially from those that were in conflict, were displaced mainly towards Mexico, the United States and Canada in largely undocumented migration flows. It appears that a minuscule percentage of these cases have requested asylum or the status of refugee, since the majority prefer to keep a low profile for several reasons; one of these is their unawareness of the bureaucratic procedure and of its consequences, real or imaginary.[11]

In this context, Mexico underwent a new experience. Because of its undocumented and clandestine nature, it is impossible to estimate the volume of migration that entered Mexican territory with the idea of remaining in the country or of crossing over to the United States. Nor is

[8]Also quoted in Del Cid (1992: 37).

[9]*See* a description and discussion of this point in Castillo (1990). Mexico, for example, included the status of refugees in its legislation as late as 1990 – a whole decade after accepting and assisting them in Mexican territory. Only in 1992 did the bylaw appear that enables a formal application to be made.

[10]A preliminary attempt to establish a typology for Central American migrations on Mexico's southern border can be found in Castillo and Martin (1990).

[11]It is worth noting that the first Guatemalans who arrived in Mexican territory in 1981, fleeing from persecution and violence in their places of origin, were returned on the argument that they were not victims of political persecution but rather "economic migrants."

The U.S. Immigration and Naturalization Service has also been particularly unbending in its policy for accepting refugees. It applies discriminatory criteria for granting admission, since it differentiates according to aspects such as the nationality of origin. Thus, during the most intense period of conflict it admitted Nicaraguans, whose regime it considered to be hostile, more easily than Guatemalans and Salvadoreans, with whose governments the U.S. government maintained friendly relations.

In regard to abuses by different agents in both countries *see*, among others, Americas Watch (1992) and Freelick (1991).

Figure 1.   Migratory Movements in Central America, 1980–1989

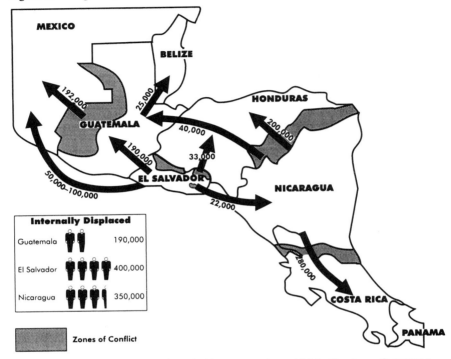

Sources: Modified version of J. R. Vargas *et al.*, *Estudio del impacto economico y social de las Migraciones en Centroamérica*, 1989, reproduced in CEPAL, *El impacto economico y social de las migraciones en Centroamérica*, Estudios e informes de la CEPAL (89) (Santiago, Chile: Naciones Unidas, 1993), 10.

Note: The figures are estimates by the source and include neither flows of returnees nor migrations towards the United States and other countries outside the region. The author, as well as the United Nations, does not necessarily accept or support these numbers.

it practicable to establish its composition and nature. We only have a few ideas based on the characteristics of those individuals identified, arrested, and expelled or deported (Castillo and Martin, 1990; Castillo and Palma, 1991).

All these Central American population movements were added to already existing migrations but with greater intensity and repercussions. The flow of Central Americans had a positive side for the countries of origin, which began to enjoy the benefits of growing remittances of sorely-needed foreign currency to their deteriorated economies.[12] This loss of human resources – be it temporary or definitive – also has a

[12]Because of the growing importance of this source of income for the economies of some Central American countries, United Nations Economic Commission for Latin America (ECLA) a study whose results can be consulted in ECLA (1991b)

negative social, cultural and family impact. However, the traditional migration of labor continued and maintained its economic importance, both for the activities that employed it as well as in terms of the income and social needs of the migrant workers.[13]

PEACE PROCESSES AND ECONOMIC ADJUSTMENT POLICIES

The end of the 1980s and the beginning of the 1990s was also the scene of hopes for changes in the countries in conflict. In Nicaragua, the elections resulted in a new regime headed by an alliance of opposition groups with the support and consent of the United States government and the participation of the sectors that had sponsored the irregular armed forces.

Increasingly persistent efforts to achieve peace were made in El Salvador within the framework of the Agreements of Esquipulas, signed by the governments of the region; these agreements were, to a certain extent, a regional mechanism to continue the initiative of the Contadora Group. These efforts concluded with the signing of the peace agreements between the government and the FMLN in January 1992, and pointed the way to the subsequent implementation of the demobilization and pacification mechanisms under international supervision.

Guatemala has also witnessed actions designed to achieve peace. The signing of the Oslo Agreement between the National Guatemalan Revolutionary Unity (URNG) and the Guatemalan government opened up the possibility of an end to the conflict. In order to achieve this, and inspired by the same spirit of searching for "a firm and lasting peace" for the region, a series of conversations and negotiations was organized under the aegis of the National Reconciliation Commission and in the presence of international observers. Even though the negotiations have several times been temporarily broken off, some basic agreements have already been reached (IRIPAZ, 1991). Shortly before the failed attempt by President Serrano to take over dictatorial control, negotiations were again interrupted. However, the new president, De León Carpio, has proposed a mechanism to rekindle talks.

Guatemala and El Salvador have fostered processes for a "return to constitutionality" and attempts to install legitimate, elected regimes headed by civilians. However, their legitimacy was also cast in doubt by those who argued that these regimes were created in a war scenario and lacked guarantees for the effective participation of the population.

[13]See Casillas and Castillo (1987, 1988), Castillo (1991a, 1991b: 173–192). See also ECLA (1992).

Furthermore, the armies' responsibility for counterinsurgency strategies gave them a large share of power and made them decisive factors in these governments' overall policies. Honduras, on the other hand, reduced its "passive" participation as a support base for the irregular Nicaraguan and mercenary forces, as well as a setting for U.S. Army military exercises. The reduction, however, implied the loss of the economic resources provided by maintaining these forces.

In any case, the end of the 1980s brought with it two closely related challenges: the need for peace and for economic recuperation as the means to achieve a solution to the social conflict. The governments in power at that time, approaching international finance agencies, had to accept the conditions imposed by the latter, including the obligation to follow adjustment policies and mechanisms. In certain cases, the governments adopted shock measures in an attempt to break with existing tendencies and to overcome accumulated deficits.

The results so far do not seem to be very promising. The levels of recuperation of production are quite weak and unstable, especially if they are compared with the rate of population growth (Table 6). Some argue that there have been partial successes in reestablishing fiscal balance, successes achieved at the cost of cutting back social spending. This weakness is even greater if the complete absence of significant efforts to change the structure of the distribution of wealth is taken into consideration. An example of this lack of interest is the evolution of the variation in real wages. They have continued to fall in recent years, and have been accompanied by a deterioration in the quantity and quality of social services.

Even though exports grew in some areas, the adjustment programs' lowering of tariffs has led to an increase in imports. The balance of the foreign current account remains high and tends to increase rapidly at the slightest sign of economic reactivation. Meanwhile, the repression of internal demand continues to maintain the deficit in balance of trade. The relation of the total foreign debt and its servicing with regard to exports of goods and services has been reduced, thanks to some relatively successful renegotiating processes and a drop in interest rates on the international market (Table 7).

However, these partial successes were not enough to overcome the accumulated backlog. Social services deteriorated even further and some of the measures included in the adjustment programs, such as the

TABLE 6

CENTRAL AMERICAN COUNTRIES: EVOLUTION OF GROSS DOMESTIC PRODUCT,
MEAN ANNUAL VARIATIONS OF CONSUMER PRICES AND REAL WAGES, FOR YEARS INDICATED

	1983	1985	1987	1989	1991
Real annual growth rate of GDP (%)	-0.1	0.3	3.5	3.0	2.3
Annual growth rate of GDP per inhabitant (%)	-2.6	-2.3	0.6	0.2	-0.4
Mean annual variation of consumer prices (%)	32.6	15.0	16.8	16.5	28.7
Variation of real wages (%)	15.0	9.1	-9.6	0.6	-4.6

Source: ECLA, *Centroamérica: Evolución económica durante 1991* (LC/MEX/L.193), México, June 29,
1992, Tables 1 and 6, pp. 39 and 44.

TABLE 7

CENTRAL AMERICAN COUNTRIES:
SOME INDICATORS FROM EXTERNAL SECTOR OF ECONOMY, YEARS INDICATED

	1983	1985	1987	1989	1991
	Annual Growth Rates (Percentage)				
Exportation of goods (f.o.b.)	0.8	-5.8	-6.0	5.4	1.2
Importation of goods (f.o.b.)	-0.3	-1.4	17.6	8.0	3.2
	Percentages				
Exportation of goods and services (GDP)	22.4	22.2	20.4	20.9	22.8
Importation of goods and services (GDP)	26.5	28.0	27.4	27.2	29.1
	Millions of Dollars				
Balance of current account	-1,589	-1,968	-2,356	-2,350	-2,097
Balance of trade account	-815	-1,167	-1,630	-1,689	-1,645
	1983	1985	1987	1989	1990
Total foreign debt/export of goods and services	308.2	366.7	392.6	400.8	394.5
Service of total foreign debt export of goods and services	47.5	46.6	44.2	34.5	—

Source: ECLA, *Centroamérica: evolución económica durante 1991* (LC/MEX/L.193), México, June 29,
1992, Tables 2, 3, 4, and 5, pp. 40–43.

increase in the cost of public services, made it more difficult for those
sectors of the population that have traditionally been marginal to gain
access to them. ECLA stated that "the population, in the majority of

Central American countries, was affected by higher levels of unemployment" (ECLA, 1991a: 8).

PERSPECTIVES FOR MIGRATION

It is not true to say that the pacification processes in the countries in conflict are a reality. Possibly the greatest advances have been registered in Nicaragua. In El Salvador the situation is still unstable; a recent proof of this was the difficulty with which both parties agreed to accept a postponement of the limits for fulfilling commitments they had both accepted. The case of Guatemala is even less certain; agreement on new terms so that the negotiation process can restart is still to come, and denunciations of violations of the population's human rights continue.[14] Nor have threats and repressive actions against human rights activists and leaders of the popular movement ceased.

The economic future is also still uncertain. The lack of mechanisms for the participation of the populace and the dearth of processes that contribute towards overcoming structural inequalities, added to the unfavorable international situation, hinder economic recovery and improvement in the social situation in the Central American countries. Adjustment policies have heightened economic difficulties, and social services and social policies have not looked to the needs of the most numerous and underprivileged sectors of the population.

It is not difficult to imagine, in this context, that population movements will continue with the same or greater intensity than in the recent past. Even though the refugees have developed movements to return home,[15] in the case of Guatemala the process has been slow and difficult. Those returning up to 1992 have been few,[16] mainly given the absence of satisfactory replies to their demands before the Guatemalan regime, whether it be headed by a civilian or a military presence.

[14]See the Resolutions of the United Nations Human Rights Commission and the Commission for the Prevention of Discrimination of Minorities and Ethnic Groups.

[15]In the Salvadorean case, the movement was developed even during the armed conflict by those settled in camps in Honduras. It would seem that the return has been completed. See Alvarez-Solis, 1992.

[16]Only 9,832 from 1984 up to November 1992 (Saenz Carrete, 1992). This figure, added to the deaths that occurred in the same period, has easily been surpassed by the births within the refugee population.

The Guatemalan refugees settled in Mexico have continued to state their desire to return. Those refugees organized in the Comisiones Permanentes de Representantes de los Refugiados en México (CCPP, their own and representative organization recognized by the international community and the Guatemalan and Mexican governments) have laid down a series of conditions for the Guatemalan government before they are prepared to actually return. In the second half of 1993 both parties finally reached an agreement for a programmed and progressive return.

The first group of 2,380 refugees traveled in January after a series of differences with Guatemalan officials regarding specific issues, such as the granting or restoring of agricultural land, or the guarantee of respect for the individual and collective rights of the refugees and their families, were solved by the mediating action of the Comisión Mediadora (an impartial negotiating group) and by international – official and nonofficial – accompaniment.

However, the persistence of political conflicts hampered a process that for many seemed hopeful and even successful; perhaps the climax was the moment of political uncertainty after Serrano's exit, although instability and human rights violations had worsened the environment of return. Organized refugees[17] decided to defer the process until general conditions in the country allow the recovery and maintenance of agreed guarantees and commitments established with the Guatemalan government.

The continued existence of a critical situation in both economic and political terms leads me to believe that the migrations will continue. Monitoring the area during the last two years seems to confirm this hypothesis (Castillo and Palma, 1991). The movement of Nicaraguans, halted with the change of political regime and the relaxation of obligatory military service has begun again. However, economic conditions and the effects of prolonged armed conflict still influence population movements towards the exterior and mainly towards the United States. The U.S. government is tackling this new presence without the same consideration that it offered those individuals that fled from Sandinista Nicaragua. Hondurans are now thickening the flow of migrants, whereas previously the contribution of Honduras was of little

[17]Dispersed nonrecognized refugees (additional to the nearby 46,000 settled in camps and assisted by Mexican and international institutions) formed their own organization and summed up coordinated efforts for "collective, voluntary and organized return" under the general and officially recognized representation exerted by the CCPP

importance. My hypothesis is that the demobilization of the Nicaraguan contras and the end of U.S. pressure on the Sandinista regime through its troops stationed at Palmerola Base have reactivated the crisis previously ameliorated by the incomes these activities meant to the Honduran economy.

In the case of El Salvador, a decrease in some migratory movements was observed, which was even combined with the movement of refugees returning home. Nonetheless, on balance the flow of migrants continues, and some of those that return are only visitors – above all those people who have legalized their position in the United States – who expressed their uncertainty with regards to a process that is still not clear.[18]

Finally, Guatemalans still live in a climate of political instability, and suffer the effects of a political and economic situation that adversely affects the majority of the population. The conditions of poverty and extreme poverty have become more acute in all countries – with the exception of Costa Rica – as is shown in Table 4, and, of them all, Guatemala and Honduras have the worst record.

In conclusion, the migratory movements of Central Americans will continue in the immediate future, although surely in a different form from that which most attracted the attention of the international community, that is, as *refugees*. This means that these migrations cannot be divorced from the factors that provoke them, nor from the policies implemented by the countries through which they pass and in which they arrive, to preserve respect for their basic rights.

REFERENCES

AID/Washington-Development Associates
1982   *Tierra y Trabajo en Guatemala: Una Evaluación.* Guatemala.

Alvarez-Solis, F.
1992   "Viabilidad de la Estrategia de Reproducción Social. El Caso de la Comunidades de Repatriados y Repobladores de El Salvador." M. A. Thesis, Social Sciences, Facultad Latinoamericana de Ciencias Sociales (FLACSO), Sede Académica de México. June.

---

[18] I have been able to verify this fact in interviews with migrants returning through Mexico, who return home only on temporary visits, to observe the development of events, or sometimes because of the economic recession in the United States, or because of specific conflicts such as the disturbances in the metropolitan zone of the City of Los Angeles in April, 1992.

Americas Watch
1992   *Brutality Unchecked: Human Rights Abuses Along the U.S. Border with Mexico.* An Americas Watch Report. New York: Human Rights Watch. May.

Casillas, R., and M. A. Castillo
1988   "Características Básicas de la Migración Guatemalteca al Soconusco Chia-paneco," *Estudios Urbanos y Regionales*, 3(9): 537–562. México: CEDDU-El Colegio de Mexico. September–December.

———
1987   "Impactos Regionales de las Migraciones Internacionales a la Frontera sur de México: El Caso de los Trabajadores Estacionales." México: El Colegio de México/Consejo Nacional de Ciencia y Tecnologia (CONACYT). December. Mimeograph.

Castillo, M. A.
1991a   "La Migración Internacional y el Problema de los Refugiados." Paper presented at the Conferencia Centroamericana, del Caribe y México, sobre Políticas de Población, sponsored by the Institute Nacional de Administración Publica (INAP), Programa Latinoamericano de Poblacion (PROLAP), Antigua Guatemala, Guatemala, April 9–12. Mimeograph.

———
1991b   "Migraciones Laborales en la Frontera sur: d'un Fénomemo en Proceso de Cambio?" In *Población y Sociedad en Mexico*, 1 ed. Ed. Humberto Muñoz. Mexico City: Coorinación de Humanidades, Universidad Nacional Autonoma de Mexico and Editorial Porrúa. Pp. 173–192. June.

1990   "Las Migraciones en la Frontera de Mexico y Centroamerica: Elemento de Vinculo o de Conflicto?" Paper presented at Segundo Congresso Internacional sore Fronteras en Iberoamerica. San Jose, Costa Rica, November 14–17.

Castillo, M. A., and E. Martin
1990   *Tipos, Volúmenes y Políticas de Inmigración a la Frontera sur de México: Interrogantes y Ambigüedades*. México: Internal Seminary, Centro de Estudios Demográficos y de Desarrollo Urbano. May 30. Mimeograph.

Castillo, M. A., and S. I. Palma
1991   "Los Transmigrantes Centroamericanos en su Ruta Hacia el Norte." Paper presented at Preparatory Conference for the International Conference on Economic Integration, Migratory Policies and Human Rights in North America. Sponsored by the Academia Mexicana de Derechos Humanos/Coordinación de Humanidades, UNAM/Center for Refugee Studies, York University, Hemispheric Migration Project and Georgetown University. México. November 15.

CSUCA, Program Centroamerica de Ciencias Sociales
1978   "Conclusiones." In *Estructura Agraria, Diámica de Población y Desarrollo Capitalista en Centroamérica*, 1 ed. San José: EDUCA. Pp. 309–327.

Del Cid, J. R.
1992   "Migración Interna e Internacional en Centroaméricana." In *Los Procesos Migratorios Centroamericanos y Sus Efectos Regionales*, 1 ed. Ed. Rodolfo Casillas. México: Facultad Latinoamericanos de Ciencias Sociales (FLACSO), Sede Académica de México. April.

ECLA, U.N. Economic Commission for Latin America
1992   "El Impacto Economico y Social de las Migraciones en Centroamérica." April 15. Mimeograph.

_____
1991a   *Bases para la Transformación Productiva y Generación de Ingresos de la Población Pobre de los Países del Istmo Centroamericano*. Mexico: LC/MEX/G.3. December 3.

_____
1991b   *Remesas y Economía Familiar en El Salvador, Guatemala y Nicaragua*. México: LC/MEX/L154 Proyecto CEPAL/Gobierno de los Países NED/89/003. June 25.

_____
1985   *Centroamérica: Bases de una Política de Reactivación y Desarrollo*. Mexico: LC/MEX/G.1/Rev. 1. May 20.

_____
1981   *Evolución de la Integración Centroamericana en 1980*. México: CEPAL/MEX/1048. May 8.

Ellis, F.
1983   *Las Transnacionales del Banano en Centroamérica*, 1 ed. San José, Costa Rica: Editorial EDUCA.

Fabregas, A., *et al.*
1985   *La Formacion Histórica de la Frontera Sur*. Cuadernos de la Casa Chata No. 125. Mexico: CIESAS del Sureste.

Freelick, B.
1991   *Running the Gauntlet: The Odyssey of Central Americans Crossing Mexico*. Washington, DC: U.S. Committee for Refugees.

Garcia de Leon, A.
1985   *Resistencia y Utopía. Memorial de Agravios y Crónica de Revueltas y Profecías Acaecidas en la Provincia de Chiapas Durante los Últimos Quinientos Años de su Historia*, 1 ed., México: Ediciones ERA.

Garcia Laguardia, J. M.
1971   *La Reform Liberal en Guatemala*. San José, Costa Rica: Editorial EDUCA.

IRIPAZ
1991   *Cronologias de Los Procesos de Paz. Guatemala y El Salvador*. Serie Cooperacion y Paz, Vols. I and II. Guatemala.

_____
1981   *La Inversión Extranjera en Centroamérica*, 3 ed. San Jose, Costa Rica: Editorial Universitaria Centroamericana.

Mayorga Quiros, R.
1983   *El Crecimiento Desigual en Centroamérica: 1950–2000*, 1 ed. Centro de Estudios Internacionales, El Colegio de México.

Montes, S., *et al.*
1992   *El Impacto Economico y Social de las Migraciones en Centroamérica.* CEPAL.
        April 15. Mimeograph.

Paniagua, A.
1983   "Chiapas en la Coyuntura Centroamericana," *Cuadernos Políticos,* 38: 36–54.
        Mexico: Ediciones ERA. October–December.

Pinto, J. C.
1989   *Centroamérica, de la Colonia al Estado Nacional (1800–1840),* 1 ed. Gua-
        temala: Editorial Universitaria, Universidad de San Carlos de Guatemala. April.

_____
1983   *Raíces Históricas del Estado en Centroamérica,* 2 ed. Guatemala: Editorial
        Universitaria, Universidad de San Carlos de Guatemala. November.

Saenz Carrete, E.
1992   "La Respuesta de México a los Refugiados Centroamericanos en el Nuevo
        Contexto Continental." Paper prepared for Reunion Sobre Dilemas Globales
        de la Migración Internacional. Sección Mexicana del Club de Roma y Centro
        Tepoztlàn, Tepoztlàn, Morelos, November.

Spenser, D.
1984   "Trabajo Forzoso en Guatemala, Bracerismo Guatemalteco en Chiapas,"
        Cuicuilco, 12: (4)5–10. Revista de la Escuela Nacional de Antropología e
        Historia, Mexico. January.

Torres-Rivas, E.
1981   *Interpretación del Desarrollo Social Centroamericano; Procesos y Estructuras
        de una Sociedad Dependiente,* 7 ed. Guatemala: Editorial Universitaria,
        Universidad de San Carlos de Guatemala.

_____
1970   "Desarrollo, Integración y Dependencia," *Estudios Internacionales,* 12:
        489–511. January–March.

Vuskovic Cespedes, P.
1986   *Centroamérica: Fisonomía de una Región,* first edition. Coor. A. Aguilar *et al.*
        México: Programa de Estudios de Centroamerica (PECA) and Centro de
        Investigacion y Docencia Económicas (CIDE). December.

8

The Mexican Dilemma

Rodolfo Casillas

Introduction

When in 1980 the Mexican government formed the Mexican Commission to Help Refugees (COMAR), it was anybody's guess what its future would be. Initially COMAR was seen as an agency designed to cope with the newly emerging and specific problem of massive Central American migration to Mexico. The problem was unexpected and supposedly of short duration. No stretch of the imagination could have foreseen that the refugee problem would turn into a Pandora's box, unleashing a series of new problems.

More than twelve years later, it is clear that the northward flow of Central American refugees and migrants was not a passing problem but part of a lasting social phenomenon that Mexico, lacking both previous experience and clear policies, was not prepared for. Historically, Mexico had developed an understanding of and policies for political asylum for special individual cases, not for refugees arriving in large numbers. We have witnessed ever-increasing migratory flows coming into Mexico from Central America. These flows have had considerable economic, social, and cultural impact in several areas within the country and now form a central part of the diplomatic agenda with bordering countries.

Over the past decade, the Mexican government has been forced to address some of the most pressing problems presented by these refugee flows and by other migrants. However, a limited legal framework and inadequate government policies have made government actions ineffectual in practice. The evidence suggests that within the Mexican public administration there are still those who underrate or undervalue the need and positive opportunity for a humanitarian response. Many administrators see the refugee and migration flows in a negative light, as trends threatening national security. On the other hand, there have been praiseworthy acts, although they have been more the exception than the rule. Mexico is far from having a humanitarian immigration policy that is enforceable and compatible with the noble tradition of political asylum of which the Mexican government is justly proud.

It would seem logical to expect that, faced with a new phenomenon that grew and changed rapidly, Mexican authorities would come up with creative policies. However, this has not been the case. One is then led to ask whether Central American migration really has a social significance that merits the development of official policies beyond those currently in use. The answer is clearly yes: steps should have been taken long ago. The reasons why this has not happened are evident when we analyze the thinking which lies behind Mexican international migration, asylum, and refugee policy over recent history.

In this paper I analyze some of the main features of the migratory flows from Central America, the social context in which they take place, and the measures adopted by the Mexican government in an attempt to find workable solutions. This analysis is based on the theoretical interpretation presented in the next section. A full answer to all the questions raised here would require more space than this paper permits. The answers provided in the present paper should be considered preliminary and partial.

CONTINUITY AND CHANGE IN MEXICO'S MIGRATORY POLICIES

Times have changed, and so have Mexican government programs, as well as the objectives they postulate in light of social changes. The establishment of new policies can expose contradictions between what has previously been done and what earlier policy sought to accomplish. Mexican immigration policy has seldom attained its objectives. This is true of early policy in the late nineteenth century, and of recent policy in the 1980s and early 1990s (Casillas, 1992a).

Mexican migration policy can be seen as having gone through three important phases.[1] The first took place during the nineteenth and earlier twentieth centuries, and was characterized by an interest in attracting immigrant masses, especially Europeans, who could establish settlements and give impetus to the country's progress. To this end, different land settlement laws were passed and a series of other initiatives was undertaken, but for various reasons these measures were not entirely successful.

The second phase began during the 1920s and continued until the end of the 1970s. It was characterized by the practice of giving asylum to politically persecuted people of diverse origins, mainly Spaniards expelled by General Franco and South Americans who arrived after the rise of military dictatorships in the southern cone. During this period there was no further discussion about settling immigrants. National progress was no longer associated with the benefits immigrants – particularly those from Europe – might bring. It was also in this period that Mexico underwent a massive social and economic transformation. Particularly in the three decades following World War II, Mexico experienced massive urbanization. It was the period when the "Mexican miracle" achieved its splendor. However, by the 1970s, the Mexican economy began to slow; the nation showed an incapacity to distribute the wealth that had been created; foreign debt rose.

The third stage began during the 1980s and continues into the present. It is characterized by both a redefinition of the state and a redefinition of its partners and methods for the growth process. For the purpose of our topic, this redefinition entails the establishment of a new international migration policy that is restrictive, protectionist, and synchronized with its United States counterpart (the partner with whom Mexico seeks much stronger ties).[2] The Mexican state no longer seeks indiscriminate immigration.[3] Nor does Mexico want hundreds of

---

[1] For a more detailed exposition of the different stages of Mexican migration policy, *see* Casillas (n.d.).

[2] In this sense, the initiatives taken to inaugurate a North American Free Tarde deal (NAFTA) are a perfect example of the government's goals. If we observe what has been done since the De la Madrid administration (1982–1988), we could conclude that the economy's integrationist tendency and the synchronizing of subordinate policies have been under way since then.

[3] This immigration policy was only indiscriminate to a point, since, as stated before, the attempt was to encourage European immigrants. Nineteenth-century Liberals and Conservatives who were in favor of "improving the race" differed on who should come. Conservatives preferred Spaniards, Italians and Poles in order to strengthen Catholic religious identity. Liberals, on the other hand, preferred English, Germans, French and others who were associated with progress, industry and cultural advancement, regardless of religious affiliation.

political refugees arriving as happened during the 1980s when, for example, the arrival of a group of Bolivian refugees caused headaches because of their lack of vocational qualifications.

From the early 1980s Mexico has attempted to receive highly qualified immigrants – investors, scientists, technicians and professionals – who could contribute their knowledge to the process of national modernization. This objective was eventually formalized in the population law of 1990 and reinforced by corresponding regulations that went into effect in 1992.

These types of immigrants obviously do not resemble the Central Americans that have arrived in this country in the hundreds and thousands. The old objective is still in place: a "quality" immigrant. The legislation has been designed to achieve that objective, while at the same time sanctioning criteria have been introduced so that all those migrants who come into the country without formally being approved for admission are to be punished.

However, what has changed, in addition to the state's desires, is the international context which drives both legal and undocumented international migration. One of the distinct features of our times is the enormous growth of political and economic pressures for international migration (Alba, 1992). Within this scenario, the Central American emergency stands out as a great expeller of people and the stage for profound displacements within the region itself. The regional flows arise from severe disequilibriums in the distribution of wealth, high levels of demographic growth, the process of economic globalization, violations of human rights, war and rape.

The governments of countries to the north have felt the potential and real pressures of the large numbers of migrants leaving Central America. To these they have responded with two courses of action. The first, a long-range plan, seeks to stimulate economic development in the countries of origin of these migrations, with the uncertain hope of encouraging potential immigrants to stay in their home countries rather than attempting to migrate.[4] The second course of action, aimed at stopping migration, which has immediate effect, has been to establish

---

[4]In recent years the United States, after Reagan's counterproductive policy toward Central America, opted for the 3-D strategy: development, democracy, and disarmament. Mexico, on the other hand, has maintained its pacifist principles about the resolution of conflicts and its opposition to foreign intervention. Furthermore, it has favored dialogue among the conflicting sectors and, through governmental protocols, the promotion of Central America's economic development.

a restrictive legal framework that allows in only "quality" immigrants, at the same time working harder at the tasks of detection and expulsion. This is how Mexico and the United States have acted, increasingly, since 1988.[5] The majority of potential migrants encounter barriers that either discourage migration or predispose them to act outside the law, which entails the risk of expulsion.

Government policies and the view of civil society are quite contradictory regarding Central American exiles. On the one hand, social conditions in Central America stimulate the emigration of the poor, ethnic minorities, and the politically dissatisfied. Central American governments are not opposed to this flight since the migration means not only an escape valve for internal conflicts, but also a subsidy for their own economies insofar as the countries all receive side benefits from the remittances that the migrants later send home (Moreno Brid, 1992). On the other hand, the governments of Mexico and the United States see Central American migrants as problems: they do not meet the skill criteria of immigration law; they break the law by migrating without required approval; they potentially take jobs from citizens, and they may be the source of ethnic conflict in their new place of residence. However, the views of the governments are not always supported by organizations of citizens. A number of Mexican and U.S. nongovernmental organizations (NGOs) have fought for a better treatment for Central American refugees and migrants (*see* Aguayo, 1991).

Since the early 1980s, Mexico has had great difficulty establishing an international migration policy that is congruent with its history and its relationship to the United States. The problem arises from the fact that Mexico is simultaneously a country of origin of migrants (nearly all of whom go the United States), a country for transmigration (Central Americans headed to the United States), and a destination country for Central American migrants. This conjuncture has created a dilemma to which the state has responded only with partial policies that often contradict each other. Current policies focus on encouraging "quality" immigrants, even if these are few in number (in fact, Mexico

[5]The Center for Information and Migratory Studies (Centro de Información y Estudios Migratorios), which works basically at the northern Mexican border, has made documented accusations against U.S. and Mexican migratory authorities of concerted attempts to stop transmigrants crossing Mexican territory in an attempt to enter the United States. Even though the Mexican authorities have denied the accusations, they have been unable to disregard U.S. public documents, particularly from the Immigration and Naturalization Service, which detail the activities carried out. *See* Casillas (1990).

does not seek a significant volume of immigrants). To facilitate Mexican emigration to the United States while discouraging Central American immigration at the same time within a single policy is problematic. Mexico has yet to find a solution. What has happened, and how conflicts arise and are dealt with, is the subject of the following sections.

BEFORE THE SOUTHERN MIGRATORY FLOWS

Before the massive migrations from Central America started in the 1980s, the only real records of migrants to Mexico were official records of foreign residents near the border[6] and a few studies of temporary workers from Guatemala hired for coffee harvests (Pohlens, 1978; Helbig, 1964) The Mexican government undertook its first serious study of this flow in response to the presence of a large group of Salvadorean migrants in Mexico City towards the end of the 1970s (Zazueta and Pablos, 1982). The arrival of thousands of Guatemalans in towns in Chiapas quickly gave rise to the formation of nongovernment organizations to aid refugees (Aguayo, 1992), the creation of COMAR and the appointment of a United Nations High Commissioner for Refugees (UNHCR). All this took place in the context of expanding media coverage of Central Americans expelled from their home towns by armed conflicts. In very little time the refugees and the events in Central America acquired a space in public opinion,[7] in academic media (Aguayo, 1985), and within government.[8]

By the mid-1980s one could speak of at least three distinct migratory flows coming from Central America: border residents, agrarian temporary workers, and refugees.[9] However, the conflict and drama associ-

[6]According to diplomatic archives, the first talks between the governments of Mexico and Guatemala regarding the emigration of citizens of both countries took place in 1832; dealt with specifically on that occasion was the issue of resident population in the border zone (González, 1988).

[7]In particular, mass media at the government's disposal offered broad coverage of the Central American conflicts. The most publicized ones were those in Nicaragua, El Salvador, and Guatemala.

[8]The administrations of José López Portillo (1976–1982) and Miguel de la Madrid (1982–1988) are particularly noteworthy for their foreign policy regarding Central America; the first for its open approval of Nicaragua's Sandinism and the fighting forces of El Salvador, and the second for Mexico's participation in the formation of the Contadora group.

[9]In this work I examine immigration from Central America through Mexico's southern border in detail, and deal very briefly with the presence of these immigrants elsewhere in Mexico. Very little is known about the activities of Central Americans living in other parts of the country, particularly those who have arrived since 1980. This examination presents some of the results of eight years of empirical research done in collaboration with Manuel Angel Castillo.

ated with refugee flight led researchers to focus only on refugees. During the second half of the 1980s more systematic research on temporary workers was undertaken (Casillas and Castillo, 1987; Grollova, 1984; Ordóñez, 1989; Mosquera, 1990) and studies were done on Central American flows arriving at other places along the Mexican southern border (César Dachary, 1990; César Dachary and Arnaiz, 1989), as were exploratory studies on other types of migrations (Salvado, 1988; Casillas and Castillo, 1989; O'Doherty, 1989). Although we are still far from having a complete and satisfactory knowledge of this situation, enough empirical evidence has been gathered to allow us to describe the main Central American migratory flows into Mexico, including those that pass through the country (Casillas and Castillo, 1992).

CHARACTERISTICS OF CURRENT MIGRATORY FLOWS

Central American migratory flows across the Mexican southern border constitute a complex phenomenon. Although it is important to avoid rigid schemes that assume that immigrants from one flow do not influence other flows, it is still possible to distinguish the following main streams of international migrants: [10]

1. temporary migratory workers;
2. commuting border residents;
3. refugees;
4. transmigrants headed to the United States and Canada.[11]

Temporary Migratory Workers

Most temporary migratory workers are hired for the cultivation of coffee, sugar cane, and bananas, but some work in fruit and chili plantations, livestock, etc. This is evident in the data for Central American migratory workers in Chiapas (Table 1), a major destination state. Since official records show that most Central Americans work on coffee, sugar cane, and banana plantations, this section examines workers on those three

[10]This classification is appropriate for the migration across Mexico's southern border. However, other records and other kinds of evidence show that there were groups of illegal Central Americans in several parts of the country as early as 1980, involved in varied economic, cultural, and social activities. *See* O'Doherty, *Centroamericanos en la Ciudad de México.*

[11]This section emphasizes migrant and transmigrant workers, with a brief discussion of border residents that makes reference to the productive activities of Central American immigrants.

TABLE 1

AGRICULTURAL WORKERS DOCUMENTED BY CHIAPAS MIGRATORY SERVICES: BY CROP, 1990

Crop	Number of workers	Percent
Coffee	51,914	73.5
Banana	6,470	9.2
Sugar cane[a]		
Cattle	6,406	9.1
Chili	2,647	3.7
Maize	1,145	1.6
Fruits	642	0.9
Coffee and cattle	642	0.9
Rice	127	0.2
Total	70,589	

Source: Unpublished data from Delegacón Regional de Servicios Migratorios del estado de Chiapas, Secretaría de Gobernación.

[a]Official records contain no information on workers in sugar cane cultuvation during 1990. We suspect that by mistake, 4,704 workers in Huyixtla county (site of the Belisario Dominguez sugar mill were counted as cattle workers. If so, sugar cane would reresent 6.7% and ranching 2.4%. For more detailed analysis, see Casillas and Castillo (1992). Volume estimates can be found in Ordóñez (1991).

crops.[12] Figure 1 depicts the border states of Mexico which have the greatest migratory exchange with Central America.

According to the Migratory Service records, a large number of short-term work permits were granted to Central Americans, as shown in Table 2. Temporary workers are peasants whose labor is vital for the cultivation of coffee; most of them come from Guatemala and stay six to eight months, from September to February, to do the harvesting. There is a collective and cyclic migration of families, neighbors and friends from the same towns, most of them from the western highlands of Guatemala. This flow is a well-established tradition, including tacit agreements with employers and set dates of arrival at the *ejidos* and

[12]Although records from Migratory Services show an increase in the volume of temporary workers during the last few years, it is impossible to estimate the total number of workers employed. Three main factors prevent a definite assessment: *1)* official records do not cover all coffee-producing units, *e.g.*, 1990 data do not include all the *ejidos*, and I doubt whether they cover all private plantations; *2)* even if the data happened to cover all units, an unknown percentage of the workforce has no documents, according to our fieldwork (*see* Casillas and Castillo, 1987); *3)* from our experience in the field, official records have been improving, so that observed increases may be due to better information rather than greater numbers, although this does not eliminate the possibility that there are more temporary workers (overwhelmingly Guatemalan).

Figure 1.   Guatemala and Refugee Areas in Southern Mexico

Location of Guatemalan
Refugees in Mexico (1992)

Registered Refugees
Chiapas: 24,650 in 125 camps
Campeche: 11,050 in 4 camps
Quintana Roo: 7,800 in 4 camps

Unregistered Refugees
50,000 to 150,000 in Chiapas,
Mexico City, and other areas.

coffee plantations. Employees typically work for the same employer each year and pass the relationship along to their descendants and kin. This kind of direct recruiting bypasses state supervision. Not all work contracts are registered and only in cases where workers are not paid do authorities intervene to enforce contractual duties.[13]

Banana cultivation, on the other hand, requires a stable supply of labor all year round. Instead of a single process (harvest) as is typical of coffee, this crop involves two separate ones: 1) continuous planting, spraying, irrigating, etc., performed by men; and 2) agro-industrial

[13]Up to now work contracts have been handled directly, without intervention of the authorities. However, workers have reported abuses and made claims to both the Guatemalan consulate and Mexican authorities. These reports have probably influenced both governments to start talks aimed at producing a binational agreement regulating work contracts.

TABLE 2

WORK PERMITS GRANTED TO MIGRANT WORKERS, 1985–1990

Year	Workers
1985	11,810[a]
1986	42,510[a]
1987	32,054[a]
1988	52,710[a]
1989	58,745[a]
1990	51,914[b]

Source: Regional Migratory Services for the state of Chiapas

[a]Activities recorded by migration offices located at Union Juarez and Ciudad Hidalgo, which issued the bulk of the work permits.
[b]Includes all migration offices of the region.

activities in packaging facilities, where women also participate. Both types of work are permanent and year-round. Consequently, the income they generate is usually the main/only one for the workers involved.

According to the Migratory Services of Chiapas, 6,470 Central American citizens were granted work permits for banana cultivation during 1990. However, this cannot be considered the total number since every day a mass of workers crosses the Suchiate River, which serves as a natural border, with no migratory control whatsoever. In contrast with coffee, small proportions of workers from Honduras and El Salvador can be found on banana plantations, as well as a significant percentage of Mexicans. According to observers within the area, in the zone nearest the Suchiate River as many as 90 percent of the workers may be from Guatemala; in the banana zones farthest from the border, the figure may be around 35 percent.

Two types of Central American workers are thus involved in banana operations: those residing in Mexico (either on the plantations or in nearby towns) and those residing in Guatemala and making frequent border crossings.[14] Banana workers living in Guatemala come from the coastal region of that country and have permanent work and income in Mexico, whereas those employed in coffee cultivation receive pay only for certain periods, so they do complementary work with comparable incomes in their home areas.

[14]Any such classification of migrants must be flexible since it must take into consideration variations introduced by factors such as economic activities, seasonality, the specific traits of each job, etc.

Sugar cane is produced in the states of Chiapas and Quintana Roo. As with bananas, "sugar production encompasses two phases: cultivation itself, culminating in cane cutting, and the product processing carried out in sugar mills, which has agroindustrial characteristics" (Casillas and Castillo, 1992: 28).[15] During cane cutting, from January to May, the number of workers peaks. At one of the two main sugar mills of the southern border region, at Huixtla in Chiapas, 1,800 temporary migrant workers were recorded (1,100 of whom came from Guatemala) (Ordóñez, 1991). At another location, Othón P. Blanco in Quintana Roo, 2,000 were recorded (over 60% of them Mexicans, from the states of Oaxaca, Tabasco, and Chiapas) (Camara, 1991).

The Guatemalans who work with sugar cane in Huixtla come from the southern coast of Guatemala, whereas those working in Othón P. Blanco come from Guatemala, from Belize, and from the refugee camps located in Quintana Roo. Like bananas, this crop involves different migratory flows revolving around a single cyclic activity. From the standpoint of income, however, temporary workers in cane earn amounts comparable to those in coffee.

Border Residents

Aside from the specific agricultural chores already mentioned, border residents also work in other crops and businesses, *e.g.*, tourism, fishing, and various jobs in the "informal" sector (such as servant, mechanic, domestic appliance repairer). Those working in the tourism industry usually have a better education, speak English, and add to Mexico's insufficient supply of qualified labor. It is worth noting that an undetermined number of people working in the towns near the Chiapas border, mainly in the informal sector, have received help from the Diocesan Border Immigrant Help Committee (CODAIF) with housing, training, and finding jobs.[16] Better-paid Central American immigrants near the southern border live in Tapachula, Tuxtla Gutierrez, Cancun, Cozumel, and Isla Mujeres.

Although several government officers have argued that there are thousands of border residents, most of them undocumented, no trustworthy sources for these numbers are available. The authorities from

[15]All translations of Spanish material are by the author.

[16]This description of the activity of border residents in Quintana Roo comes from Ken (n.d.). Opinions about residents of cities in Chiapas come from local informants.

Migratory Services act against undocumented migratory workers only when they are denounced or when, for whatever reason, campaigns are launched to arrest and expel those not having the proper migratory documents.

Transmigrants

Transmigrants form an undocumented population entering Mexico in transit to the United States. The length of the border and its geography and topography complicate the tasks of migratory authorities by permitting entry through countless points. Currently the main entrance routes lie through the states of Chiapas and Quintana Roo. Migrants usually travel by land, but also use sea and air transportation to a lesser extent.

Given its eminently undocumented nature, it is practically impossible to estimate the magnitude of this type of operation. We can only attempt characterization through records kept by Migratory Services on people arrested and expelled. According to them, since 1991 of every ten illegal aliens four are arrested. (In 1991, on average, 1,000 Central American transmigrants were expelled every week. By September 1992, 51,000 had already been expelled, a much higher weekly rate than in 1991) (Casillas, 1992a).

The turning point in the treatment received by transmigrants came in 1987, when the Ministry of Foreign Affairs released a memo instructing its foreign representatives to grant visas to only those individuals who could present extensive documentation. Under the socioeconomic conditions then prevailing in Central America it was highly improbable that those seeking visas could produce credit cards, certificates substantiating their previous employment, proof of bank accounts, photocopies of property titles, etc. As a result, transmigrants began to move outside the law. The number of Central Americans arrested and expelled from Mexico jumped from 1,308 in 1987 to 51,000 from January to September of 1992. In other words, in one week during 1992, almost the same number were arrested as in the whole of 1987.

The most important and constant portions of this transmigrant flow come from Guatemala and El Salvador, in large part related to the continuing violent conflicts in those countries. In contrast, the numbers from Honduras and Nicaragua have been fluctuating, corresponding more or less with the changing fortunes of those nations (Casillas and Castillo, 1992). News releases, through which Migratory Services publishes its figures, tell us that most arrests of Central Americans occur in the region around Tapachula, in the southern part of Chiapas. The figures also show that international migrants from other world regions (mainly Southeast Asia) are more likely to enter through Quintana Roo.

Official records of those arrested and expelled during 1988 provide the following statistics: out of 7,325 cases, 78 percent were male; 75 percent were single, and 68 percent were 19 to 29 years old. Prior to migration, 67 percent had worked at various urban jobs while 33 percent had worked in agriculture. In short, they were a young population, mostly urban, with full productive and reproductive potential. These features, together with the fact that many hired a *pollero* (clandestine travel service), help paint a picture of what some people call the "economic migrant." Nobody seemed to realize at the time that the features mentioned correspond to those individuals suffering repression and violence in their home countries (Casillas, 1992b).

RESPONSES TO MIGRATION BY THE MEXICAN GOVERNMENT AND THEIR IMPLICATIONS

Faced with growing and increasingly diversified migratory flows from Central America, Mexican authorities have responded with diverse measures aimed at 1) facilitating selective immigration (that of technicians, professionals, scientists, and investors) and 2) permitting a temporary stay, which would admit needed temporary workers to southern Mexico. The sole exceptions to this policy seem to be the creation of COMAR and the establishment of a representative of UNHCR in the country. After all, it became impossible to hide from public attention the thick clusters of thousands of Guatemalans who literally created towns where there had been none.

Ten years after their arrival, the Central American refugees saw the incorporation of the legal category of "refugee" in Mexico's 1990 General Population Law. Two years later, in October of 1992, the corresponding regulations went into effect. On one hand, it is heartening to have refugees recognized in the law, but on the other, it is distressing to see how restrictive the regulations are. The regulations concentrate many discretionary powers in a single agency; the agency's verdict cannot be revoked and mechanisms to determine the legitimacy of refugees' claims remain obscure. The activities of nongovernment organizations are completely ignored, or at least these organizations are offered no chance to participate in the process, and the regulations lack any reference to human rights organizations – to the point that they do not even mention COMAR, the pertinent government agency in Mexico.[17]

Transmigrants have also been the object of federal government actions: unprecedented arrest and expulsion campaigns, with the diligent participation of public safety authorities.[18] These procedures are perfectly consistent with the selective and restrictive migratory policy that Mexico has practiced since the end of the 1980s. It seems as though all responsibility for migratory and resident workers has been left in the hands of local public authorities. Although consultations are now being held between Mexico and Guatemala to lay the groundwork for the employment of migrant workers, there is no clear evidence of a quick and beneficial solution for the people involved.[19]

Resident workers certainly present a complex issue because they are widely dispersed and the numbers of families and individuals are unknown. Consequently, each local authority has been left to act according to its own criteria. Federal authorities have delegated their powers, but not for long. By the end of 1992, an organization of Guatemalan refugees had emerged to public view. According to the organization's own census, there are close to 60,000 undocumented immigrants in the border state of Chiapas alone. This organization's activities and its local and international impact should force the state to take it seriously, at least in the short run.

[17]For more details, see Casillas (1992a).

[18]It is possible that in the short run this campaign will help relations between Mexico and the United States, but from a broader perspective it may have grave consequences, such as the following: although it may benefit the United States, at the same time this campaign weakens Mexico's demands for decent treatment of illegal Mexican aliens north of the border; the hunt for illegal aliens increases transport prices and bribery, creating an additional problem within the fabric of government; and lack of objective analysis of migration records reduces the chances of understanding the phenomenon of transmigration, while simultaneously eliminating evidence needed to consider it in the international context, i.e., the United States and the countries from which the migrants come.

[19]Guatemala does not have studies that would allow it to make a sound proposal; the first field exploration will not start until 1993, and then only if the Labor Ministry maintains its interest in the subject, and if the party alliance that currently holds power continues to do so. The political changes that took place in Guatemala in June 1993, which are still on course, do not support any expectation that compromises will attend them soon. Mexico, on its part, faces differences of criteria and conception among officials and government agencies. Besides, no statements have been issued by the higher echelons about what to do. Elections are just over the horizon, and they may absorb attention or postpone decision making on issues like an international labor agreement, given the possible implications for relations with the United States.

FINAL REFLECTIONS

Efforts to resolve the political and military conflicts in Central America have still not been entirely successful, so that those conflicts still influence migrations coming from that region. However, even if there were an immediate total peace, certain sectors of the population would still be prone to migrate, either temporarily or permanently. The reasons are structural, having to do with poverty and poor distribution of wealth, and weak democracy throughout Central America. Also, over time, as field interviews and research already show, the first reasons that force or stimulate migration are superseded. That is, qualitative changes appear in the flows as time goes by. Migratory flows coming from Central America to Mexico and further north are likely to continue over the near future at least.

In the reforms begun by the Mexican government of 1982–1988 and intensified during the current administration, Central American migratory flows do not seem to have a significant place. They did not have an importance before, and they still do not figure seriously in the government's plans. My analysis of events suggests that the government's view goes something like this: transmigrants cause problems in our relations with the United States, so we must maintain campaigns to arrest and expel them.

Although many refugees have worked in and contributed to the Mexican economy, and have allowed Mexicans to express their long historical links with the peoples south of the Suchiate River, they have also caused the UNHCR to become active in Mexico. The UNHCR was not greeted with enthusiasm by many state officials – the organization was an unwelcome external observer of internal matters. The United States has exerted pressure to have it expelled. Guatemalan military officers complain to Mexican officials that the UNHCR hides supposed guerrillas.[20] If the refugees were to return to their homeland, this source of pressure and conflict would be eliminated. Mexican authorities, therefore, hope strongly that the situation in Guatemala changes, although this does not mean that the refugees have not evoked a certain amount of humanitarianism and compassion.

---

[20]During the 1980s, Mexico saw the emergence of nongovernment organizations as platforms in society from which to question the state and act independently of it; it is well known that Mexican authorities still find it difficult to accept the presence and activities of these organizations.

Although temporary workers introduce a dynamic element into the economy and are even vital for certain productive activities, granting them their full rights under national legislation would probably cause conflict with Mexican employees. It could also lead to a debate with the organized workers' movement in the country (with which the Mexican state is reshaping its relationship) and, if a labor agreement were signed, would create obligations to and for the government of Guatemala. Therefore the state finds it less problematic to leave relations between Mexican employers and Central American temporary workers to be regulated locally, with the authorities intervening in cases of evident abuse.

Border residents and other immigrants living in other parts of the country lack any organization or social representation. These factors, in addition to their undocumented status, have led them in the past to stay quiet, so as not to attract attention. Increasing efforts by Mexico to identify and expel those without immigration documents may be changing this situation. Undocumented migrants are now increasingly speaking for their rights. Segments of Mexican society are sympathetic, even if the state is not.

The day may not be far away when Mexican society as a whole will recognize immigrants as part of national reality, and will see in them the possibility of enriching Mexican culture and society as they have done in the past.

REFERENCES

Aguayo, S.
1992   "Del Anonimato al Protagonismo: Las Organizaciones No-gubernamentales y el Éxodo Centroamericano," *Foro Internacional*, 23(3): 323–341.

———
1991   *From the Shadows to Center Stage: NGOs and Central America*. Washington, DC: Georgetown University and Hemispheric Migration Project.

———
1985   *El Éxodo Centroamericano: Consecuencias de un Conflicto*. Mexico: Secretaría de Educación Publica, Consejo National de Fomento Educativo.

Alba, F.
1992   "Dilemmas Globales de la Migracion International," Mexico, s/e. November.

Campos Cámara, B.
1991   "Migración y Cortadores de Caña en la Frontera México-Belice." Foro Internacional: Las Fronteras National en el Umbral de los Siglos. Mimeograph.

Casillas, R.
n.d.   "Raíces Centroamericanas y Caribeñas en la Vida Mexicana." In *Cien Años de Migraciones a México*. Ed. M. E. Ota. Mexico: El Colegio de Mexico. Forthcoming.

———
1992a   "Deben Ampliarse las Politicas Migratorias." *Excelsior*. Mexico, September 25, Ideas Section.

———
1992b   "La Migración Centroamericana de Paso: Un Desafío a la Política Exterior de México." In *Migración Internacional en las Fronteras Norte y sur de México*. Mexico: Consejo Nacionales de Poblacion (CONAPO). Pp. 391–400.

———
1990   "Problemática Social a Partir de la Frontera sur de México." Paper presented at a seminar on information and analysis regarding transborder immigrants and undocumented work, organized by the Senate of the Republic. Mexico, June 20.

Casillas, R., and M. A. Castillo
1992   "Los Flujos Migratorios Internacionales en la Frontera sur de Mexico." Mexico, Secretaría del Trabajo y Previsión Social-Consejo National de Población (STyPS-CONAPO). Mexico.

———
1989   "Migraciones Centroamericanas al Estado de Chiapas, México: Presencias Desconocidas, pero no para Todos ni para Todo Propósito." Mexico: Comisión Mexicana de Ayuda a Refugiados (COMAR).

———
1987   *Impactos Regionales de las Migraciones Internacionales a la Frontera sur de México: El Caso de los Trabajadores Estacionales. Informe técnico final*. Mexico: El Colegio de México/Consejo National de Ciencia Tecnologia.

César Dachary, A.
1990   *Migraciones en la Frontera Mexico-Belice*. Chetumal, Mexico: Centro de Investigaciones de Quintana Roo (CIQRO).

César Dachary, A., and S. Arnaiz, eds.
n.d.   *Memoria del Encuentro Tres Fronteras un Destino*, third edition. Chetumal, Mexico: Centro de Investigaciones de Quintana Roo (CIQRO).

Chenaut, V.
1989   *Migrantes y Aventureros en la Frontera sur*. Mexico: SEP-CIESAS.

González, S. Mario
1988   *Relaciones Consulares y Diplomáticas México-Guatemala: 1821–1960: Guiá Documental*. Mexico: Archivo Histórico Diplomático Méxicano, Secretaría de Relaciones Exteriores de México.

Grollova, D.
1989   "Trabajo Forzado en Guatemala, Bracerismo Guatemalteco en Chiapas," *Cuicuilco*, 4(12): 5–10.

Helbig, C.
1964   *El Soconusco y su Zona Cafetalera en Chiapas*, first edition. Tuxtla Gutiérrez, Mexico: Instituto de Artes y Ciencias de Chiapas.

Ken, C.
n.d.   "Estudio Comparativo de las Fuerzas Laborales Méxicano – Beliceño: 1950–1990." In *Memoria del Encuentro Tres Fronteras un Destino*, 3 ed. Ed. A. César Dachary and S. M. Arnaiz. Chetumal, Mexico: Centro de Investigaciones de Quintana Roo (CIQRO).

Morena Brid, J. C.
1992   "Remesas Internacionales en Países Seleccionados de Centroamérica." In *Los Procesos Migratorios Centroamericanos y Sus Efectos Regionales*. Ed. R. Casillas. Colección Cuadernos No. 1. Mexico: FLACSO. Pp. 91–110.

Mosquera, A.
1990   *Los Trabajadores Guatemaltecos en Mexico*. Guatemala: Tiempos Modernos.

O'Doherty, L.
1989   *Centroamericanos en la Ciudad de México, Desarraigados y en el Silencio*. Mexico: Academia Mexicana de Derechos Humanos.

Ordóñez, C.
1991   *Demanda de Braceros Guatemaltecos en la Zafra del Ingenio Huixtla*. San Cristóbal de la Casas, Mexico: Centro de Investigaciones Ecologicas del Sureste.

———
1989   "Un Análisis Sobre Aspectos del Desarrollo Agrícola y Migracion de Fuerza de Trabajo en Regiones Fronterizas de Chiapas y Guatemala." San Cristóbal de las Casas, Mexico: Centro de Investigaciones Ecológicas del Sureste-Asociación Mexicana de Estudios de Población.

Pohlens, J.
1978   "La Formación de las Plantaciones Cafetaleras del Soconusco y el Capitalismo en Chiapas." Mexico. Mimeograph.

Salvado, L. R.
1988   "The Other Refugees: A Study of Nonrecognized Guatemalan Refugees in Chiapas, Mexico." Washington, DC: Hemispheric Migration Project, Center for Immigration Policy and Refugee Assistance, Georgetown University.

Zazueta, C. and L. Pablos
1982   "Migrantes Centroamericanos en Mexico: Primer Informe Preliminar de Trabajadores Centroamericanos a la República Mexicana." Mexico: CENIET.

Part III

The Emerging International
Division of Labor

9

Labor, Migrants and Industrial Restructuring in Electronics

M. Patricia Fernández Kelly

Introduction

The North American Free Trade Agreement (NAFTA) can be seen as the latest outcome in a process of internationalization that materialized in the 1960s. Over the past 25 years, the adjustments made by electronics production have foreshadowed distinctive features of contemporary competition on a global scale, including the movement of operations to overseas locations, the downsizing of domestic firms, the reliance on international and domestic subcontracting, and the targeting of new labor pools formed by immigrants, ethnic minorities and women. Understanding how electronics production has developed and met the challenges of internationalization can help us elucidate the probable effects of, and policy alternatives to, NAFTA.

According to some, the electronics industry is bringing forth a postindustrial era distinguished by an abundance of technical and professional jobs (Reich, 1983). The high levels of skill and flexible specialization that distinguish the electronics industry are presumed to facilitate egalitarian styles of management and workers' autonomy. High-tech industries have thus been praised as harbingers of prosperity and social progress (Bradshaw and Freeman, 1984; Glassmeier *et al.*, 1983; Castells, 1985).

Less sanguine, however, is the alternative view that the electronics industry reflects declining terms of employment for workers, including the erosion of trade unions, the constriction of blue-collar employment, and investors' diminishing loyalties to national interests (MacEwen and Tabb, 1989). Able to hopscotch from country to country in search of comparatively cheap labor and more pliable conditions for production, electronics firms need not feel responsible for the well-being of particular communities.

The removal of trade barriers will have little effect on the international leanings of the electronics industry. It is true that William Shockley's momentous invention led to the rise of silicon empires in the Santa Clara Valley, California, and in other areas throughout the United States. Nevertheless, it is also true that three years after its establishment in 1960, Fairchild Electronics, a pioneer firm and the successor of Shockley Electronics, relocated all its assembly operations first to South Korea and later to Taiwan, setting an irreversible trend (Siegel, 1984). In the succeeding years, the electronics industry deepened overseas investments to maintain its competitive edge in U.S. and world markets. Furthermore it was the electronics industry, in tandem with garment manufacturing, that gave rise to the world's largest export-processing zone: Mexico's *maquiladora* program (Sklair, 1989; Fatemi, 1990). Thus, the reorganization of production in electronics – including the growth of complementary domestic and overseas operations – may be seen as an antecedent of conditions that are likely to be generalized by the NAFTA.

Why are electronics companies continuing to produce in the United States despite the advantages derived from overseas investments? What lessons can be learned from this process that might illuminate the potential consequences of continued elimination of barriers to investment as contemplated by NAFTA? To what extent will the fledgling Mexican electronics industry represent a competitive threat to its counterpart in the United States? In partial answer to those questions, this paper offers a summary of findings from a study of electronics firms in New York and Southern California, as well as a brief assessment of the Mexican electronics industry.

To understand the relationship between industrial adjustment, immigration, and Hispanic women's employment in garment and electronics, we combined the strengths of survey and ethnographic research and took a comparative approach.[1] We collected information on a random sample of 200 electronics firms evenly divided in the two locations: New York and Southern California. We also examined existing studies on the organization of the electronics industry in Mexico. Our goal was to understand processes of industrial reorganization, but also to assess the effect of those transformations on workers employed in electronics.

NEW YORK METROPOLITAN AREA

Our study focused on the broader New York-New Jersey metropolitan area because, historically and structurally, those two labor markets have been intertwined.[2]

Overview

The New York electronics industry has experienced dramatic changes over the last 20 years. An early clustering of large, vertically integrated corporations in Manhattan has given way to a multiplicity of small companies in New York's periphery, including neighboring counties in New Jersey. Relocation within the region paralleled changes within firms, especially regarding the size of operations, types of products, and level of specialization. Reductions in plant size, an emphasis on tailored production, and a reliance on contracted work furnished new competitive advantages.

Throughout the 1980s, popular and specialized writings gave attention to smallness in plant proportions with some celebrating and others deriding downsizing. Supporters pointed to the competitive gains of lean and mean operations. Detractors saw small firms as potential sweatshops, an indication of debasement in the terms of production and employment. To some extent both interpretations were accurate. Many firms in New

[1]Between 1985 and 1988 Saskia Sassen (Professor of Urban Planning, Graduate School of Architecture and Planning, Columbia University) and the author served as principal investigators of such a project (Fernández-Kelly and Sassen, 1991).

[2]Moreover, under this broad definition of the metropolitan area we included Nassau and Suffolk Counties in New York State which recently have become a separate SMSA. We also included three additional New Jersey counties (Middlesex, Essex and Union) besides the SMSA county, Bergen. The reasons for expanding the geographic area to include Long Island and the additional counties in New Jersey were: a) the high rate of growth of the Hispanic population in these areas; b) the existence of significant concentrations of manufacturing activity in the region; and c) the possibility that the native population segments residing in those locations might not constitute a suitable labor supply for these manufacturing jobs, given the predominantly middle-class profiles of populations residing in Nassau and the growing demand for factory workers in the same county.

York exemplify the tendency towards *manucrafting*, a term used by an owner in our sample to describe his work: a paradoxical combination of advanced technology, customization, and labor-intensive production. Other small firms in our study, including home operations, illustrate the potential for the evasion of labor and tax regulations and for the deterioration of labor conditions.

Findings

After conducting a pilot study we randomly selected 100 firms for in-depth examination.[3] The largest concentration of firms in our sample was in communications equipment and electronic components, each accounting for almost one-third of the firms studied. The next largest concentration was in computers, peripherals and semiconductors with 15 and 11 percent of the sample, respectively. Since our sample was randomly selected, we can state with assurance that electronics in the New York area has a strong concentration in basic branches of the industry.

Over 70 percent of the firms in our sample had previously been located elsewhere, while 27 percent had not. The high incidence of previous location conforms with several other patterns our study uncovered, particularly the fact that many of these firms have actually broken off from larger firms that either closed down or moved to low-wage locations elsewhere in the country or offshore.

The vast majority of firms in our sample were independently owned. This held true for 78 firms, while the next largest group were subsidiaries – seventeen firms in all. The remaining firms were either publicly owned, or headquarters or divisions of multisite firms. This underscores the transformative character of electronics production in New York. An earlier stage characterized by the presence of large, vertically integrated firms has been followed by the expansion of a sector formed almost entirely by small, flexible, and highly specialized firms. Changes in type of production and the shrinking of plant size have occurred side by side with locational shifts from a core represented by Manhattan to its periphery represented by outer fringe counties, including some in the state of New Jersey.

Employment size ranged from just a handful of workers to a maximum of 2,350 employees. At least two firms had no employees; the

---

[3]The sample that controls for locations, SIC (Standard Industrial Classifications, U.S. Department of Labor) and size. A detailed description of the project's methodology is included in Fernández Kelly and Sassen (1991).

owner basically did all the work. These owners described themselves as inventors who started in their own garages. Typically, several of the smaller firms displayed the same pattern: an inventor and owner of a firm who employed just a few workers. The mean employment size of the firms in our sample was 127. This was a significantly smaller size by comparison to the California sample reviewed later in this report.

Over half of the firms customize less than 10 percent of their production. On the other hand, 30 percent customize half of their output and 17 percent, all of their production. On average, one-third of all output was produced to specification. Fully 88 percent of the firms in our sample designed at least some of the products they manufactured. Only 16 percent did not do any designing.

Almost two-thirds of the firms in the New York sample take work orders from other companies under contract; the remaining third do not. Two-thirds of these firms in turn contract work out to other firms. While many of the firms are contractors, they subcontract to a very limited extent.

We asked our respondents whether any of the subcontractors they used worked at home. Fully one-third of the respondents said they did subcontracting with homeworkers. However, 22 percent of our respondents did not answer this question. The fact that one-third of the firms in this sample used industrial homework points to the nature of the work being done in the New York area. This is a subject we return to later in more detail.

Judging from our New York sample, automated manufacturing is not widespread. Almost half of the firms had no automated work procedures. Only a handful of firms had over 20 percent automation. About 40 percent of all firms had between 10 and 50 percent automation in procedures. The mean degree of automation was about 18 percent.

The vast majority of the firms in our sample, over 80 percent, were not unionized. Only 17 percent worked with unions. We obtained from our respondents a clear impression that the small size of the firms and the fact that a majority are independently owned and are run by their owners were somehow seen as facilitating the relation with workers and making unions unnecessary. Our respondents, mostly owners, claimed that there was no need for workers' organizations because they disposed of other mechanisms for working out conflicts at the workplace.

About one-half of the firms in our sample had labor forces of which 50 percent were women. About 10 percent of the firms had between 80 and 90 percent women workers. The mean incidence of female workers was well over one-third of all workers in the firms surveyed.

By comparison to Southern California, the electronics firms in our sample employed smaller numbers of Hispanics, both foreign-born and U.S.-born: 16 percent. The percentage of female Hispanics employed in these firms was 11.3 percent. These firms employed few blacks and Asians, 7 percent and 0.5 percent, respectively.

In summary, our research in New York indicates that reorganization rather than decline has characterized the recent evolution of the electronics industry in that location. Restructuring has encompassed shifts in the spatial distribution of firms of various types and a movement towards specialized activities which in many cases resemble a new form of skilled "artisanal" production. Many of the new entrepreneurs are individuals previously associated with larger firms which pioneered development in the electronics industry. They now own small firms especially skilled in areas such as design and tend to subcontract for a variety of contractors while at the same time "putting-out" part of the production process to smaller, often informalized establishments or homeworkers. An important finding of this portion of our research was the identification of a lower echelon characterized by the widespread presence of industrial homeworkers in electronics. Although Hispanics form a fairly small segment of the electronics labor force, women represent 50 percent of those employed in the industry.

SOUTHERN CALIFORNIA

Under the term Southern California we included three counties: Los Angeles, Orange, and San Diego, comprising 9,121 square miles, that is, 5.7% of the total area of the state. Although proportionally small, 48% of the state's population lives in this southern portion. The 1980 census calculates the Hispanic population in California to be 19.2% of the total. In Los Angeles, Hispanics constitute 27.6% of the population, in Orange 14.8% and in San Diego 14.7%.

Overview

Characteristic of the area is its proximity to Mexico. The San Diego-Tijuana border is the busiest in the world in terms of the movement of commodities, information, and labor. Historically, Southern California has been an agricultural emporium linked to the employment of immigrants – first from Asia and, for the last 30 years, from Mexico. In recent times, manufacturing, defense, and aerospace have accounted for a significant proportion of the area's economy.

California has enjoyed prosperity throughout its history. However, it has also been negatively affected by shifts in its economic base that resulted in the loss of manufacturing employment and the growth of services. The growth of high-tech industries occurred within that context. The original expansion of Silicon Valley in Northern California was followed by a gradual movement of electronics companies to the southern portion of the state. That movement also paralleled restructuring strategies that have combined overseas relocation, principally to Asia and the U.S.-Mexico border, and the incorporation of Hispanic workers – many of them immigrants – in domestic points. There is a widespread belief that Santa Clara (Silicon) Valley is home to the largest number of electronics firms in the state. In fact, it is within the boundaries of Los Angeles County that the largest cluster of electronics companies in the nation is found. During the 1970s, the most intense growth spurt occurred in Orange County.

Findings

The findings reported here are based on interviews conducted with a random sample of 100 electronics employers in Los Angeles, Orange, and San Diego counties between 1985 and 1988.[4] Our objective was to obtain in-depth information about the types of adjustment that electronics companies have made in order to meet changing conditions of production both domestically and internationally. Electronics firms have followed a series of paths to reduce costs, improve competitiveness in the domestic and world markets, and make conditions for production more flexible.

The average size of electronics manufacturing plants in Southern California is just over 76,000 square feet; they had average yearly sales of $66 million between 1985 and 1987. The typical firm employed 446 workers and 41.5% of its total costs went to labor. Only 3% of the companies were fully automated, with 12.6% of employees in research

---

[4]The sample was randomly selected from sources such as official listings of firms, census reports, telephone directories and specialized directories of relevant organizations including the local chapters of the American Electronics Association.

and development and 36.7% in direct production. Approximately 20% of the firms surveyed in the random sample had 50 employees or fewer; 7% had 10 employees or fewer. Given the presence on our sample of a few giant manufacturers, these figures convey a somewhat lopsided image of Southern California. Small firms represent a growing stratum characterized by the presence of native-born owners but also by an emerging class of ethnic and immigrant entrepreneurs, mostly Hispanic and Southeast Asian.

The profile above shows that, contrary to a popular impression, the Southern California electronics industry is characterized by comparatively low levels of automation, and devotes a considerable percentage of its operation costs to labor-intensive activities. In fact, direct production accounts for the largest proportion of employment in these electronics firms.

The assembly of semiconductor components of various types represents the predominant type of production in Southern California. More than half of the firms were involved in the manufacture of hybrid microcircuits. This percentage varied when large firms were viewed separately from small firms. More than 60 percent of large firms but almost 82 percent of small firms (those with fewer than 50 workers) were dedicated to microcircuit manufacture.

Very large firms have the largest number of employees, the highest percentage of employees in research and development, and the smallest proportion of labor costs as part of total expenditures. By contrast, small firms have lower sales, a higher percentage of labor costs (almost 50 percent), and the largest percentage of all employees involved in assembly. Small firms are the most vulnerable in electronics production and, theoretically, it may be conceived as a locus for informalization.

There were 164 production workers in the average firm. Adjusted hourly wages between 1985 and 1987 were low – between $6.69 and $7.93. Almost 60 percent of direct production workers were women and more than one-third of those were Hispanic. The small and potentially informalized establishments had the largest proportion of Hispanic women involved in direct production (48.6%).

A large number of workers engaged in electronics assembly are native- and foreign-born Hispanics. Slightly over 23 percent of the Southern California population is Hispanic but 44.1% of direct production workers in our sample and upwards of 57 percent in our subsample, formed by small firms cited for Labor Code violations, belong to the same ethnic group. Perhaps more significantly, almost 35 percent of direct production workers in the sample are foreign-born Hispanics. There are fewer immigrants in very large firms (30%) and a larger proportion in small informalized establishments (43.8%). Although Asians represent 5% of the Southern California population, 20% of direct production workers in our sample are Asian. The demographic balance is reversed in the case of African-Americans who represent 12% of the Southern California population and almost half of the labor force, but only 3% of direct production workers in electronics.

The findings reported above suggest that, independently of their level of representation in the population at large, certain groups, namely Hispanics and Asians, are more likely to perform assembly work in electronics than others; for example, African-Americans. In other words, labor market selectivity does not operate randomly.

There is disagreement about the factors that explain the incorporation into or exclusion of particular ethnic groups in certain types of production. Students of immigration have noted the importance of social networks as mechanisms that provide access to employment to newly arrived immigrants. The same observation applies to women and to native-born ethnic populations who are more likely to derive their information about job opportunities from members of the group to which they belong. Interviews with electronics assemblers in Los Angeles, San Diego, and Orange Counties suggest that word of mouth is the most common means for learning about employment opportunities.

In addition to the connections established by workers with members of a common ethnic, immigrant, or gender group, we considered also the preferences of employers. From that vantage point, the contrast between the level of incorporation of blacks and Hispanics in the Southern California electronics industry is related to varying perceptions about the groups in question. Managers stated their preference for Hispanic workers, particularly the foreign-born. These groups are seen by employers as more "diligent," "hard-working," and "loyal" than native-born Americans, especially those of African descent. The opinion emerged in several of our conversations that Asians are almost as desirable as Hispanics for assembly work. However, employers complained that Asians tended to be ruthlessly competitive and, therefore, less loyal to individual companies. Echoing a widespread feeling, a manager told us that "In a flash, Asians will drop us for a 10 cent difference in wages." African-Americans are generally assumed to be less reliable, more likely to make demands, to claim rights, and to seek the backing of unions. Native-born Americans tend to have a keen awareness of their citizen status and of the rights accruing from that status. Citizen identities are embodied in aspirations for higher wages and benefits, upgraded working conditions, and stable employment. By contrast, awareness of citizen rights tends to be muted among immigrants and refugees. The undocumented status of many of the former diminish their ability or desire to make demands vis-à-vis employers. Thus, from the testimonies of managers we may envision a continuum of "employee desirability" at whose opposite extremes are located foreign-born persons and working-class African-Americans.

Labor unions have made the loss of jobs resulting from foreign competition a central issue in their agendas. However, most of the employers interviewed in our sample did not share these concerns. The reason appears to be that a large number of companies represented in this survey have turned toward tailored production and customization as a path to remaining competitive and to shelter themselves against the onslaught of large-scale standardized production. Almost 59 percent of companies in our sample offer products manufactured to specification. Larger firms exhibit an even higher tendency toward customization: 70 percent.

Customization and flexible specialization have allowed many firms a rare privilege within a highly competitive domestic and international environment. However, versatility has also been enhanced by other means, primarily the reliance of electronics firms on a complex chain formed by subcontracting arrangements. We found various forms of subcontracting, including licensing agreements, to be the backbone of the electronics industry. More than half of all companies rely heavily on various forms of domestic and international subcontracting: some firms subcontract to operations in foreign locations and to small independent firms in Southern California. The trend is towards a combination of strategies rather than full reliance on any particular form of production.

In addition, electronics companies depend on the intermittent use of homeworkers. Homeworkers are used by 13.2% of firms in our sample and by fully 30% of small firms cited by the Wage and Hour Division. This finding is in agreement with our expectation that producers at the lower end of the industrial structure – many of whom are Hispanic or Southeast Asian entrepreneurs – would be more likely to rely on the services of homeworkers. Although by comparison to the total electronics labor force, industrial home workers are a minority, their presence adds nuance to the portrayal of electronics manufacturing as a high-tech sector. Electronics is a many-layered industry that relies on a complex series of strategies to maximize access to markets, flexibility, and responsiveness to the specific needs of customers.

Subcontracting is used as a mechanism to lower production costs by displacing unskilled and semiskilled operations to small independent firms specializing in individual tasks such as coiling, sorting, counting and finishing. These firms are also the most likely to hire vulnerable workers including immigrants and women. On the other hand, subcontracting leads toward the decentralization of production, affording companies greater flexibility in adapting to fluctuating market conditions. Flexibility in production is the primary motivation cited by Southern California firms that subcontract. Subcontracting as a means to reduce costs was stressed by less than 11 percent of the firms in our sample. The trend appears to be toward the use of subcontracting mainly to increase flexibility in production and adjust to cyclical market demands.

MEXICO

Electronics products are not a major portion of Mexico's exports. Primary commodities such as crude petroleum, automotive parts and products, coffee, iron ore, textiles, and various foodstuffs and beverages represent greater opportunities for international competitiveness for Mexico (United Nations, 1991a: 131–135). Nonetheless, over the last twenty years, the Mexican government has attempted to buttress electronics production. At the same time, the U.S. and Mexican electronics industries have become increasingly interrelated through trade and investment. Mexico was the sixth largest trading partner of the United States for electronic goods in 1989; the United States was Mexico's largest trading partner. Trade in electronics between the two countries totalled $8.1 billion in 1989, with the U.S. posting a $1.3 billion deficit (Wilson, 1992; Koido, n.d.).

From an industry dominated by domestic firms and concentrated on the production of consumer electronics and components, Mexico's electronics industry has since developed into one characterized by foreign direct investment and diversification into many product areas including telecommunications, computers, consumer electronics, and electrical equipment. Electronics production now generates approximately 3 percent of Mexico's GDP. Factory shipments totalled $6.5 billion in 1989, and employment surpassed 250,000 workers. Nevertheless, limitations in technology, worker skill levels, and infrastructure will continue to constrain the development of a more robust electronics industry. In addition, the Mexican electronics industry is dwarfed by that of the United States, which had domestic shipments of over $190 billion in 1989 and employed over 2 million workers (Wilson, 1992). In other words, while employment in U.S. electronics is eight times that in Mexico, U.S. output is almost thirty times higher, signalling increased worker productivity in the United States owed in part to more automation in U.S. plants and to the types of products manufactured by U.S. workers.

Because the Mexican government has long considered electronics a key industry, it has instituted policies to attract foreign investment in local manufacturing. During the 1970s, some of those policies reflected earlier aspirations of import – substitution industrialization and attempts to replace imports with locally manufactured goods. Other policies, best exemplified by the *maquiladora* program, aimed to encourage investment in export-oriented industries.

Under protectionist trade policies, domestic production of consumer electronics flourished through an infusion of foreign technology and capital. Local manufacturers supported a large domestic supplier base that produced 75 to 90 percent of the components used in Mexican televisions during the mid-1980s. However, inefficiencies in the supplier base constrained the growth of domestic production. With the removal of import barriers in 1987, foreign competition flooded the market. By 1988, only 36 percent of the 43 plants that had manufactured consumer electronics in 1981 were still operating, and employment had fallen by a factor of three, to 2,340 employees. Total domestic manufacture of consumer electronics was expected to reach half of its 1986 level in 1991.

We can anticipate that, without a competitive supplier base, growth of an indigenous consumer electronics industry in Mexico will be slow at best. In fact, continued trade liberalization would more likely expose Mexican industry to increased competition from the United States. A reduction in tariffs under NAFTA would tend to further increase U.S. exports to Mexico.[5] However, the Mexican market for consumer electronics is considerably smaller than the U.S. market (almost $18 billion in 1991), and few additional jobs are likely to be created in the United States as a result of trade liberalization.

Mexican *maquiladoras* have to be considered in the assessment of potential effects resulting from trade liberalization. *Maquiladoras* have played a significant role in maintaining Mexico's economic stability. They generate about one-half of Mexico's industrial output and employ two-thirds of its work force, or roughly 200,000 workers. As of 1990, one-quarter of all *maquiladora* plants operating in Mexico were producing electrical and electronics products. It is important to point out that the success of the *maquiladora* sector is a result of interdependency with affiliated U.S. producers. Both the manufacture and the marketing of *maquiladora* products are dependent upon the resources and networks of U.S. affiliates.

Much of Mexico's industry is subject to strict statutes limiting the degree of foreign involvement and investment. Nonetheless, because of its outstanding economic impact, *maquiladora* operations in electronics have been exempted from many of those restrictions. Producers in the *maquiladora* sector are allowed to import inputs and production machinery duty-free and are exempted from limits on foreign ownership. Low labor costs and close proximity to the United States, the world's largest market for electronic products, make Mexico an attractive site for assembly operations. Electronic and electrical products account for nearly 45% of the output and 37 percent of the total employment in Mexico's *maquiladora* industry; in 1990 over 500 *maquiladora* electronics plants produced goods valued at $6.1 billion. Moreover, Mexico's limits on foreign ownership were removed on the production of most electronics products in early 1989 as a concession to the government's recent

---

[5]"U.S. trade in electronic equipment with Mexico grew rapidly during the 1980s, although it was marked by a U.S. deficit of $1.3 billion on total trade estimated at $8.1 billion in 1989 [the result of, among other things,the discrepancy in tariff amounts between the United States and Mexico]. The nominal U.S. tariff on Mexican electronic products averages 5% ad valorem, although some duty rates are as high as 15%. The effective trade-weighted duty averages only 2%, given the large portion of the trade that enters at reduced duties under either the *maquiladora* or Generalized System of Preferences programs. By contrast, Mexico's imports of electronic products from the United States are subject to average tariffs estimated at 16% ad valorem." Largely a result of Mexico's Buy National campaign, these high import tariffs serve to protect local Mexican industries, but they can also harm local production efforts by inhibiting the imports of many raw materials and production equipment (U.S. International Trade Commission, 1991: 4–25).

efforts at economic liberalization. Industry exemptions for electronics firms, as well as Mexico's very loose regulatory policies, make the country a very cost efficient location for foreign interests.

Production in electronics *maquiladoras* is less labor-intensive than in other sectors, including autos. Nevertheless, direct production labor accounts for nearly 80 percent of employment, a figure that has declined only slightly in recent years.[6] Wages and benefits in electronics *maquiladoras* averaged just $1.60 an hour in 1990 for direct laborers, about half the level in the Asian Newly Industrialized Countries, and one-tenth to one-seventh the level in the United States. Reliance on low-skill workers has limited *maquiladora* production to two types of electronics products: finished goods with high labor content and low profit margins, and labor intensive components or subassemblies to be shipped to the United States for incorporation into final products.

Investments in the *maquiladora* industry have been dominated by cost considerations. With wages one-seventh of those for comparable jobs in the United States, Mexican *maquiladora* labor has been used by many U.S. companies to reduce manufacturing costs and fend off competition from overseas rivals, particularly those in the Far East. However, Mexico has the added advantage of being near the U.S. market. The proximity of Mexico reduces not only time to the U.S. market, but also such logistics as coordinating design and production for U.S. firms operating overseas production sites. Time savings can result in cost savings. Products that are shipped from Mexico can enter the U.S. market in about one week compared to approximately eight weeks if shipped from Asia. Thus, *maquiladora* electronics firms can be viewed as competing directly with both U.S. and Asian jobs and can be considered more representative of the cost-driven investments likely to be seen in Mexico in the wake of NAFTA than are the investments already in place in Mexico's domestic industry.

By itself NAFTA is unlikely to radically change the patterns of investment and industrial development in the Mexican electronics industry. For the most part, these changes would have occurred in the absence of NAFTA and as a result of Mexico's unilateral attempts at market liberalization and the attempts by United States and other manufacturers to improve their competitive standing by following the

[6]This is a much higher fraction than is typical in the United States, where production workers account for only 38% of employment in computers and peripherals and 68% in consumer electronics. (*See* U.S. Department of Commerce, 1991: 27–31, 37–144.)

maquiladora strategy. On the other hand, NAFTA may, in some cases, speed up the flow of investments to Mexico by reducing uncertainty about the future of Mexico's development policy.

NAFTA includes provisions that will ease trade restrictions in all directions (U.S. International Trade Commission). As the United States is already one of Mexico's largest export markets for electronics products, the agreement would enhance the already existing relationship and provide a cost effective way by which Mexico could expand its present market. NAFTA is also likely to stimulate growth in the Mexican electronics industry by encouraging increasing amounts of direct foreign investment.[7] Improvements of local technology and industry could follow, making electronics production a fulcrum for future technological development in Mexico.

IMPLICATIONS OF FREE TRADE

NAFTA has been favorably greeted in some circles and received with alarm in others. For its supporters, the initiative represents a path for the elimination of all possible barriers to investment which in turn will lead to economic vitality and the consolidation of a vibrant consumer market on both sides of the U.S.-Mexico border. To critics, principally represented by unions in the United States, NAFTA will accentuate deindustrialization and bring about the loss of thousands of jobs in the United States as well as further debasement of wages and environmental pollution in Mexico. Which one of these two perspectives is likely to become reality after the approval of the North American Free Trade Agreement?

Our research on the electronics industry suggests that neither unqualified optimism nor apocalyptic forecasts are warranted. NAFTA is less about commerce than about investment. Its main effect will be not just to bolster trade but to further improve the conditions under which international capital is deployed. To the extent that NAFTA advances economic internationalization, it will continue to represent a massive redisciplining of labor that includes the weakening of unions in the name of flexibility in production. It is naive to believe that the same

---

[7]There are already visible changes. As a result of the economic liberalization effort spearheaded by Miguel de La Madrid, "Mexico's economy grew by about 3.9 percent in 1990, up from 2.9 percent in 1989 and 1.4 percent in 1988. Inflation was 30 percent, down from 160 percent in 1987. The Mexican peso has been appreciating in real terms (after taking inflation into account), gaining 10 percent relative to the U.S. dollar in 1990" (*Business America*, April 8, 1991, p. 12). *See also* World Bank (1984: 47–48).

initiative will not entail significant dangers of environmental debasement as well. The recent experience of the electronics industry suggests that these are all likely possibilities.

On the other hand, our study of industrial restructuring among electronics firms in New York and Southern California indicates that the outcome of NAFTA might be more complex and nuanced than either of the two scenarios sketched above indicate. There will be economic losers as well as winners. The movement of operations across international borders has been a widespread trend for three decades. The implementation of NAFTA is not likely to have a major impact upon that trend. Moreover, our research also suggests that capital migration and the establishment of overseas operations does not have to lead inevitably to the disappearance of productive activities in the United States. The process of internationalization likely to consolidate through the implementation of NAFTA has encompassed domestic rearrangements of production that include a broad range of adjustments linking specialization, just-in-time production, the streamlining of operations, subcontracting, and the targeting of new pools of labor. As a result it is improbable that the implementation of NAFTA will have a major impact upon large electronics manufacturers. On the other hand, the liberalization of the economy entailing the eradication of barriers to investment might have a positive effect upon small companies in the United States. Small, highly specialized firms like the ones found through our research in Southern California and New York, have been shaped by a highly competitive environment and will benefit from the opening of new markets.[8]

In the short term, U.S. computer manufacturers will be unlikely to establish production capacity in Mexico, even with a North American free trade agreement. Potential cost savings do not appear adequate to justify greater separation of business units. Leaders in the computer industry such as IBM, Apple, and Compaq have continued to differentiate their products through technology leadership rather than cost leadership. The Mexican market for computers, while growing, is small

---

[8]According to a recent article, "Clever design and management is helping small American companies make up for lack of size. LSI Logic in Milpitas, California, a maker of customized chips, can now produce chips smaller than those produced by the Japanese. Cypress Semiconductor, which competes in high-speed memory chips, gives factory managers an ownership stake in the factory . . . . Micron Technology of Boise, Idaho, is managing to remain profitable in the D-RAM business, the Japanese bastion. The secret is that Micron designs its chips to be smaller and to require fewer manufacturing steps than those of its competitors" (*The New York Times*, April 9, 1992).

compared to the U.S. market. By 1992, Mexico's market was expected to surpass $1 billion; the U.S. market is projected to reach $62 billion.

In a similar vein, Mexico does not provide an optimal environment for large-scale production in advanced semiconductors. Mexico has more to offer foreign investors as a location for making peripherals than for either chips or computers themselves. Direct labor represents a large portion of manufacturing costs for peripherals. But here Mexico must compete with the Far East; in fact, Mexico finds itself competing more with the Far East for jobs than with the United States. And the competition between Mexico and the United States is in labor intensive processes – those carried out in the United States by Mexican and Asian workers, particularly women.

In order to understand the potential effects of NAFTA, and to fashion fully appropriate policy responses when the treaty goes into effect, it will be necessary to consider a wide range of issues. This paper points to the wide range of interdependent social and economic patterns in the emerging North American system. Although NAFTA's direct effects will be primarily on capital flows, it will have very important indirect effects, all of which will be conditioned by other policies and circumstances. Thus, for example, international migration trends will be affected by capital investment decisions, but migration policies will have an independent influence on the availability of certain kinds of labor in the United States and Canada, and in this way will also shape the kinds of investment made under NAFTA. Laws and policies affecting how minorities are treated and their access to job retraining and schooling will have a joint impact on migration and investment decisions. Policies affecting the opportunities for minority women in the United States and Canada will be particularly important in this regard. In sum, NAFTA not only generates important questions with respect to its direct impacts, but it generates equally important questions regarding current challenges to social justice and equality in North America as an increasingly integrated system.

REFERENCES

Bradshaw, T. K., and M. Freeman
1984   "The Future of the Electronics Industry in California Communities." Institute of Governmental Studies, University of California.

Castells, M.
1985   "Towards the Informational City, High Technology, Economic Change and Spatial
        Structure: Some Exploratory Hypotheses." Working Paper No. 430. Institute of
        Urban and Regional Development, University of California at Berkeley.

Fatemi, K., ed.
1990   The Maquiladora Industry: Economic Solution or Problem. New York: Praeger.

Fernández Kelly, M. P., and S. Sassen
1991   A Collaborative Study of Hispanic Women in Garment and Electronics Industries:
        Final Report Presented to the Ford, Revson, and Tinker Foundations. Baltimore,
        MD: The Johns Hopkins University Institute for Policy Studies.

Glassmeier, A., A. R. Markusen and P. Hall
1983   "Defining High Technology Industries," Working Paper No. 407. Institute of
        Urban and Regional Development, University of California at Berkeley.

Koido, A.
n.d.   "Between Two Forces of Restructuring: U.S.-Japan Competition and the
        Transformation of Mexico's Maquiladora Industry." Ph.D. dissertation, The
        Johns Hopkins University.

MacEwan, A., and W. K. Tabb, eds.
1989   Instability and Change in the World Economy. New York: Monthly Review
        Press.

Reich, R. B.
1983   The Next American Frontier. New York: Penquin.

Siegal, L.
1984   Delicate Bonds: The Semiconductor Industry. Mountain View, CA: Pacific
        Studies Center.

Sklair, L.
1989   Assembling for Development. The Maquila Industry in Mexico and the United
        States. Boston, MA: Unwin Hyman.

United Nations
1991a   Statistical Yearbook for Latin America and the Caribbean. New York: United
        Nations.

——   1991b   Transnational Corporations and the Transfer of New and Emerging Technolo-
        gies to Developing Countries. New York: United Nations.

U.S. Department of Commerce
1991   U.S. Industrial Outlook '92. Washington, DC: Department of Commerce.

U.S. International Trade Commission
1992   Economy-Wide Modelling of the Economic Implications of a FTA with Mexico,
        and a NAFTA with Canada and Mexico. Report on Investigation No.
        332–317 under Section 332 of the Tariff Act of 1930. USITC Publication
        No. 2516. Washington, DC: U.S. International Trade Commission. May.

——   1991   The Likely Impact on the United States of a Free Trade Agreement with Mexico.
        Washington, DC: U.S. International Trade Commission.

Wilson, P.
1992 "NAFTA and the Electronic Industry in Mexico." Report prepared for the U.S. Office of Technology Assessment under Contract No. H3-7200. February.

World Bank
1984 *Local Development and Exports of Technology: The Comparative Advantage of Argentina, Brazil, India, The Republic of Korea, and Mexico.* Washington, DC: World Bank Staff Working Papers.

10

Female Migrant Labor in North America: Trends and Issues for the 1990s

Monica Boyd

Introduction

This paper examines the employment of immigrant women in North America with particular attention to the influence of economic restructuring. Evidence reviewed below suggests that immigrant women who are recent arrivals and/or from areas other than North America or Europe are most likely to be employed in low-wage, low-skill jobs in sectors of falling employment. Insofar as economic restructuring in North America means an industry separation of the labor market into "good jobs" and "bad jobs" (Economic Council of Canada, 1989), it is clear that "bad" jobs in fields such as textiles, clothing manufacturing, and personal services will be filled disproportionately by immigrant women. One may therefore conclude that extensive and effective training and other labor market adjustment policies are required to overcome the potentially negative effects of NAFTA on immigrant women. The study concludes with a discussion of the paradox created by industrial policy and immigration policy developments, with emphasis on their implications for future migration flows.

WOMEN AS INTERNATIONAL MIGRANTS TO NORTH AMERICA

Although considerable female migration occurs within major world regions, the largest flows in recent history tend to be to traditional settlement countries such as Australia, Canada and the United States.[1] By the 1980s, the United States was the country with the largest numbers of foreign-born females – nearly 7.5 million – while Canada ranked fourth with a population of nearly 2 million foreign-born females. In both countries, foreign-born females slightly outnumbered foreign-born men. The fact that females represented at least half of the foreign-born population in these two countries is neither new nor a regional aberration (Boyd, 1992a: Table 1; Houston, Kramer and Barrett, 1984; Tyree and Donato, 1986; United Nations, 1990). Figures for the top ten source countries for females admitted as permanent residents to Canada and the United States during the 1980s show that female immigrants frequently equalled or exceeded males in number (Table 1). These top ten source countries account for over half of the total female inflow to Canada and the United States during most of the 1980s.

Apart from revealing the frequent parity of females in immigration flows to North America, the data in Table 1 also indicate the changing origin characteristics of these females. Neither Canada nor any European country is among the top ten countries sending females to the United States between 1982 and 1989. For Canada, only Great Britain, Poland, and the United States are among the top ten, largely as a result of past and current economic linkages and migratory flows.[2] The top

---

[1] European countries have also been major receivers, partly as a result of the autonomous migration of women in the labor migration of the 1960s and early 1970s, but primarily as part of the resultant family reunification flows that followed male migration.

[2] Immigration from Poland reflects the ability of past migration streams to be self-sustaining when combined with facilitative immigration regulations. Until 1989 persons from Poland could enter Canada for humanitarian reasons. While they did not fall into the refugee class, immigration regulations permitted ministerial designation of certain groups as "designated groups" for whom humanitarian concerns would be grounds for entry. Relatives and church groups commonly played a role in sponsoring these groups. Following the rapprochement between Eastern and Western Europe, persons from Poland and other countries can no longer be admitted in the "designated group" category, and it seems likely that their numbers in annual flows will decline.

TABLE 1

TOP TEN COUNTRIES OF ORIGIN FOR FEMALES ADMITTED AS PERMANENT RESIDENTS TO CANADA AND THE UNITED STATES:
1981/1982–1989

To Canada: Place of Last Residence 1981–1989			To the United States: Country of Birth 1982–1989		
Rank Country	Females (N)	Females as Percent of Total	Rank Country	Females (N)	Females as Percent of Total
1 India	39,710	51.6	1 Mexico	389,819	44.9
2 Great Britain	39,634	52.8	2 Philippines	224,526	58.5
3 Hong Kong	38,442	51.0	3 Korea	151,206	56.8
4 Vietnam	32,063	47.1	4 Vietnam	127,695	43.1
5 Poland	30,616	47.3	5 China	109,140	53.0
6 China	30,477	53.6	6 India	102,423	49.3
7 United States	30,190	55.1	7 Dominican Republic	98,641	51.9
8 Philippines	29,757	58.7	8 Jamaica	85,152	52.0
9 Jamaica	17,967	57.0	9 El Salvador	64,933	51.7
10 Guyana	16,795	54.3	10 Cuba	61,863	45.1
Subtotal	310,073	52.6		1,415,398	49.5
All other countries	259,693	49.2		2,563,790	49.7
Top ten as percent of total female[a]		54.2			55.2

Source: Employment and Immigration Canada, *Immigration Statistics* (annual reports 1981–1989). U.S. Immigration and Naturalization Service, *Statistical Yearbook of the Immigration and Naturalization Service* (annual reports, 1982–1989).

[a]Calculated as subtotal divided by sum of (subtotal plus all other countries).

ten countries in fact are part of a more general pattern in which female and male migrants no longer primarily come from Canada to the United States (and vice versa), or from Europe. In this pattern historical/political ties underlie differences between Canada and the United States in the origins of previous and more recently arrived migrants. In Canada, female and male migrants are coming increasingly from Asian countries. While this trend also exists in the United States, the Mexican border and U.S. historical and political ties to the Caribbean underlie much higher inflows from Latin America and lower flows from Europe and the United Kingdom.[3]

[3]Boyd, 1992a; *see also* Table 1 (herein), where five Latin American/Caribbean countries are among the top ten source countries for females immigrating to the United States.

Theories of migration that incorporate models of global restructuring argue that origin and destination characteristics of migration flows reflect patterns of investment by firms and institutions in industrial nations (Bonacich and Cheng, 1984; R. Cohen, 1987; Fernàndez Kelly, 1989; Petras, 1981; Portes, 1981; Sassen, 1988, 1991; Zolberg, 1981; Zolberg, Suhrke and Aguayo, 1989). Investment in Third World export-based industries stimulates internal (and international) migration, establishes linkages between developed and less-developed countries, and creates unemployment either through agrarian displacement, employment policies (such as not hiring women past a certain age) or the subsequent flight of investment to cheaper wage zones. As a result of contacts, the infusion of ideology from industrial nations and the creation of surplus labor, international migration occurs in the direction of those developed countries from which the original investments came.

From the "global restructuring" perspective, international migration of women occurs partly because their employment in export industries such as electronics, garments, and toys locates them in information networks, exposes them to western ideologies and makes them vulnerable to unstable, fluctuating employment as investors relocate factories to places where wage rates are lower (Sassen, 1988: 114). In addition, the forces behind the migration of women are also indirect, through the impact of investment on the employment experiences and opportunities of men. Since international migration is often a form of household survival strategy, the migration of men often leads to the migration of accompanying female family members. This is especially true in movements to settlement countries such as the United States and Canada, where family reunification is a criterion for admission and where adults who are granted permanent residence may be accompanied by close family members. Most women enter as spouses or dependents of male migrants. However, their mode of entry does not imply that immigrant women are any less a supply of labor than men. Immigration entry data in receiving countries typically underestimate the labor force participation rates of foreign-born women when these women enter as accompanying family members. Once these "dependents" arrive, however, their labor force participation rates are frequently as high as or higher than those of the locally born female population. Further, given historical and contemporary devaluations of female labor relative to that of males, immigrant women represent a source of cheap labor. By implication, *family* migration is a way of enlarging a supply of cheap labor, directly if the principal (generally male) applicant in the family is less skilled, and indirectly if women immigrants enter as part of a family unit.

ECONOMIC RESTRUCTURING AND FEMALE LABOR

Much of the recent literature on global economy and international migration emphasizes the role of immigration in sustaining a less skilled pool of labor. This emphasis is supported by analyses that argue that the skill level of migrants is declining (Borjas, 1988). It is also strengthened by the pessimistic view of postindustrial society, in which new labor is needed to fill low-wage, low-skill "bad jobs" which emerge as the mirror image of the growth of a privatized sector of "good jobs."

Economic data document the dramatic transformation of Canadian and United States employment structures away from agriculture and into manufacturing and services during the twentieth century. By the 1950s in Canada and in the 1960s in the United States, the transformative sector, composed of manufacturing, mining and construction industries, peaked at about one-half of the total employment (Boyd, Mulvihill and Myles, 1991; Myles, Picot and Wannell, 1993; Singelmann, 1978). Thus the expression "the service economy" refers to the fact that employment in service industries is now the predominant form of employment in North American economies.

During the 1950s and 1960s the shift of employment to services was largely concentrated in business (producer services), in government employment (public administration) and in social services such as education and health. (For a more complete description of service industries, *see* Singlemann, 1978; Boyd, Mulvihill and Myles, 1991.) Employment in these service sectors in fact provided a large number of good jobs. More recently, however, the changing industrial structure of employment has involved two developments that create concern (Myles, Picot and Wannell, 1993). First, there has been an absolute, as opposed to a relative, decline, in employment in manufacturing.[4]

---

[4]During the second half of the twentieth century, the proportion of jobs in manufacturing declined as a result of very substantial increases in employment in the service industries. However, because the manufacturing sector continued to grow, although at a lower rate than service industries, the total numbers of those employed in manufacturing continued to increase. This changed by the

Second, although growth has continued in all service industries, substantial growth has occurred in retail services and consumer services (which includes personal service, accommodation and eating, and entertainment), while social services and public administration are generally characterized by many "good jobs," retail and consumer services are widely characterized by a large number of low-wage and low-skill jobs. Thus, the shift of employment within the service industries toward more jobs in consumer and retail services implies altered, and diminished, working conditions and wages (Boyd, 1991a; Myles and Fawcett, 1990; Myles, Picot, and Wannell, 1993).

In popular usage, the term "economic restructuring" refers to deindustrialization (*i.e.*, the actual loss of jobs in manufacturing) and to the expansion of low-skill, low-wage service jobs. However, the term also includes a third component of change: notably, restructuring of employment *within* industries. In their most recent research on the disappearing middle in wage distributions, Myles, Picot and Wannell (1993) observe that Canadian and American studies alike show that job losses and gains are caused primarily by the restructuring of employment within industries, a point missed by the emphasis on the interindustrial shift of employment. Further, they argue that it is this interfirm restructuring within industries (*i.e.*, intra-industry change) rather than interindustry shifts in employment, that has produced a more polarized distribution of earnings.

Underlying the earnings redistribution is a fundamental restructuring of the labor process. This restructuring includes deskilling, routinization of certain tasks and automation of others; the growth of nonunion work as well as part-time work, subcontracting, and informal work; and in the increasing use of groups divided by gender, race and nativity as sources of cheap labor and as mechanisms of labor control. These forms of restructuring of the labor process have been extensively discussed with reference to the use of female migrant labor in North America (Fernàndez Kelly, 1989; Fernàndez Kelly and Garcia, 1985, 1988; Gannage, 1986; Sassen, 1988, 1991; Tienda, Jensen and Bach, 1984).

As these analysts note, not all firms have used off-shore labor to lower their wage bill. In some cases, the nature of the activity defies moving

---

1980s. In Canada, the jobs lost during the recession of 1981–1982 in manufacturing did not return to their 1981 levels until 1989, and then fell below that 1981 level in the recession of 1990–1991 (Myles, Picot and Wannell, 1993).

production outside North America. Accommodation, entertainment, retail, hospital and cleaning services must all be provided by local workers (*see* Sassen, 1991). In other cases, notably the electronics and garment industries, some firms have moved to sites outside North America. However, others have sought new mechanisms for lessening the price of domestic labor, including expanded use of subcontracting, informal work, and homework, often involving female immigrant workers.

Migrant labor offers a ready supply of workers for these "reworked" jobs. Indeed, immigration is an important source of labor for 1) low-wage service jobs, including those consumed by a growing professional information-service class; 2) for the downgraded manufacturing sector; and 3) for the immigrant community (Sassen, 1988: 22). The demand for labor, particularly in low-wage services and manufacturing, explains why the potential supply of migrant labor, stimulated by the deployment of capital investment from developed nations to less-developed regions, becomes linked to migration flows from the latter to the former (Sassen, 1989: 825).

However, race and gender also factor into the use of migrant labor in North American economies. Students of the labor process have long noted that racial and gender divisions are used to divide workers and diffuse worker resistance. In addition, a burgeoning body of research on women points to the use of patriarchal ideology as a mechanism of control on the shop floor and to the influence of sexual stereotypes that depict women as a docile, cheap and easily disposable labor supply. The combination causes immigrant women, particularly those who are from less developed nations and/or who are women of color, to be viewed as an appropriate source of labor for low-wage, low-skill jobs and for work arrangements that because of informalization or subcontracting are marginalizing (*see* Gannage, 1986; Hossfeld, 1990). While these are "demand side" arguments, reasons also exist why these women meet such stereotypical imagery and hiring criteria: the recent entry of many immigrant women who may not have language fluency for other jobs or who face difficulty in having educational credentials recognized; the demands of their domestic roles; the dependent status assigned to many in the administrative process of legally immigrating (Boyd, 1986); and the possibility (particularly in the United States) of their undocumented (*i.e.*, illegal) status.

FEMALE MIGRANT LABOR IN NORTH AMERICA

Not all immigrants are destined to fill the low-skill, low-wage jobs that accompany North American economic restructuring. Indeed, professional and high-skilled migrants are part of recent flows to North America. However, past and current studies provide considerable evidence that immigrants, and foreign-born women in particular, are disproportionately found in manufacturing, particularly clothing and electronics, and in the lower skill and lower wage consumer segment of the service industries. In an analysis of changes between 1970 and 1980 in the United States, Tienda, Jensen and Bach (1984) found that although the service sector employed the majority of both foreign-born and U.S.-born women, immigrant women were more likely to be employed in personal services, whereas U.S.-born women were more likely to be found in social services (education and health industries). For each decade, a higher percentage of foreign-born women are employed in the transformative sector (manufacturing and construction) than are U.S.-born women. The authors attribute this concentration to the heavy reliance on immigrant women in textile industries and in the fast growing and high-technology electronics industry. In her study of employment in California's Silicon Valley firms, Hossfeld (1990) notes as well the extensive reliance on immigrant women as a labor supply. Fernàndez Kelly and Garcia (1988, 1990) also describe the extensive employment of female immigrant workers in the garment and electronics industries.

In Canada, analyses of census data between 1971 and 1986 show that foreign-born women are overrepresented in professional, product fabricating and service occupations (Basavarajappa and Verma, 1990; Boyd, 1975, 1986). Foreign-born women of color or those who are from areas other than the United States or Europe are more likely to be employed in the manufacturing and service occupations (Boyd, 1992b). Female immigrants are also disproportionately employed in clothing manufacturing industries (Gannage, 1986; Johnson and Johnson, 1982; Seward, 1990).

Tables 2, 3, and 4 highlight the selective labor market location of female migrants in Canada and the United States. These data are taken from the microdata files for the United States 1980 Census of Population and for the 1986 Canadian Census of Population. As such they are limited in detail, particularly in the Canadian case, where industry data are grouped into sixteen major categories (for the United States, detailed industry codes are provided). Further, the data refer to work actually reported by census respondents. Thus, if workers have reason to avoid either being enumerated (*e.g.*, undocumented workers) or reporting employment (*e.g.*, where payment is not formally recorded), the census will not capture the full range of economic activity. For this reason, activities that are central components to the economic restructuring of the 1980s and 1990s, such as homework or work in the unregulated economy, will be minimized in such data.[5]

Despite these limitations of census data, clear conclusions exist regarding the employment patterns of immigrant women, and they are remarkably similar for both Canada and the United States. First, women more than men have found employment in the service economy (*see also,* Boyd, Mulvihill and Myles, 1991; Tienda, Jensen and Bach, 1984). Second, despite the majority of employment in service industries, nearly 25 percent of foreign-born women in Canada (1986) and nearly 30 percent of foreign-born women in the United States (1980) are employed in the goods sector, represented by primary, manufacturing, and construction industries. Third, this representation in the goods sector is associated with the higher percentages of foreign-born women employed in manufacturing occupations. Thirteen percent of foreign-born women in Canada are in machining and production occupations, compared to 5 percent of Canadian-born women. Fourth, within the service sector, foreign-born women are as likely as, or even more likely than, foreign-born men to be employed in service occupations or in personal services industries (Table 2).

However, these findings vary by place of residence, area of birth and period of immigration (Tables 3 and 4). Foreign-born women in Canada are most likely to be employed in manufacturing (machining and fabrication) occupations and in the goods sector under three conditions: 1) residence in Montreal or Toronto, which are important sites of manufacturing in Canada; 2) birthplace other than the United States

---

[5]The data available to me also constrains the analysis. The 1986 Public Use Sample Tape (PUST) of individuals contains information on approximately 1 in 50 Canadian-born and foreign-born, for a sample of approximately 800,000. However, for the United States, a number of different data sets are produced, including the three Public Use Microfiles (PUMS) A, B, and C. The latter three represent 1 in 100 samples, representing a potential population size of 260 million. Given the resulting challenges to computer memory, most researchers work with a subset of this potentially enormous sample. In U.S. data made available to me through another project, I was able to obtain PUMS data only on the foreign born.

TABLE 2

OCCUPATIONAL AND SECTORAL LOCATION BY NATIVITY AND SEX FOR EXPERIENCED LABOR FORCE:
CANADA, 1986; UNITED STATES, 1980

| | Canada, 1986 | | | | United States, 1980 | |
| | Females | | Males | | Females | Male |
	Canada Born	Foreign Born	Canada Born	Foreign Born	Foreign Born	Foreign Born
Numbers, PUST/PUMS-C	97,975	21,667	122,381	27,539	35,621	45,441
Occupations, percent	100	100	100	100	100	100
Service	17	18	10	12	20	13
Machining, Production	5	13	17	22	17	13
All Others	78	69	73	66	63	74
Sectors, percent	100	100	100	100	100	100
Goods	15	24	39	41	29	44
Services	85	76	61	59	71	56
Services Sectors, percent[a]	100	100	100	100	100	100
Nonmarket	37	34	27	24	38	24
Distribution, Producer	23	25	40	38	26	39
Personal Service	11	12	7	12	11	8
Other Services[b]	10	12	8	9	—	—
Retail	18	17	19	17	25	29

Sources: Statistics Canada, 1986 Census of Population Public Use Sample Tape (PUST). U.S. Bureau of the Census, 1980 Census of Population, Public Use Microdata Sample (PUMS) C.

[a]Numbers may not add up to 100 because of rounding.
[b]As indicated in text, detailed industry codes exist for United States data making it possible to allocate all industries. Canadian data are in the form of a 166-category distribution for industry, in which one category is "other services." Industries in this category cannot be reassigned to other categories.

or Europe; and 3) recent immigration (Table 3). In the United States, the percentages of foreign-born women who are employed as operatives or in fabrication occupations or in the goods sector are high in urban areas of Los Angeles, Miami and New York – areas that Sassen (1991) depicts as major global cities. Percentages are also highest for persons born in the Southern Hemisphere countries (including Mexico, the Caribbean, and Central and South America) as well as for women who immigrated during the decade prior to the 1980 census (Table 4). In both countries, the percentages of women who are employed in service occupations or in personal service sectors is highest for recent arrivals or for persons not born in North America or Europe.

TABLE 3

OCCUPATIONAL AND SECTORAL LOCATION OF FEMALE FOREIGN-BORN POPULATION[a] AGE 15–64, BY AREA OF RESIDENCE, AREA OF BIRTH, AND PERIOD OF IMMIGRATION: CANADA, 1986

Immigration	Total	Major Cities of Residence				Other Area	Area of Birth[b]		Period of Immigration			
		Montreal	Toronto	Vancouver	Other CMA		USA Europe	Other	Before 1970	1971–1975	1976–1980	1981–1986
Number, PUST	16,560	1,581	5,619	1,875	3,707	3,778	10,814	5,609	9,900	3,063	2,038	1,559
Percent, Row	100	10	34	11	22	23	66	34	60	19	12	9
Occupation	100	100	100	100	100	100	100	100	100	100	100	100
Service	18	13	14	22	23	20	17	18	16	17	22	24
Machining, fabrication	13	26	15	7	11	8	12	16	11	14	16	19
All other	69	61	71	71	66	72	71	66	73	70	62	57
Sectors	100	100	100	100	100	100	100	100	100	100	100	100
Goods	24	34	27	14	19	21	23	25	22	23	26	31
Services	76	66	73	86	81	79	77	75	78	77	74	69
Service Sectors	100	100	100	100	100	100	100	100	100	100	100	100
Nonmarket	34	34	28	31	38	41	34	34	37	32	29	25
Distribution, producer	25	27	34	26	20	15	25	26	25	27	24	22
Personal service	12	9	9	13	13	14	10	13	10	11	17	17
Other service	12	13	11	14	12	11	12	12	10	12	14	19
Retail	17	16	18	16	17	19	19	15	18	18	16	16

Source: Statistics Canada, 1986 Census of Population, Public Use Sample Tape (PUST).
[a]Experienced labor force.
[b]Excludes residual group in Atlantic Provinces.

TABLE 4

OCCUPATIONAL AND SECTORAL LOCATION OF FEMALE FOREIGN-BORN POPULATION[a] AGE 16–64, BY AREA OF RESIDENCE, AREA OF BIRTH, AND PERIOD OF IMMIGRATION: UNITED STATES, 1980

	Total	Major Cities of Residence				Area of Birth[b]			Period of Immigration			
		Los Angeles	Miami	New York	Other Urban	Other	Canada Europe	Southern Hemisphere	Other	Before 1970	1970–1974	1975–1980
Number, PUMS	35,621	4,657	1,472	7,422	9,398	12,788	13,215	12,952	9,570	19,185	5,986	6,395
Percent, Row	100	13	4	21	21	26	36	37	27	61	19	20
Occupation	100	100	100	100	100	100	100	100	100	100	100	100
Service	20	19	14	18	23	20	18	22	19	19	21	23
Operations, fabrication	17	22	20	23	15	14	14	24	14	15	22	21
Other	63	59	66	59	62	66	68	54	67	66	57	56
Sectors	100	100	100	100	100	100	100	100	100	100	100	100
Goods	29	36	30	33	28	25	25	37	24	26	35	33
Services	73	64	70	67	72	75	75	63	76	74	65	67
Service Sectors	100	100	100	100	100	100	100	100	100	100	100	100
Nonmarket	38	31	28	39	40	38	35	37	41	32	36	35
Distribution, producer	26	30	35	32	19	27	27	27	24	27	26	25
Consumer	11	16	12	11	11	11	9	16	9	10	13	16
Retail	25	23	25	19	30	24	28	20	26	25	25	24

Source: U.S. Bureau of the Census, 1980 Census of Population, Public Use Microdata (PUMS)C, 1 percent sample.
[a]Worked in either 1979 or 1980.
[b]Excludes persons born in Puerto Rico and United States and/or for whom data on year of immigration are not collected.

In sum, the aggregate figures provided by national censuses confirm that newly arrived immigrants and those from either Latin America (for the United States) or from areas other than Europe and the United States (for Canada), are employed in the goods sector, in manufacturing types of occupations and in personal service activities more frequently than "old-timers." While these census data cannot provide the type of information available from case studies of the labor process and of the deliberate reliance on certain types of labor, they are consistent with arguments that minorities, represented by women, immigrants and racial groups (and their combination) are sources of labor for the less desirable jobs accompanying the restructuring of North American economies (Fernàndez Kelly and Garcia, 1988).

SEWING, SERVING, AND CIRCUITRY

Although foreign-born women are employed in consumer service industries and in manufacturing generally, they are highly concentrated in specific industries. They are employed disproportionately in textile and clothing industries, in electronics manufacturing, and in personal services. In Canada, for example, unpublished tabulations show that 18 percent of the 1986 female experienced labor force is foreign-born. However, in the industries of primary textiles, textile products and clothing manufacturing, foreign-born women represent 21, 37, and 49 percent of the female population. In electrical and electronic products, accommodation and food, and in personal and other services, foreign-born women make up 30, 18, and 21 percent of the female workforce.

These industries represent low-skill/low-pay service sector jobs in consumer services and jobs in old manufacturing industries vulnerable to restructuring as a result of offshore production. Yet, they employ at least one in five – and often more – of the foreign-born female labor force in Canada and in the United States.[6] Further, in both countries the trend for women who are recent arrivals to be employed in these particular industries is enhanced if they are born in areas other than North America or Europe. In Canada, close to half (45 percent) of employed women born outside North America and Europe who immi-

---

[6]For 1986 Canadian data on the select industries for females in the experienced labor force by area of birth and period of immigration, *see* Seward and Tremblay, 1989: Tables 12.3, 13.3. U.S. data are calculated from tabulations from U.S. Bureau of the Census 1980 Census of Population Public Use Microdata Sample (PUMS) C, 1 percent sample.

grated between 1981 and 1986 are employed in these industries, with 13.2 percent, or one in eight, employed in clothing manufacturing. Many of these women were born in Asia, particularly Southeast Asia (see Seward, 1990). Similarly in the United States, over one-third of the female labor force born in Latin and South American countries and arriving between 1970 and 1980 were employed in corresponding industries with 11.6 percent, or one in nine, employed in the garment industry or apparel products (U.S. Bureau of the Census, 1980: PUMS C).

As a result of the trends discussed above, women born in areas other than the United States or Europe tend to be overrepresented in the workforce of these industries. For example, 35 percent of all foreign-born women in Canada in 1986 were born in areas other than the United States or Europe. Yet these women represent 41 percent of foreign-born women in textile producing firms, 47 percent of those in clothing manufacturing, and 40 percent of those in electrical and electronic productions and in accommodation and food services.[7] In the United States, although women born in Southern Hemisphere countries constitute 36 percent of the foreign-born female work force, they are 51 percent of the female foreign-born workers in the apparel products industry, 39 percent in the electrical machining equipment industries and 44 percent in the accommodation and food services. Women born in other areas, notably Asia, form the backbone of female labor in the electronic and computing industry in the United States. Representing slightly over one-fourth (27 percent) of the entire foreign-born work force, these women make up 47 percent of female foreign-born women employed in electronic and computing industries and 51 percent of foreign-born women employed in entertainment and recreation services.[8]

FREE TRADE, HIGH TECH, AND CONTROLLED BORDERS: A WAY OUT, OR MORE OF THE SAME?

Will restructuring of North American economies alter the disproportionate concentration of foreign-born women in select manufacturing industries and in personal/consumer services? How will NAFTA and other trade treaties in the Americas affect this concentration and the immigration related to it?

[7]Calculated from Seward, 1990; see also Cohen, 1987.

[8]Data based on analysis of the U.S. Bureau of the Census 1980, Census of Population, PUMS C.

One might note the uncertainty of predictions in times of crisis. Optimistic and pessimistic scenarios for the future both assume substantial economic change, but they differ on the direction. An optimistic version would argue that new jobs will be created in the "good job" sectors of the North American economies. This could include an increase in manufacturing, although what kinds of jobs will be created remains unclear (*see* Thurow, 1990). In Canada, one popular assessor recently targeted service industries specializing in engineering, architecture, consulting, research, and computing services as industries best prepared for the new economy to come (Beck, 1992). Among those industries recently at the top of the growth potential list in the United States are those specializing in data base systems, biotechnologies, jet propulsion, magnetic storage information, pollution reduction and computer-based technologies (Thurow, 1992). Such growth in information-related and high technology industries could potentially draw upon an invigorated, larger pool of high-skill immigrant labor.[9] Whether it can redeploy labor from other industries remains another question, one highly relevant to discussions of female immigrants.

During the late 1980s and early 1990s, the numbers employed in primary textiles, textile products and clothing industries declined 24, 16 and 12.5 percent respectively in Canada. Comparable declines in employment in textile mill products and in apparel manufacturing industries were 11 percent and 12 percent respectively in the United States.[10] Furthermore, if NAFTA-related trade negotiations are any indications, the "winners," in Canada at least, will be those apparel industries that rely extensively on computer-assisted manufacturing and design (CAM and CAD). In the negotiations with Canada, for example, the United States tried to disqualify clothing imports from Canada made from cloth produced overseas. This attempt was neither idiosyncratic nor capricious, but rather reflected a history of protectionist activity.[11] From the Canadian perspective, manufacturers of

[9]In making assessments of growth in selected service industries, a distinction should be made between the growth in the GNP and growth in jobs. Some high-technology services may increase the GNP but have less impact on job creation.

[10]For this data, see Statistics Canada (1991: Table1) and U.S. Department of Commerce (1992: 9-1, 33-1).

[11]In 1984 the U.S. Customs Service, at the behest of the domestic textile industry, announced a restrictive rule of origin for apparel, decreeing that the nation of origin would depend not on where the fabric was finally sewn or assembled, but on the nation of origin of both the fabric and

men's wool suits, and in particular the Peerless Company in Montreal, were considered the potentially big losers. The export of men's suits to the United States had increased by more than 500 percent, rising from 50,000 suits in 1986 to 380,000 in 1991,and represented a value of $50 million and a 6 percent share of the U.S. men's suit market. However, most of the cloth was imported from Britain, Italy, Japan and South Korea, thus threatening the export capacity of manufacturers like Peerless, which accounted for 80 percent of suits exported. An agreement to increase the allowable export quota resolved this debate over men's suits. While the agreement was applauded in media reports as a success story for Canada, the fact that Peerless is highly automated went relatively unnoticed. The company relies on an array of computer-assisted cutting, sewing, and gluing machines.[12]

For both pessimists and protagonists of NAFTA (see M. Cohen, 1987), the projection of future employment in garment manufacturing is one of continued decline. One possible response is increased reliance on piecework in the home, where wages for the final product are less than on the factory floor (see Johnson and Johnson, 1982). However, another is an actual decline in employment opportunities, both formal and informal. This latter possibility raises a two-part question – where do terminated employees find new employment, and where do new entrants to the labor market, previously destined for such industries, find work?

In addressing the question of redeployment, it is important to note the characteristics of foreign-born women in the textile and clothing industries of North America. Many of these workers have low levels of education and lack fluency in the host country's language(s).[13] There-

---

of the sewing. In NAFTA negotiations over the summer of 1992, representatives from the United States built on this precedent to introduce a highly protectionist rule of origin for apparel. It required not only that clothing be sewn in North America from fabric made in North America but that the yarn the fabric was made from be also from North America – i.e., a triple rule of origin. Given the dominance of the United States textile industry, and the anticipated inability of the Canadian textile industry to compete effectively with U.S. textile manufacturers, the intent of this "yarn forward" stipulation was viewed by commentators as an attempt to oblige Mexican and Canadian apparel makers to buy yarn and fabrics from American textile mills before being allowed to sell clothing to U.S. consumers (Globe and Mail, Toronto, 1 August 1992: B1).

[12]Peerless is thus an example of the third component of economic restructuring discussed earlier in this paper, in which employment is reconfigured within industries.

[13]Analysis of the 1980 PUM data (Sample C) indicates that in the United States, 21.2% of women employed in apparel production do not speak English at home and say they speak English poorly or not at all. As might be expected from Table 4, most of these are women born in Southern

fore, their ability to find alternative sources of employment is dependent on opportunities for literacy and language training and/or job skill training (Boyd, 1991b; Seward, 1990). Compared to the United States, Canada is more proactive in language training, although the federal program, administered through Employment and Immigration and revised in June 1992, does not cover everyone and risks ignoring long-term resident migrants. In both countries, settlement services are aimed more at refugees than at other migrants. From a labor supply perspective, it would appear that massive state intervention is required to alter the future employment patterns of migrants with limited education and language skills. Yet, as liberal welfare states, neither Canada nor the United States is likely to make massive infusions. Both countries place considerable emphasis on user-pay principles and on the role of the unfettered market as mechanisms of change (Boyd, 1992a).

Pessimists also question whether changes in immigration policies will greatly diminish the numbers or origin and economic composition of immigrants to North America in general, and female migrants in particular. Although both Canada and the United States have developed mechanisms to enhance high-skill flows, two factors raise questions about their overall impact. First, in both countries, legislation permits immigration of family members unregulated by economic criteria. As observed earlier, family members can be a source of less-skilled labor, particularly when gender stratification in countries of origin ensures differences between men and women in education and employment experiences. Second, as noted in a recent conference on labor flows (Connell, 1992), where labor demand exists, attempts to restrict the immigration of the less skilled merely results in clandestine labor migration, a fact already familiar to United States analysts.

It may be argued that the immigration of less skilled female workers will continue due to the paradox created by principles of immigration legislation and the objectives of economic competitiveness in a global

---

Hemisphere countries. In Canada, 17% of the 1986 female population in the clothing industry cannot speak either English or French well enough to carry on a conversation. The percentage of those not able to speak English and/or French is very high (41%) for women employed in the clothing industry who were born in Asian regions other than southern Asia and Southeast Asia (*i.e.*, China, Hong Kong, Japan, Korea, and West Asian countries, including the Middle East) and are 16%, 18%, and 9% for women employed in the clothing industry who were born in southern Europe, Southeast Asia and Central and South America who work in the clothing industry (Seward, 1990: Table 9).

economy. Immigration policy assumes the capacity of nations to control their borders, and it includes implicit assumptions about the causes of migration flows. In her analysis of U.S. immigration policy, Sassen (1989) argues that policy makers invoke a push-pull model of forces in which immigration arises because of unfavorable conditions in the origin country, unrelated to economic needs or to larger international economic conditions. Yet, principles of economic competitiveness underlie firm investment decisions to engage in offshore production and/or to restructure domestic production, and they are the basis of international trade agreements. Models of immigration that recognize an interconnected global economy view immigration to North America as stimulated, facilitated, and sustained by economic investment decisions. Mechanisms of entry are highly variable depending on the administrative procedures (*e.g.*, refugee claimants or undocumented immigrants versus other types of migrants), but ultimately the flows are determined not by principles of border control but by the existence of economic and political linkages. These linkages ensure that countries such as Canada and the United States will continue to receive sizable numbers of migrants, many of whom are women.

REFERENCES

Basavarajappa, K. G., and R. Verma
1990   "Occupations of Immigrant Women." In *Ethnic Demography: Canadian Immigrant, Racial and Cultural Variations*. Ed. S. Halli, F. Trovato and L. Driedger. Ottawa: Carleton University Press.

Beck, N.
1992   *Shifting Gears: Thriving in the New Economy.* Toronto: Harper Collins.

Bonacich, E., and L. Cheng
1984   "Introduction: A Theoretical Orientation to International Labor Migration." In *Labor Migration Under Capitalism: Asian Workers in the United States before World War II.* Ed. L. Cheng and E. Bonacich. Berkeley: University of California Press. Pp. 1–56.

Borjas, G.
1988   *International Differences in the Labor Market and Performance of Immigrants.* Kalamazoo, MI: W. E. Upjohn Institute for Employment Research.

Boyd, M.
1992a   "Gender Issues in Immigration Trends and Language Fluency." In *Immigration, Language and Ethnic Issues: Public Policy in Canada and the United States.* Ed. B. R. Chiswick. Washington, DC: American Enterprise Institute. Pp. 305–372.

1992b   "Gender, Visible Minority and Immigrant Earnings Inequality: Reassessing an Employment Equity Premise." In *Deconstructing a Nation: Immigration, Multiculturalism and Racism in the 1990s Canada.* Ed. V. Satzewich. Halifax: Fernwood Press. Pp. 279–321.

1991a   "Changing Skill in the Service Economy: Canada, 1971–1986." Paper presented at the Annual Meeting of the Canadian Sociology and Anthropology Association. Vancouver, British Columbia, May.

1991b   "Gender, Nativity and Literacy: Proficiency and Training Issues." In *Adult Literacy in Canada: Results of a National Survey.* Catalogue 89 525E. Ottawa: Statistics Canada. Pp. 85–93.

1986   "Immigrant Women in Canada." In *International Migration: The Female Experience.* Ed. R. J. Simon and C. B. Brettell. Totowa, NJ: Rowman and Allanheld. Pp. 45–61.

1975   "The Status of Immigrant Women in Canada," *Canadian Review of Sociology and Anthropology,* 12: 406–416.

Boyd, M., M. A. Mulvihill and J. Myles
1991   "Gender, Power and Postindustrialism," *Canadian Review of Sociology and Anthropology,* 28: 407–436.

Cohen, M.
1987   *Free Trade and the Future of Women's Work: Manufacturing and Service Industries.* Toronto: Garamond Press.

Cohen, R.
1987   *The New Helots: Migrants in the International Division of Labour.* Aldershot, U.K.: Avebury, Gower Publishing.

Connell, J.
1992   "International Manpower Flows and Foreign Investment in Asia," *International Migration Review,* 26(1): 133–137.

Economic Council of Canada
1989   *Good Jobs, Bad Jobs.* Ottawa: Economic Council of Canada.

Fernàndez Kelly, M. P.
1989   "Broadening the Scope: Gender and International Development," *Sociological Forum,* 4(4): 611–635.

Fernàndez Kelly, M. P., and A. M. Garcia
1990   "Power Surrendered, Power Restored: The Politics of Home and Work among Hispanic Women in Southern Florida." In *Women, Politics and Change.* Ed. L. Tilly and P. Guerin. New York: Russell Sage Foundation.

1988   "Economic Restructuring in the United States (Hispanic Women in the Garment and Electronic Industries)." In *Women and Work: An Annual Review*, 3 ed. Ed. B. A. Gurek, A. H. Stromberg and L. Larwood. Newbury Park: Sage. Pp. 49–65.

1985   "The Making of an Underground Economy: Hispanic Women, Home Work, and the Advanced Capitalist State," *Urban Anthropology*, 14(1-3): 59–90.

Gannage, C.
1986   *Double Day, Double Bind: Women Garment Workers*. Toronto: Women's Press.

Hossfeld, K. J.
1990   "'Their Logic Against Them': Contradictions in Sex, Race and Class in Silicon Valley." In *Women Workers and Global Restructuring*. Ed. K. Ward. Ithaca, NY: IRL Press, School of Industrial and Labor Relations, Cornell University. Pp. 149–178.

Houston, M. F., R. G. Kramer and J. M. Barrett
1984   "Female Predominance in Immigration to the United States since 1930: A First Look," *International Migration Review*, 18: 908–963.

Johnson, L. C. and R. E. Johnson
1982   *The Seam Allowance: Industrial Home Sewing in Canada*. Toronto: Women's Press.

Myles, J., and G. Fawcett
1990   *Job Skills and the Service Economy*. Ottawa: Economic Council of Canada.

Myles, J., G. Picot and T. Wannell
1993   "Does Postindustrialism Matter? Evidence from the Canadian Experience." In *Changing Classes*. Ed. G. Esping-Andersen. London: Sage Publishers.

Petras, E. M.
1981   "The Global Labor Market in the World Economy." In *Global Trends in Migration*. Ed. M. M. Kritz, C. B. Keely and S. M. Tomasi. New York: Center for Migration Studies. Pp. 44–63.

Portes, A.
1981   "International Labor Migration and National Development." In *Global Trends in Migration*. Ed. M. M. Kritz, C. B. Keely and S. M. Tomasi. New York: Center for Migration Studies. Pp. 71–91.

Portes, A., and J. Walton
1987   *Labor, Class and the International System*. New York: Academic Press.

Sassen, S.
1991   *The Global City: New York, London, Tokyo*. Princeton, NJ: Princeton University Press.

1989   "America's Immigration 'Problem,'" *World Policy Journal*, 4(4): 811–832.

1988   *Mobility of Labor and Capital*. Cambridge: Cambridge University Press.

Seward, S.
1990   "Challenges of Labour Adjustment: The Case of Immigrant Women in the Clothing Industry." Discussion Paper No. 90.B1. Ottawa: Institute for Research in Public Policy.

Seward, S., and M. Tremblay
1989   "Immigrants in the Canadian Labour Force: Their Role in Structural Change." Discussion Paper No. 89.B2. Ottawa: Institute for Research in Public Policy.

Singlemann, J.
1978   *From Agriculture to Services.* Sage Library of Social Research No. 69. Beverly Hills, CA: Sage Publications.

Statistics Canada
1991   1991 Census of Canada, Industry and Class of Worker, *The Nation*, Catalogue 93-326.

_____
1986   1986 Census of Population Public Use Sample Tape (PUST).

Thurow, L. C.
1992   *Head to Head.* New York: William Morrow.

_____
1990   "The End of the Post-Industrial Era," *Business in the Contemporary World*, 2(2): 21–26.

Tienda, M., L. Jensen and R. L. Bach
1984   "Immigration, Gender and the Process of Occupational Change in the United States, 1970–1980," *International Migration Review*, 18(4): 1021–1044.

Tyree, A., and K. Donato
1986   "A Demographic Overview of the International Migration of Women." In *International Migration and the Female Experience.* Ed. R. J. Simon and C. B. Brettell. Totowa, NJ: Rowan and Allanheld.

United Nations, Population Division Department of International Economic and Social Affairs
1990   "Measuring the Extent of Female International Migration." Paper presented for the United Nations Expert Group Meeting on International Migration Policies and the Status of Female Migrants. San Minato, Italy. March 27–30.

U.S. Bureau of the Census
1980   1980 Census of Population, Public Microdata Samples (PUMS) A, B, C.

U.S. Department of Commerce, International Trade Administration
1992   *Industrial Outlook '92: Business Forecasts for 350 Industries.* Washington, DC: U.S. Department of Commerce. January.

Zolberg, A. R.
1981   "International Migration in Political Perspective." In *Global Trends in Migration.* Eds. M. M. Kritz, C. B. Keely and S. M. Tomasi. New York: Center for Migration Studies. Pp. 3–27.

Zolberg, A. R., A. Suhrke and S. Aguayo
1989   *Escape from Violence: Conflict and the Refugee Crisis in the Developing World.* New York: Oxford University Press.

11

Household, Gender and Migration in Mexican *Maquiladoras:* The Case of Nogales[1]

Kathryn Kopinak

Introduction

Mexicans have been increasingly migrating northward for at least three reasons: industry within Mexico has been moving from the center to the north; foreign investment has been establishing new factories, called *maquiladoras*, along the northern border; and declining living standards over the period since the early 1980s have stimulated an exodus from Central Mexico to the northern border and to the United States.

The number of *maquiladoras* has increased since their inception in 1966, with 2,158 plants employing almost 546,000 people at the end of May, 1993. Since the economically active population of Mexico is over 30.3 million people, *maquilas* cannot absorb very much of the

[1]The Social Science and Humanities Research Council of Canada funded the research on which this paper is based. The author would like to thank the following people for their assistance: Dolores Esquer, Liliana Ferrer, Martín Guerrero, Francisco Lara, Martha Payan, Oscar Reyes, and Daniel Paight. Institutional support for the author's work during the period of data collection was provided by the Center for U.S.-Mexican Studies at the University of California in San Diego and *El Colegio de la Frontera Norte* in Nogales. Only the author is responsible for the contents.

labor force. This is especially true in the early 1990s, when few jobs are being created due to continuing economic stagnation, together with job reduction through the privatization or elimination of government agencies.[2] However, *maquiladoras* have taken on a significance much greater than that indicated by the employment they provide for Mexican workers. With increasing economic integration throughout the continent, the *maquilas* have been the instrument used by Mexican government policy to integrate that country's economy with that of the rest of the continent. In order to attract foreign investment, conditions previously present in *maquilas* have been extended to other areas of the economy (Kopinak, 1993). *Maquilas* reflect the new regime of flexible accumulation which is being introduced worldwide (Simmons, 1993).

This paper presents findings on how the labor force of one *maquiladora* center in Mexico has been constituted through internal migration and household reorganization. The paper also discusses the implications of *maquiladora* development for international migration. These research questions are addressed through a study of *maquilas* located in and near Nogales, Sonora, with particular focus on the ten producing transport equipment. Located at Mexico's northern border, Nogales is Mexico's sixth largest *maquiladora* center. The prominent business journal *Expansion* has identified ten *maquilas* from Nogales as being among the 100 most important in the country (October 24, 1990). Two of these were part of the present study.

Nogales has been the least well studied of any *maquiladora* center in Mexico, even though it is a distinctive case with implications for emerging patterns elsewhere. Nogales has fewer plants and the number of employees per plant is much higher. This is due to the concentration of larger companies linked to multinational corporations carrying on large scale production. Sánchez notes that the Nogales Maquiladora Association has operated as one of the most closed enclaves throughout the entire border, allowing plant managers in Nogales greater independence from their head offices in the United States than that afforded to managers in other locations (Sanchez, 1990). While some

[2] In the first eight months of 1993, the Mexican Workers Confederation (CTM) reported that there had been more than 395,000 jobs lost, with over a third of them in the manufacturing sector. In the government sector, the largest reductions were made by the national railroad, the state-run oil company, the Trade Secretariat, and the National University. (*SourceMex* 4(35), September 29, 1993)

companies are unionized on paper, unions do not defend workers' rights but function to reinforce management's wishes. Although *maquila* growth has been less explosive in Nogales than Tijuana, it is considered to be more stable. *Maquilas* employ a greater percentage of the economically active population in Nogales than in all the other large *maquiladora* centers.

This paper presents findings from a survey of workers in 1991 in the ten transport equipment *maquiladoras* in Nogales and Imuris. The latter is a small village of 7,000 people located eighty kilometers south of Nogales by highway. The *maquila* in Imuris is the major source of employment in the village, and in the last decade has changed its economic base from agriculture to industry.

Seven of the ten plants produce wiring harnesses, which in 1989 was the number one manufactured good that Mexico exported to the United States. The sample of workers ($N=216$) was 10 percent of those working in all transport equipment plants in Nogales and Imuris in 1990, and was stratified by gender and size of plant. The plants ranged in size from very small (0–25 workers) to large (500+ workers).

Women constitute 43 percent of workers in the factories studied. The proportion of males among *maquiladora* workers is higher in Nogales than in any other border city.[3] Gender is an important factor in structuring the labor force, with a very clear segmentation of women workers into jobs considered least skilled (Kopinak, 1995). Newspaper ads for *maquiladora* jobs often specified gender, and women were overwhelmingly recruited as unskilled production workers. In the workplace, women receive much less training than men and do not move from unskilled to skilled jobs with seniority. However, since all production workers earn almost the same amount, and since real wages have decreased in these plants by 55 percent from 1982 to 1990, women's income is extremely important to the household, and cannot be considered supplementary. This paper focuses on how gender, migration history, and household structure are related for *maquila* workers.

---

[3]Sariego Rodríguez, 1990. In 1987, out of 22 border areas, Nogales, Sonora, was second from the lowest in the ratio of men to women employed at 44/56. The very lowest of all 22 locations was "other locations in Sonora," with a ratio of 49/51.

CONSTRUCTION OF THE MAQUILA LABOR FORCE THROUGH MIGRATION

Since the boom of the 1980s, migration has become an important mechanism supplying labor to *maquiladoras* at the border. Most of the workers and general population surveyed had migrated from within Mexico, reflecting the fact that Nogales is a "new" city whose current reason for existence is the *maquiladora* industry. Less than a fifth of workers reported that they were born in the community where they worked. Migrants reported that, on average, it had been a little more than five years since they had moved to Nogales or Imuris, and their average age at arrival was a little over 18 years.

Nogales, like Juárez, is a center of intraregional migration. It draws a smaller proportion of its population from other regions than Tijuana, Juárez, and Nuevo Laredo did in 1987 (González Ramírez, 1990: 183–211). Four-fifths of workers who had migrated to Nogales and Imuris in 1991 previously resided in the other communities in the same region of the country, the northwest.

Almost two-thirds of workers who had migrated said that they had done so for greater employment and earning opportunities, and another quarter gave family reasons. A 1978 survey of workers in several border cities, including Nogales, found the opposite, that family related reasons were far more significant than *maquila* employment in migrants' motivations, although it was predicted that the latter would become more important due to the economic crunch in Mexico and growth in *maquiladora* industries (Seligson and Williams, 1981: 81). That prediction is confirmed here.

While men and women workers were equally likely to have been migrants, women were more likely to come from nearby locations than men. Over half of women workers who had migrated previously resided in other Sonora locations, whereas only 40 percent of men workers who had migrated did. Women cited family reasons for moving only slightly more often than men. Only 1 percent of female migrants but 12 percent of male migrants reported being motivated by some kind of wanderlust (adventure, "to see what it was like," curiosity).

Migrant workers emphasized the extent to which they felt pushed to move by unemployment elsewhere. A man who had migrated to Imuris with his brothers to work in the *maquila* there said, "We'd work in something else if there was any opportunity, but if the *maquiladora* wasn't here, we'd have to sell things in the street." A 19-year-old woman worker said she had migrated from Durango with her female cousin, where she had been doing housework. She came to work in the *maquila* in Imuris because, "Where we come from there are no jobs, only cleaning houses or sweeping stores. We came here because there are more job opportunities. I regret leaving school because I would like to be promoted and have a well-paid job."

REPRODUCTION OF THE MAQUILA LABOR FORCE IN THE HOUSEHOLD

The household was operationalized as the unit which pooled costs for food. Workers were asked how many of the people who lived with them in the same dwelling shared the same grocery expenses. Workers' households ranged in size from 1 to 13, with a mean of 4.5 persons. Over a third of transport equipment workers lived in small households of three people or less, and cumulatively, 72 percent lived in households of five or fewer people. Only 7 percent of workers reported that they were not related to the head of their household, hence it may be inferred that most households were families.[4] Two-thirds or more of the workers were not only young, but also single (69%) and childless (64%).

One of the most remarkable features of workers' households is the apparent overrepresentation of men as heads of households, with three-quarters of all heads of households being male. This is higher than Staudt's finding of male headship of *maquila* households in Juárez, based on a 1979 survey (Staudt, 1986). The reason for this overrepresentation was that males in Nogales were more likely to live in single-person households, and that in multiple-person households wives were more likely to identify their husband as the head of the household.

In her groundbreaking work on *maquiladora* workers in Juárez, Fernández Kelly, found many women propelled into the *maquiladora* labor force by the absence of male economic support in their families (Fernandez Kelly, 1983, 1989). This finding, along with the fact that until the early 1980s 80 to 90 percent of the *maquiladora* labor force

---

[4]In terms of questionnaire design, respondents were asked if they were the head of their households, and if they responded that they were not, they were then asked their relationship to the head of the household. Thus, it cannot be ascertained whether those who responded that they were the head of the household were in fact kin to the other members of their household. Those who lived in single-person households were not asked how they were related to other households.

was made up of women, has led to the widespread assumption that most *maquiladora* workers are single mothers. This finding may be specific to the location and sample design (Kopinak, 1989). Stoddard has criticized Fernández Kelly's work on methodological grounds, arguing that since she relied on a support center for working women to select respondents, the findings are not at all generalizable (Stoddard, 1987: 87). The present study provides a new opportunity to investigate the questions arising from this debate.

Workers' average income of 553,000 old pesos (US$184) per month was twice the minimum wage at the time the survey was administered. Earning twice the minimum wage has been identified as the dividing line between what Rodriguez Gómez (1992) has called the absolute poor from those who are even less fortunate in Mexico. According to Gómez, 49 percent of the economically active population is absolutely poor in that they earn between two and five minimum wages, and 43 percent of the economically active population receive only one to two minimum wages.

Despite gender of worker or gender of other wage earners in the worker's household, the worker earned almost exactly the same as the average of all other wage earners in the household. This is indicative of the fact that wages for direct workers are set at the minimum by the government. Despite benefits received at different plants, or sources of income outside of the *maquiladora* sector, all wage earners make the same amount of money. As Brannon and Lucker have noted (1989), this government-set industrial minimum is not only the wage floor, but also has become the ceiling. Wage ceilings have been imposed since 1977, six months after the Mexican government signed a Letter of Agreement with the International Monetary Fund. Through the Pact of Economic Solidarity instituted in 1987, the government sets the maximum increase for the minimum wage in the public sector. In so doing, the government puts downward pressure on private sector wages as well. With the exception of 1982, wage increases have been inferior to the inflation rate for the last seventeen years. The effect has been to set Mexican wages among the lowest in the world.

Two-thirds of the members in the average worker's household in Nogales in 1991 were economically active. With an average household size of 4.5, this is 2.8 economically active persons. Given that the average industrial worker earns twice the minimum wage, with all workers in a household earning the same amount, then 2.8 economically active persons in a household would bring home over five minimum wages, which is congruent with Orozco Orozco's argument (1991) that the minimum wage set by the Mexican government covers only about a quarter of the basic necessities of the typical worker's family.

The fact that all workers earn the same wage also has implications for household strategies for survival. In this economic environment, it would seem that the best strategy for the household as an income pooling unit would be to increase its size to take advantage of economies of scale, and send as many wage earners as possible into the labor force, regardless of gender or position in the family. Women's employment outside the home, from this perspective, is absolutely essential to the household's subsistence. In a secondary analysis of survey data collected in Juárez in 1979, Young and Christopherson (1986) showed that households there increased their resources by adding an adult who worked in a *maquiladora* or took over household duties to free the wife/mother to work in a *maquiladora*.

The ratio of economically active persons per household did not differ much for the average male and female worker, but interesting patterns emerged when the sample was divided into households with both men and women wage earners ($N=125$), households with only women wage earners ($N=25$), and households with only men wage earners ($N=66$). The ratio of economically active persons per household was .68 in households with both male and female wage earners, but only .55 in households with only female wage earners. It is not surprising that the monthly incomes of the total household for these two groups are far apart, with households containing both male and female wage earners having the highest mean monthly income (1,889,500 old pesos or US $629) and households with only female wage earners having the lowest mean monthly income (811,600 old pesos or US$270).

Having a household with both male and female wage earners may be the best strategy for pooling income, since this type of household had the highest per capita income (401,400 old pesos or US$134) and the least dependence on respondent's income, since respondent's income is only 35 percent of the household income. The less the household depends on any individual's income, the less it is likely to suffer if that income is lost. Workers in households with many incomes might also be freer to switch jobs to serve their personal interests better.

Women workers who lived in households where all other workers were women appear to be in the most precarious situation. Their households have the lowest proportion of household members who are economically active (55%), the greatest reliance on the *maquiladora* industry (93% of those employed work in *maquilas*), and greatest reliance on the respondent's income (80% of household income came from the worker responding to the survey).

The major source of work for households with only male workers is also the *maquila*, and male workers who live with other male workers bring home a high proportion of the household earnings (73%) as well. They are better off, however, than women workers in households with only female wage earners, since they have the highest average income themselves (589,100 old pesos or US$196), and the highest average income for the economically active members of their household (640,100 old pesos or US$213) compared to any other subgroup within the sample.

The group of households with only women wage earners is small (12% of the sample) but comprises 27 percent of all women in the sample. This provides further support for Fernández Kelly's findings in Juárez in the early 1980s, and weakens Stoddart's critique of her work. A disproportionate number of women in Nogales are in female-headed households in which all income is provided by one woman (the dominant pattern) or two or more women (a minority pattern). Women workers from households with only female wage earners also reported being single parents much more often (36%) than men workers from households with only male wage earners (7%).

Nogales's population growth with the development of a *maquila* economy has led to an acute inadequacy of infrastructure such as housing. Twenty new residential districts appeared in Nogales in the three years between 1986 and 1989, the majority of which are substandard dwellings built by the migrants themselves on land they "invaded" (Lara Valencia, 1991). Important variations in workers' living conditions were discovered through a cluster analysis[5] of housing items in the workers' survey. While workers cannot be said to have "good" housing in any abstract sense, there are some who are worse off than others.

Three factors were found to empirically differentiate two groups of workers with regard to their housing. The most strongly differentiating

[5]For an explanation of this well-known classification technique, *see* Sneath and Sokal (1973).

factor combined the availability of electricity and durability of walls (*i.e.*, cardboard vs. wood or sheet metal), the second factor differentiated workers' housing by whether it had running water and sewage, and the third on the amount of "free" space.[6] A full 31 percent of respondents fell into the bottom cluster which had the worst housing. This variation in housing allows comparisons which help to understand how *maquiladora* workers manage their existence in new northern cities such as Nogales.

Workers improve the quality of their housing by sharing resources with others. Those with the worst housing had smaller households and were also more likely (31%) to report that they contributed the only income to the household, in comparison with those who had less poor housing (14%). This is evidence that the household mediates the effects of the economy. Inadequate housing is also one of the costs of migration, since of those who were born where they worked, 17 percent had the worst housing, but of those born elsewhere, 36 percent suffered these conditions.

Migrant workers were sometimes disadvantaged because companies would not make any allowance for the fact that they were migrants. The migration process is not usually completed in one move and may take the worker away from the plant for extended periods. One 19 year-old woman from Guasave, Sinaloa, working on an assembly line putting connectors onto circuits, gave her seniority as one year and two months, which is in the third highest quartile of seniority observed for all workers. She had come to Nogales with women friends for the first time three years previously in order to find work. Guasave is a minimum of sixteen hours away by bus, although the trip is often longer because there are many stops along the way, and the schedule runs behind. Later in the interview, however, she revealed that she had worked at the same plant twice before, the first time for nine months, and the second time for a year.

After putting in nine months at the plant, she wanted to return to Guasave to help her mother, who was over 45, and her younger brother, move to join her. Since the plant would not give her permission for a leave of absence either of the two times she had requested it, she had to quit, and lost all her seniority in the process. When the survey took

[6]Free space was defined as the number of rooms in a dwelling that were not used as bedrooms, kitchens, bathrooms, or hallways. The average for all workers surveyed was 0.3 rooms per dwelling, indicating that not only is there no free space, but that overcrowding is the norm.

place, she was living in Nogales with her mother and brother, with the latter selling souvenirs in one of the many tourist shops that line the border. Her seniority was shorter than it would have been had she been given the leaves she requested, and perhaps she would have had the opportunity to do different jobs within the plant and learn new skills. As it was, she had always done the same job.

IMPLICATIONS OF MAQUILADORAS FOR INTERNATIONAL MIGRATION

Few workers reported that they had crossed the U.S. border for work or that they had migrated to northern Mexico in order to later seek work in the United States. This finding supports the view that internal and international labor force movements in the case of Nogales are largely separate systems, each with its own chain of information flow, family support, and labor recruiting. The major policy question, then, is whether *maquiladora* growth will slow migration to the United States. This would happen if the job growth and income levels in *maquila* production within Mexico were sufficient to attract and absorb workers who would otherwise go to the United States. A related question is whether the growth of population in northern Mexico – a growth linked to the expansion of *maquila* production – will tend to create another commercial and migrant bridge to the United States. If this were to happen, it could make undocumented migration to the United States easier.

Cornelius (1991) has argued that potential growth in *maquiladoras* would not result in more migration to the United States, since *maquilas* draw the bulk of their work force from their host states and migrants to the United States tend to come from farther away than the border and bypass it entirely. This is confirmed in the present study which found that only 1 percent of all workers who had migrated said they had come in order to cross into the United States.

Whether Mexicans are likely to migrate to the United States may depend less on their location within Mexico and more on the resources available to them. De los Angeles Crummett (1985) found in her study of Calvillo, Aguascalientes, that migration to the United States predominated among the middle peasantry, and that the poorest peasants migrated only within Mexico because their precarious economic bases restricted international migration. It may be that in the future *maquila* employment will provide the poorest with more of an economic base from which they can consider migration to the United States, where higher wages are attractive.

Theoretical frameworks used to understand economic integration have important implications for understanding migration patterns. The new international division of labor perspective, which explained capital's movement in terms of the search for cheap labor to do simple assembly jobs, implied that migration would not be stemmed by transnationalization, because much of the employment made available was not sufficient to sustain workers and their families. Thus, many workers would have to migrate to other locations where they might earn more.

More recent models of "flexible" manufacturing, however, have pointed out that the kinds of jobs transplanted are not only the less skilled ones, but also those that require more training and pay more than basic assembly. Thus, while intraregional migration within a country such as Mexico might increase when people move within the country to work for new investors, this increased internal movement may not affect movement internationally, since this is driven by separate labor markets in receiving countries.

While the issue of international migration is a highly politicized one, there is strong support for the idea that NAFTA will not stop international migration from Mexico to the United States. As Velázquez Flores (1993) says,

> NAFTA will create jobs in Mexico, but not with sufficient wages. Besides, Mexicans don't only migrate because of lack of jobs, but are in reality searching for better pay. The historic experience has taught us that neither migration laws, nor border development programs, have been able to stop this phenomenon. NAFTA will not halt migratory currents because it really doesn't fight their principal cause: the search for better living standards.

One of the central characteristics of the process of maquiladorization is the lowering of wages. Wages were lowered in the Mexican auto industry, for example, when it was maquiladorized. Plants centrally located in the country closed up shop, moved north, and reopened with more modern equipment, just-in-time work organization, and more compliant unions. The average earnings of Nogales *maquila* workers in 1991 were compared to what the same plants had paid to workers in 1982, and it was found that, in terms of real buying power, in 1991 they paid only 45 percent, or less than half of what they had paid a decade earlier (Kopinak, 1995). While this calculation of real wages was based on what money could buy in Mexico, most Nogales workers, in fact, buy their groceries and other basic supplies in the United States, so that the effect of the devaluation and failure to adequately increase the minimum wage is even more extremely felt (Lara Valencia, 1992).

Redding (1991) has drawn the analogy between plantation and *maquiladora* employment in this way:

> Ethnic Spaniards continue to dominate the country's political and economic life, neglecting rural Mexico, which is overwhelmingly made up of Spanish-speaking native Americans. This social structure has fostered a plantation mentality (whose modern expression is the *maquiladora*, or low-wage assembly plant) that seeks a comparative advantage in foreign trade by repressing the labor force rather than by investing in education and new technologies in order to raise productivity and create internal markets for sustained economic growth.

It seems that Mexicans will continue to take *maquila* jobs as long as wages in Mexico do not go up substantially in real terms.

CONCLUSION

This paper has shown how *maquiladora* workers in Nogales and Imuris have purposefully sought a very active role in inserting themselves into the labor market. Many have migrated from home towns to work at the border. Once there they have organized themselves into households which attempt to mediate – through an increased number of economically active members – some of the sharpest difficulties of the economy. The household takes on an especially important role due to the absence of effective trade union organizations that might help defend workers' rights and represent their interests. It is concluded that the others with whom they undertake the active organization of their lives are in most cases family members.

The evidence presented here, and that from other research leads to the conclusion that because of harsh economic conditions, migration northward within Mexico and to the United States will continue. This does not mean that each corridor along the border will become an equally favored crossing point for people as well as goods. Nogales, for example, has never been as popular a point of entry for Mexicans into the United States as Tijuana. This may be why *maquila* workers in this study and Lara Valencia's did not report moving to Nogales in order to cross into the United States.

REFERENCES

Barajas Escamilla, R.
1989   "Complejos industriales en el sur de Estados Unidos y su relación con la distribución espacial y el crecimiento de los centros maquiladores en el norte de México." In *Las Maquiladoras: Ajuste Estructural y Desarrollo Regional.* Comp. B. González-Aréchiga and R. Barajas Escamilla. Tijuana: Fundación Friedrich Ebert.

Barajas Escamilla, R., and C. Rodríguez Camillo
1989   "Mujer y Trabajo en la Industria Maquiladora de Exportacion en Tijuana, Baja California." Tijuana. Mimeograph.

Benería, L., and M. Roldán
1987   *The Crossroads of Class and Gender.* Chicago: University of Chicago Press.

Brannon, J. T., and G. W. Lucker
1989   "The Impact of Mexico's Economic Crisis on the Demographic Composition of the *Maquiladora* Labor Force," *Journal of Borderlands Studies,* 4(1): 39–70.

Cornelius, W.
1991   "Effects of a Free Trade Agreement on Mexican Rural Migration to the United States: Alternative Scenarios." Paper presented to the Executive Policy Seminar on Agriculture in a North American Free Trade Agreement, Center for U.S.-Mexican Studies, University of California at San Diego.

De los Angeles Crummett, M.
1985   "Class, Household Structure, and Migration: A Case Study from Rural Mexico." Working Paper No. 92, Women in International Development. East Lansing: Michigan State University.

Fernández Kelly, P.
1989   "Technology and Employment along the U.S.-Mexican Border." In *The United States and Mexico: Face to Face With New Technology.* Ed. C. L. Thorup *et al.* Washington, DC: Overseas Development Council. Pp. 149–167.

———
1983   *For We are Sold, I and My People: Women and Industry in Mexico's Frontier.* Albany: State University of New York Press.

Gabayet, L., and S. Lailson
1990   "The Role of Women Wage Earners in Male Migration in Guadalajara Mexico." Working Paper No. 50. Washington, DC: Commission for the Study of International Migration and Cooperative Economic Development.

González Ramírez, R.
1990   "Evaluación de la Encuesta Socioleconómica Anual de la Frontera, 1987," *Frontera Norte,* 2(4): 183–214.

Kopinak, K.
1995   "The Continuing Importance of Gender as a Vehicle for the Subordination of Women Maquiladora Workers in Mexico," *Latin American Perspectives*. Spring.

———
1993   "Maquiladorization of the Mexican Economy." In *The Political Economy of a North American Free Trade*. Ed. R. Grinspun and M. Cameron. New York: St. Martin's Press. Pp. 141–161.

———
1989   "Living the Gospel through Service to the Poor: The Convergence of Political and Religious Motivations in Organizing *Maquiladora* Workers in Juarez, Mexico." In *Race, Class, Gender: Bonds and Barriers*. Ed. J. Vorst. Toronto: Between the Lines. Pp. 217–244.

Lara Valencia, F.
1992   "El Gasto Trasfronterizo de los Empleados de la Industria Maquiladora: Patrones e Implicaciones para Sonora y Arizona." In *Industria Maquiladora y Mercados Laborales*, Vol. II. Juárez: El Colegio de la Frontera Norte y Universidad Autonoma de Cuidad Juárez. Pp. 139–162.

———
1991   "Empleo y Migracion en la Zona Fronteriza de Sonora." Paper presented at the XVI Symposium of History and Anthropology of Sonora. Mimeograph.

Orozco Orozco, M.
1991   "Los Estragos Salariales de la Política Neoliberal," *La Jornada*, November 1.

Redding, A.,
1991   "Mexico: The Crumbling of the 'Perfect Dictatorship,'" *World Policy Journal*, 9: 255–284. Spring.

Rodriguez Gomez, J.
1992   "Los Dos Méxicos: La Pobreza de Muchos; el Privilegio de Pocos," *El Financiero*, July 20.

Sanchez, R.
1990   "Condiciones de Vida de los Trabajadores de la Maquiladora en Tijuana y Nogales," *Frontera Norte*, 2(4): 153–182.

Sariego Rodríguez, J.
1990   "Trabajo y Maquiladoras en Chihuahua," *El Cotidiano*, 33: 15–25, January–February.

Seligson, M. A., and E. J. Williams
1981   *Maquiladoras and Migration. Workers in the Mexico-United States Border Industrialization Program*. Austin, TX: Mexico-United States Research Program.

Shaiken, H.
1990   *Mexico in the Global Economy: High Technology and Work Organization in Export Industries*. Monograph. Series No. 33. San Diego: Center for U.S.-Mexican Studies, University of California at San Diego.

Simmons, A. B.
1993   "Migration and Flexible Accumulation." Paper presented at the workshop on Nuevas Modalidades y Tendencias de la Migracion Internacional Frente a Los Procesos de Integracion. Montevideo, Uruguay.

Sneath, P., and R. Sokal
1973   *Numerical Taxonomy*. San Francisco: W. H. Freeman.

Staudt, K.
1986   "Economic Change and Ideological Lag in Households of Maquila Workers in Cuidad Juarez." In *The Social Ecology and Economic Development of Ciudad Juárez*. Ed. G. Young. Boulder, CO: Westview.

Stoddard, E.
1987   *Maquila*. El Paso: Texas Western Press.

Velazquez Flores, R.
1993   "El TLC y los Indocumentados," *El Financiero*, September 7. P. 27A.

Welti, C.
1993   "Políticas Púbicas de Población: Un Tema en Debate Permanente," *Fem*, 17(128): 16–18.

Young and Christopherson
1986   "Household Structure and Activity in Ciudad Juárez." In *The Social Ecology and Economic Development of Ciudad Juárez*. Ed. G. Young. Boulder, CO: Westview.

Part IV

Refugees and Asylum in the Hemisphere

12

Asylum Policies in Developed Countries: National Security Concerns and Regional Issues

Charles B. Keely
Sharon Stanton Russell

Introduction

This paper assesses asylum policies in Europe and argues that the logic of national security and regionalized approaches to issues of asylum and refugees are applicable to North America. Canada, the United States, and Mexico already show an inclination toward collective solutions similar to those being developed in Europe. This is evident in Canadian concerns with bilateral agreements to return screened-out asylum applicants, the U.S. policy of avoiding being a country of mass first asylum for the hemisphere, and the introduction of the strategic concept of national security into Mexican foreign-relations thinking. However, the immigrant tradition and the focus on trade and investment solutions related to NAFTA (as opposed to aid) differentiate the North American and European cases. They also underscore the basis for regionalized approaches. National security and regional concerns are not necessarily inimical to humanitarian actions and a human rights emphasis in future refugee policy in North America. Such a presumption may forestall the inclusion of a humanitarian and human rights dimension into national-security dominated approaches to refugee and asylum policies.

The industrial countries of Europe and North America are searching for policies and mechanisms to meet the diverse demands presented by current asylum and refugee realities. Asylum demands have grown so great numerically, so diverse in sources, so complex in internal and external implications that an increasing number of countries seek collective solutions. In diverse forums, refugee-receiving countries in the North try to work out coordinated or "harmonized" solutions that fit well with political realities at home. In Europe the process has advanced to a degree that may provide insights into developments in North America. While many aspects differ between the European and North American contexts, some of the logic of events in Europe may well apply in the New World.

This paper has three parts. The first reviews European trends in migration policy. The second part analyzes developments in North America that indicate policy outcomes similar to those in Europe, but with important differences. Finally, the paper draws implications for humanitarian and human rights organizations interested in refugee issues.[1]

EUROPEAN ASYLUM AND REFUGEE CONCERNS

European governments feel buffeted by international migration that raises fundamental questions about the shape of their societies. Migrants of concern include the remnants from "temporary workers" who were not required to leave when new recruitment generally ceased about 1973 (Collinson, 1993a: 46–63). Many of these workers were permitted to reunite their families in the European countries where they worked. In some cases citizenship was a realistic goal, in others it was not. In virtually all cases, there was the issue of social integration. Most notably, Europeans discussed the "second generation problem." The reference was to children of migrant workers born or raised in a European country. Even in cases where a child held citizenship, segre-

---

[1]This paper draws on interviews and review of documents that are part of a study of the diplomacy of migration policy among industrial countries. Details about the various forums and the results to date can be found in Russell and Keely (n.d.) and in Keely and Russell (n.d.).

gation was more the norm than integration into the society that recruited their parent(s) to work (Rogers, 1985; Collinson, 1993a: 103–108; Kubat, 1993).

In the 1980s, a second group was added, namely the asylum seekers who entered Europe. Many were viewed as abusers of asylum systems that were not geared to handle the large numbers who requested asylum. In the eyes of asylum granters the use of routes through the former Warsaw Pact countries to gain entry into Western Europe to make asylum claims undermined the legitimacy of many applicants.

Third, illegal migrants have been a persistent issue, usually a low-grade irritant. The severity of illegal migration is thought to have been mitigated by the availability of the asylum procedures to gain at least temporary access to European labor markets (Collinson, 1993b: 85–87; Kinzer, 1993: A7). Tightening of asylum procedures may lead to increased illegal migration.

In these cases (the remnants of temporary worker programs, mounting asylum applications, and illegal migration), European countries were reluctant and certainly inefficient in removal of those without valid residence permits or whose asylum applications were turned down (Kamm, 1993: 14; Kinzer, 1993: A7). While the numbers mounted, questioning of social, political, and economic impact also grew apace. For a period, governments, nevertheless, seemed unwilling or unable to take action.

Gradually, European governments moved toward discussion about coordinated solutions. The Dublin Agreement among the European Community states and the Schengen Agreement among five (now nine) states addressed issues of control of asylum applicants and their removal if denied admission (European Union, 1989, 1990). Meetings have taken place in many forums to discuss harmonization of policy and mechanisms like information sharing on asylum applicants.

It was in a context of heightened concern about the remnants of guestworker programs and increased asylum applications that the end of the Cold War came. In Europe, it was not long before a fear of massive East-West movement arose. The former Soviet Union was seen as a possible breeding ground for massive displacement that could well spill over into Europe. Emigration is considered a likely concomitant of the social revolutions taking place in Warsaw Pact countries that have been shedding Communist governments and are involved in political and economic changes whose outcome is far from settled. Albanian boats on the Italian shore were proof that mass movement could happen and were viewed by some as a foretaste of things to come (Binder, 1991; Los Angeles Times, 1991).

Other East-West movements were taking place. Germany's Basic Law permitted the "return" of ethnic Germans to their fatherland. The numbers were large and compounded migration issues in the largest European receiver of migrants (SOPEMI, 1992: 131). The social tensions and notoriety surrounding minority and "foreigners" issues has disproportionate influence because of the importance of Germany (Mehrlander, 1993; Kamm, 1993: 14; Fisher, 1992a, 1992b). Other population movements were taking place in less dramatic fashion as minority nationalities sought refuge in a mother country. The potential for population transfers is great. Ethnic sorting had roots in the post-World War I era and was exacerbated by events during and after World War II. Nationalist expression had been frozen by Soviet hegemony in Eastern Europe but was rapidly spreading its tendrils in the spring that followed the end of the Cold War. Western Europe was and remains concerned.

The East-West movements due to ethnic sorting have not yet come in the numbers feared. Europe is exercised currently about even greater emigration from former Yugoslavia. The outflow in the winter of 1992–1993 was not as large as expected (Maass, 1992; Robinson, 1992; IGC, 1993). Subsequent events have gone badly in Bosnia. The winter of 1993–1994 can produce attempts at large-scale exits from fighting and desperate conditions. Germany, Austria, Switzerland and, to an extent, Sweden have felt the major effects of migration to escape Bosnian fighting (IGC, 1993; Washington Post, 1993). Further pressures on Croatia from Bosnian refugees and demands by Croatia for cash payments for their costs may lead the Croatian government to push current non-Croatian and future Bosnian refugees out of and across their territory and into the German-speaking border states. Political tensions in Kosovo are hardly settled. Germany estimates, at a minimum, 300,000 former Yugoslavs resident as temporary asylees (Washington Post, 1993).

Events in Germany have been a dramatic example of the impact of these cumulative migration movements and prospects in parts of Europe. Numbers, cultural differences, feelings of events being out of control have resulted in a strong segment of political opinion supporting a stop to the movement. German and Austrian leaders and opinion makers are discussing possible threats to the foundations of their democracies. The concern is not limited to the migrants, but includes the reaction of the citizenry to them. In societies built on an ethnically-based national identity, threats to that identity, which is seen as the foundation of social integration and legitimacy of the state as a protector and enhancer of the people and their culture, are serious. The issues are not confined to a rightist fringe. What is it that holds a nation and a state together? If a minority has rights on the basis of nationality, does not a majority population? What is to be done when "rights" come into conflict?

This paper does not pretend to answer these questions or even to analyze adequately their sources in the nation-state organizing principle of contemporary geopolitics. What is important for this analysis is that unease is deep and raises concern and even fear about the very basis of democratic societies and their futures.

The discussions about asylum, refugees and migration have moved into high gear in Europe. The optic for analysis is changing from seeing refugee movements in Europe as predominantly a humanitarian issue to seeing them also as an issue of national security. Efforts to deal with the collective threat, as refugee and asylum movements are coming to be seen, are being regionalized. This development is at once ostensibly supported by and a challenge for the United Nations agencies, especially in the political sphere.

As the lead agency in caring for the Croatian-based refugees of the former Yugoslavia, the U.N. High Commissioner for Refugees has a grave burden. While the winter of 1992–1993 did not produce the expected numbers of refugees outside the territory of former Yugoslavia, the movement was not negligible. Germany, Austria, Switzerland and Sweden have been less than impressed at the willingness of European countries to share the burden of providing refuge. But the job was done. Will future refugee protection be as successful (in relative terms) as in the past? Success in the eyes of European states in this instance will include prevention of large-scale movement into Austria, Germany, Switzerland and other Western states. Many Western European states have adopted visa and other procedures that virtually preclude a former Yugoslavian from claiming asylum on arrival at a port of entry. If the U.N. in general and the UNHCR in particular are not successful in preventing a large refugee exodus from the former Yugoslavia, their roles may well be redefined.

One possibility that has been discussed is a European refugee or migration convention and a new council or other mechanism to carry out common policy. Events do not seem to be going in the direction of such new mechanisms and joint action. Rather, states seem to be enacting similar laws and adopting similar policies, of a deterrent nature, and developing bilateral agreements to provide resources to Eastern European countries to allow them to establish asylum procedures and review applications. The hope is that this sort of burden sharing will discourage unfounded asylum applications when would-be asylees realize they will get a "safe haven" (or access to the labor market), for example, not in Sweden or Germany but in Poland.

In short, asylum and refugee issues in Europe are moving from a humanitarian to a national security optic and from global (U.N.) to regional solutions in the form of similar, but still unilateral, policies, supplemented by bilateral agreements. Extensive diplomatic discussions have resulted so far in a harmonization by consensus about directions and actions to be taken by each state rather than by formal, collective, multistate operations. These processes have not produced identical policy actions by states, but have resulted in legislation and regulations that are quite similar in their reduction of asylum applications. Other policy outcomes are possible in the future, perhaps a regional regime developed by states' collective action. The cumulative effect of prior migration policies of the European Community (EC) and the inauguration of the European Union (EU) in November 1993 by the Maastricht Treaty should lead to increased collective action about migration by the Twelve. This may eventually spill over to other EC associated and nonassociated states in Europe. Our assessment at the present, however, is that harmonization of asylum and refugee policy for the foreseeable future will take the form of consistent policies adopted by states in their sovereign capacity. European trends and especially the logic behind them have implications for North America.

TRENDS IN NORTH AMERICAN REFUGEE POLICY

Each of the three North American countries has refugee concerns and policies that are peculiar to it, yet there are common interests that unite them. These shared interests may lead and already show signs of leading to outcomes that exhibit national security and regionalization tendencies similar to those developing in Europe.

Canada

The Canadian government has been concerned about asylum seekers from two sources: large boats landing on its shores bringing would-be refugees from Third World countries and, second, Central Americans, primarily but also others, arriving via the United States either after being denied asylum by the United States or simply using the United States as a transit country. Canada has been pursuing a policy of facilitating removals by agreements to return asylum applicants to a country that already denied an application or through which an asylum applicant travelled but did not seek asylum. The intent is to have the transit country, not Canada, return a denied asylum applicant to his or her country of origin. Canada has pursued this topic in a variety of diplomatic forums. Recently these include the Intergovernmental Consultations on Asylum, Refugee and Migration Policies in Europe, North America and Australia (IGC) which comprises thirteen European states, Canada, Australia, and the United States. Canada in 1992 held the chair of the Informal Consultations (as this process is generally known). The Chair's country hosts an annual major meeting of the group (called a full-round). The June 1992 meeting hosted by Canada at Niagara-on-the-Lake focused to a large extent on removals, prevention of asylum seeking by nonqualified applicants, information sharing on individuals seeking asylum to avoid asylum shopping, and coordinated mechanisms (IGC, 1992). These interests are not peculiar to Canada. They are at the heart of the consultation process in this and other forums.

Canada also has exerted a great deal of effort to obtain a memorandum of understanding (MOU) with the United States on the return to the United States of those who are denied asylum by or transit through the United States and subsequently enter Canada and request asylum. The United States government has yet to sign the agreement. The flow would mostly be from Canada to the United States and would lead to very few returns by the U.S. government of asylum applicants previously denied by the Canadian government. The low priority for this issue in the United States suggests that it may be stalling the Canadian government in order to avoid a straightforward refusal.

In addition to the MOU with the United States, Canada is interested in establishing a series of bilateral agreements to weave a protective shield against asylum shoppers on its shores. Canadian attempts at similar agreements with European states have to date been equally unsuccessful as those with the United States.

Under international agreements and customary international law, a country may not refoule (return) a person in danger of being killed or deprived of freedom. It remains a disputed question whether a country meets its nonrefoulement obligations when it sends a person back to a country that made a negative decision about the application and lets that country bear the responsibility of returning the applicant to the country of origin.

Although organized boatloads of asylum seekers are a concern to Canada (as happened in the case of a boat from Germany to its Atlantic shores), the numerical flow over its southern border is greater. Latin American and Caribbean migration provides the basis of a common interest with the United States and Mexico in protecting against hemispheric flows of false asylum applicants who abuse the system.

United States

A consistent policy goal of the United States in the 1980s has been to avoid becoming a country of mass asylum for the Western Hemisphere. The lessons of the Mariel boat lift from Cuba in the spring of 1980 were traumatic (Bach, 1987; Keely, 1993: 73; Keely and Barrett, 1992).

The United States also has an aversion to putting people in camps for long periods. Japanese internment in World War II is but one searing memory of the use of camps. On the other hand, permitting large groups of asylees to live among the general public with work authorization is presumed tantamount to permanent admission and an open invitation to abuse.

The policy objective of not being a first asylum country has been pursued by the executive branch under presidents of both parties from Jimmy Carter, through Reagan, Bush and Clinton. During the Reagan and Bush presidencies, opponents to U.S. policy in Central America and human rights advocates found sympathetic ears in Congress, which passed the "temporary protective status" as part of the 1990 immigration legislation. The courts also found fault with the execution of this nonarticulated, executive branch policy. The *American Baptist Case* (*ABC*), which required a rehearing of denied asylum applications and permitting late filings by those who were scared off by the low approval rates of the Immigration and Naturalization Service in the 1980s, underscores the complexity of U.S. governance (Mason, 1991; Papademetriou, 1991).

The Caribbean and Central America continue to present real possibilities of large-scale asylum seeking. Now, organized smuggling presents the possibility of multiple shiploads of people coming from as far as China. The United States, like European counterparts, tries to convince domestic and world opinion that some countries sending forth many asylum applicants are really "safe countries," or not producers of refugees from a strictly legal standpoint. Such countries may be poor, even desperately so. They may have political instability. There may even be political persecution of some elements in the country. These conditions do not necessarily translate into personal persecution of all individuals of that country for reasons of race, nationality, religion, political opinion, or membership in a social group. "If everyone is a refugee, then no one is a refugee" is the gist of the argument.

The U.S. government shares the view of many European governments and Canada that many asylum applicants are desperate people in great need but not necessarily refugees. International migration, especially unregulated, is not a solution to the economic or political problems of the exiles; it also poses a threat, proximately or remotely, to the domestic stability of the receiving country.

What Canada and the United States are doing mirrors steps taken in Europe. Legislation is proposed: C-86 in Canada, which received Royal Assent on December 17, 1992; the Simpson-Kennedy bill in the United States; and President Clinton's proposals announced at a press conference on July 28, 1993. Such legislative initiatives basically permit a border triage that attempts to weed out the manifestly unfounded cases. Safe countries are defined that are presumed not to produce refugees and an applicant would have to show very strong evidence to counteract the presumption of no persecution. The United States did this in the case of the election of the Solidarity government in Poland and other elected governments in Central Europe.

Mexico

The movement of asylum seekers across Mexico's southern border, their settlement in the country's southern region, their spread throughout Mexico, their use of Mexico as a transit alley northward, and reported incursions by the Guatemalan army all were linked in Mexican foreign policy discourse to the concept of national security. In the past, Mexican security was provided by a U.S. umbrella. In this, as in much else of its relation to its northern neighbor, Mexico's main problem was to maintain an independence of operating space. Migration over its southern border is Mexico's direct problem and will not be mediated by a U.S. defensive shield. The movement is a Mexican national security issue.

Mexico has been involved in moving into the orbit of the international refugee regime as it proceeds to develop refugee policy, law and practice. It is also cooperating with U.S. immigration authorities to deal with procedures and resources to control its borders.

Despite poor coordination by the White House staff concerning prior discussion and agreement, Mexico was not indisposed to handling the July, 1993, case of three boats of smuggled Chinese off the west coast of North America (Devroy and Williams, 1993). The Mexicans understood the U.S. reluctance to take the passengers onto U.S. soil because the passengers could claim asylum and enter a lengthy adjudication procedure even though the circumstances of the trip, the cost and the arrangements involved with participants to the scheme in the United States, Taiwan and China all pointed to their being nonrefugees (Rotella, 1993; DePalma, 1993; Robberson, 1993). Mexico had no such elaborate procedures. The Mexican government, however, wanted to do it its own way and not at all appear, least of all to its own citizens, as if sovereign Mexico were being used as a Guantànamo by the United States.

Collective Interests in Coordinated Action

This telegraphic tour of the policy interests and issues of the three major North American countries indicates confluence of interests and conditions that have resulted in trilateral discussions on migration issues among Mexico, Canada, and the United States. Not to be confused with the North American Free Trade Agreement (NAFTA) negotiations, in which migration was excluded (except for technicalities about temporary business-related entries similar to the U.S.-Canada trade agreement), these trilateral talks focus on common interests. The logic of state interests seems to point in the direction of a regionalized approach to migration into North America. The three countries currently have a mutual interest in asylum and illegal migration from Central America and the Caribbean. They have a shared interest in preventing boat loads of smuggled migrants from China or elsewhere arriving under the guise of asylum seekers. The hoped-for economic success of NAFTA will further increase collective migration interests regarding migration to a prosperous North America that includes Mexico. Some prefiguring of such an eventuality, echoing the experience of Spain and Italy vis-à-vis Europe, is already apparent in the migration into Mexico. Mexico is no longer just an emigration country. It already is a magnet for immigrants, even in the early stages of its economic integration in North America.

As in Europe, North American events indicate the presence of a national security optic in the bargain. The main difference in the northern part of the Western Hemisphere compared to Europe is that, at this point, the migrants in the Americas are not yet seen as a threat to the internal foundations of democracy. Such specters in North America are remote at this point, even if rising anti-immigrant feelings are evident. In some European capitals, threats to democracy's foundations are seriously discussed. In the New World the national security dimension is real, but as a preventative lest the situation get out of hand. The immediate security dimension involves Mexico's southern border and the political and economic stability of Central America and the Caribbean. The anti-immigrant sentiments in the United States to date translate into calls for restrictions on immigration. They have not spilled over into widespread anti-immigrant episodes. While there can be disagreement in interpretation of the severity and implications of incidents of racial or ethnic tension, the level of public clamor and concern and the depth of questioning the effects of immigration on fundamental national unity has not gone as far as in leading European countries. Anti-immigrant sentiments in Canada and Mexico are even more muted than in the United States.

North America, like Europe, reveals tendencies to treat asylum and refugee issues in regionalized ways and with a decided security dimension. That said, there are important contextual differences between the two regions' approaches and the underlying factors that shape responses to asylum challenges.

DIFFERENCES BETWEEN EUROPE AND NORTH AMERICA REGARDING ASYLUM

The fundamental difference between Europe and North America is the relative openness of Canada and the United States to immigration and refugee reception given the historical and continuing role of migration. Mexico also has a long and important tradition of exile reception. Though strained by the movements from Central America, this tradition is an important part of the political culture and defining characteristics of Mexico. North America, in short, and especially the two northernmost countries, think of themselves as immigrant countries in ways not shared by European countries. The issues around the integration of immigrants consequently are topics about which the traditional immigrant receiving countries have experience and values. This does not at all mean the absence of tensions; rather, the public policy challenges and the level of concern are different from the general European case.

The concerns about migration from southern countries in the North American context have resemblances to Europe's prior concerns about migration from the poor cousins of southern Europe. This is quite different from concern about migration from poor southern countries that seem to be endless reservoirs of workers and to have few prospects for genuine development. In North America, the first concern is with reinforcing economic growth in Mexico. Among many other beneficial results, the presumption is that this will lead, with a lag time, to lower Mexican migration. Even beyond Mexico, NAFTA discussions include invitations to other Latin countries to join the framework. Chile and Argentina have shown interest. The focus, as earlier in Europe, is on trade and investment for sustained economic development. In Europe today, there is much talk of aid programs to migrant-sending countries, scarcely disguised as programs to keep people home, rather than to develop partner economies to increase markets and bring economic prosperity to all participant countries.

In both Europe and North America, concern over asylum is leading to adoption of a greater role for national security in migration policy development and moves to increased regionalization of policy and program as opposed to reliance on a global strategy and U.N. agencies. This conclusion, however, should not overlook the important differences in the policy contexts in the two major regions analyzed. Those differences are part of the reason why regionalization, based on specific coincidence of interests, results in attempts to harmonize responses.

IMPLICATIONS FOR HUMANITARIAN AND HUMAN RIGHTS ACTIVITIES

It is all too easy to react to the words "national security" and "regionalization" as codes for the wholesale violation of human rights and acceptance of needless suffering. Have not horrors enough been perpetrated in the name of national security, and in the very countries from which many asylees come to North America these days? Are the persecutors going to win by making us like them? Have the human rights movement and the refugee protection community worked so hard for universal standards and global approaches only to see regionalism reemerge?

These concerns are real and we cannot deny their force. On the other hand, national security does not preclude humanitarian action or holding governments to their responsibilities to respect and protect their citizens. If human rights are to be actively pursued in foreign policy, they must be integrated with national security concerns. They are not contradictory or antithetical. Reducing asylum claims, including reduction of the need for genuine claims for relief from persecution, are advanced by holding governments responsible for their actions. Would not reduction of military abuses in Central America lead to both a lessening in the rights violations and a reduction in the movements over Mexico's southern border? To the extent that migration remains high on government agendas, human rights will emerge from the margins to be a central foreign policy problem.

The logic of events in Europe has similarities to that in North America. If so, the development of industrial governments' migration policies will incorporate greater attention to national security and receiving country efforts will be increasingly regional in nature. The results will be a reconfigured global refugee regime. That, we suggest, will be the environment. To fight to change it may be tilting against windmills.

Assistance to the uprooted and persecuted would not be advanced by denying a security dimension or resisting regional discussion and initiative. If humanitarian goals and universal principles are not by definition contradictory to national security and regional approaches, than the struggles for dignity and rights can proceed, even in the new context. In fact, the new context may move human rights from the margins to a more central place on foreign policy agendas of immigrant receiving countries. That, we propose, will be the additional challenge in an already difficult effort on behalf of people unjustly victimized.

REFERENCES

Bach, R. L.
1987   "The Cuban Exodus: Political and Economic Motivations." In *The Caribbean Exodus*. Ed. B. B. Levine. New York: Praeger. Pp. 106–130.

Binder, D.
1991   "Thousands of Albanians Flee Aboard Ships to Italy," *The New York Times*, March 3. A5.

Collinson, S.
1993a   *Europe and International Migration*. London: Pinter.

1993b   *Beyond Borders: West European Migration Policy towards the 21st Century*. London: Royal Institute for International Affairs and Wyndham Place Trust.

DePalma, A.
1993   "Refugees Are Sent Back to China Hours after They Dock in Mexico," *The New York Times*, July 18. 1.

Devroy, A., and D. Williams
1993   "Diplomatic Mishaps Set US Migrant Policy Adrift," *The New York Times*, July 14. A17.

European Union
1990   Convention Applying the Schengen Agreement of 14 June 1985 between the Governments of the States of the Benelux Economic Union, the Federal Republic of Germany and the French Republic, on the Gradual Abolition of Checks at Their Common Borders. English text.

1989   Convention Determining the State Responsible for Reexamining Applications for Asylum Lodged in One of the Member States of the European Communities. English text.

Fisher, M.
1992a   "Violence Seen Hurting German Economy," *The New York Times*, December 1. A27.

1992b   "Germany Looks Inward," *The New York Times*, December 21. 1.

Intergovernmental Consultations (IGC)
1993   "Asylum Applications in Participating States – 1983–1992 and 1993 Fore-
          cast." Mimeograph.

───────
1992   "Annotated Agenda: Full Round of Consultations, Niagara-on-the-Lake, 29–30,
          June 1992." Mimeograph.

Kamm, H.
1993   "In Europe's Upheaval, Doors Close to Foreigners," *The New York Times*,
          February 10. 1*ff.*

Keely, C. B.
1993   "The United States of America: Retaining a Fair Immigration Policy." In *The
          Politics of Migration Policies: Settlement and Integration, The First World into
          the 1990s.* Ed. D. Kubat. New York: Center for Migration Studies. Pp. 60–84.

Keely, C. B., and R. C. Barrett
1992   "The Office of the United States Coordinator of Refugees: An Experiment
          in Legislating Crisis Management." Center for Immigration Policy and Refu-
          gee Assistance. Draft Mimeograph. June 1.

Keely, C. B., and S. S. Russell
n.d.   "The Response of Industrial Countries to Asylum Flows," *Journal of Interna-
          tional Affairs.* Forthcoming.

Kinzer, S.
1993   "Germany Closing Migrants' Hostels," *The New York Times*, September 8.
          A7.

Kubat, D., ed.
1993   *The Politics of Migration Policies: Settlement and Integration, The First World
          into the 1990s.* New York: Center for Migration Studies.

Los Angeles Times
1991   "Europe's New Flood of Refugees," *Los Angeles Times*, August 13. B6.

Maass, P.
1992   "Bosnia Saturated with Refugees." *The New York Times*, November 4. A3.

Mason, J.
1991   "Immigration Act of 1990." American Public Welfare Association. Mimeo-
          graph.

Mehrlander, U.
1993   "Federal Republic of Germany: Sociological Aspects of Migration Policy." In
          *The Politics of Migration Policies: Settlement and Integration, The First World
          into the 1990s.* Ed. D. Kubat. New York: Center for Migration Studies.

Papademetriou, D. G.
1991   "The Immigration Act of 1990." Washington, DC: U.S. Department of Labor,
          Bureau of International Affairs. Mimeograph.

Robberson, T.
1993   "Mexican Navy Seizes Third Migrant Ship," *The Washington Post*, July 19.
          A1.

Robinson, E.
1992   "Refugees Challenge a Continent's Stability," *The New York Times*, December 20. 1.

Rogers, R., ed.
1985   *Guests Come to Stay: The Affects of European Labor Migration on Sending and Receiving Countries*. Boulder, CO: Westview.

Rotella, S.
1993   "Mexico Ready to Send Chinese Voyagers Back," *Los Angeles Times*, July 17. 1.

Russell, S. S., and C. B. Keely
n.d.   "Regional Efforts in Industrial Countries." In *Toward a New Global Refugee System*. Ed. R. Rogers and S. S. Russell. Forthcoming.

SOPEMI
1992   *Trends in International Migration*. Paris: OECD.

Washington Post
1993   "Refugees from Former Yugoslavia as of April 1993," *The Washington Post*, July 14. 14.

13

United States Refugee Law and Policy: Past, Present and Future

T. Alexander Aleinikoff

United States refugee law has three major components: 1) selection of refugees overseas; 2) adjudication of asylum claims of aliens physically present in the United States; and 3) responses to "refugee-like" situations (Salvadorans, Haitians, Mariel Cubans). In this paper, I will briefly summarize the law relating to each category and comment on current policies.[1]

SELECTION OF REFUGEES OVERSEAS

For U.S. refugee law and policy, 1980 was a watershed year – witnessing both enactment of the Refugee Act of 1980 and the arrival of more than 125,000 Mariel Cubans in southern Florida.

Before 1980, U.S. refugee policy had been largely ad hoc. Special statutory programs had authorized entry of 400,000 displaced persons in the aftermath of World War II and 30,000 refugees following suppression of the 1956 Hungarian revolt. In 1965, as part of the repeal of the 1920s national origins quota system, Congress established a small quota for annual refugee admissions (the so-called "seventh prefer-

---

[1]For references to sources regarding legislative and policy developments described herein, *see* Aleinikoff and Martin (1991).

ence") available only to refugees fleeing either a Communist-dominated regime or countries in the Middle East. The number of admissions allotted to the seventh preference (up to 17,400 by 1978) could not begin to accommodate the hundreds of thousands of Cubans and Southeast Asians who sought entry as refugees in the 1960s and 1970s. These groups were permitted to enter the United States by way of exercise of the Attorney General's "parole" power. Because parole conferred no formal status, subsequent federal legislation was adopted to permit attainment of lawful permanent residency.

The 1980 Refugee Act was enacted to regularize refugee admissions and to conform U.S. law to the international conventions on refugees (the United States had acceded to the 1967 Protocol in 1968, but had not amended its immigration or refugee statutes to reflect the new international obligations). The major features of the Refugee Act are as follows:

1) Annual designation of the number and source of overseas refugees, to be established after executive branch "consultation" with congressional committees (and repeal of the ideologically and geographically limited seventh preference). (Immigration and Nationality Act (INA) § 207)

2) Incorporation of the 1951 Convention's definition of refugee (as amended by the 1967 Protocol) into U.S. law. (INA § 101(a)(42))

3) Incorporation of the 1951 Convention's mandatory prohibition on refoulement of refugees (through amendment of the previously discretionary power bestowed by INA § 243(h)).

4) Limitation of the Attorney General's parole power to prevent large-scale admission of refugees outside the structure of the Refugee Act (INA § 212(d)(5)).

5) Statutory recognition of a right, for aliens in the United States, to apply for asylum. (INA § 208)

6) Creation of refugee assistance programs and restructuring of the federal bureaucracy to coordinate such efforts.

With the ink barely dry on the Refugee Act, Fidel Castro opened up Mariel harbor and more than 125,000 Cubans came to the United States. Despite INA restriction of Attorney General parole power and the demand by some in Congress that the Cubans be designated refugees under the new statutory provisions, the Mariel Cubans were "paroled" into the United States, pending congressional resolution of their status. (In 1986, Congress finally provided for their regularization.) The Mariel boat lift – occurring so soon after passage of the Refugee Act – demonstrated a lesson still being learned by U.S. policy makers: that world events largely beyond the control of Washington frustrate attempts to "regularize" refugee admissions into the United States.

The 1980 Refugee Act: Thirteen Years After

Despite the 1980 Refugee Act's repeal of the seventh preference's ideological and geographical restrictions, U.S. overseas admissions remain overwhelmingly dominated by refugees fleeing (now former) Communist regimes.[2] The fall of the Berlin Wall and the Eastern bloc governments notwithstanding, the designations for fiscal year 1993 follow the familiar pattern. Of the 132,000 authorized admissions, the vast majority will be provided to aliens from the former Soviet Union, Eastern bloc countries and Southeast Asia (*see* Table 1).

It is certainly arguable that the overseas admission program has, for aliens coming from former Communist countries, shifted its underlying premise from refugee protection to family reunification. This is most apparent in U.S. policy regarding refugee admissions from the former Soviet Union. In 1988, the Attorney General raised concern that many Soviet citizens granted refugee status appeared not to meet the rather narrow standards of U.S. law, and that overseas determinations should proceed on a case-by-case basis. This policy shift coincided with the radical restructing of Soviet society under *glasnost* and *perestroika*. Thereafter, INS approval rates for Soviet refugee applicants, many of whom had secured exit documents, plummeted. Under pressure from domestic interest groups, Congress intervened in 1990, enacting legislation (the "Lautenberg amendment") that effectively adopted a presumption of refugee status for Soviet Jews, Evangelical Christians, and members of the Ukrainian Catholic Church and Orthodox Church. The Lautenberg amendment has been reenacted and still controls refugee admissions from the former Soviet Union. Thus 50,000 admissions are designated for the former Soviet Union for fiscal year 1993, and the State Department has announced that these numbers will be allocated to members of groups covered by the Lautenberg amend-

---

[2]For tables on refugee admissions to the United States, *see* Refugee Reports (1991b).

TABLE 1

FY 1991 AND 1992 REFUGEE ADMISSIONS AND FY 1993 CEILINGS

Region	FY 1991 Actual	FY 1992 Authorized Levels	FY 1992 Estimated Arrivals	FY 1993 Proposed Ceilings
Africa	4,424	6,000	6,000	7,000
East Asia	53,486	52,000	52,000	52,000[a]
Eastern Europe	6,855	3,000	3,000	1,500
Latin America/Caribbean	2,237	3,000	3,000	3,500
Near East/South Asia	5,359	6,000	5,500	7,000
Soviet Union/Former Soviet Union	38,661	61,000	60,000	50,000
Unallocated Res.	n/a	1,000	200	1,000
Subtotal	111,022	132,000	129,700	122,000
Privately Funded	1,789	10,000	1,500	10,000
Total	112,811	142,000	131,200	132,000

Source: *Refugee Reports*, "FY 91 and 92 Refugee Admissions and FY 93 Ceilings," 13(7): 16. July 31, 1992.

[a]Includes Amerasian immigrants and their families who enter as immigrants under a special statutory provision, but receive benefits as refugees.

ment. The vast majority of these refugees will be joining family members living in the United States.

In sum, while the Refugee Act has established a flexible and efficacious system for annual overseas admissions, implementation of the act continues to favor groups traditionally benefitted by U.S. refugee programs, despite dramatic changes in the home countries of such refugees. Whether or not most of the persons admitted would meet the standards applied in asylum cases filed in the United States is in doubt.

ASYLUM: POLICY AND PROCEDURES

Until the 1980s, the United States had no statutory asylum policy or procedures. The occasional Soviet ballerina or Chinese tennis star who "defected" was granted asylum under the authority of INS officials. The Refugee Act required the Attorney General to establish by regulation "a procedure for an alien physically present in the United States or at a land border or port of entry, irrespective of such alien's status, to apply for asylum" (INA § 208). Importantly, the INA asylum provision establishes no limit on the number of aliens who may apply for or be granted asylum in any year (although the statute limits the number of those who may obtain permanent residency status to 10,000 per annum); nor must an alien be in a lawful status in order to apply for asylum. The result is that any alien who arrives in the United States has the right to request asylum and usually can remain in the country until various levels of appellate review are completed. Unlike the numerically limited overseas admission program, the asylum process constitutes (to use David Martin's phrase) "a wildcard in the immigration deck" (1982: 112). These considerations have led the executive branch to adopt measures aimed at deterring the arrival of asylum applicants, such as interdiction, detention and funding of Mexican efforts to return Central Americans.

Aliens granted asylum may in due course obtain lawful permanent resident status and, ultimately, citizenship. Their spouses and children are entitled to enter the United States and are also granted asylee status. Asylees are entitled to most state and federal benefit programs made available to permanent resident aliens and citizens. Thus, the granting of asylum goes far beyond the nonrefoulement protection required by the refugee Convention and Protocol, which enjoins state signatories from returning persons to countries in which they will face persecution but does not require the receiving states to grant refugees formal status.

Since 1980, the annual number of applications has ranged from less than 20,000 to more than 100,000.[3] In 1992, 103,447 applications from the top 25 sending countries (92% of the total) were filed with the INS.[4] (An additional several thousand cases were initiated in deportation or exclusion proceedings before immigration judges.) Over the past twelve years, asylum has been granted in approximately 50,000 cases. Calculating an "average approval rate," however, would be misleading because approval rates for particular countries vary significantly: until the collapse of Communist regimes, claims filed by aliens coming from Eastern bloc countries were approved at far higher rates than applications filed by Salvadorans, Haitians, and Guatemalans. There is little doubt that U.S. foreign policy interests have played a major role in the differential approval rates.

A decade of objections to the apparent bias in the adjudication process finally produced a new set of asylum regulations in 1990. Under the new procedures, asylum claims are heard by specially trained "asylum officers," State Department influence has been reduced, and a documen-

[3]*See* tables on asylum cases filed with INS District Offices (Refugee Reports, 1990, 1991b).

[4]*See* table on asylum applicant countries of origin (Refugee Reports, 1992a).

tation center (modelled after the Canadian center) has been established (Beyer, 1992). Initial reports indicate that the process is improved, but serious defects remain (National Asylum Study Project, 1992).

One of the major problems facing the asylum adjudication process is a current backlog of more than 200,000 cases. A substantial portion of the backlog has resulted from the settlement reached in *American Baptist Church v. Thornburgh* (760 F. Supp. 796 [N.D.Cal. 1991]), or *ABC*, a case that had challenged the government's adjudication of Salvadoran and Guatemalan asylum claims. Under the settlement, aliens from El Salvador and Guatemala whose claims had been adjudicated under the old asylum rules (or who were present in the United States prior to 1990 and had not requested asylum) may file for asylum under the new procedures. While their claims are pending they will be granted authorization to work and will not be deported. It is estimated that more than 100,000 aliens may benefit from the settlement.

The 1991–1992 influx of Haitian asylum seekers (discussed below) further strained the adjudication process. To deal with the crisis, asylum officers were diverted from usual tasks and sent to Guantànamo Naval Base to prescreen Haitians picked up at sea by the U.S. Coast Guard. A federal district court eventually held that the Attorney General had exceeded his authority in establishing the prescreening process at Guantànamo.[5]

REFUGEE-LIKE SITUATIONS: MARIEL, TPS, AND HAITIAN SCREENING

The formal categories of "refugee" and "asylee" tell only one part of the story of U.S. approaches to involuntary migrants. Presented below are two refugee-like groups seeking entry to the United States, the Cubans of the Mariel boat lift in 1980 and the so-called Haitian boat people, along with the U.S. administration of extended voluntary departure or temporary protected status programs in response to their situations.

Mariel Cubans

As mentioned above, more than 125,000 Mariel Cubans were permitted to enter the United States in 1980 in an informal status. They were never granted refugee status; rather, they have obtained permanent residency

---

[5]*Haitian Centers Council, Inc. v. Sale*, Civ. No. 92-1258 (SJ) (E.D.N.Y., June 8, 1993). This conclusion seems doubtful as a matter of law, and is likely to be appealed by the Government.

status under the 1966 Cuban Adjustment Act or a provision in the 1986 Immigration Reform and Control Act. (The latter provision also permitted several thousand Haitians in INS proceedings to adjust status.)

EVD and TPS

The United States has also utilized a number of administrative devices for granting "safe haven" to groups of aliens in the United States whose home countries are embroiled in civil strife. This forestalling of deportation was granted whether or not a particular alien could establish that he or she would face persecution if returned home; that is, the safe haven policies were extended on humanitarian grounds to aliens who might not qualify for the protection against nonrefoulement provided by the refugee Convention and Protocol and § 243(h) of the U.S. Immigration Code.

Until 1990, such programs were known as "extended voluntary departure" (EVD). Under EVD, deportable aliens from designated countries were not returned until conditions in their countries of origin stabilized. The decision to grant EVD was made by the Attorney General upon recommendation from the State Department. Groups that have benefitted from EVD include: Ethiopians (1977), Ugandans (1978), Iranians (1979), Nicaraguans (1979) and Afghans (1980). Following the Tiananmen Square massacre in 1989, the Bush Administration ordered the "deferral of enforced departure" (effectively, EVD) of Chinese nationals in the United States.

For most of the 1980s, refugee advocates urged the government to extend EVD to Salvadorans and Guatemalans in the United States. The argument was made that these groups faced far more serious situations upon return than Poles and Nicaraguans, who had been granted EVD. The State Department resisted, suggesting that circumstances in the home countries were not generally dangerous and that any EVD program would only serve as a magnet for further arrivals of undocumented "economic migrants." (Most observers believe that foreign policy considerations were in fact the primary reason for the EVD denials.) In 1990, as part of the omnibus immigration reform legislation, Congress added a new provision to the Immigration Code (INA § 244A) authorizing the Attorney General to grant "temporary protected status" (TPS) to aliens in the United States whose home countries are facing unsettled conditions due to ongoing armed conflict, natural or environmental disaster, or other serious threats to safety. Initial TPS designations may last up to eighteen months, and may be renewed. Aliens granted TPS are authorized to work.

In the 1990 legislation, Congress mandated the granting of TPS to Salvadorans (a measure also supported by the Salvadoran government in order to prevent the mass return of Salvadorans, many of whom are currently working in the United States and sending millions of dollars to relatives in El Salvador). At the expiration of the statutory grant, the Bush Administration elected not to renew TPS for Salvadorans. However, President Bush granted covered Salvadorans deferred enforced departure (DED) status (the same designation used for the Chinese following Tiananmen) until June 30, 1993. President Clinton extended DED until mid-1994. In practice, both TPS and DED are merely different names for EVD: all three statuses prevent deportation and authorize work; none permits family unification or automatic conversion to permanent residency status.

The Attorney General has extended TPS to other nationalities. Included among these are Kuwaitis, Lebanese, Liberians, Somalis, and Bosnians.

Haitians

The major refugee-like situation facing the United States today is the (now staunched) flow of Haitian boat people. The phenomenon is hardly new. During the Carter Administration, the INS initiated mass deportation hearings to clear up a backlog of several thousand Haitian asylum claims. The program, later ruled by the courts to have violated constitutional protections of due process, was justified on the grounds that virtually all Haitian asylum seekers were "economic migrants" who were abusing the asylum process in order to escape from the poorest nation in the Western Hemisphere. The Reagan and Bush Administrations continued to so characterize Haitian asylum applicants, despite solid documentation of gross violations of human rights in Haiti.

Under the Reagan Administration, two policies were initiated aimed at deterring the flow of Haitians. First, reversing a policy adopted in the 1950s, the INS announced that it would detain all aliens who could not demonstrate a legal right to enter, pending proceedings to remove them from the United States. The new policy fell most heavily on asylum seekers (Salvadorans in the southwest, Haitians in Florida, and

Afghans arriving at airports in the northeast), many of whom spent many months in detention while their claims were being adjudicated. (Undocumented Mexican migrants could avoid detention by accepting voluntary return to their country of origin – an option usually not desired by asylum seekers.) Court challenges to the detention policy generally failed, with some courts issuing disturbing rulings that aliens at U.S. borders had no constitutional rights of due process or equal protection in regard to their applications for entry.[6] The detention policy remains in effect, although most long-term detainees have eventually been granted parole into the United States.

The second Reagan Administration policy innovation was interdiction. Under an agreement with the Haitian government, the United States was authorized to stop Haitian vessels on the high seas bound for the United States in order to enforce U.S. and Haitian laws. In an attempt to appear to comply with international prohibitions against refoulement, U.S. immigration officers were stationed on board the Coast Guard cutters and charged with determining whether any of the interdicted Haitians legitimately feared return to Haiti. Haitians with credible claims for asylum were to be brought to the United States for processing. As was obvious from the start, the likelihood that Haitians would identify themselves in such a manner was extremely low; for the first ten years of the policy fewer than a dozen Haitians were brought to the United States, while more than 20,000 were returned.

The interdiction program was relatively successful at reducing the flow of Haitians to Florida until the September 1991 military coup that overthrew the first democratically elected President in Haitian history, Jean-Bertrand Aristide. With the increase in repression following the coup, thousands of Haitians took to boats, and the U.S. interdiction program was quickly overwhelmed. After unsuccessful efforts to find other havens in the Caribbean region, arrangements were made to bring the Haitians to the U.S. Guantànamo Naval Base on Cuba, where they were prescreened by asylum officers. Initially, large percentages were held to have stated a credible basis for fearing return, and thus were "screened in" (meaning that they were brought to the United States, granted parole, and given a year to file an asylum claim). Apparently, State Department officials complained that the number of those

[6]*Jean v. Nelson*, 727 F.2d 957 (11 Cir. 1984) (en banc), modified on other grounds, 472 U.S. 846 (1985).

screened in was too high, and the approval rate declined. Over the course of the program, more than 30,000 Haitians were screened, and approximately one-third were brought to the United States for the formal filing of an asylum claim. The remainder were returned to Haiti. (The relatively high rate of "screening in" is no doubt a result of the new corps of asylum officers recruited and trained after promulgation of the new asylum regulations.)[7]

With the continued flow of boat people, conditions at Guantànamo worsened. In May 1992, President Bush issued the so-called "Kennebunkport Order," which terminated the screening procedure, and announced that henceforth all interdicted Haitians would be returned to Haiti *with no opportunity for applying for asylum*. The Bush Administration maintained the view that most of the Haitians were "economic migrants" (despite an aggregate screened-in rate of about one-third), and that the screening procedure was enticing Haitians to undertake life-threatening sea voyages. The Administration denied that the new policy violated the legal obligation of nonrefoulement, arguing that the obligation only applied on U.S. territory. They suggested that Haitians could come to the U.S. embassy in Port-au-Prince in order to request refugee status.

Lawsuits were brought challenging the Bush Administration policies. The technical legal question presented was whether a provision in the immigration laws prohibiting refoulement (INA § 243(h)) applied beyond the territorial limits of the United States. It was thought that the election of President Clinton would moot the case, since candidate Clinton had condemned the interdiction policy. However, shortly before taking office, Clinton announced that he would maintain the interdiction program "for the time being" in order to forestall a "humanitarian tragedy" – that is, the loss of life at sea that American policy makers believed would accompany a mass exodus by boat from

---

[7]Some 200 screened-in Haitians remained at Guantànamo because they, or close family members, tested positive for HIV. Such aliens are excludable under U.S. immigration law, and the INS refused to permit them to come to the United States to file asylum claims. These aliens were finally permitted to enter the United States in the summer of 1993 after a federal district court held that their detention and treatment at Guantànamo violated their constitutionally protected right to due process; *see Haitian Centers Council, Inc. v. Sale*, Civ. No. 92-1258 (SJ) (E.D.N.Y., June 8, 1993), following affirmance of preliminary injunction in *Haitian Centers Council, Inc. v. McNary*, 969 F.2d 1326 (2d Cir. 1992). There is an obvious (and unresolved) tension between the holding in the Guantànamo case and the earlier cases ruling that detained and excludable Haitians in the United States have no constitutional rights to assert regarding their applications for entry.

Haiti if the interdiction policy were revoked.[8] Thus the Clinton Administration defended the Bush policy before the Supreme Court, and the Court, in an 8 to 1 decision, held that the interdiction order violated neither U.S. nor international law (*Sale v. Haitian Center Council, Inc.,* 1993 US LEXIS 4247 [June 21, 1993]).

THE FUTURE OF REFUGEE POLICY

Although there is a growing trend in the developed world to deter refugee influxes, it is not likely that U.S. refugee and asylum policy will change radically in the next few years. Overseas admissions programs are likely to continue to bring not insignificant numbers of refugees to the United States each year. This is so because such flows are controlled and controllable; U.S. policy makers designate the groups and numbers authorized to enter. Furthermore, the process initiated by the Refugee Act of 1980 has become regularized and it has strong interest group support in the United States. The executive and legislative branches have established a modus operandi that seems to work reasonably well – even if the overseas program is not targeted at the most needy of the world's refugees. Indeed, because overseas admissions decisions favor groups and individuals with existing communities or family members in the United States, absorption costs are not viewed as prohibitively high.

The unregulated asylum process is another matter. The U.S. government is certain to adopt new asylum procedures and standards aimed at deterring frivolous claims and expediting adjudication. Currently on the table are recommendations to establish "summary exclusion" procedures at the border. Such legislative proposals are based on the perception that increasing numbers of persons arrive at U.S. borders with fraudulent documents (or having destroyed travel documents), request political asylum, and either enter into lengthy proceedings testing the merits of their claim or disappear into the United States. Relying in part on the Guantànamo experience, the legislation would assign INS officials to screen such aliens at the border, summarily returning aliens who cannot establish a "credible basis" for their claim of feared persecution.

---

[8]Clinton also announced that he would step up in-country processing in Haiti under which persons who demonstrated to U.S. officials in Haiti that they met the "refugee" definition would be brought directly to the United States. As of this writing, the government has not released official data on the in-country processing program.

An additional problem is the large (and growing) backlog of asylum cases. It is estimated at more than 200,000. Part of the backlog could be cleared by legislation that would "legalize" the status of those in the backlog. This strategy might be appropriate for Salvadorans and Guatemalans covered by the *ABC* case, and perhaps for "screened-in Haitians." It is also likely that streamlining of procedures will be considered, such as restricting administrative and court review of asylum denials.

European nations (particularly Germany) have provided other mechanisms for expediting the asylum process which no doubt will undergo scrutiny in the United States. These include: agreements among receiving nations that asylum claims be adjudicated by the country in which the asylum seeker first arrived (Canada and the United States have produced a draft agreement of this kind, patterned after European efforts[9]), and legislation denying refugee status to asylum seekers whose countries of origin are deemed "safe" or who travelled through "safe" countries prior to arrival. As the United States considers these options, a crucial factor will be its assessment of Mexico's treatment of asylum seekers (Frelick, 1991; Aguayo and Fagan, 1988; Friedland and Rodriguez y Rodriguez, 1987).

The policy options just mentioned would apply to asylum seekers who have reached the territory of the United States. It is quite likely that significant attention will also be paid to policies that deter arrival in the United States. Of major importance here is the Supreme Court's ruling in the Haiti interdiction case holding that neither U.S. nor international refugee law applies to the acts of the U.S. government taken outside U.S. territory. Also likely to continue is U.S. financial assistance to Mexican efforts to stem the flow of Latin American asylum seekers and undocumented aliens through Mexico to the United States.

REFERENCES

Aguayo, S., and P. W. Fagen
1988   *Central American Refugees in Mexico and the United States.* Washington, DC: Hemispheric Migration Project, Center for Immigration Policy and Refugee Assistance, Georgetown University.

---

[9]*See* European Union (1990a, 1990b).

Aleinikoff, T. A., and D. A. Martin
1991   *Immigration: Process and Policy,* 2 ed. Saint Paul, MN: West Publishing Co.

Beyer, G. A.
1992   "Establishing the United States Asylum Officer Corps: A First Report," *International Journal of Refugee Law,* 4(4): 454–480.

European Union
1990a   Convention Determining the State Responsible for Examining Applications for Asylum Lodged in one of the Member States of the European Communities, June 15, 1990. Reprinted in *International Journal of Refugee Law,* 2(469).

——— 1990b   Convention on the Application of the Schengen Agreement of June 14, 1985, relating to the Gradual Suppression of Controls at Common Frontiers, between the Governments of States Members of the Benelux Economic Union, the Federal Republic of Germany, and the French Republic, June 19, 1990. Reprinted in *International Journal of Refugee Law,* 3(773): 780–786.

Frelick, B.
1991   *Running the Gauntlet: The Central American Journey through Mexico.* Washington, DC: U.S. Committee for Refugees. January.

Friedland, J., and J. Rodriguez y Rodriguez
1987   *Seeking Safe Ground: The Legal Situation of Central American Refugees in Mexico.* San Diego, CA: Mexico-U.S. Law Institute, University of California at San Diego.

Martin, D. A.
1982   "The Refugee Act of 1980: Its Past and Future," *Michigan Yearbook of International Legal Studies,* 91–123.

National Asylum Study Project, Harvard Law School Immigration and Refugee Program
1992   "An Interim Assessment of the Asylum Process of the Immigration and Naturalization Service." December.

Refugee Reports
1992a   Asylum applicant countries of origin, *Refugee Reports,* 13(10): 20. October 30.

——— 1992b   "FY91 and FY92 Refugee Admissions and FY93 Ceilings," *Refugee Reports,* 13(7): 16. July 31.

——— 1991a   Refugee admissions to United States, *Refugee Reports,* 12(12): 9–11. December 30.

——— 1991b   Asylum cases filed with INS District Offices, *Refugee Reports,* 12(12): 12. December 30.

——— 1990   Asylum cases filed with INS District Offices, *Refugee Reports,* 11(7): 16, July 20; 11(12): 12, December 21.

14

Refugee Claimants: Canadian Law and North American Regionalism[1]

H. Patrick Glenn

Introduction

Growth in world population movement has coincided with other
challenges to the nation-state. States, therefore, find themselves defending national policies on population, trade and the environment
while at the same time participating in the creation or adjustment of
regional political units, designed to regulate more effectively those
problems which have come to be recognized as transnational. Of the
world's population movements, that of refugees is the most critical,
since it is based on immediate and overwhelming human need in a
volume incapable of resolution at the national level. In North America,
as in Europe, nation-states thus find themselves responding separately
to refugee demands while seeking some broader form of regional
cooperation, compatible with the cooperation already established in
other, related fields of transnational concern.

---

[1]Portions of this paper are derived from an earlier paper entitled "Procedural Rights of Refugee
Claimants," now in press for a special number of the review *Migration* devoted to Canadian
immigration and refugee policy.

National treatment of refugee claims is thus a product of refugee movement, national policy (as it is expressed in constitutions, legislation, executive regulation or judicial decision) and regional institutions or bilateral forms of cooperation. These sources may not always be harmonious.

As well, North American refugee movement is directed unequally at Mexico, the United States of America and Canada. Refugee movement reaches Canada from Latin America through the United States; from the rest of the world, though again following passage through the United States; or directly from overseas. The nature of refugee flow is thus differentiated. The response of the Canadian State to refugee claims is thus a function of the particular refugee flow, the national source of policy which has obtained dominance, and the susceptibility of the refugee flow to regional forms of regulation.

Of the relevant sources of Canadian law, the Constitution and judicial decisions are of the most general application. The Constitution speaks in terms of abstract guarantees available to "everyone"; in implementing the constitution or fundamental guarantees of procedural justice the judiciary does not make fine distinctions between groups of people or refugees. Legislation and executive regulation lend themselves to more managerial forms of regulation of population flow, including that of refugees. Policies reflecting a particular national response to refugee flow will therefore be found in legislation or regulation; the implementation of such national policies will be rooted in executive agencies of the government as opposed to the judiciary. To the extent that regional cooperation is the object of intergovernmental agreement, the normal means of implementation will also be through legislation and executive regulation. The national response is here harmonized with regional efforts.

Two types of response have thus characterized the reaction of the Canadian State to refugee claims. The first is rooted institutionally in the Canadian judiciary and is formulated in terms of the procedural rights of refugee claimants, regardless of their geographical origin. The second is rooted institutionally in the Canadian executive, which both represents Canada abroad and controls the Canadian Parliament, and is formulated in terms of regulation and control of immigration and refugee movement at both national and regional levels. There is currently tension in Canada between these two types of response to refugee claims.

PROCEDURAL RIGHTS OF REFUGEE CLAIMANTS IN CANADA

A number of countries which have traditionally regarded refugee determination as a purely executive function, unencumbered by constitutional restraints and involving essentially no procedural guarantees for the refugee claimant, have been slowing evolving towards a more adjudicative form of procedure. An adjudicative procedure is one which entails procedural guarantees, of varying description, for the refugee claimant. Even absent a constitutional guarantee of asylum, procedural guarantees may emerge as principles of natural justice, adopted by national legislators or articulated by national courts.

Canada is one of these countries which have moved towards an adjudicative model for refugee determination, and its procedural regime will be examined more fully in the remainder of this paper. In other countries the same phenomenon is observable. Australia has thus recently begun to decentralize the refugee determination process, and a hearing or interview before the decision-making officer appears to be an essential part of the new procedures (Glenn, 1992: 52–53). In the United States the determination process effected in district offices of the Immigration and Naturalization Service has been replaced since 1991 by a process of hearings before asylum officers who enjoy particular status within the governmental hierarchy (Anker, 1991: 34–36). In France within the last year the percentage of refugee claimants accorded interviews by agents of the Office Français de Protection des Réfugiés et Apatrides has increased from 20 percent to 56 percent and further progression is expected (Lott, 1992). These developments appear to be part of a broader movement in which state institutional structures are becoming, in many respects, more permeable to claims by foreigners and nonresidents. The theoretical justification for this development will be examined first, in the cadre of refugee claims, before examining in greater detail the Canadian procedural response.

The State and the Refugee Claimant

Procedure and substantive law have always been closely related to one another. In the common law tradition a hypertrophied concept of procedure prevented the development of substantive law and individual rights, and citizens were entitled to address common law courts only with permission of the chancellor. In the civil law tradition, rights emerged once access to official tribunals became unlimited, and the right of action, or right to sue, may thus be seen as the necessary precursor of individual, substantive rights. It is thus possible, and the history of the civil law is the best illustration of the process, to develop procedural rights in the absence of any concept of underlying, substantive rights. The common law may now be going through this same process, given that access to common law courts has become unlimited, at least within national territories.

In the absence of a right to asylum or any related right, a court could therefore conclude that the claim of a refugee required a judicial hearing as a principle of natural justice. To the writer's knowledge this has not happened anywhere in the world, and traditional language has justified the exclusion or procedural disentitlement of the alien or nonresident because of a status which is merely that of a "guest," or which is merely "privileged" as opposed to being as of right. The existence of the state has thus traditionally prevented the extension of procedural rights to the alien nonresident, and in particular to the refugee claimant. There appear, however, to be two main reasons for the current decline in the concept of a procedurally impregnable state.

The first relates to the concept of the state itself. While some states are more "natural" than others, in the sense of exhibiting coincidence between political, cultural, racial and linguistic boundaries, the modern state is increasingly recognized as a fragile alliance, *un plébiscite de tous les jours*, in the phrase of Renan. As an impermanent political alliance the state is thus essentially consensual, and necessarily open to consensually-based claims to membership, of whatever duration. Since the principal characteristic of the consensual, liberal state is the rule of law, it becomes increasingly difficult to deny the rule of law to claimants to membership. They are already subject to conditions of membership which did not apply to original members, or arrivals, and which are the creation of national, political will. Original members thus had to meet no conditions of membership and are now in principle entitled to adjudication of any claims they raise. Are later arrivals to be denied membership and even the possibility of adjudication of the claim to membership, when the state appears more and more demonstrably as a consensual institution? The pressures towards adjudication of such claims are greatest in countries of immigration such as Canada, where multiculturalism has become an official policy of the federal government, but they are present today in all states.

The second reason for the decline in national barriers to procedural justice is the pervasive influence of right-based thinking, which is now widespread in both civil and common law countries. This has not of course given rise to a right of asylum at the level of international law, since the fundamental element of any right, a viable means of enforcement, is lacking at the international level. Rights are more frequently found to exist in national law, however, and rights rooted in national law may be of great importance to refugee claimants, in a variety of ways. The Canadian example, as shown in the 1985 decision of the Supreme Court of Canada in *Re Singh* ([1985] 1 S.C.R. 177), indicates how rights found to exist at the national level can profoundly affect the procedural regime of the refugee claimant.

In *Re Singh*, refugee claims had been made according to the procedure then prevailing in Canada, by virtue of which claims were determined administratively with no oral hearing. On rejection of their claims, the claimants challenged the legality of these procedures. Their arguments were not based on the existence of a right to asylum, since neither the Canadian Constitution nor Canadian legislation articulates such a right. The Supreme Court of Canada found, however, that certain rights had been conferred on Convention refugees by Canadian federal legislation. These rights included the right to consideration by the Minister for an entry permit once refugee status had been found to exist, the right not to be returned to a country where the refugee's life or freedom would be threatened, and the right to appeal against an order of removal. While almost all persons found to be Convention refugees in Canada are granted permanent residence, Canadian law thus clearly allows expulsion of Convention refugees from Canada, and provides only these slender means of formal protection. The enjoyment of these rights by Convention refugees, however, came to be crucial for the creation of a regime of procedural guarantees for simple refugee claimants, and for the extension of other constitutional guarantees to them (Brun, 1988; Brunelle, 1987).

Since Convention refugees enjoyed such rights, the Supreme Court reasoned, their violation could result in a violation of the general right to "life, liberty and security of the person" which is enjoyed by "everyone," in accordance with Section 7 of the Canadian Charter of Rights and Liberties. Violation of these specific rights of Convention refugees could take place if a refugee claimant was treated in a procedurally unfair way, was found erroneously not to be a Convention refugee, and was removed to a country where personal security was threatened. The existing Canadian procedural regime for determination of refugee status therefore did not adequately protect against possible violations of the rights of Convention refugees. Since the effect of such a violation would affect the security of the person, the violation of the specific rights of Convention refugees also constituted a violation of the right to security of the person protected by the Charter. The Supreme Court therefore invalidated the existing form of administrative refugee determination and remanded the claims to the Ministry for a hearing.

From minimal rights accorded Convention refugees the Supreme Court thus concluded that the general constitutional right to security of the person was applicable and that appropriate procedural guarantees were necessary to prevent eventual violation of this right. The decision illustrates how rights which fall short of a right to asylum may nevertheless be used to justify an appropriate procedural regime, and suggests two further forms of reasoning. First, even in the absence of the specific rights granted by Canadian law to Convention refugees, the general right to security of the person granted by the Canadian or other constitutions to "everyone" might be found to extend to Convention refugees and hence to require procedural safeguards for refugee claimants. Second, in the absence of any constitutional guarantee of the security of the person (in countries lacking written Charters or Bills of Rights), any statutory rights granted to Convention refugees such as those granted by Canadian law may justify procedural guarantees, and national legislation may be unable to overcome such a judicially-imposed requirement of procedural fairness in individual cases.

Individual rights established by national law may thus play an important role in justifying procedural guarantees for refugee claimants and the rights used for this purpose may be of varying description, falling well short of a right to asylum. Given the increasing permeability of the contemporary state, any type of right conferred by national law on Convention refugees is likely to yield significant procedural protection.

This is the probable reason for the refusal of some jurisdictions to legislate in relation to refugee claims, preferring to proceed exclusively by informal executive action. In a country such as Canada, however, where there is a commitment to immigration, official multiculturalism and constitutionally guaranteed rights, the procedural guarantees are likely to be particularly developed. This development has occurred in Canada since the decision of the Supreme Court in 1985 in *Singh*. The question may be asked, however, as to whether the procedural guarantees subsequently adopted in Canada are the most appropriate ones for refugee claims.

Procedural Rights of Refugee Claimants in Canada

Canadian refugee determination procedures have been necessarily integrated into wider systems of immigration control, court structures and legal aid, which provide further guarantees to the refugee claimant. A word on the relation of refugee determination procedures to broader forms of immigration control is therefore in order.

Persons seeking to immigrate to Canada must follow established procedures for obtaining an immigration visa overseas, while those seeking to enter Canada as visitors must establish that they fall within the categories of visitors allowed by law. Immigration officials at ports of entry may however decide that a visa has been unlawfully obtained, or is fraudulent, or may decide that a person seeking entry as a visitor is improperly seeking to evade immigration requirements. It has been a noteworthy feature of Canadian immigration law, in this regard paralleling that of the United States, that no person could be excluded from Canadian territory in such circumstances by virtue of a simple executive order on the part of immigration officials. The executive "turnaround" has been illegal. Departure on the part of the allegedly illegal entrant had to be either voluntary or pursuant to adjudication of the claim to entry by an adjudicator appointed under the federal Public Service Employment Act for the purpose of adjudication under the Immigration Act. Adjudicators do not have access to individual files, are expected to decide on the basis of evidence presented at the adjudication inquiry, and are members of a distinct Adjudication Branch of the Ministry. Their decisions are not reviewable by executive authority and their function has been described, in the traditional language of administrative law in common law countries, as "quasi-judicial." The illegal entrant is thus entitled in principle to a form of adjudicative hearing of the claim to entry, with attendant procedural guarantees. The extension of adjudicative proceedings and procedural guarantees to refugee claimants by the Supreme Court in Canada in the *Singh* case may thus be seen as placing refugee claimants on an equal procedural footing with illegal entrants. It is not evident why refugee claimants should be in a worse position than illegal entrants, and the extension of procedural guarantees to refugee claimants thus ensured that all claims of entry into Canada were subject to an adjudicative system of determination, with attendant procedural guarantees.

The refugee determination procedures eventually established in 1989, following *Singh*, were modeled to some extent on existing immigration adjudication procedures, but an effort was made to adapt them to the particular circumstances of refugee claims. Following the model known in Germany and France, a distinct refugee determination authority was established, whose members are not subject to executive control in the determination process. This authority, the Convention Refugee Determination Division (CRDD) of the Immigration and Refugee Board, is now the largest administrative tribunal in Canada, with approximately 250 members active in the refugee determination process. Its members are politically appointed by the federal cabinet for terms of from two to five years (renewable), and have no responsibilities other than those of refugee determination. The CRDD granted refugee status in approximately 90 percent of the cases referred to it in its first year of existence; the acceptance rate has now declined to approximately 50 percent.

Determination decisions are taken by CRDD members sitting in panels of two, and the vote of one member is in principle sufficient for the determination of refugee status. In certain limited circumstances, such as those where the claimant has destroyed identity documents, unanimity is now required. All refugee claimants whose claims are referred to the CRDD are entitled to an oral hearing, as a consequence of the decision of the Supreme Court of Canada in *Singh*. It is the nature of this oral hearing which is of interest in the context of refugee determination procedures generally. Following the *Singh* decision a major effort was made to ensure that Canadian determination procedures adhered to standards of procedural fairness and provided appropriate procedural guarantees to the refugee claimant. The procedural model adopted was largely that of the adversarial civil trial, though it is questionable whether such an expensive and cumbersome procedure is suitable to the nonadversarial character of refugee determinations (Glenn, 1992: 58–59, 91–92). The CRDD now has adopted a fast-track procedure which permits an affirmative finding of refugee status following an interview with a Refugee Hearing Officer and a brief confirmatory hearing before a single member of the CRDD. It is only through the use of this fast-track procedure that the CRDD succeeds in processing the approximately 30,000 claims now being received annually in Canada. Following a negative determination of refugee status a claimant may seek judicial review in the Federal Court of Canada, with leave of the Court.

The procedural rights of refugee claimants in Canada are thus guaranteed by the Constitution and neither legislation nor executive regulation can affect this entitlement. The precise content of the constitutional rights is always subject to interpretation, however, and Canadian legislation which came into force in 1993 seeks to expand the regulatory authority of the Canadian executive over refugee movement.

REGULATION AND CONTROL OF REFUGEE MOVEMENT

Prior to the *Singh* decision of the Supreme Court of Canada in 1985, treatment of refugee claims in Canada was largely subject to executive control. No constitutional requirements were imposed; both legislation and regulation could be used for regulatory purposes; implementation was in the hands of executive agencies with no institutional concessions made to the particular character of refugee claims. Following *Singh* and the constitutional entitlement of refugee claimants that flowed from it, a period of radical judicialization took place. This led to the imposition of an obligatory oral hearing before the quasi-independent CRDD and the adoption of adversarial-style proceedings before the CRDD. In the meantime refugee population flow continued, with only a slight decline from the figures reached in the late 1980s. From the perspective of regulation and control of refugee movement, this created two problems. In the first place, the determination procedures established following *Singh* were both slow and expensive. This resulted in alternative, fast-track procedures, as has been seen, while the procedure used by the CRDD remains the object of discussion and investigation.

In the second place, access to the determination procedure became very broad, with no expeditious, executive-controlled means of screening claims considered to be abusive. A screening procedure involving an oral hearing before an adjudicator and a member of the CRDD, which allowed rejection of refugee claims which were ineligible or lacked a credible basis, was abandoned in 1993 as itself too cumbersome and inefficient. The absence of any means of screening access to the hearings of the CRDD meant that the CRDD was functioning at near total capacity, with little ability to absorb an increase in refugee claims. Legislation which came into effect in Canada in 1993 thus sought to reassert executive control over access to the refugee determination process.

The principal effect of Bill C-86 (S.C. 1992, C. 49, in force February 1, 1993) is to reintroduce executive decision-making into the process of entry into Canada. Thus, § 23(4) of the Immigration Act will now allow a senior immigration officer to make an exclusion order against a person seeking entry into Canada where the person does not possess a valid and subsisting passport or other appropriate documentation. The undocumented alien may thus be excluded without resort to normal adjudicative mechanisms. This is an important deviation from the existing principle of adjudication of all disputed claims of entry to Canada. The procedure used by senior immigration officers in making such exclusion orders may be subject to challenge on constitutional grounds or on more traditional grounds of the principles of natural justice. In practice, however, the effect of the exclusion order may be avoided through the making of a refugee claim. In this case access to Canadian territory for purposes of adjudication of the refugee claim has traditionally been assured. The claim may now be subject, however, to a new and different process of screening.

Bill C-86 attempts to establish an executive screening of refugee claimants, in the cadre of an as-yet-undefined system of regional collaboration. Section 45 of the Immigration Act thus allows a senior immigration officer to decide on the eligibility of a person to have a claim determined by the Refugee Division, and the criteria of ineligibility include coming to Canada, "directly or indirectly," from a country prescribed as a safe third country (§§ 46.01(1)(b) and 114). Section 108.1 of the act, moreover, authorizes the conclusion of agreements with other countries for the purpose of sharing the responsibility for examining refugee claims and for sharing information concerning persons who travel between countries that are parties to such agreements. As a result of these provisions the Government of Canada would conclude regional bilateral or multilateral agreements with other countries for sharing of refugee determination, prescribe such countries to be safe third countries and thereby authorize senior immigration officers to exclude from the Canadian determination process refugee claimants coming "directly or indirectly" from such countries. The decision of the senior immigration officer in such a case has been described as purely "mechanical" or "administrative," but the complexity of such decisions is indicated by §§ 45(4) and 46.01(3) of the act, providing respectively that the burden of proof of eligibility is on the refugee claimant and that "subject to any agreement entered into pursuant to section 108.1, a person who is in a country solely for the purpose of joining a connecting flight to Canada shall not be considered as coming to Canada from that country. . . ." In the summer of 1993, the Government of Canada also announced that the border control units of the Department of Employment and Immigration were to become part of a new and larger ministry of Public Security, including other federal forces of police. The publicity given to these legislative and institutional changes has brought about a significant decline in refugee claims being made at the U.S.-Canada border, though as of yet Canada has concluded no international agreements for the sharing of the refugee determination process and has prescribed no safe third countries.

These recent efforts to increase the national and regional control of refugee movement raise important legal questions in Canada. Two questions may be identified. The first relates to the adequacy of the procedures undertaken by a senior immigration officer in excluding a refugee claimant from Canada on the grounds that the applicant has come from a prescribed country. The second relates to the permissibility, by whatever means, of denying a refugee claimant access to the refugee determination process, on grounds unrelated to the possible merits of the individual claim.

As to the adequacy of procedures of exclusion undertaken by a senior immigration officer, it cannot be said that the decision of the Supreme Court of Canada in *Singh* provides precise guidance. The decision in *Singh* invalidated previous procedures because they did not allow refugee claimants to state their case adequately or to know the case which might be made against them. To the extent that a senior immigration officer hears any representations that a refugee claimant wishes to make concerning arrival from a safe third country, it is possible that such a hearing satisfies the requirements of the Constitution. However, a number of features of such a hearing raise doubts as to such a conclusion. First, the senior immigration officer is making a decision crucial to eventual refugee determination while benefiting from none of the institutional guarantees of CRDD members. Moreover, as has been indicated, in the future such officers may be part of a governmental department whose functions are those of national security, unconnected to matters of refugee determination or immigration. This may be of no consequence if the decision to exclude a claimant is a "mechanical" or purely administrative one. Given the complexity of modern transport, however, it is inevitable that a jurisprudence will be established as to how much contact with a safe third country is necessary to justify exclusion. What is a "connecting flight," for example, in the context of § 46.01(3) of the act? Where complex decisions are made by an immigration or security officer to deny access to the refugee determination process, with no guarantee of the presence of legal counsel or an interpreter, a finding of constitutional infirmity must be considered a possibility.

Even if the procedure undertaken by a senior immigration officer is considered adequate, the question still remains as to the permissibility of exclusion on the ground of arrival from a safe third country. The justification for such exclusion is that such claimants could and should have made their claim to refugee status in the first safe country they reached, or that their claim in such country was rejected and should not be reheard. The regional bilateral and multilateral agreements contemplated by § 108.1 of the Immigration Act would thus prevent asylum shopping by refugee claimants, either initially or following earlier rejection of their claim. The national barrier constituted by the senior immigration officer's exclusion order would be the most efficient means of ensuring this regional sharing of responsibility for examining refugee claims.

Exclusion by a senior immigration officer on the grounds of arrival from a safe third country has the effect, however, of preventing a determination of refugee status in Canada. The claimant who is in reality a refugee would thus be deprived of the rights of a refugee which are now accorded by Canadian law, as found in the *Singh* decision, and would be deprived of the right to security of the person guaranteed by the Constitution. Deprivation of such rights would have to be justified on the ground either that the claimant could have obtained enjoyment of similar rights in the safe third country but chose not to, or because the decision of the safe third country refusing refugee status must be accepted in Canada. Are these adequate justifications for denying adjudication of the claim to refugee status, by whatever procedure? The Constitution presently guarantees, it should be recalled, fundamental justice *in the adjudication* of the claim to refugee status (*Singh* [1985] 1 S.C.R. 177 at 210, per Wilson, and 231 per Beetz). Can this be refused on the basis of prior presence in another country or on the basis that the prior decision of another country must be followed in Canada? Neither of these conclusions is self-evident.[2]

Regional sharing of responsibility for refugee determination is a reasonable and efficient goal. When its effect is to *preclude* refugee determination in Canada, however, in the absence of refugee determination elsewhere, it is difficult to see how such preclusion is compatible with the constitutional guarantee of fundamental justice in the refugee determination process. The constitutional right is one which is presently enjoyed by the refugee claimant in Canada; its constitutional nature does not appear immediately compatible with a governmental directive that it be exercised elsewhere on grounds of efficiency. Nor are there evident reasons why a foreign decision denying refugee status must be followed in Canada. Res judicata is a tenuous doctrine internationally, and there are few legal bases for the view that a decision on refugee status made for purposes of entry onto U.S. soil, for example, is binding for purposes of a subsequent claim of access to Canadian soil. Judicial decisions in matters of public law are traditionally accorded no recognition beyond the state of their origin. Why then would such recognition be accorded when the consequence would be violation of a right guaranteed by the Canadian Constitution? *Singh* casts a long shadow over efforts in Canada to implement regional collaboration in

---

[2]Eligibility requirements for refugee determination have already been challenged on constitutional grounds, even where the basis of ineligibility was prior determination of refugee status in Canada within the previous 90 days. See *Berrahman v. M.E.I.* (1992), 132 N.R. 202, in which J. A. Marceau stated (at p. 213): "One can easily imagine conditions of eligibility in legislation dealing with aliens seeking refuge which would infringe the precepts of the Charter."

the refugee determination process, where such collaboration is based on the concept of the safe third country.

CONCLUSION

The constitutional protection accorded refugee claimants by Canadian law places limits on the extent of executive control of refugee movement. The precise nature of these limits has not been fully determined. It does not appear to make a difference, however, whether such executive measures of control are being implemented pursuant to purely national policy or pursuant to regional forms of collaboration. In either case there may be denial of fundamental justice in the *process* of adjudication of the refugee claim, or denial of fundamental justice through denial of the *possibility* of adjudication of the refugee claim. The judicial determination of these questions will continue to be informed by debate as to the nature of the Canadian State.

REFERENCES

Anker, D.
1991   *The Law of Asylum in the United States.* Washington, DC: American Immigration Law Foundation.

Brun, H.
1988   "Les Statuts Resectifs de Citoyen, Résident et Étranger, à la Lumiére des Chartes des Droits," *Cahiers de Droit*, 29: 689–731.

Brunelle, C.
1987   "La Primauté du Droit: La Situation des Immigrants et des Réfugiés en Droit Canadian au Regard des Chartes et des Textes Internationaux," *Cahiers de Droit*, 28: 585–624.

Glenn, H. P.
1992   *Strangers at the Gate: Refugees, Illegal Entrants and Procedural Justice.* Cowansville: Editions Yvon Blais.

Lott, F.
1992   Declaration made to Collque de l'Office Française de Protection des Refugiés et Apatrides, Les Refugiés en France et en Europe. June 11–13.

15

Haitian Refugees and U.S. Policy

Lucas Guttentag[1]

Introduction

For more than two decades Haitian refugees have been the victims rather than the beneficiaries of the United States asylum system. The seeming obsession of four American Presidents with repelling and deporting fleeing Haitians has caused these innocent victims of persecution to be denied both safety and justice by the United States.[2]

Overt discrimination against Haitian refugees began in the 1970s when the Carter Administration adopted a "Haitian program" to deny thousands of Haitians in South Florida any opportunity to obtain

---

[1]The author would like to express his appreciation to Ann Parrent, Jinsoo Kim and Tracey Chambers for their invaluable help in preparing this article and to Harry D. Snyder for his ever-patient production assistance.

[2]The asylum process itself has also been denigrated by its discrimination against Haitians. For example, the decision to detain Haitians in 1981 caused the abandonment of a 30-year policy of release and the adoption of new rules that now cause thousands of "excludable" aliens, including countless asylum applicants, to languish in detention centers. Similarly, the Haitian interdiction program has been emulated off the coast of California to intercept Chinese refugees on the high seas and on the southern border of Mexico (via funding to Mexican authorities) to intercept Central American refugees before either can reach the United States. *See* U.S. Committee for Refugees (1991); The New York Times (1993a).

Moreover, Haitians have not been the only victims of a discriminatory or hostile asylum system. Court decisions document a decade of discrimination against Central American refugees and other

272

asylum.[3] It continued when, a few years later, the Reagan Administration adopted a preemptive "interdiction" program applicable only to Haiti and a detention policy aimed at Haitians.[4] And it reached a zenith when President Bush, in 1992, abandoned modest improvements to the interdiction program and instead promulgated the infamous Kennebunkport Order that summarily returns *all* interdicted Haitians directly to Haiti regardless of the persecution they face. The Kennebunkport Order compounded the Bush Administration's callousness toward Haitian refugees as reflected in its earlier decision to imprison hundreds of interdicted Haitians with bona fide asylum claims in a detention camp at the United States Naval Base in Guantànamo, Cuba, solely because they had tested HIV-positive. Finally, in 1993, the discrimination continued unabated when President Clinton's new administration, despite his campaign and preinaugural statements to the

---

abuses of the asylum system by the executive branch. *See, e.g., American Baptist Churches v. Thornburgh*, 760 F. Supp. 796 (N.D. Cal. 1991) (all Salvadoran and Guatemalan nationals in the United States in 1990 entitled to de novo asylum adjudication); *Mendez v. Thornburgh*, No. 88-04995-TJH (C.D. Cal. 1989) (Los Angeles asylum office ordered to offer new asylum interviews to 30,000 applicants of all nationalities due to hostile and incompetent interviews by INS officials); *Orantes-Hernandez v. Smith*, 541 F. Supp. 351 (C.D. Cal. 1982), aff'd, 919 F. 2d 549 (9th Cir. 1990) (nationwide injunction against INS and Border Patrol to prohibit abusive treatment of Salvadoran refugees).

[3]The Carter "Haitian program" was designed to process and deport Haitians regardless of their claims of persecution. In other words of the district court, which enjoined the program:

[T]here was a program at work within INS to expel Haitians. Their asylum claims were prejudged, their rights to a hearing given second priority to the need for accelerated processing. . . . The violations [of due process] were discriminatory acts, part of a Program to expel Haitians. . . . The [INS] did not grant a single request for asylum. . . . During that time thousands of Haitians were processed. Those denials were not case-by-case adjudication, but an intentional, class-wide, summary denial.

The court is therefore presented with a pattern of discrimination which [apparently] began. . . in 1964. Over the past 17 years, Haitian claims for asylum and refuge have been systematically denied, while all others have been granted. The recent Haitian Program is but the largest-scale, most dramatic example of that pattern. *Haitian Refugee Center v. Civiletti*, 503 F. Supp. 442, 519 (S.D. Fla. 1980), aff'd *sub nom. Haitian Refugee Center v. Smith*, 676 F. 2d 1023 (5th Cir. Unit B 1982).

The court found that the program violated "the Constitution, the immigration statutes, international agreements, INS regulations and INS operating procedures." (*Id.* at 452)

[4]After the closing of Ellis Island in 1954, arriving aliens were routinely paroled into the United States unless they posed a security risk or a risk of absconding. In 1981, the Reagan Administration instituted a new policy, without statutory or regulatory authority, that resulted in disproportionately detaining Haitians and denying them access to counsel.

Having made a long and perilous journey on the seas to Southern Florida, these refugees, seeking the promised land, have instead been subject to a human shell game in which the arbitrary Immigration and Naturalization Services has sought to scatter them [out

contrary,[5] maintained and defended both the Kennebunkport Order and the HIV detention policies.

The domestic legal challenge to these policies is the subject of this paper. Litigation initiated in March 1992 by a coalition of legal groups[6] ended in June, 1993, with significantly divergent results. On June 8, 1993, all of the men, women and children who remained detained in the HIV prison camp at Guantànamo were ordered released by a federal district court in Brooklyn, New York, and shortly thereafter the notorious Guantànamo camp was permanently closed (*Haitian Centers Council v. Sale*, 823 F. Supp. 1028, E.D. N.Y. 1993). In contrast, the Kennebunkport Order's forcible interdiction and summary repatriation was upheld by the U.S. Supreme Court less than two weeks later (*Sale v. Haitian Centers Council*, 113 S. Ct. 2459 1993). As a result, that policy continues to this day.

BACKGROUND

The Haitian Interdiction Operation was initially established by President Ronald Reagan in 1981. By executive order, he authorized the Coast Guard to interdict on the high seas and to return to Haiti any Haitians seeking to come to the United States in violation of Haitian

---

of Miami where there is a substantial immigration bar as well as volunteer lawyers] to locations that, with the exception of Brooklyn are all in desolate, remote, hostile, culturally diverse areas, containing a paucity of available legal support and few, if any, Creole interpreters. *Louis v. Meissner*, 530 F. Supp. 924, 926 (S.D. Fla. 1981).

See also Louis v. Nelson, 544 F. Supp. 973, 1000 (S.D. Fla. 1982) ("[i]t is undisputed that the Haitians are impacted to a greater degree by the new detention policy than aliens of any other nationality. . . .") *See generally Jean v. Nelson*, 472 U.S. 846, 849 (1985).

[5] During the campaign, candidate Clinton excoriated the Bush interdiction policy as immoral and illegal. "This [interdiction] process must not stand. It is a blow to the principle of first asylum and to America's moral authority in defending the rights of refugees around the world." (May 27, 1992.) During his acceptance speech at the Democratic National Convention, nominee Clinton stated that he would accept and implement the recommendations of the National Commission on AIDS, one of which was the elimination of the HIV exclusion in U.S. immigration policy. The majority of Commission members later specifically called on President Clinton to bring the Haitians incarcerated at Guantànamo to the United States. (Letter of Feb. 17, 1993, from seven members of the National Commission on AIDS to President Clinton.)

[6] The *Haitian Centers Council v. McNary* suit, as it was originally denominated, was litigated on behalf of local and national Haitian organizations by the American Civil Liberties Union Immigrants' Rights Project, the Yale Law School Lowenstein International Human Rights Clinic, the Center for Constitutional Rights, the Lawyers Committee for Civil Rights of the San Francisco Bay Area, and the New York law firm of Simpson Thacher & Bartlett.

or U.S. immigration laws.[7] The Reagan order expressly recognized, however, that international legal obligations under the U.N. Refugee Convention[8] barred the return of political refugees to Haiti against their will. To honor this duty, the United States implemented a screening process to identify putative political refugees and to permit them to enter the United States to apply for asylum. To be "screened-in," interdicted Haitians had to demonstrate that their asylum claims had merit (or, after 1991, that they had a "credible fear of persecution") at a cursory on-the-spot interview conducted on Coast Guard cutters (*Haitian Refugee Center v. Baker*, 953 F. 2d 1498, 1501–1502, 11th Cir., cert. denied, 112 S. Ct. 1245 1992). In the view of many, the gross inadequacies of this procedure and its bias against Haitian claims were confirmed by the barely measurable number of Haitians who satisfied the standard during the first ten years – a time of uncontroverted human rights violations in Haiti.[9]

After the September 1991 coup overthrowing Haiti's first democratically elected president, Jean-Bertrand Aristide, the number of Haitians fleeing in boats increased dramatically while the human rights conditions in the country deteriorated drastically (Amnesty International, 1992; Lawyers Committee for Human Rights, 1992). Nonethe-

---

[7]Executive Order No. 12,324, 46 Fed. Reg. 48109 (1981). On September 29, 1981, President Reagan authorized the interdiction of vessels of foreign nations containing undocumented aliens where the United States had arrangements with the foreign nation authorizing the United States to stop and board such vessels. Proclamation No. 4865, 46 Fed. Reg. 48107 (published October 1, 1981); Executive Order No. 12,324, 46 Fed. Reg. 48109, 48110 (published October 1, 1981). A few days earlier, on September 23, 1981, the United States had entered into such an agreement with Haiti. T.I.A.S. 10241.

[8]United Nations Convention Relating to the Status of Refugees, July 28, 1951, 19 U.S.T. 6259, T.I.A.S. 6577, 189 U.N.T.S. 150 (to which the United States had become a party in 1968 upon signing the United Nations Protocol Relating to the Status of Refugees, 11 January 1967, 19 U.S.T. 623, T.I.A.S. 6577).

[9]In ten years, the Coast Guard interdicted approximately 25,000 Haitians of whom only 28 (or 0.1%) were screened in to the United States to pursue asylum claims. *See, e.g.*, Lawyers Committee for Human Rights (1990) (noting that only 6 of 21,461 interdicted Haitians had been screened in); Helsinki Watch (1989) (noting that only 5 of 20,421 interdicted Haitians had been screened in). "The entire procedure is highly objectionable from a human rights and humanitarian point of view. The Administration's Interdiction Program fails to give appropriate weight to the extremely unstable and continuing repressive political situation in Haiti." (51–52). Challenges to legality of the original interdiction program were unsuccessful. See *Haitian Refugee Center v. Gracey*, 600 F. Supp. 1396 (D.D.C. 1985), aff'd on other grounds, 809 F.2d 794 (D.C. Cir. 1987).

less, the Bush Administration continued the interdiction policy using a recently-instituted modified screening process. As before, interviews were conducted on Coast Guard cutters on the high seas and those screened-in were permitted to apply for asylum in the United States while those screened-out were returned directly to Haiti.

In November 1991, the Haitian Refugee Center in Miami filed suit to challenge the screening process on the ground that prevailing conditions made adequate interviews impossible and that bona fide refugees were being returned to Haiti in violation of U.S. obligations under the Refugee Convention and the U.S. Refugee Act. The suit was dismissed in February 1992 on several grounds, including that Haitian plaintiffs outside the United States were not protected by domestic or international refugee law, and that the Refugee Convention was not a "self-executing" international agreement (*Haitian Refugee Center v. Baker*, 789 F. Supp. 1552, S. D. Fla. 1991, rev'd, *Haitian Refugee Center v. Baker*, 949 F. 2d 1109, 11th Cir. 1991; 953 F. 2d 1498, 11th Cir., cert. denied, 112 S. Ct. 1245–1992).

Though ultimately unsuccessful, the Florida litigation resulted in the screening process being moved from the decks of Coast Guard cutters to the U.S. naval base at Guantànamo Bay, Cuba. But the interdictions and repatriations continued apace. More ominously, just five days after the Supreme Court declined to review the *Haitian Refugee Center* litigation, the INS issued a memorandum regarding the processing of screened-in Haitians at Guantànamo. Written by the then-INS General Counsel, it directed that some screened-in Haitians would no longer be brought directly to the United States to apply for asylum. Instead, those who tested HIV-positive would remain at Guantànamo and would be required to apply for asylum while incarcerated at the naval base. The claim for asylum would be decided while the individual remained imprisoned, and the determination of the claim would be final and unreviewable. Anyone deemed not to satisfy the "well-founded fear of persecution" standard necessary for asylum would be immediately repatriated to Haiti. Furthermore, even those who demonstrated a well-founded fear would be eligible for release only if they obtained an HIV waiver under criteria that were never articulated or, apparently, determined.[10] Throughout the asylum adjudication and

---

[10]Memorandum of Grover Joseph Rees, III, INS General Counsel, 29 Feb. 1993 (the "Rees Memorandum"). *See Haitian Centers Council v. McNary*, 969 F.2d 1326, 1335 (2d Cir. 1992).

waiver processing, the screened-in Haitians would remain at Guantànamo under military guard behind coils of barbed wire.

THE RIGHTS OF HAITIANS AT GUANTÀNAMO

In March 1992, the *Haitian Centers Council v. McNary* (HCC) suit was filed in Brooklyn, New York, to challenge the processing and detention of screened-in Haitians at Guantànamo. The suit attacked the government policy that singled out HIV-positive Haitians and denied them procedural rights (especially access to lawyers) in their asylum adjudications.[11] The suit asserted that reliance on HIV infection to deny substantive or procedural protections to screened-in Haitians was unlawful. The new policy was contrary to the rights of asylum seekers in the United States for whom HIV infection is not a factor, much less a bar, in applying for or receiving asylum. It was inconsistent with prior practice since, until the Rees Memorandum, HIV status had never been a basis for barring the entry of any screened-in boat person into the United States. It was without statutory authority since nothing in the law required – or authorized – the sudden imposition of such a bar. And it was plainly discriminatory since Cuban "rafters," picked up in the same international waters by the same Coast Guard, were routinely transported directly to the United States without any HIV testing or inquiry.

The government's principal response to the Haitians' challenge, at the outset of the suit and consistently thereafter, was that aliens outside the United States, like the detained Haitians, could not invoke the jurisdiction of the federal courts, the U.S. Constitution or the Immigration and Nationality Act (INA). The government argued that the interdiction, detention and processing of Haitians outside the United States were not subject to any legal limitation or to any oversight by the federal judiciary.

---

[11]Among the rights applicable to asylum adjudications in the United States that were denied Haitian refugees at Guantànamo were the right to collect, prepare and submit supporting evidence (8 C.F.R.208.9(b), (e)), to be represented by counsel or a representative before and at the asylum interview (8 U.S.C. 1362; 8 C.F.R. 208.9(e)), to be informed in writing if asylum is to be denied, including the reasons for denial (8 C.F.R. 208.17) and to rebut materials from other sources if they form the basis of decision (8 C.F.R. 208.12), to renew the asylum application in an adversary proceeding before an immigration judge (8 C.F.R. 208.4), and to judicial review of any negative decision in that proceeding (8 U.S.C. 1105).

Conditions at Guantànamo

While the case progressed through the courts, lawyers representing the Haitians – accompanied by independent doctors – were finally permitted the first of several monthly visits to the Guantànamo detention camp in October 1992. By that time, many of the refugees – men, women and young children – had been detained at Guantànamo for almost a year. The lawyers witnessed the frustration, desperation, anger and despair of their refugee clients and saw firsthand their heart-wrenching living conditions.

The detention area was a camp-like prison surrounded by a perimeter fence and a guarded entrance. Coils of barbed wire and several gates divided the prison camp into sections, which included the hut area for sleeping, a clinic, an exercise and day activities area, the military control compound and other restricted areas. The wooden huts or "hooches" were constructed of plywood and wire-mesh siding set on top of concrete slabs and roofed with corrugated metal. Toilet facilities consisted of a cluster of port-a-johns far removed from the single building with running water. Bathing took place in a communal shower before a row of partially-functioning sinks or in a fully-exposed outdoor shower area. In the words of the Center for Disease Control doctors who had visited the camp, congregating so many immune-suppressed people in a single location was "a potential public health disaster."[12]

After the first camp visit, the lawyers complained to the INS of the most egregious conditions. These included:

1) The absence of flush toilets, the lack of nearby sinks and the poor maintenance of the port-a-johns, all of which had been criticized as a danger to health by the Center for Disease Control in March 1992. These conditions were unchanged in October.

2) Walls of the residence huts that provided little protection against the elements, especially rain. Water entered the huts and soak bedding and belongings. The wire-mesh sections of wall lacked shutters or other covering. Many of the Haitians tied plastic garbage bags over the mesh in an effort to keep out the rain.

[12]Memorandum from Paul Effler, M.D., to Charles McCance, Director, Division of Quarantine (March 1, 1992).

3) Walls of huts that did not extend to the roof and left many large openings. Haitians complained of bugs, snakes, scorpions, banana rats and other flying and crawling animals entering the huts.

4) Bedding that consisted only of military cots and huts that afforded no privacy. No mattresses, beds or cribs were available. The only means of creating privacy within the huts was by stretching sheets from the rafters to screen off a small area.

5) The lack of any facilities to launder clothes.

Over the ensuing months, only a few of these conditions received attention. The overall camp conditions and, more profoundly, the state of mind of the refugees, deteriorated significantly. In February 1993, the Haitians began a lengthy hunger strike to call attention to their ordeal.

The Guantànamo Litigation

In March 1992, the district court issued a preliminary ruling on the plaintiffs' challenge to the asylum processing at Guantànamo. Judge Sterling M. Johnson, Jr., rejected the government's assertion of pervasive and unreviewable power and issued a temporary injunction that halted any further processing without counsel and that allowed Haitian service organizations to have access to the refugees. Due to a flurry of governmental requests for stays and appeals, the district court injunction was temporarily suspended pending appellate court review. Although the order prohibiting processing without lawyers was later affirmed, the government's appeal permitted the INS to repatriate many of the Haitian refugees in the interim. By the time the preliminary injunction was upheld by the court of appeals, approximately 300 Haitians remained at Guantànamo.

The appellate ruling, on June 10, 1993, agreed that asylum processing could not proceed unless the Haitians were permitted to have access to lawyers. The court based its decision on the Constitution's guarantee of due process and rejected the government's argument that the Constitution could not be invoked by persons outside the United States.[13] The

[13]*HCC v. McNary*, 969 F.2d 1326 (2d Cir. 1992), rev'd sub. nom *Sale v. Haitian Centers Council*, 113 S. Ct. 2549 (1993). The independent First Amendment claim of the lawyers and legal service organizations in the United States seeking access to the Guantànamo Haitians for the purpose of providing counsel was left to be determined at trial. *See In re Primus*, 436 U.S. 412 (1978); *NAACP v. Button*, 371 U.S. 415 (1963).

court held that due process protections applied to the Guantànamo Haitians because of the authorization in the Rees Memorandum of a "de facto" asylum proceeding at Guantànamo "identical in form and substance" to one conducted in the United States; the detention of the Haitians on property subject to the exclusive jurisdiction and control of the United States; and the INS's own finding that the Haitians possessed "credible" fears of persecution if returned to Haiti (*HCC v. McNary*, 969 F. 2d at 1345–1346).

In response to this ruling, the government suspended all asylum processing rather than permit the Haitians to have legal representation. As a result, the refugees were condemned to further indefinite incarceration at the Guantànamo camp until their legal rights were conclusively determined at trial.

The trial challenging the refugees' detention and processing at Guantànamo began in March 1993. By then, approximately 250 screened-in Haitians, including young children, remained at Guantànamo. Many had been imprisoned for as long as eighteen months.[14] While the case had initially focused on the right to legal counsel, by the time of trial it had evolved into a much broader challenge. The evidence presented to the court fell into several broad categories: 1) inadequate medical care for the HIV-positive population; 2) inhumane living conditions at the camp; 3) the indefiniteness of the detention; 4) the absence of any legal basis for an asylum adjudication process that comported with neither the overseas refugee system nor the domestic asylum system (INA § 207, 8 U.S.C. 1157; INA § 208, 8 U.S.C. 1158); 5) the discriminatory treatment of Haitians compared to other nationalities, particularly Cubans; 6) the discriminatory exclusion of lawyers from access to the detained Haitians; and 7) the duty to afford Guantànamo Haitians the same basic procedural protections attendant to asylum processing in the United States.

As before, the government argued that the Constitution and laws of the United States do not apply outside U.S. territory. It further contended that the Coast Guard had "rescued" the interdicted Haitians from unseaworthy boats and that the detained Haitians were "free" to go anywhere but the United States.

---

[14]A number of pregnant women were evacuated to the United States as their delivery dates approached after one baby, born at Guantànamo, died shortly after being evacuated to the United States. A few other Haitians were brought to the United States for medical treatment.

The trial consumed almost three weeks. It included dozens of witnesses, extensive deposition testimony, and hundreds of exhibits. During its course, the government was forced to concede that it could not provide adequate medical care at Guantànamo for refugees whose condition met the clinical definition of AIDS (Trial Tr. at 836–837, March 15, 1993). At the conclusion of the evidence and before he issued a final decision, Judge Johnson expressed incredulity at the government's policies.[15] Shortly thereafter he issued an interim order requiring the immediate medical evacuation from Guantànamo of all Haitians with AIDS (*HCC v. Sale*, 817 F. Supp. 336, E.D. N.Y. 1993). As a result, 51 were brought to the United States the week of April 5.[16]

On June 3, 1993, Judge Johnson issued his final decision and ordered that *all* the Haitians remaining at Guantànamo be released immediately (*HCC v. Sale*, 823 F. Supp. 1028, E.D. N.Y. 1993). In a 50-page opinion he condemned the camp: "The Haitian camp at Guantànamo is the only known refugee camp in the world composed entirely of HIV positive refugees. The Haitians' plight is a tragedy of immense proportion and their continued detainment is totally unacceptable to this Court. . . ." He further found that "[Guantànamo] is nothing more than an HIV prison camp presenting potential public health risks to the Haitians held there. . . ." In response to a remark by an INS official defending the medical treatment because "they're going to die anyway, aren't they?" Judge Johnson decried the government's attitude: "It is outrageous, callous and reprehensible that defendant INS finds no value in providing adequate medical care even when a patient's illness is fatal" (823 F. Supp. at 1038).

The opinion described the general conditions at Guantànamo in words that few could ignore.

> Today there are approximately 200 "screened in" HIV+ Haitians remaining at Guantànamo. They live in camps surrounded by razor barbed wire. They tie plastic garbage bags to the sides of the building to keep the rain out. They

---

[15]On one occasion, Judge Johnson pointedly asked: "Does [U.S. immigration policy] permit the United States Government to take, kidnap or abscond, whatever you want to call it, and take a group of people and put them into a compound, and no matter how you slice it, whether you call it a humanitarian camp or prison, keep them there indefinitely while there has been no charge leveled against them and there is no light at the end of the tunnel?" (Trial Tr. at 1603–1604, Mar. 19, 1993).

[16]Private voluntary agencies working with municipal governments took responsibility for the resettlement of all of those individuals, many of whom are now residing with family members.

sleep on cots and hang sheets to create some semblance of privacy. They are guarded by the military and are not permitted to leave the camp, except under military escort. The Haitian detainees have been subjected to pre-dawn military sweeps as they sleep by as many as 400 soldiers dressed in full riot gear. They are confined like prisoners and are subject to detention in the brig without a hearing for camp rule infractions. (823 F. Supp. at 1037)

The opinion also emphasized that the government had not and could not provide adequate medical care at Guantànamo and that the INS intentionally ignored the medical advice of military doctors.

[T]he Government acknowledges that the medical facilities on the Guantànamo Naval Base are inadequate to provide medical care to those Haitians who have developed AIDS, particularly patients with T-cell counts of 200 or below or a percentage of 13 or less. . . . Defendant INS has repeatedly failed to act on recommendations and deliberately ignored the medical advice of U.S. military doctors that all persons with T-cell count below 200 or percentages below 13 be transported to the United States for treatment. Such actions constitute deliberate indifference to the Haitians' medical needs in violation of their due process rights. (823 F. Supp. at 1038, 1044)

Judge Johnson also condemned the indefinite detention of persons who "are merely the unfortunate victims of a fatal disease" whose detention serves no valid purpose.

[T]he detained Haitians are neither criminals nor national security risks. Some are pregnant mothers and others are children. . . . The Government has failed to demonstrate to this Court's satisfaction that the detainees' illness warrants the kind of indefinite detention usually reserved for spies and murderers. . . . Where detention no longer serves a legitimate purpose, the detainees must be released. (823 F. Supp. at 1045)

Finally, Judge Johnson concluded that the processing of well-founded fear claims at Guantànamo had no statutory basis, that affording access to attorneys and to the procedural rights available to asylum applicants in the United States provided a significant benefit to the applicant and no burden on defendants (823 F. Supp. at 1043), and that refusing to release the Haitians from detention constituted an abuse of discretion.

Where HIV+ detainees have been held for nearly two years in prison camp conditions likely to further compromise their health, where each year other individuals carrying the HIV virus are allowed to enter the United States, and where the admission of the Haitians is unlikely to affect the spread of

AIDS in this country, the Government's continued imprisonment of the Screened In Plaintiffs serves no purpose other than to punish them for being sick. . . . (823 F. Supp. at 1049)

Shortly after the court's decision, all the Guantànamo Haitians were transported to the United States to relatives and friends. By June 18, 1993, the ignominious camp was closed.

INTERDICTION AND IMMEDIATE REPATRIATION (KENNEBUNKPORT ORDER)

While the Guantànamo issues were being litigated, President Bush drastically altered the interdiction policy. A new executive order, issued on May 23, 1992, from his vacation home in Kennebunkport, Maine, authorized the immediate repatriation of all interdicted Haitians without any screening (Executive Order No. 12, 807, 57 Fed. Reg. 23, 133 1992). Since the Kennebunkport Order, the Coast Guard has returned all interdicted Haitians directly to Haiti without regard to – or even any inquiry concerning – their fear or risk of persecution. This occurred despite the INS's own determination that the percentage of interdicted Haitians who should be screened-in based on a showing of a credible fear of persecution had ranged from as high as 90–95 percent in January 1992 to an average of approximately 40 percent in February 1992 (deposition of Asylum Quality Control Officer, May 6, 1992). Overall, the screen-in rate had been 30–35 percent. In short, the government's own asylum officers were finding that roughly one-third of the fleeing Haitians presented credible fears of persecution and should be allowed to present and pursue their claims. After the Kennebunkport Order, none were permitted to do so and all were summarily returned.

The HCC plaintiffs sought to enjoin this forced repatriation through additional proceedings in the pending suit. Plaintiffs argued that the Kennebunkport Order violated the nonrefoulement obligation embodied in Article 33 of the Refugee Convention and incorporated into U.S. domestic law by the Refugee Act of 1980. Article 33 provides that "[n]o Contracting State shall expel or return (refouler) a refugee in any manner whatsoever to the frontiers of territories where his life or freedom would be threatened on account of his race, religion, nationality, membership in a particular social group or political opinion." The 1980 Refugee Act amended INA § 243(h) to provide that "the Attorney General shall not deport or return any alien . . . if the Attorney General determines that such alien's life or freedom would be threatened" on account of any of the five grounds enumerated in the Refugee Convention.[17] The suit argued that these dual proscriptions impose an absolute prohibition against the United States returning a refugee to his or her persecutors, regardless of where the government's action occurs. The government responded with jurisdictional as well as substantive defenses of the summary repatriation policy. As in the Guantánamo part of the litigation, the primary defense was that the Haitians could assert rights only in relation to acts occurring within the physical territory of the United States. The government also argued that the conduct of the Coast Guard in international waters is not governed by the Refugee Act and is not addressed by the Refugee Convention.[18]

Under the government's view, the United States' affirmative reaching out onto the high seas to capture fleeing Haitians in order to prevent them from reaching U.S. territory (where the Refugee Act indisputably applies) was not subject to the same international constraints against returning refugees to persecution as when the seizure occurs within U.S. territorial limits. The government asserted a right to extend its power to control immigration by moving the border far out to sea while ignoring the legal limitations on the exercise of that power applicable within the United States. Under the government's view, the power of the state to exercise control over individuals may be extended indefinitely, but the duty to protect individual rights remained anchored to shore. Thus, fleeing Haitians could be denied the rights they would have upon arriving at the U.S. border by the simple expedient of preventing them from ever reaching that destination. The district court felt bound by appellate precedent to permit the forced repatriations. However, Judge Johnson decried the new interdiction policy in the sharpest terms:

> It is unconscionable that the United States should accede to the [U.N.] Protocol and later claim that it is not bound by it. This Court is astonished

[17]INA 243(h), 8 U.S.C. 1253(h). Notably, the Refugee Act, in addition to other changes, specifically deleted language in INA 243(h) that previously limited its application to aliens "within the United States."

[18]In addition, the government contended that the Refugee Convention is not self-executing so that whatever obligations it may impose on the United States could not be asserted by individual Haitian refugees. The government did not contest that the Refugee Act intended to bring the United States into full compliance with the Refugee Convention, and that any rights under the Refugee Convention could presumably be enforced through this domestic statute.

that the United States would return Haitian refugees to the jaws of political persecution, terror, death and uncertainty when it has contracted not to do so. The Government's conduct is particularly hypocritical given its condemnation of other countries who have refused to abide by the principle of non-refoulement. As it stands now, [the U.N. Protocol] is a cruel hoax and not worth the paper it is printed on. . . . (*HCC v. McNary*, No. 92 CV 1258 E.D.N.Y. 7 June, 1992[19])

On appeal, the Second Circuit recognized the legal force of the district court's outrage. The appellate court held that the Kennebunkport Order violated the plain language of the Refugee Act and ordered the interdiction policy stopped (*HCC v. Sale*, 969 F. 2d 1350, 2d Cir. 1992). The court found that interdicted Haitians were encompassed within the statutory term "any alien" and that their summary repatriation by the Coast Guard constituted a "return" within the prohibition of INA § 243(h). The court also found that the President's emergency powers under the INA to control the *entry* of aliens did not support an interdiction operation that prevented foreign nationals from *leaving* their own country for an unspecified or unknown destination.

The Bush Administration immediately sought and received a stay from the Supreme Court pending its review of the case. Despite earlier statements by candidate Clinton condemning the Kennebunkport Order and praising the court of appeals decision, the Clinton Administration pursued the Supreme Court appeal and did nothing to alter the policy or the arguments presented to the Court.[20] On March 2, the Court heard the case; on June 21, 1993, it upheld the interdiction policy, ruling that neither Article 33 of the Refugee Convention nor INA § 243(h) apply outside the territorial limits of the United States

---

[19]LEXIS Genfed Library.

[20]The new Administration initially contended that maintaining summary repatriation was a temporary measure undertaken in tandem with steps to restore President Aristide to office. That claim has been all but publicly abandoned and the policy is now reportedly subject to widespread criticism even within the administration. (*See* The New York Times, 1993.)

The Clinton Administration also proffered various other justifications for its continuation of the Bush policy, but there was no dispute that genuine political refugees were being sent back to Haiti under the Kennebunkport Order. Instead, President Clinton cited to the danger to Haitians of fleeing in small boats, the U.S. fear of a massive outflow, and the existence of a process within Haiti for applying for refugee status. Yet none of these rationales addressed the duty to protect Haitians who are actually fleeing, the fact that persons on dangerous or sinking boats can be saved without being repatriated, the evidence that government projections of massive flight were demonstrably exaggerated whenever subjected to the scrutiny of sworn testimony, and the obvious and severe deficiencies of the in-country process, particularly for those who are the most at risk.

(*Sale v. HCC*, 113 S. Ct. 2549 1993). Justice Stevens, author of the two major decisions interpreting the 1980 Refugee Act, wrote for the majority.[21] Only Justice Blackmun dissented.

The majority opinion concluded that INA § 243(h) does not apply to conduct outside the United States because 1) the statute's language is limited to "the Attorney General," 2) the dual prohibition of "deport or return" signifies only the statute's applicability to the technically-different exclusion and deportation proceedings, 3) deletion in 1980 of the language that the protection applies solely to aliens "within the United States" only expanded the statute to apply to exclusion proceedings, and 4) the legislative history is not sufficient to overcome the presumption that statutes do not apply extraterritorially. The Court also held that Article 33 does not apply outside the territorial limits of a contracting state because 1) the *limitation* on Article 33's applicability (contained in Article 33.2) refers to aliens within a country and that the entire provision should be read as so limited, 2) the French *refouler* is a limited term that implies a defensive act of resistance "at the border," and 3) the negotiating history does not reflect a clear extra-territorial intent.

Justice Blackmun as the lone dissenter systematically refuted each premise of the majority decision. He began with the uncontroverted premise that the Refugee Act of 1980 was enacted to conform U.S. law to Article 33 of the Refugee Convention and with the fundamental interpretive principle that the plain language of the Convention and statute govern (113 S. Ct. at 2568–2569). He found that the French prohibition against *refouler* in the Convention and the English "shall not return any alien" language in INA § 243(h) are consistent and clear in prohibiting the United States from "returning" Haitian refugees to persecution. In doing so he showed why the language in Convention Article 33.2 (incorporated into INA § 243(h)(2)(c)) on which the Court relies does not support the interpretation of nonrefoulement the majority adopted (113 S. Ct. at 2570), that the term "return" is used throughout the INA with the same plain meaning that the Haitian plaintiffs sought to apply in § 243(h) (113 S. Ct. at 2575 n. 12), that the government's interpretation of the Convention would render it redundant (113 S. Ct. at 2569 n.4), and that the negotiating history of

---

[21]*See INS v. Stevic*, 467 U.S. 407 (1984) (standard applicable to the nonrefoulement requirement of INA 2434(h); *INS v. Cardoza-Fonseca*, 480 U.S. 421 (1987) (standard applicable to the "well-founded fear" determination of INA 208).

the Convention – if relevant at all – supports the plain reading of the nonrefoulement prohibition that he endorses (113 S. Ct. at 2572).

Justice Blackmun's analysis carefully distinguished the right of a country to prevent the "admission" of an alien (or refugee), which the Haitian plaintiffs were not seeking, from the prohibition against forcibly returning refugees to persecution (113 S. Ct. at 2572). He also recognized that the linchpin of the majority's decision is its "heavy reliance on the presumption against extraterritoriality" (113 S. Ct. at 2576) and explained why the presumption has no force when a statute "regulates a distinctively international subject matter: immigration, nationalities and refugees" (113 S. Ct. at 2577). In contrast to the majority, Justice Blackmun recognized that abstract concepts of extraterritoriality are beside the point when the United States is affirmatively reaching out into international waters to interdict and return fleeing refugees who are far from this country's shores. "This is a case in which a Nation has gone forth to *seize* aliens who are *not* at its borders and *return* them to persecution. Nothing . . . even hints at an intention on the part of the drafters to countenance a course of conduct so at odds with the Convention's basic purpose" (113 S. Ct. at 2572; footnote omitted, emphasis in original).

In reaching its conclusion, the Court majority conceded its begrudging and hypertechnical reading of the statute and Convention. The Court acknowledged the "moral weight" of the Haitians' argument and recognized that the language of Article 33 might not explicitly prohibit the extraterritorial interdiction and summary return precisely because "[t]he drafters of the Convention and the parties to the Protocol . . . may not have contemplated that any nation would gather fleeing refugees and return them to the one country they had desperately sought to escape" (113 S. Ct. at 2563). Such actions, the Court agreed, "may even violate the spirit of Article 33" (113 S. Ct. at 2565). In short, the Court virtually conceded that the United States is acting contrary to the purpose and spirit of the nonrefoulement principle and that interdiction and forcible repatriation were never anticipated by the drafters of this safeguard. Yet except in brief asides, the Court refused to confront the uniqueness of the interdiction program. Instead, it considered the issue solely as an abstract question of the extraterritorial reach of U.S. law. The majority failed to address that the Haitians relied on U.S. law only because the United States first seized them. Hence, the question is not whether Convention Article 33 or INA § 243(h) should apply extraterritorially in all cases and to all persons wherever and whenever the government acts. Rather, the issue is whether a country should be permitted to reach out affirmatively to capture persons in international waters while simultaneously ignoring or renouncing its legal duty not to return those persons to persecution. Having elected to establish an interdiction program on the high seas for the express purpose of controlling access to our shores, the United States should not be able to use the very fact that it is acting in extraterritorial waters to escape its obligations under international and domestic law. The artifice of interdiction cannot alter the reality of refoulement. Haitians are being returned to persecution, not protected against it.

Ultimately, only Justice Blackmun appreciated the moral and historical dimensions of the Court's decision and accepted the full implications of the interdiction policy for the United States and the world:

> The Convention that the Refugee Act embodies was enacted largely in response to the experience of Jewish refugees in Europe during the period of World War II. The tragic consequences of the world's indifference at that time are well known. The resulting ban on *refoulement*, as broad as the humanitarian purpose that inspired it, is easily applicable here, the Court's protestations of impotence and regret notwithstanding.
>
> The refugees attempting to escape from Haiti . . . demand only that the United States, land of refugees and guardian of freedom, cease forcibly driving them back to detention, abuse, and death. That is a modest plea. . . . We should not close our ears to it. (113 S. Ct. at 2577)[22]

CONCLUSION

The prospects for restoration of democracy in Haiti remain dim. Yet the interdiction program continues unchanged and unscrutinized. An entire people are being held hostage in their country – not by their own repressive

---

[22]One other aspect of the majority's opinion bears note – the Court's silence on the self-executing status of the Refugee Convention. While not explicitly addressing whether the Convention is self-executing, the Court's discussion of the territorial reach and substantive protections afforded by the Convention assumed that it was properly invoked by the Haitian plaintiffs. The discussion of Article 33 was in part to determine the reach of INA 243(h), but the Court did not shy away from treating the Convention as having independent force and being self-executing. "[T]he Convention might have established an extraterritorial obligation which the statute does not; under the Supremacy Clause, that broader treaty obligation might then provide the controlling rule of law." *Sale v. HCC*, 113 S. Ct. at 2562; *cf. HRC v. Baker*, 949 F.2d 1109 (11th Cir. 1991) cert. denied, *112 S. Ct. 1245 (1992). See also, HCC v. McNary*, No. 92 CV 1258 (E.D.N.Y. 7 June 1992) (citing *Bertrand v. Sava*, 684 F.2d 204, 218–219 (2d Cir. 1982)). *See also, HRC v. Gracey*, 600 F. Supp. at 1406 ("United Nations Protocol is not self-executing").

regime, but by the conscious policy of the United States. Never before has the United States sought to justify reaching out beyond its borders to snatch fleeing refugees from their desperate flight and to return them directly to the perpetrators of violence, oppression, and death.

On October 12, 1993, a boatload of U.S. soldiers was ordered to abandon a landing in Haiti because the danger was too great. Yet fleeing Haitians refugees are interdicted almost daily and summarily returned. By international standards the number fleeing is not large in light of the size, wealth and diversity of the United States, the number is tiny. The danger the Haitians pose is not from their arrival on our shores. Instead it is our nation's response to their plight that is doing inestimable damage to international refugee protection and the rule of law. The fugitive slave laws forced fleeing slaves back to slavery and the *Dred Scott* decision denied them the protection of our courts. Now the United States has adopted a "fugitive refugee law" that returns fleeing refugees back to persecution, and the Supreme Court has denied them the protection of our laws.

REFERENCES

Amnesty International
1992   "Haiti: Human Rights Held Ransom." August.

Helsinki Watch
1989   *Detained, Denied, Deported: Asylum Seekers in the United States.* Pp. 51–52. June.

Lawyers Committee for Human Rights
1992   *Haiti: A Human Rights Nightmare.* August.

_____
1990   *Refugee Refoulement: The Forced Return of Haitians Under the U.S.-Haitian Interdiction Agreement.* March 3.

The New York Times
1993a   "Crackdown Fails to Stem Smuggling of Chinese to U.S.," *The New York Times*, A1, Col. 6. August 23.

_____
1993b   "U.S. Aide to Seek New Policy on Fleeing Haitians," *The New York Times*, A7. December 15.

U.S. Committee for Refugees
1991   *Running the Gauntlet: The Central American Journey through Mexico.* January.

16

Displaced Central Americans: Mexican NGOs and the International Response

Sergio Aguayo Quezada

Introduction

The end of the Cold War hastened changes that had already appeared in the agenda of international priorities. Preoccupation with confrontation between two blocs and ideologies shifted to concern over the environment and human rights within the context of the globalization of the world's economy and a communications revolution. These facts are forcing a redefinition of the concepts of nationalism, sovereignty, and borders.

A simultaneous phenomenon has received less attention but bears directly on the above tendencies: the internationalization of politics. Governments and political parties have traditionally been regarded as the main protagonists of political systems and international order. This view has been modified by a loss of credibility in governments and parties, and a proliferation of social and nongovernmental (or intermediate) organizations permanently striving to influence public policies in novel ways. One method has been to develop independent diplomatic activities through citizens' networks, creating a web of contacts between societies.

This phenomenon, still insufficiently researched, manifested itself after 1990, when the three North American countries – Canada, the United States, and Mexico – embarked on a process of formal economic integration. During the years of negotiations for a North American Free Trade Agreement (NAFTA), in all three countries social and nongovernment coalitions arose to support or oppose it. Whether for or against all or part of the Agreement, these coalitions did everything in their power to change the shape and features of NAFTA.

In November of 1993, NAFTA was approved. Assessing various coalitions' effects on government decisions is difficult. My impression – reinforced by some interviews – is that the influence of nongovernmental organizations (NGOs) and the alliances they established with other actors had much to do with their increasing political importance. The main variable, however, was the openness of the political system. Some participants in the process suggest that NGOs were more influential in Canada than in Mexico, with those in the United States in an intermediate position.[1]

Regardless of the exact importance these coalitions may have had, their very existence was a further indication of the internationalization of politics. In this essay, I will explore a direct precedent of this collaboration between societies: the work carried out by Mexican NGOs to protect and defend Central American populations displaced by wars that plagued the region for more than a decade. Although the greatest emphasis is placed on Mexico, I will also refer to various Central American countries, the United States, and Canada (Aguayo, 1991).

From the end of the 1970s onwards, three Central American countries were affected by armed conflict and economic devastation. Although there are many differences between the conflicts, Guatemala, El Salvador and Nicaragua each registered the phenomenon of massive displacement. The most accurate estimates set the number of people who left their place of residence to return to their country of origin or to seek refuge in neighboring countries at between 2 and 3 million. Migration occurred on a huge scale, especially if we take into account that in 1985 these three countries had a combined population of 16 million.

[1]Interviews with members of the Red Mexicana Frente al Acuerdo de Libre Comercio (RE-MALC), November 1993.

In the case of those who travelled to other countries, the exodus occurred from Central to North America. Eighty-seven percent of the 1 or 2 million who left El Salvador, Guatemala and Nicaragua went to Mexico and the United States. Between 165,000 and 400,000 remained in Mexico; 600,000 to 1,130,000 came to the United States, with most of them using Mexico as an overland corridor. A much smaller figure landed in Canada.[2] Thus Mexico played a key role as a host country or transit area for those going north.

In Central and North America, most governments and certain sectors of the population regarded the Central Americans' arrival with concern (and in some cases hostility). In spite of this rejection, Central Americans managed to reach Mexico, settle there, or continue their journeys north. This was the result of several factors, including the corruption of petty authorities, the area's open borders, and the existence of land routes and migratory networks in use since before the conflicts. However, one of the most important factors, one present throughout the region, was the solidarity among some sectors of society that was organized and expressed through the work of NGOs. This study focuses on the NGOs that supported Guatemalans or Salvadoreans.

In 1992, the European Commission Delegation prepared a highly revealing directory of institutions involved in the phenomenon of displaced Central Americans in Mexico.[3] According to this document, there are 36 Mexican NGOs, nine organizations representing Guatemalan or Salvadorean refugees or displaced persons, eleven international NGO agencies, five research centers concerned with the topic, three international United Nations' organizations and four Mexican government institutions. There is also a Coordinadora Nacional de ONGs (Mexicanas) de Ayuda a Refugiados (CONONGAR) that groups together fifteen of the 36 Mexican NGOs involved in the subject (González, 1992).

A list of all those who have participated in the policy-making process towards Central Americans would require the addition of the United

---

[2]Estimates are based on the systematization of data from various sources. *See* Aguayo and Fagen (1988: 78–79).

[3]Throughout the text, I use the concept of displaced persons to include both refugees recognized by the United Nations High Commissioner for Refugees and those who were not. My reason is that recognition was occasionally determined by political factors, meaning that it was not granted to all those who warranted it.

States, Canadian, and European governments' embassies and a fair number of donor agencies or NGOs from these countries that were not included in the European Commission's Directory. The present study, however, concentrates on NGOs as a particular form of social organization.

Part of the difficulty in categorizing and conceptualizing NGOs lies in the fact that they have a negative identity. That is, they are neither parties nor social movements, they are not linked to governments, and they are nonprofit. As a result, they do not fit the model of most existing institutions although they are influenced by some of them. For example, at least half the NGOs included in the European Commission's Directory are somehow influenced by a church or by the Christian tradition.

NGOs can be roughly defined as small organizations created with one or more very specific aims. The most common of these is to provide support for unprotected sectors of society to enable them to organize themselves, defend their rights and influence public policies affecting them. A relative lack of ideology has made it easy for them to become a point of encounter for different social classes and groups, whether lay or religious. There has been a recent tendency among NGOs to set up formal or informal networks, national or international, according to the type of problem they are dealing with. Their political importance is generally limited, except when they act in coordination.[4]

In this essay, I will provide an overall view of this little-known aspect of the history of Central American conflicts. After a brief summary of the history of Mexican NGOs and a tentative assessment of their achievements and limitations. I suggest that this experience goes far beyond defending Central Americans and devote a few pages to explaining some scarcely visible effects. For example, part of the importance of this experience is that it provided NGOs in Mexico and other countries with an international outlook that made it easier to establish more effective operational relations with U.S. and Canadian society when the process of formal economic integration began.

---

[4]Two of the most useful documents on NGOs are the International Council of Voluntary Agencies' *Documents in Development, 1981–1989* (ICVA, 1989) and the magazine *Development in Practice* published by OXFAM, Oxford, England.

STAGES IN THE HISTORY OF NGOs ASSISTING CENTRAL AMERICANS

The Mexican NGOs' work to protect and defend displaced Central Americans can be divided in fairly clearly-defined stages. The approximate dates are:

1) 1979–1984, a period characterized by isolation, dispersal and marginality;

2) 1984–1990, when they became more organized, thus having an important effect on the asylum, protection, and assistance policies adopted by governments and multilateral organizations;

3) 1990–1993, when the organizations underwent a double process. On the one hand, the NGOs still working with refugees and displaced persons experienced an extremely difficult transition period; on the other, some NGOs in Mexico, the United States and Canada were attempting to establish some kind of regional coordination that would allow them to preserve the asylum tradition and defend labor rights in North America.

Central Americans began to reach Mexico in the late 1970s, and some sectors of society immediately devised means of protecting them. Initially, a few already existing social, church and nongovernmental organizations set up assistance programs; a year or two later, NGOs were established with the sole aim of attending the Central Americans who were arriving. There were only a few NGOs. Those that did exist were scattered and isolated, and had very little weight in official policies. This was partly due to the fact that the organizations did not know each other or felt a strong mutual distrust. The only points they had in common were their solidarity with the displaced and the hostility towards government authorities and the United Nations High Commissioner for Refugees (UNHCR), which carried out a delicate balancing act between protecting part of the displaced population (the Guatemalans who reached Chiapas) and trying not to antagonize a government that did everything in its power to reject the displaced people.

For various reasons distrust was entirely logical. The Mexican NGOs had sprung up and developed in the shadow of an authoritarian regime that found it difficult to accept independent organizations. (In Central

America, with the exception of Costa Rica, the situation was just as bad or worse.) The NGOs could be roughly divided by their origins – Christian or secular – or by the populations they attended (the clearest distinction was between Guatemalans recognized as refugees by UNHCR and the Central Americans who were not). Another reason for the atomization that existed among the NGOs derived from the way in which displacement was regarded. The general view was that it was a temporary form of migration for which only emergency relief had to be provided as a means of supporting the processes of change in El Salvador and Guatemala. This view came from a very widespread belief that the insurgent forces were close to taking over power in both of these countries, exactly as the Nicaraguan Sandinistas had done. If the displaced people were going to be here for only a short time, there did not seem to be a need for any coordination between the NGOs that attended them.

The sum of these factors meant that early attempts to create some form of collective effort among the NGOs in 1981 and 1982 failed. For example, the coordination of policies for the assistance of NGO refugees, created by the Dioceses of San Cristóbal las Casas and Tapachula, Chiapas (a state bordering Guatemala) did not last long, in spite of their proximity. Nor was there any form of communication between the NGOs that attended nonrecognized Central Americans in Mexico City and the Centro de Investigación y Estudios Migratorios (CIEM) on the border with the United States.

Moreover, most of these organizations harbored traditions of distrust towards foreigners, particularly Americans. At that time in Mexico, there was still a very strong nationalistic tradition, fueled by history and the government, that all foreigners were regarded as a potential threat to the country's sovereignty. This attitude was to be rapidly modified by an unavoidable reality.

Mexican NGOs lacked resources to carry out their aim of providing emergency relief and protection for Central Americans, and these resources could not come from Mexico, where the philanthropic tradition is quite weak. But some foreign organizations and agencies that came to the region and to Mexico with the aim of helping Central Americans had these resources, and they wished to provide them through the NGOs since this was their mandate, and also because of a unique aspect of Mexico. In the Central American countries, foreign private organization offices and even operational programs could be set up (Honduras was the most significant example). In Mexico, the government refused to allow this type of institution to operate in national territory, much less for such a thorny issue as displaced Central Americans. Other factors that influenced the decision of foreign organizations to work through Mexican NGOs was the myth of the Mexican political system's complexity, and the desire not to antagonize the Mexican government which, though authoritarian in its own country, had a progressive foreign policy towards Central America that they fully supported.

Interviews with those directly involved would seem to suggest that during the early years, the relationship between Mexican and foreign NGOs was a marriage of convenience. However, relations improved because Mexican NGOs realized that the foreigners gave their support while respecting local criteria and provided a certain degree of political protection, which was indispensable given the conditions under which the NGOs worked. A bond of trust was gradually forged between the Mexican NGOs and the European, U.S., and Canadian agencies and foundations. During this period, organizations such as the International Council of Voluntary Agencies (ICVA) adopted a very clear policy of encouraging the coordination of local NGOs. In spite of their resistance, the local NGOs began to communicate with each other and reduce mutual distrust. As opinion surveys have shown, trust is a key factor for carrying out activities of this sort (Inglehart, 1990: 10).

At the same time, another form of collaboration between societies emerged. It has never been publicly discussed, but it illustrates vividly the differences among North American societies. In the United States, one method that churches, social organizations and NGOs used to protect Central Americans was to provide "sanctuary" to some of those who, according to the U.S. government, did not qualify for asylum. It should be mentioned in passing that the origin and modern revival of this practice is further proof of the internationalization of political practices. The tradition of providing sanctuary to those pursued by the law dates from the Middle Ages. It was revived in this hemisphere after the 1973 *coup d'état* in Chile and, as far as I can tell, the example was followed by Americans who had undergone the experience in Chile.

The "Sanctuary Movement" was complemented by what was known as the "Underground Railway," a term originating from the practice of certain groups in the North who helped black slaves to escape from the South during the nineteenth century. The modern, regional version of the railway consisted of taking some of those who were being persecuted in El Salvador or Guatemala to the United States. The escape route passed through Mexico, where Mexican NGOs were in charge of receiving them at the southern border, taking them across Mexico, and handing them over to U.S. organizations at the northern border who put them in sanctuaries.

The declaration of sanctuary in churches, universities and towns was widely publicized by the Americans. They saw it as a form of civil disobedience whose aim was to draw society's attention, through the mass media, to the plight of Central Americans in the United States and to protest against Republican administrations' policies towards the region, which they regarded as morally reprehensible. The Mexicans had a completely opposite attitude: given the methods and practices of their own regime, they preferred to keep silent about their role. The contrast illustrates well the vast differences in the nature of the two political systems.

The activities of Mexican NGOs were either ignored or viewed with profound suspicion by the Mexican government. The intrusion of these groups of citizens was resented by Mexican officials because they knew nothing about the NGOs, because they were convinced that the NGOs were instruments of foreign intervention, and because the issue of Central Americans was classified as a security problem at the time.

The Mexican government was not alone in distrusting the NGOs; the same occurred throughout the region. There could be no better proof of this than the Cartagena Conference in Colombia in November, 1984, from which emerged a declaration that broadened the concept of refugee status. In spite of the importance of this meeting, not a single local NGO or refugee organization was represented.

The year of the Cartagena Conference, 1984, can be considered as a watershed in the NGOs' evolution. It marked the beginning of a second stage that lasted until 1990. By 1984 there had been a fundamental change in the perception of massive population movements. The impasse reached in the conflicts showed governments, multilateral organizations and NGOs that population displacement was not a short-term problem.

If displaced persons were to remain for a long time, then durable solutions would have to be provided, which would require stable programs and/or the creation of new organizations especially designed for them. There was also the need to attend to legal and psychological aspects, and to take care of special groups (widows, unmarried mothers, orphans, Indians suffering the shock of urban living, etc.) It also necessitated stronger and more sophisticated interaction with the government, UNHCR, donor countries' embassies and the national or international press, all of which were following this aspect of the conflict with growing interest.[5]

All this implied a broader and more permanent financial commitment than the Northern agencies were willing to provide. Their disposition was influenced by the priority given to the Central American conflict in various parts of the world. Two examples will give an idea of the economic magnitude of this aid and interest. The Project Counselling Service for Latin American Refugees (PCS) is a coalition of European and Canadian agencies operating throughout the area, with headquarters in Costa Rica. Between March, 1986, and September, 1991, PCS channelled $10,440,000 through Latin American NGOs in the area (PCS, 1992). As for research funds, Georgetown University's Hemispheric Migration Project (HMP) channelled almost $2 million into approximately 50 studies on economic and political migration.[6]

The complexity of this phase affecting displaced populations, whether in camps or dispersed throughout the region, made it essential that coordination begin among the NGOs that had been growing in Mexico and the other countries. Eric Holt-Giménez comments (1989), with a trace of irony, that the armies and NGOs were the only institutions that flourished in Central America during the war. These years were characterized by a notable increase in NGOs organization and influence.

In short, between 1984 and 1990 increased coordination was the consequence of four factors: 1) requests made by the financing agencies (with ICVA acting as a catalyst) that led to two NGO regional meetings in 1984 and 1986 in San José, Costa Rica; 2) the contribution of academics

[5]In Mexico, the refugees' cause was greatly assisted by the creation of an independent newspaper, *La Jornada*, in 1984. Information and support regarding the protection of displaced persons was one of its editorial and news priorities.

[6]Interview with Mary Ann Larkin, Program Coordinator, February, 1992.

and research centers throughout the region that showed the complexity and dimensions of the displacements; 3) the peace process that begun with Contadora and continued with Esquipulas; and 4) the United Nations' call, through UNHCR and the United Nations Development Program (UNDP) for a grand Conferencia Internacional sobre Refugiados Centroamericanos (CIREFCA), in which representatives from governments and international organizations were to participate.

Local NGOs were excluded from the planning stages of CIREFCA. In spite of this and after several delays, when CIREFCA was held in Guatemala City in May of 1989, NGOs played a key role. The difference between this conference and the 1984 Cartagena Conference was remarkable. In fact, it was this external point of reference, and the aforementioned changes, that provided the final incentive for NGOs in Mexico and the whole region to participate more fully in the coordination process. The initiative came from two Mexican NGOs, (Academia Mexicana de Derechos Humanos and Servicio, Desarrollo y Paz), and, after a number of preparatory meetings, led to the First International Conference of NGOs Working with Central American Refugees, Displaced Persons and Returnees, which was held two months before CIREFCA, in Mexico City, in March, 1989.

NGO delegations from all countries with displaced Central Americans (from Panama to Canada) participated in this Conference, and consequently national coordinating bodies were set up in nearly all countries. In Mexico, fifteen NGOs established the Coordinadora Nacional de ONGs de ayuda a Refugiados, CONONGAR. The Asociación Regional de Coordinadoras Nacionales que trabajan con Refugiados, Desplazados y Retornados, was created for the region (and formally constituted in October, 1989). That same year, a Mexican NGO – Servicio, Desarrollo y Paz (SEDEPAC) – requested its affiliation to the International Council of Voluntary Agencies headquarters in Geneva. It was the first Mexican NGO to do so, and an indicator of the need for NGOs to have their own international activities.

From then on and with the support of Northern NGOs, local NGOs acquired a degree of prominence that would have been unthinkable only a few years before. Delegates from 52 NGOs and representatives from Guatemalan and Salvadorean refugee organizations took part in CIREFCA II in New York in June 1990. The fact that NGOs were able to reach these levels of prominence was due to the degree of maturity they had acquired, the alliances they had established with academic sectors, their reconciliation with UNHCR and other international organizations, the trust vested in them by certain donor governments dissatisfied with the inefficiency and high cost of official aid programs for refugees, and above all, to the degree of unity they had achieved with NGOs and foundations in the North. CIREFCA was a culminating moment in the development of civic diplomacy aimed at defending refugees, displaced persons, and returnees from Central America.

Although this progress was made possible by the levels of coordination achieved between NGOs of the South and North, the former still had reservations about their wealthier neighbors. For example, in March 1989 at the First International NGOs conference, the NGO delegations from the United States and Canada were participants. However, when the Regional Association was created in October, 1989, the Central American NGOs decided that U.S. and Canadian NGOs should be relegated to the category of "honorary members." Mexican NGOs were accepted with great difficulty. This attitude sprang from a very widespread desire among Central Americans to control their own processes and from a traditional resentment towards their northern neighbors. Thus, although the small size of the NGOs ought to make it easier to have equal relationships, in practice enormous difficulties arise.

Yet there is no doubt that the NGO coordination affected international and domestic policies towards displaced persons. In Mexico, it was remarkable that CONONGAR should have succeeded in making Congress modify a bill in May-June 1990, to reform the General Population Law issued by the Mexican executive branch and proposed to cover refugees. This was particularly noteworthy because of the traditional submission of the Mexican legislative branch to the president, and because it was the first time a group of NGOs had managed to influence migratory policy so clearly.

Indeed, this degree of influence was possible because the Mexican government had modified its perception of the phenomenon of displaced Central Americans. While the government initially saw them as a national security issue, by the end of the decade it had transferred them to the category of a human rights issue. In addition, with the creation of the governmental National Human Rights Commission (CNDH) in June 1990, human rights were now legitimated. Some officials I interviewed identified a key factor in this change as the dialogue established with the NGOs which served to dispel their previous image as instruments of intervention. Another factor affecting official perception was the collapse of the revolutionary economic model in the mid-1980s, which forced the Mexican economy to open its doors to other countries. Mexico's entry into the global economy dealt a death blow to the version of nationalism that branded as traitors Mexicans who dared form alliances with any foreign group.

Paradoxically, it was just when NGOs had reached their peak of influence that problems began to arise. This leads me to the third stage, still incomplete at the point of finishing this writing (December 1993). By the late 1980s, the peace process in Nicaragua, El Salvador and Guatemala had advanced and the most visible aspect of displacements abroad had begun to be solved. Recognized refugee camps began repatriating people to Nicaragua and El Salvador. Repatriation, together with the emergence of crises in Eastern Europe and the Middle East, reduced the international attention that the region had received for over ten years. It was a recurrence of the phenomenon whereby humanitarian (and economic) aid is greatly determined by the visibility of the crisis. One very obvious consequence has been a reduction in the flow of international funds towards the NGOs dealing with refugees and displaced persons with the result that, after 1990, there was a relative reduction in the ability of both the national coordinating bodies (*e.g.*, CONONGAR in Mexico) and the regional association to wield any influence.

In April 1990, it was announced that the Mexican government had begun to approach Washington to explore the possibility of a North American Free Trade Agreement, to be joined later by Canada. Given the attention these negotiations have received, I think it is unnecessary to describe them. The process I wish to highlight was the emergence of NGO coalitions (in Canada, Common Frontiers; in Mexico, REMALC) that established a common agenda to try to influence NAFTA. It is not my goal to evaluate how successful they were, in an area in which success is hard to define. From a long-term perspective, what is really important are the implications for the future of citizen diplomacy. It was the first time in history in which social organizations of the three countries cooperated on an issue affecting the three. As economic integration proceeds, the impact of this networking will be felt in the field of politics.

There is an evident need to coordinate or to establish relations in groups not directly related to NAFTA, as in the case of NGOs working with displaced populations and migrants. From the outset, the three governments agreed to exclude the subject of economic or political migrations from NAFTA negotiations. In spite of these intentions, formal economic integration will obviously have some effect on the type and intensity of migration among the three countries. There is also documentary evidence that Mexican authorities have discreetly begun to adapt their immigration policies to those of the United States (Frelick, 1990). This adaptation means that Mexico has tightened control over the migration of citizens from other countries (not just Central Americans) who have continued to use Mexico as a corridor to the United States. The governments seem to be quietly constructing a sort of North American fortress rather like what has been happening in Western Europe.

In this context, and with its eight years' experience of work with displaced persons, in 1991 the Academia Mexicana de Derechos Humanos proposed convening a regional meeting of NGOs and research centers in Mexico, the United States and Canada that are interested in the issues of asylum and economic migration. Its initiative was seconded, and later led, by the Georgetown University Hemispheric Migration Project and the Center of Studies on Refugees (CSR) at York University, Toronto. The main aim was to start a process enabling a regional approach toward the phenomenon of economic and political migrations, to be adopted in a spirit of equality between NGOs and researchers. This would provide the basis for designing a program that would combine research with activism so as to protect labor rights and preserve the tradition of asylum in the three countries. In the light of previous experience, attempts were being made to correct earlier mistakes.

The Conferencia Internacional sobre Integración Económica, Políticas Migratorias y Derechos Humanos en América del Norte (International Conference on Economic Integration, Migratory Policies and Human Rights in North America) was held in Mexico in February 1992. One of the main conclusions was the need to create a "permanent, trinational structure to investigate hemispheric migration, with a special focus on problems of protection." This structure is called the Foro de los Países de América del Norte para los Derechos de los Refugiados y los

Migrantes (CONAFORRAM) (Academia Mexicana de Derecho Humanas, 1992: 3). A resolution of this Conference was to hold a followup conference – organized by York University in Toronto in November 1992 – during which discussions progressed and it was decided that Georgetown University should organize a third meeting to be held in Washington in September 1993 (CONAFORRAM III).

This has not been an easy process for a number of reasons, among them the sharp differences of approach between academics and activists: complementary, but not always easy to reconcile in practice. A second hindrance to the coordination process is the current period of transition at all levels, posing fundamental problems in all three societies. Any debate about migration or any other specific issue is overshadowed by the complexities of three extraordinarily different societies. In this context, NGOs have to decide on the kind of role they can (or should) have. There are no definite answers, but I will put forth a few ideas based on a general assessment of the NGOs' experience.

AN ASSESSMENT AND A FEW ADDITIONAL IDEAS

I earlier mentioned the lack of research or reflections on the subject of nongovernmental organizations in Mexico and the region. In spite of this, the experience described here shows the importance of these civic organizations and the need to continue delving more deeply into the subject and its implications.

First of all, NGOs that assisted or protected Central American populations displaced by the conflict grew in both quality and quantity. As they established coordination mechanisms and set up operational networks, they became a determining factor, at times able to influence government policies affecting these nuclei of population. A key element in this was the prestige they acquired as efficient, committed institutions who offered donors the far from negligible incentive of lower operating costs than those of government or international bureaucratic institutions. A crucial factor in their effectiveness and coordination was the support they received from Northern NGOs, foundations, governments (European and Scandinavian in particular), and international organizations such as UNHCR, whose mandate included establishing mechanisms of coordination with NGOs.

At the end of 1992, for a number of reasons, NGOs working with displaced persons in the region face a difficult transition. Over time the

NGOs acquired a dependence on international funds, and neglected to develop local sources of financing. Once foreign funds began to grow scarce because of Central America's lowered priority, the NGOs faced serious difficulties. Some have already disappeared while others reduce their activities, which implies a considerable loss of accumulated experience.

The situation is also affected by a more complex problem. With few exceptions, donor agencies from the North were obsessed with financing projects and only rarely supported what is generically known as institutional development. This means that several organizations lacked the resources to become professional, making their transition all the more difficult. A related complication was that Northern agencies began their cooperation without clarifying the terms of reference; for instance, it would have been extremely useful to establish a time frame for their cooperation. Simple facts like this one must not be minimized because Southern NGOs sometimes lack sophistication on the mechanics of international aid.

Obviously, not all NGOs have had the same experience. Some Mexican and Central American NGOs detected the change of priorities in time and began to orient their work in other directions. A recurrent phenomenon has been to redirect work towards human rights, which has become a Mexican and worldwide priority. Although it is not the only reason, this reorientation explains the current success of nongovernmental human rights organizations in Mexico. To give some idea of the increase in this type of NGO, suffice it to say that in 1983 there were about 20 nongovernmental human rights organizations, while, by the end of 1993, there were almost 300 across the country (Coordinación de Educación, Academia Mexicana de Derechos Humanas, n.d.). This proliferation of NGOs is also occurring in the fields of environmental protection, development, popular education, feminism, etc.

At the same time, NGOs working with displaced populations had other, less visible, effects worth mentioning. The first concerns the battle for Central America waged in the United States by groups of Americans that were divided as to American policy in that region. Several sectors of American society put up a remarkable degree of opposition and were surprisingly effective in obstructing Republican policies during the Central American conflicts. Although the history is extremely complex, two interrelated factors explaining this opposition are the presence of hundreds of thousands of Central Americans in the United States, and the measures that some of them consciously adopted to promote solidarity in the United States with El Salvador, Nicaragua or Guatemala. In this sense, the fact that NGOs facilitated the passage of Central Americans to the United States had an effect on the way in which the conflicts evolved.

Another effect is that of NGO collective action in Mexico. The coordinating body for NGOs that worked with displaced people – CONONGAR – was among the early NGO networks set up in Mexico. Since its creation, the number of social networks in other areas has increased. One of the most important at the moment is Convergencia de Organismos Civiles por la Democracia (COCD), a coalition of 150 NGOs operating in nineteen states with work programs that affect some 4 million Mexicans. Convergencia's importance lies in its promotion of democracy. Thus, Central America is indirectly affecting changes in Mexico.

A third effect is that, through the refugee issue, NGOs hastened the creation of formal or informal collaboration agreements with NGOs in other countries. This is a most significant achievement because, for several decades, Mexican society was shut in behind the walls of a brand of nationalism that regarded anything that came from abroad with suspicion. (Not until the 1970s was the first research center dedicated to the United States created in Mexico.) The costs of this isolation were a scant knowledge of other countries and an inability to understand their cultural and political codes. A parallel process has occurred whereby the presence in Mexico of NGOs from the North has served to familiarize a fair number of activists from industrial countries with the complexities of Mexican life.

This relationship with the outside world has been difficult, for it implies the maturing and/or abandonment of the old nationalistic Mexican culture. Overcoming distrust of foreigners has been extraordinarily traumatic, because we Mexicans were brought up with the belief that the border was a wall defending the country from ambitious foreigners bent on stealing our riches. Until very recently, a pillar of Mexican nationalism was the belief that the main potential threat to the country's sovereignty came from the United States. Because of the experience of the past few years – and the new economic opening to the North – many NGOs have been able to distinguish more clearly between American government and society. The relationship with Canadian NGOs, more recent, is still at the initial stages (with one or two exceptions). In any case, the ripple effect cannot be ignored regarding the perception of foreigners in Mexico's political culture.

There is an additional, less visible but equally important, effect. In the early 1980s, only a few NGOs had faxes or computers with modems. Nowadays, the reverse is true, and more and more NGOs are venturing into increasingly sophisticated forms of communication (especially electronic mail, of which there are already a number of networks). This is proving extremely important in the struggle to democratize the system.

Finally, these transformations facilitated the swift creation of Mexican NGO networks that, in conjunction with networks in the United States and Canada, attempted to obstruct or impose conditions on the negotiations and approval of NAFTA. Given the authoritarian nature of the Mexican political system, Mexican NGOs had much less impact than did their counterparts in the other two countries. Nonetheless, the fact that they managed to get organized so quickly has partly to do with the cumulative experience of NGOs that worked with displaced people. It is even possible to identify activists who moved from NGOs that worked with Central Americans to NGOs created to oppose NAFTA.

I do not intend to exaggerate the importance of Mexican NGOs, for their presence is relatively recent. However, their very existence is not well understood in Mexico and should be taken into account when speculating about the future. In this sense, there is no doubt that Mexico's future will be linked to that of its Northern neighbors, and the Free Trade Agreement will have profound effects on all aspects of Mexican life.

It is difficult to go beyond these generalities because there are no historical precedents for this current form of integration. Mexico, the United States, and Canada are different in many respects. In spite of this, I think that in the short term, the greatest changes in Mexico will take place in the field of politics. In Mexico's authoritarian political tradition, even the numerical majority may count for little. In great contrast, the open nature of the political system in the United States and Canada often allows well-organized minorities to influence government policy, by shaping its direction or by slowing and obstructing its implementation.

The Mexican political system is beginning to change, and some of the strongest pressures to become more democratic and approach the model of any representative liberal democracy come from NGOs. Since 1991, the struggle for democracy has taken several forms, some of which have no precedent in this country. For example, the observation of elections by Mexican NGOs is an adaptation of a practice that has become popular all over the world as a means of assessing a country's level of democracy. In 1993 and 1994, Mexico will witness a definitive battle for democracy. Having observed the tendencies in Mexico, I think that some of the strongest pressure for the country to be democratized will come from NGOs that will enjoy the support of their counterparts in Canada and the United States.

This virtual internationalization of Mexican politics raises a host of questions about its implications for other aspects of reality. The internationalization of political life means vulnerability to external factors, and increased interest in Mexico abroad. One consequence is that the regime is inhibited to use force as in the past. That has reduced fear, which is one of the most important glues holding together authoritarian societies, and has given an added impetus to democracy.

I will not go deeper in this matter but simply stress that the hospitable reception of displaced Central Americans by Mexican society hastened the strengthening and maturity of social forces that are having an effect on other internal and external dimensions. Thus NGOs can be said to be sketching part of the new international system whose outline we are only just beginning to glimpse.

REFERENCES

Academia Mexicana de Derechos Humanos
1992   "Informe Narrativo de la Conferencia Internacional sobre Integración Económica, Políticas Migratorias y Derechos Humanos en América del Norte," Mexico, D.F.

Aguayo, S.
1991   *From the Shadows to Center Stage: Non-government Organizations and Central American Refugee Assistance.* Washington, DC: Georgetown University, Hemispheric Migration Project.

Aguayo, S., and P. W. Fagen
1988   *Central Americans in Mexico and the United States.* Washington, DC: Georgetown University, Hemispheric Migration Project.

Coordinación de Educación, Academia Mexicana de Derechos Humanos.
n.d.   "Directorio de ONGs de Derechos Humanos en Mexico." Academia Mexicana de Derechos Humanos. In press.

Frelick, W.
1990   *Closing the Faucet*. Washington, DC: U.S. Committee for Refugees.

González, A. L.
1992   "Recopilación de Organismos Internacionales Gubernamentales y No-gubernamentales para el Trabajo con Refugiados en México." Mexico: European Commission Delegation. July 24.

Holt-Giménez, E.
1989   "NGOs in Central America: The Crisis and the Potential." Paper presented at the Twenty-Fifth International Congress of the Latin American Studies Association. Miami, FL, December 4–6.

Inglehart, R.
1990   *Culture Shift in Industrial Society*. Princeton, NJ: Princeton University Press.

International Council of Voluntary Agencies (ICVA)
1989   *Documents in Development, 1981–1989*. Geneva: ICVA.

Project Counselling Service for Latin American Refugees (PCS)
1992   "Historical Expenditure Analysis by Country. From March 1986 to 1991." San José, Costa Rica.

17

Refugees and the Guatemalan Peace Process

Carlos Ochoa Garcia[1]

Introduction

Rigoberta Menchú, winner of the 1992 Nobel Peace Prize, has argued that "real measures" to address the rights of indigenous people in Guatemala can be implemented only once a general accord on human rights has been achieved (*Excelsior*, December 17, 1992, 22A). Since the first meeting in Mexico (April 26, 1991), the Guatemalan peace process has given particular attention to the question of human rights – it is the second item in a list of ten negotiating points. The antagonistic parties have agreed on democratization (July 1991), the first point on the list. However, they have not yet concluded negotiations on human rights. This is despite the fact that other important items further down the list, such as repatriation (No. 7), have been successfully negotiated. Proceeding with repatriation without a human rights accord is obviously a risky matter, but one which refugees are willing to pursue since the "return" is viewed as an important step towards peace.

A "basic agreement on repatriation" between the Guatemalan government and refugee representatives was signed on August 10, 1992. However, the actual return has been only partial and has taken some time to organize. Whether future events will lead to a massive refugee flow from Mexico is an open question. All will depend on specific features

[1]The assistance of Nat Holmes in the preparation of this text is gratefully acknowledged.

of the peace process, particularly those concerning human rights and respect for indigenous peoples. Rigoberta Menchú has stated his definite return will only take place when Guatemalan refugees will be able to return with dignity, to rebuild their homeland; many others feel the same. Yet, hesitant and partial steps toward a return are being organized. These are very important steps for the peace process and for building human rights guarantees. A historical perspective on the refugee problem, maps delineating the geographical context, and an analysis of the five factors which facilitate/impede the return of large numbers of Guatemalan refugees resident in Mexico are provided below.

BACKGROUND TO THE REFUGEE FLIGHT

The refugee problem in Guatemala is a direct result of armed conflict. Population and territorial control has been a central tenet of Guatemalan military strategy in the last decades. Militarization of indigenous and peasant territories has led to massive population flight which has in turn facilitated military control over these areas.[2]

The repercussions of armed military repression of the civil population in indigenous territories of Guatemala were immediately felt in the Mexican border region. Areas in Mexico adjacent to Guatemala received an increased flow of refugees and exiles starting in May 1979, with high intensity between 1982–1983 and very low intensity with the first civil government in 1985 (see Table 1). The first flows streamed toward the Mexican State of Chiapas (Castaneda, 1987: 85).

In addition, very large population displacements took place within Guatemala. Most moved from villages facing violence to safer zones in their own provinces or in neighboring provinces. The provinces of Huehuetenango, El Quiché, Alta Verapaz and San Marcos registered the highest numbers of displaced people. "Approximately 80% of the citizens (1.3 million people) living in these areas at least temporarily abandoned their villages between 1981–1982." (PAVA, 1981: 3). As many as one in seven Guatemalans were affected by internal displacement (Aguilera Peralta, 1992: 11)

As shown in Figure 1, conflict and refugee flight have been highly concentrated. A 1984 report of the Mexican Commission for Refugees

---

[2]The implications of violence in Guatemala were expressed in the CACIF (enterprise representatives) protocol speech at the 1990 Ottawa meeting with the URNG. They are also illustrated by CEAR (1991: 9), INFORPRESS (informe 1982) and Falla (1992).

TABLE 1

MEXICO-GUATEMALA BORDER INCREASE IN REFUGEE FLOWS

Year	Increase in Refugee Flows
1979	First indeterminate flows
1981	First flows to Honduras: 600 refugees (CEAR, 1991: 6)
1982	Approximately 20,000 people flee Guatemala, mostly to Mexico (COINDI, 1991)
1983	Approximately 50,000 people flee Guatemala, leading to 60 refugee villages, 17 camps in Mexico
1984	Refugee camps in Chiapas alone have a population of 42,000
1989	CIREFCA estimates 53,000 refugees in Mexico (CIREFCA, 1989: 23)

(COMAR)[3] shows 85.4% of the Guatemalan refugees to be from the province Huehuetenango. Another 10.4% from Quiché, and 4.1% from El Peten. Densely settled zones such as Ixil, Ixcan, Huista and Kanjobal in the provinces of El Quiché and Huehuetenango were particularly affected.

The border region between Guatemala and Chiapas makes up more than two-thirds of the overall Guatemala-Mexico border. As a result of its proximity to the conflict areas, Chiapas has received the main flow of Guatemalan refugees. In 1991 Chiapas had 23,000 refugees located in 120 small villages. The most populous refugee areas are: Las Margaritas (12,000 people; 32 camps), Trinitaria (4,500) and Comalapa (4,550) (CEAR, 1991: 5; Bauer Paíz, 1989: 20).

The first refugee camps were established between 1980 and 1983 close to the Mexican-Guatemalan border. As a result of Guatemalan military presence close to the Mexican border, the Mexican government decided to resettle the camps further to the north.[4] In 1984 a total of 18,500 refugees were resettled: 12,500 in Campeche and 6,000 in Quintana Roo (for principal camps, *see* Table 2).

NEGOTIATING PEACE AND RETURN

The issues which lie behind Guatemalan refugee flight – civil war, repression, lack of civil rights, and underdeveloped democratic institutions

---

[3]COMAR was founded July 22, 1980. COMAR belongs to the Secretaries of Interior, Foreign Relations, Work and Social Security.

[4]On March 30, 1984, armed groups penetrated the refugee camps of "El Chupadero" (Chiapas); other similar cases were reported in this period.

TABLE 2

PRINCIPAL REFUGEE CAMPS IN 1985

Campeche:	Maya Tecun	Chiapas:	Margaritas
	Quetal Etzná		Independenciz
			Trinitaria
Quintana Roo:	Cuchumatan	Comalapa Frontera	
	Los Lirios	San Pedro Bella V.	
	Maya Balam	Amatenango	

Sources: Castañeda, 1987: 103; CEAR, 1991: 4

– are unique to Guatemala's history and current situation. At the same time, Guatemala's problems are part of a constellation of regional issues affecting all of Central America. It is not surprising therefore that recent progress in Guatemala has been closely linked with progress at the regional level. In fact, the first step on the way to progress in Guatemala's problems was a 1987 regional peace proposal, known as the Esquipulas Plan, described further below. A second important step was the greater involvement of the international community and nongovernment parties through the so-called Oslo Round of discussions and through two Guatemalan peace process meetings in Mexico (1991). Through these foundational steps, direct discussion between the representatives of Guatemalan refugees and the Guatemalan state gradually became possible, leading to a Basic Accord for Repatriation (1992). Following this, gradual progress in establishing guarantees for initial refugee return (in 1993) and the conditions for a possible expanded return in the future are being established, although slowly and painstakingly. Each of these steps is discussed further in the points which follow.

First Steps: Interstate Frameworks

The Esquipulas Central American Peace Plan of 1987 saw national reconciliation as the only possible means of achieving peace. National reconciliation was to be achieved through the utilization of four mechanisms outlined in Figure 2.

The leader of Nicaragua, El Salvador, and Guatemala proposed these mechanisms to stop armed conflict in their own countries and to bring an end to U.S. intervention in Nicaragua and El Salvador.

The Esquipulas Peace Plan established the first measures for the return of Guatemalan refugees. The plan called for respect of the

Figure 1.   Guatemalan Refugee Flow

principle of voluntary repatriation and resettlement, as well as protection of and assistance for the refugees. (*See* Table 3.) Establishing this principle opened the door to a chain of subsequent steps.

Expansion of Involvement of International and Nongovernment Organizations

The next stage in the internal Guatemalan peace process was The Oslo Agreement which opened a round of meetings between March 1990

TABLE 3

Repatriates from Mexico to Guatemala, 1987–1991

Guatemalan Provinces	No.	Percent
Huehuetenango	4,090	67.63
El Quiché	1,317	21.78
Alta Verapaz	375	6.20
Peten	90	1.49
San Marcos	60	0.89
Izabal	29	0.48
Chiquimula	18	0.30
Escuintla	9	0.15
Suchitepequez	9	0.15
Quetzaltenango	8	0.13
Guatemala	4	0.07
Totonicapán	3	0.05
Without Specification	36	0.60
Total Repatriates (1991)	6,048	100.00
Total Number of Refugees Registered by CIREFCA	53,000	

Source: National Commission for Attention to Repatriates, Refugees, and the Displaced (CEAR), (*Caracterizatión de la Poblacion Repatriada en Guatemala*. Anexo IX).

and October 1990 in Madrid, Ottawa, Quito, Metepeq, and Atlixco (Mexico). These meeting were conducted under interstate auspices in the presence of diverse church and nongovernment groups (NGOs).[5] Refugee representatives participated in the Metepec (Mexico) talks along with union representatives, popular leaders and the URNG, under the mediation of the conciliator and a U.N. observer. The Metepec Declaration called for respect for human rights, fundamental liberties, modification of the constitution, and the summoning of a national dialogue.

A new period of refugee participation began in 1991 after the Mexico Accord (April 29, 1991) and the Queretaro Accord (July 25, 1991), two important steps in the current Guatemalan Peace Process. The Queretaro Accord places refugee issues within the peace process agenda. "The effective settlement of the populations displaced by the

[5]Meetings: Madrid (June 1, 1990, with political parties); Ottawa (January 9, 1990, with enterprise representatives); Quito (September 29, 1990, with church representatives), and Mexico (October 25, 1990, with civil sectors).

Figure 2.   Mechanism to Reach Peace and Refugee Return

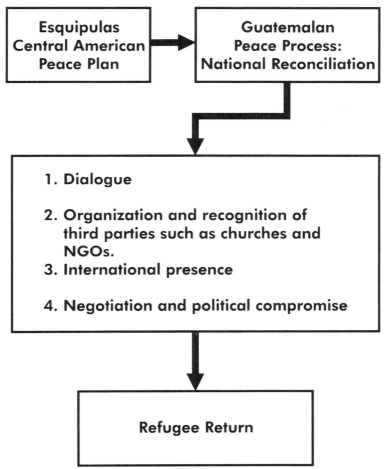

internal armed conflict"[6] is now one of the principal objectives of the
Guatemalan peace process. The Queretaro Accord establishes that
democratization and the search for peace by political means are important conditions for the return of the displaced populations of Guatemala. The substance of this agreement is clearly important, but so too
is the extent to which NGOs, including those representing Guatemalan
refugees, were involved in its evolution. The Permanent Commissions

[6]Queretaro Accord: Point 1, objective i.

(CCPP) was established under international auspices to represent refugee concerns. The CCPP expanded its activity through the discussions leading to the two Mexican accords. The involvement by the CCPP further strengthened its legitimacy in efforts to speak directly to the Guatemalan government. As would be expected, the Serrano government, which was in power in Guatemala at the time of the Mexican accords, did not want to deal directly with the CCPP and its demands. However, the pressure of events eventually did lead to direct talks between the CCPP and the government.

In February 1991, the Serrano government took its first official measures regarding refugees by modifying the status of the National Commission for Attention to Repatriates, Refugees, and the Displaced (CEAR).[7] The new Serrano government wanted to directly control the refugee problem by not allowing members of the CCPP to participate in internal dialogue initiatives.[8] This consequently eliminated important independent refugee initiatives such as the Peace Plan for El Quiche, which was presented by Ramiro De Leon Carpio, Guatemalan Human Rights Procurator (Ombudsman) on March 21, 1991. The Serrano government's refugee policy was clearly demonstrated by its Total Peace Initiative implemented on April 8, 1991, less than three months after Serrano took office. Through this peace initiative the government aims to independently develop a series of mechanisms:

1) An information system for population repatriation (which began in May, 1991);
2) A National Fund for Peace (FONAPAZ)[9] which aims to create the necessary infrastructure and basic services;
3) A Presidential Commission for Human Rights (COPREDEH);
4) A security system.

---

[7]Vice-president Gustavo Espina was designated as the director of the Presidential Commission for Human Rights (COPREDEH) and became governmental representative for refugee policy. *See* Final Report of Propositions for Civilian Sectors and National Dialogue, CRN, Guatemala, 1989; and refugees' initiative, February, 1989.

[8]In January 1992, representatives of CCPP were not authorized to enter the country to participate in the Conference for Peace and Human Rights.

[9]FONAPAZ was created on June 28, 1991, by Governmental Accord 408-91. The areas known as ZONAPAZ are the departments of San Marcos, Huehuetenanago, El Quiche, Chimaltenango, Solola, Alta Verapaz, and the Peten.

These initiatives were obviously positive in terms of their stated objectives, but in the context of limited democracy and continuing human rights abuses there was reason to have concern about the extent and ways in which they would be implemented. The CCPP and its supporters continued to push for greater involvement of civil society, refugee organizations, and international human-rights monitors in the peace and return process. Other changes in public awareness and consensus were required before this would come to pass.

Clearly the presence of the NGOs constitutes a reference point for the operational plans for subsequent returns. The NGOs support local response capacity. In the Guatemalan case their role is clearly defined and subject to mechanisms of coordination. There are six principles that guide the NGOs' coordination:

1) Accompaniment, including all aspects related to collecting information on the conditions of return, disseminating findings, providing legal support and protecting human rights, as well as providing technical cooperation for the returnees;
2) Humanitarian work with respect to food, medicine, etc.;
3) Fortification of community organization and self-management;
4) Strengthening civil society and its organized expressions;
5) Supporting the victimized populations;
6) Credibility, which means always seeking and acting on the truth.

Direct Dialogue between Refugee Representatives and the Guatemalan State

As a result of the sixth meeting of the Oslo Round, Guatemalan civil society now considers the return of the refugees and international mediation as two of the most crucial points of national reconciliation. There is a consensus that reconciliation will not be viable if a substantial percent of the national population remains outside the country for political reasons.

The Guatemalan peace process has been managed by the National Reconciliation Commission (CNR). This Commission was created in 1987. Since the end of 1987, the Commission for Refugees had been trying to negotiate the return of refugees with the former Cerezo government (Letter of March 20, 1988). However, the Cerezo government did not respond to these requests. Cerezo wanted to address the refugee problem through CEAR.[10] Under Cerezo, the CEAR ignored refugee demands that were presented in the National Dialogue. These included demands for freedom of organization, security, free mobilization and the acceptance of an international presence.

As a result of the failure of the preceding initiatives, refugee representatives have presented their demands in the national forum of civil society through which The National Dialogue was created in March, 1989, by CNR. Unfortunately, this dialogue initiative was unable to survive the three *coup d'état* attempts against the Cerezo government. The political space needed for free dialogue and organization has thus been reduced.

Since the Oslo Accord (March1990), the role of mediator in the peace process has been assigned to the "conciliator"[11] and the role of advisor and consultant has been assigned to the U.N. observer. However, in practice U.N. observation has decreased, thus depriving the peace process of external mediation. The refugee issue could pose a major challenge which will help to promote an increased international presence within the Guatamalan peace process.

The Guatemalan peace process has utilized a variety of different modalities for conducting refugee negotiations. The current modality involves a process of direct dialogue between the Permanent Commissions of Refugees and the president. Pressure from internal organizations has been fundamental in influencing the Serrano government to negotiate with the CCPP without resorting to the use of force or employing pressure tactics (*see* Peace and Human Rights Conference Resolution, January 31, 1992).

The dialogue between the government and the Permanent Commissions that represent the refugees covers a range of issues, from recognition of the CCPP to minimum guarantees for the return. Three characteristics of the dialogue – directness, coverage of a multitude of issues, and recognition of the refugee community – mark it as a historic precedent. It has allowed the refugees an opportunity to acquire a new negotiating capacity, and it has led to concrete results: a framework repatriation accord (October 7, 1992), and an operational accord (May 8, 1993).

[10]CEAR was created September 26, 1986, in Cerezo's Governmental Accord No. 765-86.

[11]The Oslo Agreement created the "conciliator" figure. In practice the conciliator became the leader of the CNR. Conciliator characteristics are analyzed in Padilla, 1991: 130

The first accord, the Basic Agreements on Repatriation, defines the bases and the conditions for the return of the refugees to Guatemala, including the following:

1) Nature of the return to be of an individual and voluntary nature, but organized in a collective form, taking indigenous customs into account;

2) Recognition of the right to free association and organization of the returnees, without intervention by the Guatemalan army; governmental recognition of the civil and peaceful character of the return;

3) The accompaniment by national and international NGOs during the return, resettlement, and reintegration of the refugees;

4) Freedom of movement in and out of the country; the freedom to choose place and mode of residence;

5) The necessary guarantees of respect for life and for the integrity of the person and the community;

6) The certainty and the means of access to land;

7) International mediation, follow-up, and verification.

The second accord, reached in May 1993, builds on the framework of the earlier 1992 accord. Its objective is to define operational matters, such as the preparation of complete listings of the returnees and the accompanying organizations, documents of personal identification, land ownership deeds, basic humanitarian assistance, and the coordination of operational plans.

Discussion of refugee issues has strengthened the role of the mediator in internal third parties. Groups playing the role of mediator include the Instances of Mediation (Catholic Church, the Human Rights Ombudsmen, Human Rights Guatemalan Commission, and UNHCR), the CNR, and the International Consultant and Support Group for the Return (GRICAR group). As well, this discussion has led to a popular consensus on points that are fundamental to the peace process:

- consciousness of the implications of violence and the demands of the rule of law;

- the need for constructive dialogue;

- the need to establish cultural, political, economic and social reforms; and

- the need for international mediation.

Toward Establishment of Guarantees for Executing the Accords

Unfortunately, the Guatemalan peace process has not benefitted from sufficient international presence. U.N. Secretary General observer Fransisco Vendrell has been the only international representative assisting the Guatemalan negotiations. If we look at El Salvador's peace negotiations we can see how positive international mediation and assistance has helped to resolve the Salvadorean armed conflict. "Clearly, Guatemala has not yet arrived at the situation of U.N. peacekeeping and peace-building" (Padilla, 1991: 140). Stressing the relationship between peace and the subsequent return of refugees may seem overly idealistic; however, it is clear that peace provides the fundamental framework in which the entire spectrum of refugee-related problems can be addressed.

Even though Guatemala has not benefitted from an international presence at the peace table, we can see a positive international trend in refugee-related assistance and programs that emerged as a response to the Esquipulas II Plan (*see* Table 4).

In May, 1988, the General Assembly of the United Nations created the Special Plan with Economic Cooperation with Central America (PEC)[12] This plan directly supported the Esquipulas Plan and gave priority to the grave situation of refugees in Central America.[13]

The Basic Accord for Repatriation (August 1, 1992) between the government and CCPP clearly established the use of mediation and verification as a way to guarantee the execution of the accords. This responsibility has been assigned to the GRICAR group. GRICAR is a coalition formed by part of the World Church Council, the International Council of Voluntary Agencies (ICVA), and the Canadian, French, Mexican, and Swedish embassies.

The process of negotiating the return of refugees and the displaced has revealed the capacity of civil society and international bodies to mobilize in joint efforts. Repatriation is now perceived as a national and international issue to be solved by consensus and multiparty negotiating teams. This has set a solid example for other peace process agenda items.

---

[12]United Nations General Assembly in support of the peace plan and a special plan for Economic Cooperation with Central America (PAECA) (UN/GA Resolutions 42/1, October 7, 1987, and Resolution 42/204, December 27, 1987).

[13]"Approximately 2,000,000 Central Americans have had to abandon their place of origin due to the internal violence, political tensions and wars that have affected the history of the region for the last decade" (PRODERE, 1991: 3).

FUTURE STEPS

Negotiations and political compromise between refugees and the government will need to take into account the demands of refugee communities and representatives if they are to solve the refugee problem. Many questions need to be addressed: Will the preparations for the return be a separate issue in the peace process? Can the movement for repatriation create new conditions and hopes, facilitating the rebuilding and resettling of a more democratic Guatemala? The following is a brief synthesis of refugee demands.

1) *Voluntary Repatriation:* refugees call for respect of the principle of voluntary repatriation and resettlement, and for the principle of respect and decisionmaking of cultural minorities.

2) *Collective and Organized Return:* refugees demand guarantees that repatriation will be in the form of the return of entire communities (not simply individuals).[14]

3) *Observance:* refugees request the physical presence of neutral, humanitarian observers during the three phases of the return (transport, resettlement, and reintegration).

4) *Access to Land:* refugees call for access to their original properties and facilities (credit, land reform, return of confiscated or appropriated realty) to obtain land.

5) *Free Mobilization:* refugees request freedom of mobilization and self-organization. They also request there be no obligatory military service.

6) *Security:* refugees request the establishment of mechanisms to guarantee the protection, security, integrity, and liberty of refugees and their communities, as well as security of assistance to their communities.

Based on the Basic Agreements on Repatriation, the first massive return of refugees to Guatemala began January 16, 1993. A total of 828 families or 2,480 persons registered in this first group. The majority settled in the zone known as Polígono 14 (now called Comunidad Victoria 20 de enero). The second return, initially scheduled for May 1993 but postponed several times, finally took place on December 3, 1993. In this group there were 1,347 registered returnees.

---

[14]This plan for the return was presented by refugees at the second CIREFCA meeting in San Salvador (April, 1992).

TABLE 4

INTERNATIONAL ACTION FOR REFUGEES

Year	Assistance and Programs
1987	Esquipulas II Agreement/Plan
1988	U.N. Resolution: PEC
1989	PRODERE program (PNUD-Italia)
1989	CIREFCA Conference
1991	Tri-Party Commission: COMAR/CEAR/UNHCR
1992	Mexico-Guatemalan Technical Commission
1992	UNHCR-Guatemalan Government Agreement

However, if the real difficulties confronted by the first returnees consisted primarily of logistical problems and of basic needs that went unsatisfied, the main problem of the second return is that of security. The Guatemalan Minister of Defense emphatically declared that he would not be responsible for what might happen to the returnees in light of the fact that they are settling in an area considered "red" (a zone of military confrontations).

The current peace process has been significantly affected by ongoing refugee negotiations. It is clear that the peace process can derive important lessons from the refugee negotiations. Among these are:

- *The clear need to construct a judicial background for negotiations.* Negotiations to date have produced a solid body of jurisprudence on refugee issues that will serve as a reference point for other agenda items facilitating the search for genuine compromises. An impressive framework of 24 different accords on refugee issues has been established. Half of these agreements have been created internally and half of them are internationally accepted.

- *The recognition that items under negotiation are interconnected and should not be dealt with in a predetermined order.* It is better to live with inconsistencies and piecemeal accords since it is only through agreeing one by one on individual points that progress can be made. Illustrative of this point, on October 8, 1992, the government reached a bilateral Basic Accord for Repatriation with the CCPP. These negotiations were complicated by Rigoberta Menchú's candidacy for the Nobel Peace Prize (which the Serrano government openly opposed) and by vocal opposition from Indian organizations to state promotion of the celebration of the 500th anniversary of the "discovery" of the Americas by Columbus. Serrano seems to have decided to deal with mounting criticism and opposition by agreeing to the repatriation item in the peace process. Thus, the Basic Accord for Repatriation was signed before the conclusion of the clause of the Mexico Agenda dealing with human rights. Subsequently, progress on the theme of human rights has been stuck on three points: continuing civil-military patrols, difficulties in finding ways to apply international humanitarian law, and how the accords are to be executed (Padilla, 1991: 141). The government and the URNG have reached an agreement on all of the other points dealing with human rights.[15] Bit by bit, progress is being made, even if the process is rife with inconsistencies.

- *To negotiate on principles under international observance.* In the past ten years, refugees have accumulated a very rich cross-cultural experience and have developed organizational capabilities to solve specific community problems. The conditions that refugees will confront upon arrival will require these communities to continue to develop their cultural and organizational resources in order to resettle into peaceful communities. The negotiations surrounding the return of refugees have strengthened the right of self-determination in Guatemala. This fundamental liberty will have to be further developed in accordance with the needs of returning refugees. Self-determination is especially important in Guatemala because of its multiethnic and multicultural population. As Rigoberta Menchú concluded, the role of the international community in establishing and maintaining global human rights will be essential in future progress on peace and repatriation in Guatemala.

RECENT DEVELOPMENTS IN THE PEACE DISCUSSIONS

The twelve months of 1993 were not very successful for the advance of the negotiations between the Guatemalan government and representatives of the refugees. This owes to two basic considerations: 1) a major political crisis in the Guatemalan state; 2) unexpected problems and continuing conflict in the resettlement process

---

[15]These points are: 1) the need to strengthen human rights protection; 2) respect for the rule of law and the need to stop impunity; 3) the elimination of paramilitary bodies; 4) the purification of the armed forces and arms control; 5) the guarantee that there will be no obligatory military service; 6) the protection of human rights workers; 7) retribution for victims of violence; 8) the establishment of a commission for truth and justice; 9) the establishment of a commission for human rights verification.

The first return and resettlement process took place in the context of the worst political crisis of the state since the end of the military regimes. The first half of 1993 witnessed political instability, threats against the press and civilian leaders, and the reappearance of the dreaded death squads. Finally, on May 25, the crisis culminated in an extremely unusual *coup d'état* led by the President of the Executive in the face of army indifference. The new authoritarian state dissolved Congress, repealed certain articles of the constitution, and modified the composition of the Supreme Court of Justice and the Constitutional Court. The new president quickly demonstrated his incapacity to manage the consequences of the crisis. While respect for human rights noticeably improved, no progress was made in the peace process, the conversations with civilian leaders, or the negotiations with the representatives of the refugees. Tension between executive, legislative, and judicial powers increased and polarized all political initiatives between July and November.

In this political context it was practically impossible to introduce initiatives to facilitate the return. Negotiation for the return of additional refugees were stalled as were the development of new operational plans for the return. In addition, the returns already agreed to were slowed and troubled by several unforseen circumstances, including: 1) the discovery of mined fields on the return route; 2) confrontations between the guerrillas and the government forces in the zones where returnees plan to resettle; 3) the fact that military bases have been established in the resettlement zone; 4) the return route itself is in bad condition.

What is needed in the immediate future are agreements that can best facilitate incorporation and integration into the productive activity of the country, along with guarantees of political freedoms for those refugees who have already returned. Fruitful negotiations for subsequent returns depend on these conditions being fulfilled.

It is important to point out that for the refugees, repatriation has not meant an improvement in living conditions. The majority of the returnees demonstrate deficiencies in health, nutrition, education and housing, and have access to insufficient implements and natural resources. So far, the major efforts made to cooperate with and assist the refugees and to plan for the immediate future come from international and/or nongovernmental sources.

REFERENCES

Aguayo, S.
1985   *El Exodo Centroamericano*. Mexico: CONAFE/SEP.

Aguilera Peralta
1992   "Negociación, Avanzando Sin Que Se Mire," *La Hora*, 11. January 11.

ASIES
1991   ASIES Momento Estadistico, 10. Guatemala.

Bauer Paíz, A.
1989   "Los Refugiados Guatemaltecos," *La Oltra Guatemala*, 2(6–7): 1921. April Mexico.

Carmack, R.
1991   *Cosecha de Violencias*. Costa Rica: FLACSO.

Castañeda
1987   *Guatemala, Crisis Social, Politica Exterior y Relaciones Con Mexico*. Guatemala: PECA CIDE.

Castillo, G., M. A.
1989   "La Frontera Mexico – Guatemala un Ambito de Relaciones Complejas," *Estudios Latinoamericanos*, 6–7. January–December.

———

1986   "Algunos Determinantes y Principales Transformaciones Recientes de la Migración Guatenmalteca a la Frontera sur de Mexico," *Estudios Sociales Centroamericanos*, 40. January–April.

CEAR (*See* National Commission for Attention to Repatriates, Refugees, and the Displaced)

CEIDEC
1990   *Guatemala. Polos de Desarrollo. El Caso de la Desetructuración de las Comunidades Indigenas*, 2 vols. Mexico.

CIASO
1992   *Boletin del Consejo de Informacion y Analísis Silverio Ortiz*, 4(47). August. Guatemala.

CIREFCA (*See* International Conference for Central American Refugees)

CNR (*See* Comisión Nacional de Reconciliación)

COCIPAZ
1992   *Prouesta de Plan de Trabajo de las Instancias Civiles que Participan en el Proceso de Paz*. July. Guatemala.

COINDE
1991   *Diagnostico sobre Refugiados Retornados y Desplazados de Guatemala*. April. Guatemala.

COMAR-UNHCR-CEAR
1991   *Minuta de la CII Reunión Tripartita*. September 23. Guatemala.

Comisión Nacional de Reconciliación (CNR)
1992   *Propuesta de los Sectores Civiles Acera de su Participatión en el Proceso de Paz y Negociaciones*. Guatemala: CNR. July 30.

1991   *Acuerdo de Queretaro* (Queretaro Accord). Guatemala.

1990   *Dialogo Nacional. Informe de Ponencias Presentadas al Diaogo Nacional.* Guatemala.

Conferencia Episcopal de Guatemala
1991   *Visita a los Guatemaltecos Refugiados.* August 22. Guatemala.

Conferencia por la Paz y los Derechos Humanos
1991   *Declaracion.* January. Guatemala.

Cordova Macías, R., and R. Benitez Manaut
1989   *La Paz en Centroamérica. Expedientes de Documentos Fundamentales 1979–1989.* Mexico: UNam.

Dominguez, G. *et al.*
1991   *Refugiados e Indocumentados Centroamericanos en México. Un Retorno Incierto.* Mexico.

Falla, R.
1992   *Masacres de la Selva.* Guatemala: Ed. Universitaria.

Fuerza Obrera
n.d.   *Organo Informativo STINDE,* 6(80–92). Guatemala.

Gobierno de la Republica de Guatemala
1992a   *Carta de Entendimiento entre el Gobierno de Guatemala y las Comisiones Permanentes de Refugiados Guatemaltecos en Mexico, Palacio Arzobispal.* December 23.

1992b   *Acuerdo Básico de Repatriación entre el Gobierno de Guatemala y las Comisiones Permanentes de Refugiados Guatemaltecos en México.* October 8.

1992c   *Acuerdo de Repatriación entre el Gobierno de Guatemala y las Comisiones Permanentes de Refugiados Guatemaltecos en México.* September 23.

1992d   *Peace Commission.* July.

1991a   *Carta de Entendimiento entre el Gobierno de la República de Guatemale y la Alta Comisionada de las Naciones Unidas para los Refugiados Guatemaltecos.* November 13.

1991b   *Asamlea Permanente de Grupos Cristianos Resultados de los Diálogos y Conversaciones entre CNR, Sectores, Gobierno y la URNG.* November.

Hathaway, J.
1991   *The Law of Refugee Status.* Toronto: Butterworths.

International Conference for Central American Refugees (CIREFCA)
1992a   *Segunda Reunón del Comite Internacional de Seguimiento. Documento Oficial del Gobierno de la República de Guatemala.*

1992b   *Informe sobre los Avances en la Ejecución Delplan de Acción.* San Salvador.

IRIPAZ
1991   *Cronologías de los Procesos de Paz.* Guatemala: IRIPAZ.

Mack, M.
1992   *Donde esta el Futuro.* Guatemala: AVANSCO.

Naciones Unidas
1992   *Desarrollo Humano: Informe 1992.* Colombia: PNUD.

1988   "La situación en Centroamérica amenazas a la paz y seguridad internacionales
         e iniciativas de paz," *Journal*, May 11. New York.

National Commission for Attention to Repatriates, Refugees and the Displaced (CEAR)
1992a   *Caracterizacion de la Poplación Repatriada en Guatemala.* January–June.
         Guatemala.

1992b   *Politica, Estrategias y Acciones Dirigidas a Favor de Poblaciones Desplazadas.*
         Guatemala.

1991   *Caracterización de la Poblacion Repatriada en Guatemala.* October 1991.
        Guatemala.

1988   *Informe 1er semestre 1988.* August 30.

1987   *Informe al 31 de diciembre de 1987.* December 31.

Ochoa Gárcia, C.
n.d.   "Identidad, Procesos Culturales y Conflicto," *Revista de IRIPAZ*, 2: 113–130.
        Guatemala.

1991   *Guia para el Analísis y Resolución de Conflicto.* Guatemala: IRIPAZ.

Padilla, M. L.
1992   "Conflict Resolution Theory and Its Applications to Guatemalan Social
        Context." In *Internal Conflict and Governance.* Ed. K. Rupesinghe. New
        York: St. Martin's Press.

1991   "La Intermediación un Analísis Comparativo," *Revista de IRIPAZ*, 4:
        130–142. Guatemala.

Panorama
1987   *El Proceso de Paz en Centroamérica: Temas y Documentos.* Panorama C.a.
        11–12. Guatemala.

Programa de Ayuda para los Vecinos del Altiplano (PAVA)
1981   *Final Report.* Washington, DC. USAID Project No. DR-520-84-04.

Programa de Desarrollo para Desplazados Refugiados y Repatriados en Centroamérica
(PRODERE)
1991   *Publicación de PRODERE.*

Reeencuentro
1992   *Reeencuentro*, 1–2. June–August.

Rivas Cifuentes, A. F.
1990   *Medidas para Recuperar la Poblacion en Resistencia. Estado Mayor de la Defensa Nacional.* Guatemala.

UNSITRAGUA
1992   *Resultado y Declaraciones Surgidas entre la CNR, Sectores Civiles, Gobierno y URNG en el Proceso de Paz.* February. Guatemala.

URNG
n.d.   *Guatemala una Paz Justa y Democrática: Contenido de la Negociación s.d.e.*

n.d.   *The Negotiations Process in Search of a Political Solution to the Armed Conflict in Guatemala, s.d.e.*

INDEX

A

Academia Mexicana de Derechos Humanos, initiative, 302
aerospace center, European, 129
Afghan migrants to U.S., 251, 253
Afro Americans, 11
agricultural migrants, 91
agriculture, 38, 76, 126, 130, 137, 138–142, 161
    See also specific subjects, e.g., bananas; coffee; labor migration
agro-processing, 130, 134, 164
AIDS (Auto-Immune Deficiency Syndrome) 257–259, 281
American Baptist Church v. Thornburgh (ABC), 237, 250, 256
American Popular Revolutionary Alliance in Peru (APRA), 55, 58
Anguilla, 124, 126, 131
anti-immigrant sentiments, 239
Antigua, 131
apparel manufacture See garment industry
Argentina, 49, 55
Aristide, Jean-Bertrand, 253, 275
Aronson, Bernard, 57
Asian Americans, 11
Asian migrants
    to Canada, 90, 96, 116, 118, 206
    to U.S., 182
Asociación Regional de Coordinadoras Nacionales que trabajan co, 299
asylum See refugees; specific subjects
Australian refugee policy, 235, 260
Austria, 232–234

B

Bahamas, 126–127, 129, 131–132
Baja California, 38
Baker, James, 53
Banamex, 51
bananas, 123, 126, 131, 134, 139, 162, 164–165
banking, 126, 131
Barbados, 100–103, 125, 132
Basic Accord for Repatriation to Guatemala, 312, 319–321, 323
Belize, 125, 130–132
Belmont, Ricardo, 59
Berlin Wall opening; 1989, 247
Bermuda, 124, 131
Bolivian migrants
    to Argentina, 118
    to Mexico, 159
border residents as migrants, 161, 166
Borja Navarrete, Gilberto, 51

Bosnia, 208–210, 232
Bosnian migrants to U.S., 252
bracero programs, 93
Brazil, 48, 49
Bush, George H. W., 27–29, 53, 236, 252, 254, 273, 276, 285

C

Caicos Islands, 124, 126, 129
California, 11
Cambodian migrants, 97
Campeche, 311
Canada
    See also specific subjects
    admission to, 264
    apparel trade, 36
    automobile insurance, 34, 81–103
    Charter of Rights and Liberties, 263
    diplomacy, 268
    economic policy and NAFTA, 52
    Employment Authorization Programme of 1973, 109
    employment structure, 197
    exchange rate, 31
    garment industry, 12
    Guatemalan peace process, 320
    health insurance, 31
    immigration law, 37
    labor market, 8–10, 35
    language training, 209
    migrant women's employment, 200, 206
    refugee law, 258–271
    refugees, 235
    regional development programs, 31
    registration of refugees, 237
    social services, 39
    textile sector, 12, 36
    U.S.-Canada relations, 30–38, 207
    Visitors Data System, 105
    women immigrants, 194
Canada-U.S. Free Trade Agreement (CUFTA), 3, 21, 119, 239
capital, 130
capital flows, 18, 32, 34, 139, 187–190, 196
Caribbean, 123–136
. Caribbean Basin Initiative (CBI), 126
Caribbean Common Market (CARICOM), 125, 127, 131–132
Caribbean migration
    balances by country, decade, 128
    population loss, 127
    refugees to North America, 236–237
    to Canada, 6, 90, 115, 133
    to Cuba, 131

329

Caribbean migration *(continued)*
  to Europe, 127
  to North America, 127
  to Panama, 131
  to United States, 6, 86, 133
Cartagena Conference of 1984, 297, 299
Carter, James Earl, 236, 252, 272
Cayman Islands, 124, 126, 129, 132
Cemex, 51
Center of Studies on Refugees (CSR), 302
Central America
  See also specific subjects
  military activity, 146, 241
  zones of conflict, 146
Central American Common Market, 141
Central American migrants
  to Belize, 144, 146
  to Canada, 90, 116
  to Mexico, 6, 144, 146, 160, 292
  to United States, 86, 305
  within the area, 137, 146
Centro de Investigación y Estudios
  Migratorios (CIEM), 295
Chiapas, 13, 138, 161, 166
Chile, 47, 240, 296
  migrants to Argentina, 118
  overthrow of government; 1975, 96–97
Chinese migrants
  to Canada, 84
  to North America, 238
  to United States, 251
Chretien, 35
civil law and refugees, 261
class migration, 36
Clinton, William J., 29, 35, 42, 54, 236,
  252, 254–255, 273, 285
clothing industry *See* garment industry
coffee, 13, 139, 162–163
cold war, 99, 231–232, 290
Colombian migrants to Venezuela, 118
Comisión Mediadora, 151
Comisiones Permanentes de Representantes
  de los Refugiados en Mexico, 151
common law and refugees, 260–261
compensation to investors under NAFTA, 33
computers, 189
Conferencia Internacional sobre Refugiados
  Centroamericanos (CIRC), 299
connecting flight's implications for
  first-asylum concept, 269
Consultations on Asylum, Refugee and
  Migration Policies in Europe, 235
continuity of employment, 222
Convention Refugee Determination
  Division (CRDD) of the Immigration and
  Naturalization Service, 265–267
Convergencia de Organismos Civiles por la
  Democracia (COCD), 305

Coordinadora Nacional de ONGs
  (Mexicanas) de Ayuda a Refugiados, 292
Coordinadora Nacional de ONGs de ayuda a
  Refugiados, CONONGAR (CIREFCA), 299
Coordinadora Nacional de ONGs de Ayuda
  Refugiados (CONONGAR), 305
Costa Rica, 143, 146, 152, 295, 298
Croatia, 232–264
Cuba, 125, 127, 132
Cuban migrants to Canada, 84
Cuban Adjustment Act of 1966; U.S., 251
Cuban revolution of 1959, 96

D

De Leon Carpio, Ramiro, 316
de Mello, Collor, 48
Declaration of Cartagena, 145
defection, 248
deferred enforced departure (DED), 252
democracy
  market economy, 60
  NAFTA, 41
  supported by other social institutions, 47
Democratic Constituent Congress; Peru
  (CCD), 58–60
Democratic Revolution Party; Mexico (PRD), 51
detention, 252
dictablanda, 58
Diocesan Border, 166
Dominican Republic, 125, 127, 130, 132, 135
Dred Scott v. Saneford, 289
Dublin Agreement, 231
Dutch migrants, 84

E

Eastern Europe, 231, 234, 249, 301
economic restructuring, 193–213
El Salvador, 98, 141, 144, 146, 147, 150,
  291, 295, 301, 312
electronics, 174–192, 199, 205
  NY/NJ metropolitan area, 176–179
electronics sector, 11
employment *See* specific subjects
enclave sector, 134
Enrique Guzman y Valle University, 59
entrepreneurs
  as immigrants, 181
  as migrants, 91, 94
Esquipulas II Plan, 320
Esquipulas Peace Plan of 1987, 312
Ethiopian migrants to U.S., 251
ethnic conflict, 18
Europe, 22
European Economic Community, 3, 234
European migrants to U.S., 118
European nations' refugee policies, 230, 256
European Union (EU), 234
Evangelical Christian migrants from
  U.S.S.R., 247

expulsion of migrants, 169
extended voluntary departure (EVD), 251

F

family reunification, 133, 247
Canada, 93
United States, 68–69, 93
Farabundo Martí Front for National
Liberation (FMLN), 141, 147
Filipino migrants to Canada, 84
first-asylum countries, 235–236, 256, 268
Fordism, 41
Foro de los Países de América del Norte
para los Derechos de lo, 302
France
Guatemalan peace process, 320
migrants to Canada/U.S., 84
refugee law, 265
refugee policy, 260
free markets and political power, 51
free-trade zones, 12
French Antilles, 131, 134
French Guyana, 124, 129
Fujimori, Alberto, 54–61

G

García Pérez, Alan, 54–55
garment industry, 12, 36, 193, 199, 205
Garza Sada, Bernardo, 51
GATT, 3, 21, 29, 34, 37
Germany, 232–234
migrants, 84
refugee law, 265
globalization of migration, 118
González, Claudio, 30
government social services, 5, 132, 148, 209
Grupo Alfa, 51
Guadeloupe, 124
Guantànamo Bay, 276–293
Guantànamo Naval Base, 250, 253–254, 273
Guatemala, 142–144, 146, 147, 150,
165–166, 170, 238, 291, 295, 301
migrants/refugees from, 98, 152, 309–328
to Canada, 292
to Chiapas, 294
to Honduras, 311
to Mexico, 138, 146, 151, 157–159, 161,
163–165, 167, 309–328, 292
to United States, 92, 249–241, 256, 292
migration policy, 158
NGO activity, 313–319
NGOs and, 292–310
Guatemalan peace process, 311–317
Guyana, 125–127, 130–132

H

Haiti, 10, 57, 125, 127, 130–131, 135, 272
Haitian Centers Council, 283
Haitian Centers Council v. McNary, 277

Haitian migrants
to Caribbean, 129, 131
to North America, 129
to United States, 92, 249–252, 254
Haitian Refugee Center, 276
Hemispheric Migration Project (HMP),
298, 302
Hermoza, General, 60
Hernández, Roberto, 51
Hispanic Americans, 11
Hispanic workers, 179–180
Hispanics, 181
HIV-positive migrants, 273–274, 276–281
homework, 178, 183, 201, 208
Honduran migrants, 151, 165, 167
Honduras, 143–144, 146, 148, 296
Hong Kong, 37
Hong Kong migrants
to Canada, 84, 95
to United States, 94
hours of work, 76
household organization among migrants
218–223
housing, 221–223
Huixtla, 166
human rights, 65
Hungarian uprising of 1956, 95–96, 245

I

Immigrant Help Committee (CODAIF), 166
Immigration Act in Canada, 267
Immigration Act of 1924; U.S., 93
Immigration Act of 1976; Canada, 94, 97
Immigration Act of 1990; U.S., 94–95
Immigration and Nationality Act of 1952;
U.S., 93
Immigration and Nationality Act of 1965;
U.S., 93, 96
Immigration and Naturalization Service, U.S.
278–281, 283
Immigration Reform and Control Act (IRCA)
of 1986; U.S., 83, 92, 251
import substitution, 134
Imuris, 217
Indian migrants to Canada, 84
industrial workers as migrants, 76–77
informal sector of economy, 166
Institutional Revolutionary Party in Mexico
(PRI), 67
interdiction
Haitian migrants, 283
Haitian refugees, 272–289
U.S. Policy, 253, 288
internal conflicts, 160
internal migration, 137, 166, 214–228
international migration and, 223–226
International Conference of NGOs Working
with Central Americans (CIREFCA), 299

International Conference on Economic
   Integration, Migratory Policy of 1992, 302
International Consultant and Support
   Group for the Return (GRIC), 319
International Council of Voluntary Agencies
   (ICVA), 298–299, 320
International Monetary Fund (IMF), 19, 34,
   37, 54, 56, 61
international peace and migration, 20
intracompany transferees, 91
Iranian migrants to United States, 251
Irish migrants , 94
Italian migrants, 84

J

Jamaica, 125–127, 132
Jamaica migrants
   in Caribbean, 131
   to Canada, 84
Japan, 55
Jewish migrants
   from U.S.S.R, 247
   in World War II, 288
Johnson, Sterling M., Jr., 279, 281–282, 284
Juárez, 217, 220–221

K

Kennebunkport Order, 254, 273, 274, 283, 285
Korean migrants to Canada, 84
Kuwaiti migrants to United States, 252

L

labor legislation, 65–79
labor market, 34–39
labor migration, 36, 90, 109–127
labor unions, 41, 178, 183, 188, 198, 216
   California, 77–78
   Canada, 75
   Mexico, 73–78
   United States, 75
language fluency, 209
Laotian migrants, 97
Larrea Ortega, Jorge, 51
Latin America, 46–64, 118
Latin American migration
   refugees to North America, 236–237
   to Canada, 115
   to United States, 115, 206
Lautenberg amendment, 247–248
Lebanese migrants to United States, 252
Leeward Islands, 125–127
liberalization, 8, 46–64, 189
Liberian migrants to United States, 252
Lomé Agreement, 134
Los Angeles, 179–184
Los Angeles County, 180

M

Maastricht Treaty, 234
maize section, Mexico; NAFTA, 38
Malca, Victor, 59
maquiladoras, 12, 38, 68–69, 78, 175,
   185–188, 214–228
Mariel boatlift, 236, 246, 250
Marielitos, 97
Martinique, 124
Menchú, Rigoberta, 281, 282, 309, 322
mestizos, 69
Mexican Commission to Help Refugees
   (COMAR), 156, 168, 317
Mexican migration to U.S., 76–77
Mexican-U.S. relations, 158–159, 169, 238
   electronics trade, 184
   migration policy, 302
   refugees, 256, 272
Mexico, 12, 40–42, 49–56, 65–79
   See also specific subjects
   agriculture, 38
   Asian competition, 190
   Constitution; 1917, 66, 75, 77
   ejido, 98, 163–164
   electronics industry, 185
   emigration, 38
   employment, 1985–1992, 70
   exchange rate, 31
   free-trade zones, 12
   General Population Law of 1990, 168, 300
   government economic planning, 30–31
   government social services, 35
   Guatemalan peace process, 320
   internal migration and, 223–226
   internationalization of national politics, 307
   labor market, 37–39
   migrants to U.S., 6, 15, 86, 92–93, 160
   migration policy, 168–170
   Ministry of Foreign Affairs, 167
   national security, 238
   nationalism, 305
   NGOs, 292
   principal exports, 184
   relations with foreign NGOs, 296
   work hours, 76
Mexico Accord of 1991, 314
Middle East, 301
migration causes, 2, 5
migration flows, 170
migration law; Canada, 37
Migratory Services of Chiapas, 165, 167
military activity, Central America, 241
Miller, Agusto Blacker, 56
minerals, 126
Montesinos, Vladimiro, 60
Montserrat, 124, 130–131
Mulroney, Brian, 29, 35

N

NAFTA *See* North American Free Trade Agreement
nation-states' denial of access to courts to refugees, 261
National Action Party in Mexico (PAN), 51–52
National Commission for Attention to Repatriates, Refugees, and the Displaced (CEAR), 316
National dialogue in Guatemala, 318
National Guatemalan Revolutionary Unity (URNG), 147, 314, 323
National Human Rights Commission (CNDH), 300
National Politechnic Institute; Mexico, 70
National Reconciliation Commission (CNR), 317–319
national security and migration, 239–241
Europe, 233
natural justice and refugees, 261
neoconservatism in NAFTA, 29–44
neoliberalism, 46–64
Netherlands Antilles, 124–125
New Jersey, 176–179
new trends in international migration, 8
New York, 11, 176–178
NGOs, 291, 309
See also specific subjects
Nicaragua, 144, 147–148, 150, 291, 295, 301, 312
Nicaraguan migrants
internally displaced, 146
to Canada, 292
to Mexico, 167, 292
to United States, 151, 251, 292
Nicaraguan revolution of 1979, 98
Nogales, 215–228
Nogales Maquiladora Association, 215
nongovernmental organizations (NGOs), 291–309
Nonimmigrant Information System in U.S., 106
nontariff barriers (NTBs), 30
North American Free Trade Agreement (NAFTA), 65, 186–187
See also specific subjects
codifying trends, 21, 99, 133
economic policy, 52
electronics, 188–190
garment industry, 207
government regulation, 33
history, 29, 301
internal and international migration, 224–226
nongovernmental organizations, 291, 302
provisions, 3
refugees, 229–242
refugee policy, 258–286
social services, 20, 39–43

numbers of migrants
Canada, 83
United States, 83, 91

O

Obras party in Peru, 59
Ontario, 34, 42
Orange County, 179–184
Organization of American States (OAS), 48, 57
Organization of Eastern Caribbean States (OECS), 125
origin of migrants to Canada/U.S., 83–85
Orthodox Christian migrants from U.S.S.R., 247
Oslo Agreement of 1990, 147, 313, 318
Oslo Round of Guatemalan peace negotiations, 312

P

Palmerola Base, Honduras, 152
Paraguayan migrants to Argentina, 118
part-time work, 198
Peace Process in Guatemala, 323
peacemaking and migration, 241
Pease, Henry, 59
Peerless Company (men's suits), 208
Pérez, Carlos Andres, 48
Permanent Commissions (CCPP); Guatemala, 315, 318
Permanent Commissions of Refugees, 318
personal service, 193, 200, 205
Peru, 54–61
Peruvian migrants, 55
petroleum, 126, 141
Poland, 234, 237
Polish migrants, 84, 251
political leaders as migrants, 138
pollero, 168
Popular Action party in Peru, 58
Presidential Commission for Human Rights (COPREDEH)in Guatemala, 316
preventing migration, 240
professionals as migrants, 7, 91, 138
Project Counselling Service for Latin American Refugees (PCS), 298
Public Service Employment Act, 264
Puerto Rico, 124, 127, 130, 132
purchasing power of migrants, 225

Q

Queretaro Accord of 1991, 314
Quintana Roo, 166–168, 311

R

racial discrimination, 69
Re Singh decision, 262, 264–268, 270
Reagan, Ronald W., 236, 252–253, 273–275
recent migrants as workers, 205
Rees Memorandum, 277

Rees, Grover Joseph, III, 276–277, 280
refoulement, 236, 251, 254, 283, 286–288
Refugee Act of 1980; U.S., 97–98,
    245–248, 255, 283–288
Refugee Hearing Officer; Canada, 266
refugee policy, 245–286, 272–289
refugees
    See also specific subjects
    asylum in the Hemisphere, 13
    Canada, 14, 95, 258–271
    from Central America, 144, 150, 152, 156,
        161–162
    limited status, 13
    Mexico, 14
    United States, 95
regionalization, 2–4, 115, 241, 270
religious persecution, 247
relocation of business internationally, 180
remittances, 146, 160
repatriation, 301, 321
    Guatemalan migrants, 309
    Haitian migrants, 283
    Haitian refugees, 274
Republican party in United States, 297, 304
residence status, 82
return migration, 150, 309
Revolutionary Institutional Party in Mexico
    (PRI), 49–53
right-based thinking, 262
Robles, Rodolfo, 59

S

safe third country, 235, 236, 256, 268
Saint Kitts-Nevis, 131–132
Saint Maarten, 129
Sale v. Haitian Center Council, Inc., 255
Salinas de Gortari, Carlos, 4, 29–30, 50,
    53–55, 68, 70, 74
Salvadoran migrants, 98, 152
    NGOs and, 292–309
    to Canada, 292
    to Mexico, 161, 165, 167, 292
    to United States, 92, 249–252, 256, 292
San Cristóbal las Casas, diocese of, 295
San Diego, 179–180
sanctuary movement, 296
Sandinista Front of National Liberation
    (FSLN), 141, 143–144
Santa Clara, 175
Santa Clara (Silicon) Valley, 180
Scandinavian aid to Mexican NGOs, 303
Schengen Agreement, 231
seasonal migrants, 130
Sendero Luminoso; Peru, 57–58
service sector, 197, 200
Servicio, Desarrollo y Paz (SEDEPAC), 299
Simpson-Kennedy bill in U.S., 237
Sinaloa, 38
Singh decision; Canada, 107

skilled migrants, 7, 17–18, 94, 133, 197
skilled workers as migrants, 91
social service workers, 200
Soconusco, 138
Somali migrants to United States, 252
Sonora, 12, 38, 214–228
South American migrants to United States, 206
South Korea, 30
Southern California, 179–184
Soviet migrants
    to United States, 247
    to Western Europe, 231
Soviet migration, 116
Spanish-American War, 124
Special Plan with Economic Cooperation
    with Central America, 320
Stevens, John Paul, 286
students as migrants, 7, 90, 108
subcontracting, 178, 184, 198
Suchiate River, 165, 170
sugar, 123, 126, 139
sugar cane, 162, 166
summary exclusion migrants, 255
Suriname, 125, 132
Sweden, 232–234
    Guatemalan peace process, 320
Switzerland, 232–234

T

Tapachula, 168
tariffs, 16, 186
taxes, 20, 36
Teachers' Union in Mexico, 74
temporary migrants
    Canada, 86, 105, 109
    relative importance, 114
    United States, 86, 87, 106, 112–130
temporary protected status (TPS), 251–252
textile industry, 36, 193, 205
textile sector, 12
Tijuana, 216
Toronto, 36, 40
Total Peace Initiative in Guatemala, 316
tourism, 126, 131–132, 135, 166
transmigration, 160, 162, 167, 235, 292
transnational corporations (TNCs), 31
transportation equipment sector, 216
Trinidad and Tobago, 125–128, 131
Turks Islands, 124, 126, 129

U

Uganda
    Asian migrants to Canada, 96
    migrants to United States, 251
Ukrainian Catholic migrants from U.S.S.R., 247
underground railway, 296
undocumented migrants, 18, 38, 145, 167, 171,
    199
undocumented workers, 201

unemployment, 132
  insurance, 35
  Mexico, 67–70, 77
  U.S. Hispanic, 69
Union of Soviet Socialist Republics, 52, 232
unionization *See* labor unionization
United Kingdom migrants to Canada/U.S., 84
United Nations Convention and Protocol
  Relating to the Status of Refugees; 1951,
  1967, 96, 262, 275–276, 283–288
United Nations Development Program
  (UNDP), 299
United Nations High Commissioner for
  Refugees (UNHCR), 98, 145, 161, 168,
  170, 233, 294, 298–299, 303, 319
United States
  See also specific subjects
  Coast Guard, U.S., 275–276, 280, 283–284
  Constitution and migrant rights, 279
  electronics industry, 11, 185
  employment structure, 197
  growth industries, 207
  language training, 209
  origins of women immigrants, 194
  refugee policy, 245–257
  trade laws, 31
  women immigrants, 194, 200, 206
United States Convention and Protocol of
  1967, 249
Universal Charter of Human Rights, 66
unskilled workers as migrants, 17–18, 91, 209
URNG party; Guatemala, 147, 314, 323

V

Vargas Llosa, Mario, 56
Vendrell, Francisco, 320
Venezuela, 48
Viet Nam War, 97

Viet Namese migrants, 84, 97
Virgin Islands, 124, 126, 129, 131–132
Visitors Data System; Canada, 105

W

wages
  California, 77
  maquiladora, 219
  Mexico, 70–71, 77, 187
  unreported, 201
Warsaw Pact countries *See* Eastern Europe
Windward Islands, 125, 127, 130, 132,
  134–135
women, 7, 12, 18, 36, 38, 69, 135, 165,
  179, 181, 190, 193–213, 216
workplace safety
  Canada, 73, 74
  Mexico, 73, 74, 77
  United States, 73, 74
World Bank, 19, 34, 54, 61
World Council of Churches, 320
World War I, 93, 232
World War II, 93, 95, 127, 130, 139,
  158–160, 232, 236, 245, 288

X

xenophobia, 239

Y

young workers, 38, 135
Yugoslavia, 232–234
Yugoslavian migrants, 84

Z

Zambrano, Lorenzo, 51

Other Recent Titles in This Series

POPULATION
DISPLACEMENT AND
RESETTLEMENT:
Development and Conflict
in the Middle East
edited by Seteney Shami

THE IMMIGRATION
EXPERIENCE IN THE
UNITED STATES:
Policy Implications
*edited by Mary G. Powers and
John J. Macisco, Jr.*

THE POLITICS OF
MIGRATION POLICIES.
Settlement and
Integration: The First
World into the 1990s
edited by Daniel Kubat

THE DEMOGRAPHICS OF
IMMIGRATION:
A Socio-Demographic
Profile of the Foreign-Born
Population in New York State
by Nadia H. Youssef

REFUGEE POLICY:
Canada and the United States
edited by Howard Adelman

WHEN BORDERS DON'T
DIVIDE:
Labor Migration and
Refugee Movements in the
Americas
edited by Patricia R. Pessar

PACIFIC BRIDGES:
The New Immigration
from Asia and the Pacific
Islands
*edited by James T. Fawcett and
Benjamin V. Carino*

Forthcoming in 1996

CARIBBEAN CIRCUITS:
Emigration, Remittances,
and Return
edited by Patricia R. Pessar